Advance Praise for *Perspectives on Intellectual Capital: Multidisciplinary Insights into Management, Measurement, and Reporting*

"Outstanding! Bernard Marr has drawn on the top pioneers and experts in intellectual capital to provide an indispensable resource for investors and executives. Each chapter shines alone but as a whole they provide a clear, lucid, yet in-depth exploration of the most important themes and issues around the new fundamentals for understanding and valuing intangible assets. This collection of essays will prove useful for those new to the field as well as those who have been applying these principles for some time."
—**Verna Allee**, author of *The Future of Knowledge: Increasing Prosperity through Value Networks*

"Marr has managed to bring together some of the brightest minds in the field to discuss the important concept of intellectual capital from a variety of perspectives. A major achievement!"
—**Daniel Andriessen**, Professor of Intellectual Capital, INHOLLAND University; Author of *Find your Real Value in a Future of Intangible Assets* and *Making Sense of Intellectual Capital; Designing a Method for the Valuation of Intangibles*

"For many, intellectual capital remains a fad-ridden minefield. Bernard Marr negotiates a route through the distracting complications to prove that intellectual capital is the essence of modern business."
—**Stuart Crainer**, Editor, *Financial Times Handbook of Management*, and Editorial Fellow, London Business School

"The last decade has witnessed a substantial amount of literature on intellectual capital. Here, for the first time, is a comprehensive, multi-disciplinary perspective on intellectual capital, setting a milestone for reaching a common understanding on intellectual capital, its usage and relevance to public, private and third sector business management in the 21st century.
  An impressive result, which opens up new horizons for understanding the 'how's', 'why's' and 'what's' of intellectual capital. This book sets a standard for management thinking now and into the future. It promotes cross-disciplinary awareness and collaboration, appealing to a wide audience, encompassing business executives, academics, investors, students and policy makers alike. This book is highly recommended as a text for undergraduate and post graduate teaching, as well as being a substantial contribution to the research literature."
—**Professor James Guthrie**, Discipline of Accounting and Business Law, Faculty of Economics and Business, The University of Sydney, Australia

"In the context of the European Union setting itself the strategic goal to become the most competitive and dynamic knowledge based economy in the world, this book should become one of the 'must reads' for managers and all those who create the economic environment. Why? Because intellectual capital is the key value-creating factor of the knowledge economy and everyone who wants to cope with the ongoing transition successfully will have to learn as much about it as fast as they can.
  This book provides valuable insights for absolute IC-beginners as well as for IC-pioneers, like myself, and I highly recommend it to all who are interested in leveraging their company's, regions or nations value creating potential."
—**Dr. Ante Pulic**, Professor of Finance, University of Zagreb, Croatia

"Excellent new book on intellectual capital. With academic rigor, Bernard Marr examines key topics on intellectual capital, organizational learning, knowledge management and their connections."
—**Patricia Ordóñez de Pablos**, Professor of Business Administration, The University of Oviedo, Spain, Executive Editor of the *International Journal of Learning and Intellectual Capital*

"Although executives around the world consider intellectual capital as the most relevant factor for the future success of their business, their approaches of managing it are still poor or non-existent. Bernard Marr tries to disentangle the main reasons of this frustrating gap. His book **Perspectives on Intellectual Capital** is, as for as I know, the first systematic and scientific approach on the way to elucidate the concept of intellectual capital and on the critical process of deploying intangible assets to establish and sustain competitive advantages."
—**Dr. José Ma. Viedma Martí,** President of Intellectual Capital Management Systems and Professor of Business Administration at Polytechnic University of Catalonia

Perspectives on Intellectual Capital

Edited by
Bernard Marr

ELSEVIER
BUTTERWORTH
HEINEMANN

AMSTERDAM • BOSTON • HEIDELBERG • LONDON
NEW YORK • OXFORD • PARIS • SAN DIEGO
SAN FRANCISCO • SINGAPORE • SYDNEY • TOKYO

338.5
P467

Elsevier Butterworth-Heinemann
30 Corporate Drive, Suite 400, Burlington, MA 01803, USA
Linacre House, Jordan Hill, Oxford OX2 8DP, UK

Library of Congress Cataloging-in-Publication Data
Perspectives on intellectual capital / Bernard Marr.
   p. cm.
   Includes bibliographical references.
   ISBN 0-7506-7799-6
   1. Intellectual capital.   I. Marr, Bernard.   II. Title.

   HD53.P47 2005
   338.5–dc22
                        2004022862

British Library Cataloging-in-Publication Data
A catalogue record for this book is available from the British Library.

ISBN: 0-7506-7799-6

For information on all Elsevier Butterworth-Heinemann publications
visit our Web site at www.books.elsevier.com

05 06 07 08 09 10   10 9 8 7 6 5 4 3 2 1

Printed in the United States of America

I dedicate this book to
my wife Claire
and with loving memory
to my mother.

Contents

Foreword, *Robert Grant*   ix
Preface   xi
Introduction   xiii

Part One Disciplinary Views   1

Chapter 1 An Economics Perspective on Intellectual Capital, *Mie Augier and David Teece*   3

Chapter 2 A Strategy Perspective on Intellectual Capital, *Bernard Marr and Göran Roos*   28

Chapter 3 An Accounting Perspective on Intellectual Capital, *Baruch Lev, Leandro Cañibano, and Bernard Marr*   42

Chapter 4 A Finance Perspective on Intellectual Capital, *Sudi Sudarsanam, Ghulam Sorwar, and Bernard Marr*   56

Chatper 5 A Reporting Perspective on Intellectual Capital, *Jan Mourtisen, Per Nikolaj Bukh, and Bernard Marr*   69

Chapter 6 A Marketing Perspective on Intellectual Capital, *Lisa Fernström*   82

Chapter 7 A Human Resource Perspective on Intellectual Capital, *Ulf Johanson*   96

Chapter 8 An Information Systems Perspective on Intellectual Capital, *Joe Peppard*   106

Chapter 9 A Legal Perspective on Intellectual Capital, *L. Martin Clotier and E. Richard Gold*   125

Chapter 10 An Intellectual Property Perspective on Intellectual Capital, *Patrick H. Sullivan, Jr.*   137

Part Two Interdisciplinary Views   153

Chapter 11 An Interfirm Perspective on Intellectual Capital, *Giovanni Schiuma, Antonio Lerro, and Daniela Carlucci*   155

Chapter 12 A Public Policy Perspective on Intellectual Capital, *Ahmed Bounfour and Leif Edvinsson*   170

viii *Contents*

Chapter 13 A Knowledge-Based Perspective on Intellectual Capital, *J.-C. Spender and Bernard Marr* 183

Chapter 14 An Epistemology Perspective on Intellectual Capital, *Göran Roos* 196

Part Three Discussion and Final Thoughts 211

Chapter 15 The Evolution and Convergence of Intellectual Capital as a Theme, *Bernard Marr* 213

Index 227

Foreword

It is becoming increasingly apparent that the beginning of the twenty-first century marked a watershed in both world history and the development of business management. In international relations, the events of September 11, 2001, and its aftermath—the U.S.-led invasions of Afghanistan and Iraq and the decline of multilateralism—provided a dramatic end to the euphoria that followed the breakup of the Soviet Union, the collapse of communism as a viable politicoeconomic system, and the end of the Cold War.

The world of business also entered a new era of uncertainty. The year 2001 saw the end of the TMT (telecommunications, media, and technology) boom, the onset of a bear market for stocks, and a host of corporate scandals that engulfed some of the world's most prominent and successful companies. The resulting uncertainties rose partly from the conditions in the business environment (anemic growth, high energy and raw material prices, and growing protectionism) and partly from waning confidence in corporate leaders' ability to manage in a complex and turbulent environment. The dominant management model of the 1990s, that of shareholder value maximization, lost much of its credibility. At the same time, the very success of strategies based on this model (cost cutting, refocusing, outsourcing, reengineering and delayering) meant that most of the potential gains from these restructuring activities are largely exhausted.

Hence, corporate executives face two critical strategic questions. First, what will be the main sources of future profitability now that most of the low-hanging fruit on the tree of profit has been harvested? Second, what principles and theories of management can guide companies in exploiting these future sources of profitability? The emerging field of intellectual capital can help us in relation to both.

Despite nearly a decade when knowledge management in its various forms has been prominent, it is clear that, in most firms, the major areas of inefficiency lie in the utilization of intellectual capital. In almost every organization I have close contact with, I see human effort, human creativity, and individuals' desire to excel being squandered. The most important factor distinguishing high performance companies, whether at the frontiers of science such as Intel or in the unglamorous world of discount retailing such as Wal-Mart, is the ability to access and deploy the knowledge resources available to them.

Managing intellectual capital requires working at multiple organizational levels and at different levels of complexity and uncertainty. At the most fundamental level, companies need to recognize the different types of intellectual capital they possess and the characteristics of these assets. Considerable progress has been made in relation to managing distinct categories of intellectual capital, most notably in human resource management and intellectual property management. Yet, for many companies, top management's understanding of the company's asset base remains bounded by the irrelevancies of balance sheet accounting. Looking beyond the awareness, identification, and evaluation of intellectual capital, some of the greatest challenges lie in deploying these assets to establish and sustain competitive advantage.

The increasing intensity of international competition means that sustainable advantage requires building of multilayered capabilities. In most industries, it is insufficient to compete on the basis of cost, quality, or innovation—companies must achieve all of these simultaneously. Toyota is a classic example of a company that leads its industry through combining capabilities in cost efficiency, world-class quality, design, fast-cycle new product development, and flexibility.

In the same way that we lack scientific explanations of why the talent-rich soccer teams of Italy, Spain, France, and England are outperformed by upstarts such as Greece, Croatia, and Denmark, we also lack scientific explanations of how the intellectual capital embodied in people and proprietary technologies is translated into competitive advantage and why it remains underdeveloped. However, we have a number of promising pointers. In particular, we know that the quest for answers must draw on multiple disciplines and look across multiple business functions.

This book offers an up-to-the-minute view of the field of intellectual capital by some of the world's most prominent experts, as well as providing repetition valuable pointers for future development. It is the first book that makes the multidisciplinary character of the intellectual capital field explicit by presenting the different disciplinary and interdisciplinary perspectives on intellectual capital. Highly relevant for practicing managers as well as firmly grounded in academic theory, this book addresses the opportunities and challenges in each of these perspectives and makes a first attempt to synthesize the different strands of thought. The chapters dealing with the measurement and valuation of intellectual capital focus on better-developed areas of intellectual capital and offer a foundation for firms' understanding and appreciation of their knowledge-based assets. The chapters dealing with strategic, evolutionary, epistemological, and interfirm dimensions of intellectual capital extend the frontiers of the field and offer penetrating insights into some of the more challenging questions concerning a firm's need to adapt its strategies, structures, and management systems to better deploy its intellectual capital.

The next few years promise to be interesting ones for both management thinkers and management practitioners. The management challenges facing firms call for new theories and new techniques. The principles and practices of intellectual capital management offer tremendous potential both in focusing managers' attention on what is important and in forging links between the human and intangible resources of the firm and the organizational capabilities that drive superior performance.

Robert Grant
Georgetown University
Washington, D.C.

Preface

The idea for this book resulted from my frustration in reading articles on or hearing people talk about intellectual capital, intangible assets, and knowledge assets. Most writers and presenters shared the notion that something had changed in our economy and intellectual capital had become more important. However, it often seemed that even though the same words, such as *intellectual capital* or *intangible assets*, were used, people often referred to completely different constructs. This led to many misunderstandings, endless and often useless discussions. It seemed that concepts such as intellectual capital meant different things to different people, and this difference was often due to the different backgrounds and perspectives taken.

One day, over a cup of coffee, I made my frustration known to Karen Maloney, saying that it would be great if we could make these differences a bit more explicit, so people could avoid misunderstandings and the useless discussions about taxonomies. Karen happened to be the senior acquisitions editor for Butterworth–Heinemann in the United States, and the idea for this book was quickly born. In my role as chairman of the PMA Intellectual Capital Group, I approached potential authors. Everyone I talked to was excited about the idea. After many months of hard work, the book is finished, and I would like to express my gratitude to everyone who contributed to it. Not only the authors of chapters have made this book happen, but also many colleagues and friends with their suggestions, help, and support. Without all these people, the book would never have materialized. I would like to thank everyone who contributed in any way.

Special thanks go to all members of the PMA Intellectual Capital Group who have not written a chapter but contributed their insights and discussions. These include Guy Ahonen, Verna Allee, Debra Amidon, Daniel Andriessen, Max Boisot, Nick Bontis, Bino Catasus, Jay Chatzkel, Christina Chaminade, Jürgen Daum, Chris Evans, Robert Grant, Karin Grasenick, James Guthrie, Richard Hall, Clive Holtham, Jon Low, Sarah Mavrinac, David O'Donnell, Patricia Ordonez de Pablos, Steven Pike, Ante Pulic, Hanno Roberts, Robin Roslender, Hubert Saint-Onge, Paloma Sanchez, Harry Scarborough, David Snowden, Karl-Erik Sveiby, José Viedma Marti, Stefano Zambon, among many others.

Of course, I would like to express special appreciation for the authors who believed in the value of this book and gave up some of their valuable time to contribute a chapter. Thank you Mie, David, Göran, Baruch, Leandro, Sudi, Guhlam, Jan, Per Nikolaj, Lisa, Ulf, Joe, Martin, Richard, Pat, Antonio, Gianni, Daniela, Ahmed, Leif, and J.-C. for all your efforts.

In addition, I thank my colleagues at the Centre for Business Performance at Cranfield School of Management for providing me with a continuously stimulating and challenging environment, for support, friendship, as well as many valuable insights. Therefore, I thank Chris Adams, Mike Bourne, Monica Franco, Mike

Kennerley, Dina Gray, Mark Wilcox, Steve Mason, Pietro Micheli, Karim Moustaghfir, Veronica Martinez, Angela Walters, Eva Barton, Alison Isham, and Jacqueline Brown. Special thanks go to Andy Neely for all the valuable guidance as well as the friendship provided over the years.

Finally I would like to express my deepest appreciation for the support of my family, my brother Marc André Marr, Julie and Alan Parkins, and especially my wife Claire. They have, with their love and support, enabled me to engage in another book venture.

Bernard Marr
Cranfield School of Management

Introduction

Bernard Marr

Cranfield School of Management

Intellectual capital scores highly on the agenda of executives, managers, and academics as they try to disentangle such problems as how to value intangibles, how to identify and measure knowledge resources, and how to report invisible assets. Few people doubt the importance of managing intellectual capital; and most are in agreement that intangible assets such as knowledge, brands, relationships, organizational culture, and intellectual property are primary drivers of competitiveness in today's global economy. The consulting firm Accenture recently commissioned the Economist Intelligence Unit to conduct a survey of executives around the world to understand their views on intellectual capital. Most executives responded that intellectual capital is critical for the future success of their businesses. However, at the same time, most agreed that their approaches of managing it were poor or nonexistent (Molnar, 2004).

The growing interest in this topic is also reflected in an onslaught of new books and journals dedicated to the topic. Articles on intangibles appear at an increasing rate and currently average about two per day in the English language alone. More and more conferences are being organized to address the management of intangibles, software companies are developing tools to assist managers in their search to master their "soft" assets, and a basic search on the Internet will produce over 250,000 websites on the topic.

Governments, research bodies, and private institutions sponsor projects to develop our understanding of intellectual capital, which in turn leads to an increase in publications and awareness. Tools are being developed to address some of the gaps in the way we handle intellectual capital and intangible assets. These include strategic approaches and frameworks, methods to value intangible assets such as brands, and methods to measure human capital, to name just a few. In addition, instruments are being developed for the disclosure of intellectual capital, including new guidelines and accounting rules.

So far, I used the notions of intangibles and intellectual capital interchangeably. This brings us to a significant problem many people face when they first delve into this area: The definitions are not very clear and neither are the boundaries. This is due, to a large extent, to the multidimensional nature of the topic. When one talks to accountants, they might refer to intangibles as "non-financial fixed assets that do not have physical substance but are identifiable and controlled by the entity through custody and legal rights," as defined by the Accounting Standards Board in FRS 10, their main standard for reporting intangibles and goodwill. Such a stringent definition excludes many commonly accepted intangibles, like customer satisfaction and knowledge and skills of employees, as they cannot be controlled by the firm in an "accounting" sense. A human resources manager might refer to intellectual capital as the skills, knowledge, and attitude of employees. A marketing manager might argue that intellectual capital, such as brand recognition and customer satisfaction, is at the heart of business success; whereas the IT manager might view key intangibles as being software applications and network capabilities.

This brief scenario illustrates the definition problems that occur when different people talk about the same concept from different perspectives or disciplines, using the same language to describe different constructs. The issue is further complicated by the nature of academic research. Traditionally, academic careers are based on functional specialization. Accounting professors, for example, go to accounting conferences and are published in accounting journals, whereas marketing professors go to marketing conventions and are published in their dedicated periodicals. A marketing professor could very well be working on intellectual capital, yet never come across work conducted by an accounting professor operating in the same field. Academics tend to read publications in their dedicated field and rarely reference or build on work conducted in other disciplines. The result is little cross-fertilization of ideas and concepts. This seems to be especially problematic for a field like intellectual capital, where developments take place in diverse disciplines.

In summary, the field of intellectual capital is truly multidisciplinary, spanning most functions and disciplines. Unfortunately, there is little agreement and much confusion regarding the definition of *intellectual capital*, available management tools, their intended usage, and the extent to which such tools are applied in organizations.

The aim of this book it to address exactly these issues. First, it provides a comprehensive, multidisciplinary introduction to the topic of intellectual capital and intangible assets. Second, it is intended to help bridge some of the disciplinary gaps and facilitate knowledge transfer across disciplines. To meet these objectives, the book deliberately offers functional perspectives and therefore a comprehensive understanding of what intellectual capital is, what it stands for, what is the state of the art in each discipline, and where it will go in the future. The breadth of the book means that it should appeal to a wide audience, encompassing academics and practitioners, novices as well as experts. It is a starting point to elucidate the concept of intellectual capital and a base for deeper understanding of a complex, exciting, and important field with utmost relevance to today's business world.

The book features views on intellectual capital from an economics, strategy, accounting, finance, reporting, marketing, human resource management, information systems, and legal position. It also offers interdisciplinary views on intellectual capital from an interfirm, public policy, knowledge-based, and epistemology perspective. The final chapter of the book summarizes the overall evolution of intellectual capital as a multidisciplinary theme, extracts the key trends and developments, and tries to highlight possible bridges across disciplines to open trajectories for future developments, learning, and practice.

The book is structured methodologically, designed to provide a multifaceted understanding of the field. The structure of each chapter is similar and starts with an explanation and review of the background and development of intellectual capital in relation to the discipline being discussed. It covers a historic review to explore the triggers and reasons why intangibles have become important, and above all, it provides definitions and clarifies the language used to describe intellectual capital. This part addresses the key beliefs and theoretical foundations on which views on intellectual capital are based in the corresponding perspective.

Each chapter then outlines the evolution of theoretical concepts and gives the reader insight into which theoretical tools and techniques have been developed to manage intellectual capital in the corresponding perspective. It is intended to demonstrate the status quo and theoretical diversity. This is then contrasted with the extent to which these tools and techniques are used in practice. The chapter might include a selection of best-practice examples of how real organizations apply these tools and techniques and might uncover possible gaps between theory and practice. Different disciplines face different gaps; in some, theory leads practice, whereas in others, theory might lag practice. In this way, the reader sees the potential for both transfer of theoretical concepts into practice and grounding practical concepts in theory.

The final part of each chapter looks to the future. It tries to identify how mature the theme is in each disciplinary view and discuss how intellectual capital might develop. In this, the authors seek to identify the major challenges to be addressed in the future and give an outline of possible barriers and enablers.

Overview of the Chapters

This book contains 15 chapters by a total of 22 authors, all of whom are recognized as thought leaders in the area of intellectual capital in their specific discipline.

Part I. Disciplinary Views

An Economics Perspective on Intellectual Capital

In Chapter 1, *Mie Augier* and *David Teece* provide an excellent introduction to the topic by highlighting the economic importance of intellectual capital. The authors provide a historical overview of the growing significance of knowledge and intellectual capital as a driver for innovation and R&D and describe the features of such assets in terms of replicability, imitability, and appropriability. Finally, the authors highlight how the nature of intellectual capital offers big challenges for their measurement and management.

A Strategy Perspective on Intellectual Capital

In Chapter 2, *Bernard Marr* and *Göran Roos* outline the development of strategy from a market-based to a resource-based paradigm. The authors discuss the strategic importance of intellectual capital resources and differentiate between the static and dynamic nature of these assets. Then, the authors outline the tools for the strategic management of intellectual capital.

An Accounting Perspective on Intellectual Capital

In Chapter 3, *Baruch Lev*, *Leandro Cañibano*, and *Bernard Marr* provide an accounting perspective on intellectual capital. The chapter clarifies the definition of *intellectual capital* from an accountant's view and discusses some of the difficulties and inconsistencies in the way intellectual capital is treated in accounting, posing many challenges for accounting professionals. The authors then outline the current practice and latest changes in accounting rules and regulations for intangibles, before they take a look into the future of accounting for intangibles.

A Finance Perspective on Intellectual Capital

In Chapter 4, *Sudi Sudarsanam, Ghulam Sorwar,* and *Bernard Marr* discuss the financial valuation of intellectual capital. The chapter outlines the importance of intellectual capital for future cash flow and growth opportunities. It then discusses a selection of valuation approaches, which are split into static and dynamic models. In the final part of the chapter, the authors focus on real option models for the valuation of intellectual capital, by highlighting both the benefits and the limitations of such an approach.

A Reporting Perspective on Intellectual Capital

In Chapter 5, *Jan Mourtisen, Per Nikolaj Bukh,* and *Bernard Marr* discuss how organizations could voluntarily report on intellectual capital, both internally and externally. This perspective is related to management accounting but does not take a disciplinary perspective as such. The chapter discusses the voluntary reporting experience in Europe, where several initiatives have developed guidelines on how to report and disclose information on the knowledge-based value drivers. The chapter discusses the need for reporting on intellectual capital, then discusses what organizations should include in such reports and outlines European guidelines for intellectual capital reports. The chapter includes a case study example of how a firm produced intellectual capital reports for external disclosure.

A Marketing Perspective on Intellectual Capital

In Chapter 6, *Lisa Fernström* discusses the importance of brands, customer satisfaction, and customer relationships. The chapter outlines the development of modern marketing, with a strong emphasis on intellectual capital. It then discusses the different intellectual capital components relevant from a marketing perspective. The chapter also outlines how an intellectual capital perspective might shed light on the valuation and measurement of assets such as brand and relationships.

A Human Resource Perspective on Intellectual Capital

In Chapter 7, *Ulf Johansson* discusses the role of intellectual capital in a human resource management environment. The chapter defines *intellectual capital* in this context and then discusses various tools developed to manage intellectual capital from this perspective. These include the human resources scorecard, human resource accounting, and human resource costing. The chapter outlines the measurement trap many of these tools fall into and the conflicting interest concerning human resource measures. Case studies show how firms have managed their intellectual capital from a human resources perspective, before the author takes a look into the future.

An Information Systems Perspective on Intellectual Capital

In Chapter 8, *Joe Peppard* discusses the role of intellectual capital from an information systems perspective. The chapter puts intellectual capital into the context of information systems and technology. It distinguishes between data, information, and knowledge as organizational assets and the role of information systems and technology in the management of these assets. The chapter discusses how to value information system assets and how information systems management can help transform human capital into structural capital.

A Legal Perspective on Intellectual Capital

In Chapter 9, *Martin Cloutier* and *Richard Gold* discuss intellectual capital from a legal perspective. The chapter outlines the various legal mechanisms and instruments companies have at their disposal to protect their intellectual capital. As part of this chapter, the authors discuss the application of instruments such as trade secrets, patents, copyrights, contracts, and licenses.

An Intellectual Property Perspective on Intellectual Capital

In Chapter 10, *Patrick Sullivan, Jr.*, outlines how organizations can strategically manage their intellectual property. Related to the legal perspective, this perspective outlines the practical business application of intellectual capital in an intellectual property paradigm. Based on the experience of various firms, the author outlines some best practices for managing intellectual property for business value.

Part II. Interdisciplinary Views

An Interfirm Perspective on Intellectual Capital

In Chapter 11, *Giovanni Schiuma*, *Antonio Lerro*, and *Daniela Carlucci* outline a framework for managing intellectual capital in clusters of firms. Much research to date has focused on the firm level; however, with increasing integration of supply chains and increasing collaboration among firms, this perspective gains importance. The chapter outlines the importance of knowledge in firm clusters and then discusses the different intellectual capital components important for interfirm collaboration.

A Public Policy Perspective on Intellectual Capital

In Chapter 12, *Ahmed Bounfour* and *Leif Edvinsson* discuss implications of the increasing importance of intellectual capital for public policy. The authors outline the importance of intellectual capital in the performance of regions and entire countries. The chapter contrasts European, American, and Japanese investment in intellectual capital and outlines the various policy initiatives implemented in different countries. In their look into the future, the authors outline possible approaches of intellectual capital management for nations and regions.

A Knowledge-Based Perspective on Intellectual Capital

In Chapter 13, *J.-C. Spender* and *Bernard Marr* discuss the importance of knowledge as intellectual capital and implications for its management. The chapter outlines the increasing importance of knowledge-based assets, the different views of what knowledge is, and how it evolved in the business context. The authors draw some conclusions for the management of knowledge assets based on the diverse views of knowledge.

An Epistemology Perspective on Intellectual Capital

In Chapter 14, *Göran Roos* discusses the notion of corporate epistemology. Introducing three different epistemological concepts (connectionist, cognitivist, and autopoietic), the chapter outlines their implications for the management of intellectual capital. The way people believe knowledge is created has an impact on the way knowledge is managed, and a mismatch between the way knowledge is managed and corporate epistemology might cause problems. Reporting on various case studies, the author highlights the different epistemologies and their suitability with different value creation logics.

Part III. Discussion and Final Thoughts

The Evolution and Convergence of Intellectual Capital as a Theme

In Chapter 15, *Bernard Marr* provides an interdisciplinary overview of the evolution of intellectual capital. The chapter provides a historic perspective, with the major milestones and developments in each perspective. The chapter then draws some implications of this multidisciplinary evolution and provides a starting point to bring together the views on intellectual capital from the different perspectives and disciplines to create a holistic understanding of the subject and facilitate cross-disciplinary awareness and collaboration.

The selection of perspectives is not thought to be exhaustive, and I believe there are other interesting perspectives on the subject of intellectual capital. Furthermore, the individual perspectives included in this book are not thought to present an all-encompassing view but *one* view from *one* perspective. This is why the chapters are called *a* perspective and not *the* perspective. The intention, however, is to highlight the major perspectives on the topic to facilitate cross-disciplinary learning and provide readers a broad understanding of intellectual capital—the most important driver of value and competitive advantage in today's economy.

Reference

Molnar, M. J. 2004. "Executive views on Intangible Assests." Insights From the Accenture/Economist Intelligence unit Survey. "Accenture Research Note Intangible Assets and Future Value".

Part I
Disciplinary Views

An Economics Perspective on Intellectual Capital[1]

Mie Augier
Stanford University

David J. Teece
Haas School of Business, University of California, Berkeley

> Technological advance, resting in the new knowledge and occurring accidentally or mechanically, seems to be the only possible offset to this "natural" tendency to diminishing returns.
>
> Frank H. Knight, "Diminishing Returns from Investments," *Journal of Political Economy*

Introduction

Business organizations employ knowledge. They generate and process information, formulate plans and strategies, make decisions, monitor behavior and experiences, and learn, create, and use know-how. Although economists have traditionally modeled firms as employing capital, labor, and other factors of production to increase output—possibly with exogenous technical change as a shift parameter in the production function—it is increasingly realized within the economics profession that knowledge and intellectual capital (IC) are the primary creators of value in the economy (i.e., the creation and use of intangible rather than tangible [physical] assets are the keys to wealth creation), and technological change is not exogenous but, in fact, generated in large measure by firms themselves. As Peter Drucker suggested: "The traditional factors of production—land, labor and capital—have not disappeared. But they have become secondary. Knowledge is becoming the only meaningful resource" (1993, p. 42).

Economists and management it was probally scholars (as well as scholars from other disciplines) have done much to advance our understanding of the central issues around intellec-tual capital. While classical economists were aware of the role of technology and knowledge in economic growth, Schumpeter who brought innovation to the fore. Unfortunately, Schumpeterian economics until quite recently was ignored by mainstream economists. Notable exceptions to this include Paul David, Giovanni Dosi, Chris Freeman, Zvi Griliches, Edwin Mansfield, David Mowery, Richard

---

[1] We are indebted to Bernard Marr for encouragement and suggestions and to Patricia Lonergan for skillful assistance.

Nelson, Nathan Rosenberg, Sidney Winter, and occasionally Kenneth Arrow and Robert Solow. These economists took innovation issues seriously, and while small in number, they initiated several streams of research that helped build a rich understanding of the economics of technological change. In recent years, business economists and management scholars added considerably to the understanding of technological change and intellectual capital.

In short, economists provided early insights into many of the issues around knowledge and technological innovation. As an example, at least since Arrow (1962), knowledge has been well appreciated (among economists) for its "public good" characteristics (i.e., the nonrivalrous nature of consumption) because of high levels of nonexcludability. The attributes of knowledge have been used to explain, for instance, why imitation can (but need not be) easy, why diffusion of new technologies depends on the mobility of engineers and scientists, and why know-how markets do not work well (Teece 1977a, 1981a). Also, more-recent research on the generation of new knowledge made it possible to understand the role of technological externalities and the positive feedback effects on technological innovation (David, 1993).

Despite the development of important insights by a few economists, it is unfortunately the case that the production and utilization of technological and organizational knowledge is still handled in a rather cavalier way within mainstream (neoclassical) economic theory. The challenges posed by technological change for economic theory have been recognized since at least Frank Knight (1921), but it wasn't until Teece (1981a, 1986), Nelson and Winter (1982), and Nonaka (1991) that issues such as the tacit nature of much technological and organizational knowledge came to be widely recognized and the ramifications explored.[2] Because of the tacit (i.e., difficult or costly to articulate) nature of know-how, those practicing a technique may be able to do so with great facility, but they may not be able to transfer the skill to others without demonstration and involvement.

The growing recognition of the importance of knowledge and intangible assets, their tacit nature, and the desire to understand what creates competitive advantages at both the level of the firm and the level of the economy has stimulated many diverse (but not always consistent) streams of research on technological innovation and knowledge management. The intention of this chapter is to review some of the key insights and contributions to the economics and management of intellectual capital. The following section focuses on the organization of research and development (R&D) and the production of new technology. The next section outlines classical contributions to understanding the role of knowledge in the economy and the increasing awareness of the importance of innovation. The section after that surveys central concepts in the economies of knowledge and intellectual property as they exist in the literature today. Then we highlight the measurement issues and review some of the relevant recent empirical literature on intangibles before the chapter concludes.

---

[2] Frank Knight is an often-neglected advocate for the fact that technological change makes economic predictions difficult; as he stated: "The most fundamentally and irretrievably uncertain phases or factors of progress are those which amount essentially to the increase of knowledge as such. This description evidently holds for the improvement of technological processes and the forms of business organization and for the discovery of new natural resources. Here it is a contradiction in terms to speak of anticipation, in an accurate and detailed sense, for to anticipate the advance would be to make it at once" (Knight 1921, p. 318).

Organizing Research and Development and Knowledge Production Activities

Intellectual assets created by businesses are developed through learning, experience, and at least since the early twentieth century, of course, organized industrial research and development (R&D) activities. R&D encompasses several different activities that can occur in any order. Basic research is aimed purely at the creation of new scientific and technical knowledge. Its purpose is to advance understanding of phenomena. Its core foundations are usually quite abstract. Applied research is designed to implement new scientific and technical knowledge, which is expected to have a practical but not necessarily a commercial payoff. While basic research is aimed at new knowledge for its own sake, the goal of applied research is practical and has utility. In development, the new knowledge is embedded in a product or process and honed for commercial application. Boundaries among these activities are quite fuzzy, and the manner in which they have been organized and linked has changed over time (Teece, 1989). For almost a century and a half, organized research activities have placed an important (although ever changing) role.

The first organized research laboratory in the United States was established by Thomas Edison in 1876. In 1886, Arthur D. Little, an applied scientist, started his enterprise, which became a major technical services, consulting organization to other enterprises. Eastman Kodak (1893), B. F. Goodrich (1895), General Electric (1900), Dow (1900), Dupont (1902), Goodyear (1909), and American Telephone & Telegraph (1907) followed soon thereafter. The industrial laboratory constituted a significant departure from an earlier period of U.S. history, when innovation was largely the work of independent inventors like Eli Whitney (the cotton gin), Samuel Morse (telegraph), Charles Goodyear (vulcanization of rubber), and Cyrus McCormick (the reaper).

The founding of formal R&D programs and laboratories stemmed in part from competitive threats, which necessitated a more proactive strategy toward innovation. For instance, AT&T at first followed the telegraph industry's practice of relying on the market for technological innovation. However, the expiration of the major Bell patents and the growth of large numbers of independent telephone companies helped stimulate AT&T to organize Bell Labs. Competition likewise drove George Eastman to established laboratories at Kodak Park in Rochester, New York, to counteract efforts by German dyestuff and chemical firms to enter into the manufacture of fine chemicals, including photographic chemicals and film.

During the early years of the twentieth century, the number of research labs grew dramatically. By World War I, perhaps as many as 100 industrial research laboratories were in the United States. The number tripled during that war, and industrial R&D even maintained its momentum during the Depression. R&D activity conducted in centralized laboratories of American business enterprises increased still further during World War II and maintained momentum through the 1950s and the 1960s. Significant breakthroughs included the transistor, electronic computing, synthetic fibers, and lasers.

By the early 1970s, however, management was beginning to lose faith in the science-driven view of industrial research and technological innovation, primarily because few blockbuster products emerged from the research funded during the 1950s, 1960s, and 1970s. As a result of this and other factors, from the mid-1970s on, there has been a marked change in organization and strategy, as both industry and government have come to recognize that the classical form of R&D organization, with centralized research and a science-driven culture, was simply not working, in part because new technology was not getting into new products and processes soon enough and imitation rates had increased. Foreign competitors began undermining the traditional markets of many U.S. firms.

Many firms realized that extracting value from intellectual capital is a much more-complicated and risky process than extracting value from physical capital. Many were confronted by the paradox of being leaders in R&D and the creation of intangibles but laggards in capturing value from their investments. The fruit of much R&D was being appropriated by domestic and foreign competitors, and much technology was wasting away in many research laboratories. In telecommunications, Bell Lab's contribution to the economy at large far outstripped its contribution to AT&T. Xerox Corporation's Palo Alto Research Center made stunning contributions to the economy in the area of the personal computer, local area networks, and the graphical user interface that became the basis of Apple's Macintosh computer. Xerox shareholders were well served, too, but most of the benefits ended up in the hands of Xerox's competitors.

By the 1980s and 1990s, a new model for organizing research became apparent. First, R&D activity came to be decentralized inside large corporations themselves, with the aim to bring it closer to the users. Intel, the world leader in microprocessors, spent over $1 billion per year on R&D but had no separate R&D laboratory. Rather, development was conducted in the manufacturing facilities. It did not invest in fundamental research at all, except possibly through its funding of university research. It did, however, participate actively in the development and sharing of new process knowledge through its funding of Sematech.

Second, many companies were looking to the universities for much of their basic or fundamental research, maintaining close associations with the science and engineering departments at the major research universities. Indeed, over the century, the percentage of academic research funded by industry grew from 2.7% in 1960 to 6.8% in 1995. However, strong links between university research and industrial research are limited primarily to electronics (especially semiconductors), chemical products, medicine, and agriculture. For the most part, university researchers are insufficiently versed in the particulars of specific product markets and customer needs to configure products to the needs of the market. Moreover, in many sectors, the cost of research equipment is so high that universities simply cannot participate.

Third, corporations embraced alliances involving R&D, manufacturing, and marketing to get products to market quicker and leverage off complementary assets already in place elsewhere. (It is important to note, however, that outsourcing R&D is a complement, not a substitute, to in-house R&D.) Outsourcing and codevelopment arrangements had become common by the 1980s and 1990s (e.g., Pratt & Whitney's codevelopment programs for jet engines), as the costs of product development increased and the antitrust laws were modified to recognize the benefits of cooperation on R&D and related activities. The National Cooperative Research Act of 1984 and its amendment in 1993 provided greater clarity with respect to the likely positive antitrust treatment of cooperative efforts relating to technological innovation and its commercialization. Cooperation was also facilitated by the emergence of capable potential partners in Europe and Japan.

These developments meant that, at the end of the twentieth century, research and development and the creation and exploitation of intangible assets was being conducted in quite a different manner from the early decades of the century. Many corporations closed their central research laboratories or dramatically scaled back, including Westinghouse, RCA, AT&T, and Unocal, to name just a few. Alliances and cooperative efforts of all kinds were of much greater importance in both developing and commercializing new knowledge.

Importantly, a transformation in industry structure brought about through venture-capital-funded startups was well underway. New business enterprises, or "startups," were in part the cause for the decline of research laboratories; but in many ways the startups still depended on the organized R&D labs for their birthright. Beginning in the late 1970s, the organized venture capital industry, providing funding for new enterprise development, rose to significance. This was particularly true in industries such as biotech and information services. While venture capital in one form or another has been around for much of the twentieth century—the Rockefellers, Morgans, Mellons, Vanderbilts, Hilmans, and other significant families had been funding entrepreneurs for quite some time—institutional sources of money, including pension funds and university endowments, had become significant sources by the 1980s. This dramatically increased the funds available, as well as the professionalism by which "the money" provided guidance to a new breed of entrepreneurs, eager to develop and market new products incorporating new technology.

As a result, venture funded startups proliferated in many sectors. While, in the 1970s, Apple Computer significantly "bootstrapped" (although it did take modest venture funding from Arthur Rock and others) itself into the personal computer industry, in the 1980s, Compaq and others received much larger infusions of venture capital to get started in the personal computer industry. In biotechnology, venture funding also grew to great significance. However, it is extremely unusual for venture funds to support the efforts of companies making investments in early stage research. Rather, venture funding tends to be focused more on exploiting intangibles, less in creating them. Successful startups frequently begin with a product or process concept (and often personnel) that has been "incubated" to some level in a research program of an already established firm. Nevertheless, the phenomena of venture funding is significant, as it is now a very important channel by which intangible assets are employed and new products and processes brought to market.

The Economics of Knowledge: Some Historical Roots

Antecedents

The inclusion of knowledge as a factor in the study of modern economic growth was advanced by post-World War II scholars studying the sources of productivity improvement in the U.S. economy. However, the linkage of knowledge to economic performance in fact had been made much earlier. Issues of knowledge externalities and learning were present in Smith (1776) and Marshall (1925); the tacit nature of knowledge had been recognized by Hayek (1945) and Knight (1921); and Schumpeter (1943) focused on entrepreneurship, the organization of innovation, and innovation-driven competition.[3] These antecedents are given only a cursory and selective review in what follows.

Adam Smith was aware of the importance of learning and knowledge for economic growth. His now famous discussion of the pin factory demonstrated how repeated

---

[3] As Schumpeter noted, "The fundamental impulse that sets and keeps the capitalist engine in motion comes from the new consumers' goods, the new methods of production or transportation, the new markets, the new forms of industrial organization that capitalist enterprise creates" (Schumpeter, 1943, p. 83).

exposure to individual tasks in the pin-making process enabled workers to increase production. As he wrote,

> The great increase of the quantity of work which, in consequence of the division of labor, the same number of people are capable of performing, is owning to three different circumstances; first, to the increase of individual dexterity in every particular workman; secondly, to the saving of time which is commonly lost in passing from one species of work to another; and lastly, to the invention of a great number of machines which facilitate and abridge labour. (Smith 1776, p. 112).

In other words, learning by doing increases output from individual skills in part because of product innovations. Wealth and growth in Smith is a coevolutionary process, in which growing markets support the division of labor.[4] In effect, Smith recognized that the division of labor and increasing returns follows from organizational change and learning. Others recognized that the capacity for individuals and organizations to create and absorb new knowledge is important (Loasby 2004). These elements were subsequently developed further in theories of the firm by Edith Penrose (1959), Nelson and Winter (1982), Teece (1982, 1984), and others.

Another important contribution by a classical economist to the economics of knowledge was Alfred Marshall's early discussion of "external economies" arising from the interaction between industrial districts. He recognized that positive externalities were available to all firms in a given industry. Marshall thus flagged early on the importance of spillover and appropriability issues. Others agreed. For instance, Allyn Young noted that, "not all of the economies which are properly to be called external can be accounted for by adding up the internal economies of all the separate firms" (Young 1928, p. 528).

However, while ideas relating to the study of innovation were mentioned by the classical economists, they provided no in-depth analysis or analytical apparatus to help us better understand the particulars of technological innovation and the creation and commercialization of intellectual capital and other intangibles. A rather limited number of economists, including Nelson and Winter, Abramovitz, Kuznets, Mansfield, and Rosenberg, kept the study of innovation alive and added to our understanding of knowledge generation, storage, and use.

Knowledge (know-how) and information (know-of) are related but analytically separate concepts. Nevertheless, it is important to recognize that issues surrounding ignorance and asymmetric information did receive attention. For instance, Simon (1955, 1978) studied the impact of bounded rationality, and Akerlof and others studied the impact of limited information on market failure. In particular, Simon criticized assumptions of perfect information and unlimited computational capacity and aimed to replace the assumption of global rationality with an assumption more in correspondence with how humans (and other choosing organisms) made decisions, their computational limitations, and how they accessed information in their current environments (1955, p. 99).

Furthermore, the injection of the entrepreneur into economic theory by Knight (1921), Schumpeter (1934), and others was also clearly significant; but as with innovation and learning, not much analytical structure was provided for analyzing the role

---

[4] As Young (1928) wrote: "Adam Smith's dictum amounts to the theorem that the division of labour depends in large part upon the division of labour ... change becomes progressive and propagates itself in a cumulative way" (p. 533).

of knowledge in organizations in a detailed way, and so conceptual development of issues related to intangibles failed to become mainstream. This left economics as a field being perhaps the first of the social sciences to flag the importance of innovation to economic and social development; yet economic theory was extremely slow to incorporate this understanding into its mainstream. Most economists preferred to ignore the subject, as it tended to make economic modeling more difficult. Static rather than (technologically) dynamic models held the attention of the profession for quite a number of decades.[5]

Innovation and Economic Growth

The notion that innovation is not just an important phenomenon but the primary driver of economic growth was long suspected by classical economists.[6] Economic historians consistently recognized the importance of knowledge (e.g., Kuznets 1967, Abramovitz 1962) and kept knowledge on stage in the study of economic growth.[7] As discussed previously, outlines of modern theories of technological change and growth are of Smithian origins. Considerable additional impetus to the importance of innovation and intangible assets came when Solow (1957) provided the important calculation that 87.5% of the growth in output in the United States between the years of 1909 and 1949 could be ascribed to technological improvements alone. The "Solow residual" was not just substantial, it appeared to be of overwhelming importance. However, one early reaction was to try and explain the "residual" by reference to improvements in the quality of the capital stock.[8]

Indeed, growth theorists did not take the full import of empirical studies by productivity/growth scholars seriously for quite some time. Nicholas Kaldor argued for the existence of a "technical progress" function: Per-capita income was a function of

---

[5] The use of mathematic modeling in economics has been debated for centuries, at least in part because excessive formalism often undermines dynamics (Nelson and Winter 1982; Teece 1984). Alfred Marshall for instance wrote to a student and colleague: "(1) Use mathematics as a shorthand language, rather than as an engine of inquiry. (2) Keep to them till you have done. (3) Translate into English. (4) Then illustrate by examples that are important in real life. (5) Burn the mathematics. (6) If you can't succeed in 4, burn 3." (in Krugman 1998). Debreu's textbook of course promotes a different view: "The theory of value is treated here with the standards of rigor of the contemporary formalist school of mathematics" (1959, p. x). The problem is that the rigor of mathematics undermines the empirical validity of the theory. Nelson and Winter (1982) distinguish between "formal" and "appreciative" theorizing in economics, with appreciative referring to empirically relevant and applied work.

[6] See, for instance, Schumpeter (1943): "The essential point to grasp is that in dealing with capitalism we are dealing with an evolutionary process. . . . The fundamental impulse that sets and keeps the capitalist engine in motion comes from the new consumer goods, the new methods of production or transportation, the new forms of industrial organization that capitalist enterprise creates. . . . In the case of retail trade the competition that matters arises not from additional shops of the same type, but from the department store, the chain store, the mail-order house and the super market, which are bound to destroy those pyramids sooner or later. Now a theoretical construction which neglects this essential element of the case neglects all that is most typically capitalist about it; even if correct in logic as well as in fact, it is like Hamlet without the Danish Prince."

[7] Kuznets remarked, "all empirical knowledge, all scientifically tested information, no matter how abstract and remote it may seem, is potentially applicable in economic production" (1967, p. 61).

[8] Solow argues, for instance, that increased capital-intensive investment embodies new machinery and new ideas as well as increased learning for even further economic progress.

per-capita investment. In a series of important studies, Edward Denison (1962), Zvi Griliches (1963), and Dale W. Jorgensen and Zvi Griliches (1967) argued that there were errors in measurement in the early growth work. One such error, it was argued, was that the Solow residual actually was substantially less than first estimated, because if technical progress usually arrives "embodied" in new capital goods, then a lot more growth can be ascribed to simply the "qualitative growth" of capital inputs.

Further progress began to be made when Kenneth Arrow argued that the level of the "learning" coefficient is a function of cumulative investment (i.e., past gross investment) (Arrow 1962). Arrow recognized that because new machines are more productive versions of those in existence, capital investment not only induces labor productivity through augmenting the capital stock (as in Kaldor) but also improves productivity through the use of higher-quality capital, where quality improvement stems from innovation.

Despite a burst of inquiry in the immediate postwar period, interest by growth theorists in innovation was minimal in the 1960s, 1970s, and 1980s and macroeconomists in general pursued business cycle and rational expectation issues. Interest in growth was renewed in the mid-1980s, in particular with Paul Romer's 1986 article on "Increasing Returns and Long Run Growth." This article heralded the emergence of the "new growth theory."

Innovation and intangibles are now somewhat recognized by growth theorists. In particular, Romer described the macroeconomic importance of intellectual assets and growth (Romer 1993):

> Every generation has perceived limits to growth that finite resources and undesirable side effects would pose if no new recipes or ideas were discovered. And every generation has underestimated the potential for finding new recipes and ideas. We consistently fail to grasp how many ideas remain to be discovered. The difficulty is the same one we have with compounding. Possibilities do not add up. They multiply. (p. 3)

The *new* in the new growth theory, compared to the classical Solow model (Solow 1957), is that long-term growth is explained, not by the growth of the population, but by knowledge accumulation. Knowledge generates increasing returns and growth, in part because of its public good characteristic.

One central insight is the effects of the positive externalities of technological knowledge. As Romer (1986, p. 1003) remarks, "The creation of new knowledge by one firm is assumed to have a positive external effect on the production possibilities of other firms, because knowledge cannot be perfectly patented or kept secret." Because of zero (or close to zero) marginal costs of using new knowledge and lower costs of using existing knowledge to lower the costs of producing new knowledge, there is dynamic scale economics in knowledge accumulation, an insight arguably already provided by the classical economists. Assuming only partial excludability, the "new growth theory" showed that there could be positive externalities from (private) knowledge accumulation efforts. In short, the "new growth theorists" began to pay attention to what the classical economists and a small group of business economists and business historians had been saying for decades. Nevertheless, the new growth theory does represent progress.

In short, widespread recognition of the importance of innovation and intangibles in both economic theory and growth theory has been very slow in coming. Moreover, mainstream theory is still not particularly insightful with respect to the causes and nature of technological progress and learning. The reason for this is the inherent limitations of neoclassical theorizing, and its inability so far to incorporate such phenomena as the tacit nature of knowledge, the role of entrepreneurship, and the importance of disequilibrium (Simon 1978; Teece and Winter 1984).

Firm-Level Developments

For quite some time, microeconomic analysis has been out in front of macroeconomics with respect to the study of intellectual capital. Eclectic approaches to the study of innovation at the firm have been pursued with vigor by a few economists and several notable social scientists at least since 1950. In particular, evolutionary ideas of technological change have become widespread. For example, one can reference the early Nelson and Winter work on technological change (1977, 1982) and the early work of Teece (1977a, 1977b) and Dosi (1982) on technology transfer and technology paradigms.

Microeconomic work on spillovers and appropriability has proceeded unabated since Alfred Marshall. Teece (1986), Rosenberg and Steinmueller (1988), and Mansfield (1988) noted the importance of externalities and "spillovers" and studied processes of technology transfer. "Spillovers" may be generated by rival firms, universities, and government research organizations. Indeed, March and Simon (1958) argued earlier that organizations may learn by imitating or borrowing from their rivals.

Also, knowledge spillovers are important at the intraorganizational level, and research suggests that a firm's innovative performance is strongly influenced by knowledge generated outside the firm's formal R&D (Mansfield 1968; Teece 1992; Chesbrough 2003). Teece (1986) developed the concept of appropriability regimes to explicitly recognized industry- and firm-level differences in appropriability.

Microeconomic studies focused on issues relating to creating and maintaining a competitive advantage at the firm level. Issues around learning and intangibles have become especially salient. Whereas learning in neoclassical theory was mainly about productivity gains in human capital resulting from increasing quality or speed of job performance as a result of previous experience in a given task (Arrow 1962) or experience improving individual skills and productivity through investing experience in training (Becker 1964), organizational learning theorists emphasized competency traps in learning and the coevolution and adaptation of individual and organizational learning (March 1991).

Issues in (organizational) learning are central to the recent economics of intellectual capital (Teece, Boerner and Macher 2001). Learning enables businesses to modify and develop new technologies, structures, and operating practices in the face of changing economic conditions. It also enables the creation of intangible assets as the basis for creating sustainably competitive advantages.

This literature also produced insights into the complex nature of technology development. Developing a new product or process is a highly uncertain venture, entailing the interaction of a host of frequently complex technological and market factors (Kline and Rosenberg, 1986). Successful new product development involves bringing together knowledge from a variety of sources and effectively meeting performance criteria that differ across multiple dimensions (Patel and Pavitt, 1998).

Increasingly, researchers recognized that knowledge is frequently embedded in business processes and "routines." As Nelson and Winter (1982, p. 106) point out, "skills, organization and 'technology' are intimately intertwined in a functioning routine, and it is difficult to say exactly where one aspect ends and another begins." This suggests that the "cospecialization" of "complementary assets" (Teece 1986) and activities is thus not just about physical assets, it also embraces interconnectedness and close coupling between knowledge and physical assets.

Nelson and Winter's work on routines began to explore the internal process by which firms learn and develop new, strategically relevant competencies. Research examining the dynamic nature of the capabilities of the business firm further developed these issues.

First outlined in Teece and Pisano (1994) and elaborated in Teece, Pisano, and Shuen (1997), the dynamic capabilities approach to the business firm and strategy builds on the theoretical foundations provided by Schumpeter (1934); Penrose (1959); Williamson (1975, 1985); Cyert and March (1963); Rumelt (1984); Nelson and Winter (1982); Teece (1982); and Teece and Pisano (1994). In particular, it is consistent with the Schumpeterian view that the emergence of new products and processes results from "new combinations" of knowledge. In a similar vein, it is argued in the dynamic capabilities approach that competitive success arises from the continuous development and reconfiguration of firm-specific assets (Teece and Pisano 1994; Teece et al. 1997). Whereas Penrose and the resource-based scholars recognize the competitive importance of firm-specific capabilities, researchers of the dynamic capabilities approach attempt to outline specifically how organizations develop and renew internal competencies. Therefore, the latter approach is concerned with a subset of a firm's overall capabilities, namely, those that allow firms to create new knowledge and invest in the commercialization of new technologies. As these developments suggest, intellectual capital and intangible assets have become increasingly important and discussed in the literature. We turn to some of the recent developments in the sections that follow. Consistent with several authoritative definitions of intellectual capital (for instance, OECD), we use the term as referring to organizational and individual human capital (knowledge) and nonmonetary assets that can be used to generate wealth.

Central Concepts in the Economics of Knowledge and Intellectual Property

As seen already, classical economists laid the foundation for much of the work on the economics of knowledge and intellectual capital in a business context. While progress has been slow, what now exists in economic theory and business studies is an important set of concepts routinely employed to study the role of intellectual capital in business performance. These concepts are critical to the formulation of technology strategy. In what follows, we outline some of the new wisdom on the role of knowledge and intangible assets more generally.

The Nature of Knowledge

Understanding the very nature of knowledge itself and other intangible assets remains perplexing. Know-how is not a physical commodity—it is arguably not a commodity at all. Accordingly, new concepts, language, and terminology had to be developed so that one could begin to understand and grasp the fundamental nature of knowledge. Key concepts that have been developed over the years and accepted into the literature include what follows.

Codified versus Tacit

Tacit knowledge is that knowledge which is difficult to articulate in a way that is meaningful and understood.[9] It is often hard to explain to others things one knows intuitively. The fact that we know more than we can tell speaks to the tacit dimension of knowledge. Moreover, stand-alone codified knowledge (knowledge that can be written down such as blueprints, formulas, or computer code) need not convey much meaning. This is more akin to information than knowledge.

Consider how to sail a yacht. It can be readily explained by simple mechanics. But if one gives such instruction and puts the student into a sailing dinghy with a good breeze afoot, for sure the dinghy will soon be capsized. The transfer of codified knowledge is insufficient. Tacit knowledge built with just a few hours of real experience—how to hold the mainsheet, where to put one's weight, just how to "point" as the wind shifts, and the like—is critical to establish even a modest level of proficiency.

There appears to be a simple but powerful relationship between the codification of knowledge and the cost of its transfer. Simply stated, the more a given item of knowledge or experience has been codified, the more economically at least part of it can be transferred. This is a purely technical property that depends on the ready availability of channels of communication suitable for the transmission of well-codified information, for example, printing, radio, telegraph, and data networks. Whether information so transferred is considered meaningful by those who receive it depends on whether they are familiar with the code selected as well as the different contexts in which it is used (Shannon and Weaver 1949).

Tacit knowledge is slow and costly to transmit. Ambiguities abound and can be overcome only when communication takes place face to face. Errors or interpretation can be corrected by prompt personal feedback.

The transmission of codified knowledge, on the other hand, does not require face-to-face contact and often can be carried out largely by impersonal means, such as when one computer "talks" to another or a technical manual is passed from one individual to another. Messages are better structured and less ambiguous if they can be transferred in codified form.

Observable versus Nonobservable in Use

Much technology is available for public examination and reverse engineering the moment the product that embodies it is sold into the market. This is simply an unavoidable consequence of engaging in commerce; reverse engineering and copying, with or without improvements, is the harsh reality that must often be faced. For example, a new CT scanner, laser printer, or microprocessor is available for conceptual imitation and reverse engineering once it has been released into the market. The technology behind new products typically is ascertainable and, absent patents, may well be imitable.

Process technology, however, is often different. You cannot easily find out the manufacturing process by which something was made simply by inspecting the product. Rarely is the "signature" of a process ascertainable through reverse engineering. While clues about a manufacturing process may sometimes be gleaned by closely inspecting the product, much about process technology can be protected if the owners

---

[9] The classical insights on the nature of tacit knowledge are provided by Hayek (1945) and Polyani (1962) and early applications to the study of technology, including Teece (1981a).

of the process technology are diligent in protecting the trade secrets used in the factory. In short, absent patents, process technology is inherently more protectable than product technology.

Positive versus Negative Knowledge

Technological innovation involves considerable uncertainty. Research efforts frequently go down what turns out to be a blind alley. It is well recognized that a discovery (positive knowledge) can focus research on promising areas of inquiry, thereby avoiding blind alleys. However, it is frequently forgotten that negative knowledge— knowledge of failures ("this approach doesn't work")—is also valuable, as it can help steer resources into more promising avenues. For this reason, firms often find it desirable to keep their failures as well as their successes secret, even setting to one side issues of embarrassment.

The Paradigmatic Nature of Technological Innovation

One of the best modern contributions to understanding technological change comes from Dosi's analogy between technological evolution and Thomas Kuhn's view on scientific evolution: "In broad analogy with the Kuhnian definition of a 'paradigm', we shall define a 'technological paradigm' as 'model' and a 'pattern' of solution of selected technological problems, based on selected principles derived from the natural sciences and on selected material technologies" (Dosi 1982, p. 152). Even more Kuhnian is the view that a technological paradigm is constituted by the existence of an "exemplar" and a set of heuristics for elaborating the relevant paradigm. The broad characteristics of technological evolution begins with a preparadigmatic phase, where product design and technology is flexible, then a paradigmatic phase follows with the emergence of a standard.[10]

Intangible Assets, Tangible Assets, and Intellectual Property

Knowledge assets are simply one class of intangible assets; they differ from tangible assets in several important respects. These are summarized in Table 1.1.

First, knowledge has aspects of what economists refer to as public goods; as discussed earlier, consumption by one individual does not reduce the amount left for another. This is especially true for scientific knowledge. One engineer's use of Newton's laws does not subtract from the ability of others to use the same laws. However, the distinction erodes quickly as one moves toward industrial knowledge and away from scientific knowledge. While multiple use need not take away from knowledge—indeed, it may well be augmented—the economic value may well decline with simultaneous use by multiple entities. This is saying little more than the obvious. Imitators can dramatically lower the market value of knowledge by augmenting its supply in the market.

Competition simply drives down the price of knowledge, even though its utility has not declined. In a related manner, while knowledge does not wear out like most physical assets (tractors, trucks, refrigerators, and disk drives), it is frequently exposed to rapid depreciation because of the creation of new knowledge. Therefore, leading edge

---

[10] Dosi's use of technological paradigms as a frame for understanding technological change can also accommodate the insights of dominating designs, technological regimes, and so forth. See Dosi (1982) for details.

Table 1.1

Differences between Intangible Assets and Tangible Assets		
	Knowledge (Intangible) Assets	Physical (Tangible) Assets
Publicness	Use by one party need not prevent use by another	Use by one party prevents simultaneous use by another
Depreciation	Does not "wear out" but usually depreciates rapidly	Wears out; may depreciate quickly or slowly
Transfer costs	Hard to calibrate (increases with the tacit portion)	Easier to calibrate (depends on transportation and related costs)
Property rights	Limited (patents, trade secrets, copyrights, trademarks, etc.) and fuzzy, even in developed countries	Generally comprehensive and clearer, at least in developed countries
Enforcement of property rights	Relatively difficult	Relatively easy

products in the computer industry are often obsolete in a matter of months, not years. In fact, the depreciation may be so radical that a technological breakthrough drops the value of current practice technology to zero, or very nearly so.

An important difference between intangible and tangible assets is the availability and enforceability of property rights. Physical assets (land, cars, yachts, etc.) are generally well protected. Ownership is relatively easy to define, and the "boundaries" of the property can be clearly delineated. Whether theft has occurred is relatively easy to ascertain, and in many jurisdictions, there is a decent chance of getting police assistance in property recovery if the asset is of significant value—not so with intangibles.

It may be natural to think that the different forms of intellectual property (patents, trade secrets, trademarks, copyrights, etc.) as providing similar ownership rights, with readily available protection against theft and misuse; but this is not so. There can be "holes" and "gaps" in intellectual property coverage, and ascertaining whether trespass or theft has occurred can be difficult. Moreover, patents and copyrights eventually expire and cannot be extended. This is generally not so for physical assets.

Patents, trade secrets, and trademarks provide protection for different mediums in different ways. The strongest form of intellectual property is the patent. A valid patent provides rights for exclusive use by the owner, although depending on the scope of the patent, it may be possible to invent around it, albeit at some cost. Trade secrets provide no rights of exclusion over any knowledge domain, but they protect covered secrets in perpetuity. Trade secrets can well augment the value of a patent position. Different knowledge mediums quality for different types of intellectual property protection. The degree that intellectual property keeps imitators at bay may also depend on other external factors, such as regulations, which may block or limit the scope for invent-around alternatives.[11]

---

[11] Contributions to the discussions of patent and patent protection include the early survey data from Mansfield, Schwartz and Wagner (1981) and Levin et al. (1987). An extension and discussion of these studies can be found in Schankerman (1998).

Replicability, Imitability, and Appropriability of Knowledge

The economic value of knowledge depends not just on its ultimate utility, but on the ease of transfer and replication. If it can be replicated, it can be "scaled" and applied in new contexts. Replicability is closely related to transferability. If it can be transferred, from one geography to another or from one product market context to a different one, then it can potentially yield more value. But the catch is that, if it can be readily transferred, it is also prone to being lost to competitors.

Replication

The replication of know-how involves transferring or redeploying competences from one economic setting to another. Since productive knowledge is typically embodied, this cannot be accomplished by simply transmitting information. Only in those instances where all relevant knowledge is fully codified and understood can replication be collapsed into a simple problem of information transfer. Too often, the contextual dependence of original performance is poorly appreciated, so unless firms have replicated their systems of productive knowledge on many prior occasions, the act of replication is likely to be difficult (Teece 1993). Indeed, replication and transfer are often impossible without the transfer of people, although this can be minimized if investments are made to convert tacit knowledge to codified knowledge. However, such transfer may not be possible.

In short, knowledge assets are normally rather difficult to replicate. Even understanding the relevant routines that support a particular competence may not be transparent. Indeed, Lippman and Rumelt (1982) have argued that some sources of competitive advantage are so complex that the firm itself, let alone its competitors, does not understand them.

Imitation can also be hindered by the fact that few routines work well in all contexts. Therefore, imitating a part of what a competitor does may not enhance performance at all. Understanding the overall causal structure of organization and superior performance is often critical to successful imitation and replication. This observation provides the foundation for the concept of uncertain imitability (Lippman and Rumelt 1982). Because key performance factors in an organization are not understood (externally and possibly internally as well), replicating observable attributes is no guarantee of success.

At least two types of benefits flow to the firm from expertise in replication if it can be achieved. One is simply the ability to support geographic and product line expansion ("scalability"). To the extent that the organizational capabilities in question are relevant to the customer needs elsewhere, replication can confer value. Another is that the ability to replicate indicates that the firm has the foundations in place for learning and improvement.

Second, understanding processes, in both production and in management, is the key to process improvement; an organization cannot improve what it does not understand. Deep process understanding is often required to accomplish codification and replication. Indeed, if knowledge is highly tacit, it indicates that the phenomenon may not be well understood, except at an experiential level. When knowledge is tacit, the rate of learning may be limited because scientific and engineering principles cannot be systematically applied. Instead, learning is confined to proceeding through trial and error, and the amplification to learning that might otherwise come from the application of modern science is denied.

Table 1.2

Appropriatability Regimes for Knowledge Assets		
Intellectual Property Rights	Inherent Replicability	
	Easy	Hard
Tight	Weak	Moderate
Loose	Moderate	Strong

Imitation

Imitation is simply replication performed by a competitor. If self-replication is difficult, imitation is likely to be even harder. In competitive markets, the ease of imitation determines the sustainability of a competitive advantage. Easy imitation leads to the rapid dissipation of supernormal profits.

Factors that make replication difficult also make imitation difficult. Therefore, the more tacit the firm's productive knowledge, the harder it is to replicate, by the firm itself or by its competitors. When the tacit component is high, imitation may well be impossible, absent the hiring away of key individuals and the transfer of key organizational processes.

In advanced industrial countries, intellectual property rights may impede imitation of certain capabilities. These rights present a formidable imitation barrier in particular contexts. Several other factors, in addition to the patent system, cause the difference between replication costs and imitation costs. The observability of the technology or the organization is one such important factor. As mentioned earlier, while insight into product technology can be obtained thorough strategies such as reverse engineering, this is not the case for process technology, as the firm need not expose its process technology to the outside to benefit from it. Firms with product technology, on the other hand, confront the unfortunate circumstances that they must expose what they have to complete a sale. Secrets, therefore, are more easily protected if there is no need to expose them in contexts where competitors can learn about them.

Appropriability

Appropriability is a function of the nature of knowledge, ease of replication, and efficiency of intellectual property rights as a barrier to imitation. Appropriability is strong when a technology is both inherently difficult to replicate and the intellectual property system provides legal barriers to imitation. As shown in Table 1.2, the owners of valuable intangibles that are inherently easy to replicate might enjoy different layers of "protection," depending on the inherent ease of replication and the availability and effectuality of intellectual property protection; without these, appropriability is weak.[12]

---

[12] A description of the results of an inquiry into appropriability conditions in manufacturing industries is found in Levin et al. (1987). Their data and discussion are consistent with the views discussed here.

The Distinction between Innovation and Intellectual Property

Much confusion has been caused by ignoring the significant distinction between an innovation and the intellectual property that embodies it. The latter is merely a legal right (more precisely, a collection of various legal rights, some procedural and some substantive).

An inventor develops, say, a new technology for cracking petroleum. The technology exists when it has been developed and tested. But it becomes covered by intellectual property only once it is legally recognized as such: In the case of patents, this occurs when a particular country's patent office recognizes the inventor's application and grants a patent. An issued patent is presumed valid, but its ultimate validity is never established until it is challenged and upheld in a court of law. This distinction between the innovation and legal "intellectual property" rights is most readily seen when the property right grant expires. Beethoven's copyright in his compositions has long since expired. But Beethoven's creations live on. An innovation may be just as valuable to society, in the sense that it represents an advance over the available alternative technologies, the day after the patent on that innovation expires as it was the day before the patent expired. But the legal rights of the innovator are radically different before and after the expiration date; after that date, the innovator has no right to exclude others from using the innovation. The private value falls, but the social value does not decline and may in fact increase.

One other key distinction is that the innovation and the legal rights are often not coextensive. An innovator may obtain legal rights over only part of the totality of the innovation. Confusion can sometimes arise when individuals seek to assess the value of the "technology" per se, rather than the value of the patent rights, namely, the right to exclude others from using the patented aspects of the technology. If the two are sold together, it may not matter. When they are not, it does.

Capturing Value from Intellectual Capital

As mentioned earlier, extracting value from intangible capital is a much more complicated and risky process than extracting value from tangible (physical) capital. Intellectual property, standing alone, generates little or no value to the final consumer. A patent, for instance, is merely a piece of paper that conveys the right to exclude others. The vast majority of patents are never practiced. Rather, value typically arises only after inventions are embedded in devices, which are then combined with other (complementary) assets to produce a product or service sold in a market.

To take a simple example, merely coming up with an idea for a new semiconductor device or even obtaining a patent or copyright on a design for a better semiconductor device does not generate economic value. Value is generated only when some entity combines an invention or a new design with the manufacturing, marketing, after-sale support, and other capabilities necessary to actually produce and sell semiconductors. Complementary assets typically assist in the extraction of value from intellectual property. Such assets generate a return that is analytically separate from the intellectual property itself.

In short, frequently, significant hurdles must be cleared and significant risks undertaken before an innovative idea can be successfully commercialized. Often, the individual(s) or firm(s) that supplies the necessary complementary assets and skills needed to commercialize the innovation or that takes the necessary risks is not the inventor. When this is the case, the gains from innovation get split not only with the consumer but also with the owners of the relevant complementary assets. Getting the commercialization strategy right is therefore very important, as discussed in Teece (1986).

Appropriability Regimes

A fundamental reason why innovators with good, marketable ideas fail to open up markets successfully is that they operate in an environment where appropriability is weak. This constrains their ability to capture the economic benefits arising from their ideas. The two most important environmental factors conditioning this are the efficacy of legal protection mechanisms and the nature of technology (Teece 1986).

It is well known that patents do not generally block competitors. Rarely, if ever, do patents confer perfect appropriability, although they afford considerable advantage in some industries, such as with new chemical products and rather simple mechanical inventions (Levin et al. 1987). Very often, patents can be "invented around" (Mansfield et al. 1988; Mansfield 1986). They are especially ineffective at protecting process innovations. Often patents provide little protection because the legal and financial requirements for upholding their validity or proving their infringement are high.

The degree of legal protection a firm enjoys is not necessarily a "god given" attribute. The inventor's own intellectual property strategy enters the equation. The inventor of a core technology need not only seek to patent the innovation but can also seek complementary patents on new features or manufacturing processes and possibly on designs.

Of course, the more fundamental is the invention, the better the chances that a broad patent will be granted and granted in multiple jurisdictions. It must be recognized that exclusionary rights are not fully secured by the mere issuance of a patent. While a patent is presumed to be valid in many jurisdictions, validity is never firmly established until a patent has been upheld in court. The strongest patents are those that are broad in scope and have already been upheld in court.

In some industries, particularly where the innovation is embedded in processes, trade secrets are a viable alternative to patents. Trade secret protection is possible, however, only if a firm can put its product before the public and still keep the underlying technology secret. Usually only chemical formulas and industrial-commercial processes can be protected as trade secrets after they are "out."

The degree to which knowledge about an innovation is tacit or easily codified also affects the ease of imitation. Tacit knowledge, by definition, is difficult to articulate and, so, hard to pass on unless those who possess the know-how can demonstrate it to others. It is also hard to protect using intellectual property law. Codified knowledge is easier to transmit and receive and more exposed to industrial espionage. On the other hand, it is often easier to protect using the instruments of intellectual property law. Appropriability regimes can be divided into "weak" (innovations are difficult to protect because they can be easily codified and legal protection of intellectual property is ineffective) and "strong" (innovations are easy to protect because knowledge about them is tacit or they are well protected legally). Despite recent efforts to strengthen the protection of intellectual property, strong appropriability is the exception rather than the rule. This has been so for centuries and will never be substantially different in democratic societies, where the migration of individuals and ideas faces few governmental constraints.

Standards and Timing Issues

The success of the strategies, methods, and procedures by which innovators endeavor to develop new technology and capture value from it are frequently severely affected by factors over which they may have little control. Standards and timing issues are among such factors.

Standard issues are particularly important when technologies must work closely together as a coupled or intertwined "system." Examples include telecommunications and computer equipment (interconnection is usually required) or even photocopiers (all the aftermarket products, such as paper and toner, must conform to certain standards for the machine to work or at least work well).

These factors lead to efforts by companies to promote proprietary standards (when they believe they have a good chance of success) or open standards when the success of a competitor's proprietary standard is of greater concern. Many factors affect a firm's success, or lack thereof, in establishing standards. Achieving overall critical mass is frequently an issue, particularly when the phenomenon of two-sided (or multisided) markets is at issue (Rochet and Tirole 2004; Evans 2003). When standards are at issue, success may beget further success and dominant standards emerge. When customers adopt a standard, they implicitly (and sometimes explicitly) abandon others. Inasmuch as innovations are often developed around existing or prospective standards, the rise and decline of certain standards is likely to have an impact on competitive outcomes.

Other Issues

A plethora of research by economists working in intellectual capital or related fields (like management and organization) is endeavoring to come to grips with the economics and management of intellectual capital. This chapter has barely scratched the surface of existing contributions. It is also selective. Omitted areas clearly worthy of mention, had space permitted, are important empirical work on patents and trends in patent activity, R&D and venture capital funding, licensing and cross-licensing issues, and technology transfer. Some of these topics are covered elsewhere (e.g., Teece 1977a, 1977b; Grindley and Teece 1997). These omissions are not meant to signal their unimportance.

Measurement Issues: Accounting and Market Metrics (Tobin's Q)

It is undisputed that the creation of intangible assets and intellectual capital is a source of economic growth and productivity enhancement. It is also undisputed that private enterprise businesses, in the aggregate, generate value from various investments, including investments aimed at creating valuable technological assets. Quite simply, firms would stop investing in R&D unless they continued to perceive that, as a result, such research generates an acceptable rate of return; and venture capitalists would be unable to raise money if they could not deliver the prospect of a positive return, commensurate with the risk. But quantifying the value of intangibles and the returns they generate is not easy. It is also a very important matter, for several reasons. First, it is extremely hard to manage assets that one cannot describe or measure. One has difficulties, not only in setting priorities, but in determining success or failure in asset management activities. Also, if intangibles are not measured correctly, an organization might appear to be doing poorly when it fact it is simply investing in intangibles. Accounting practices in the United States and elsewhere do not recognize many forms of intangibles, and this renders accounting data of limited value and causes discrepancies to emerge between the market value and the book value of the business enterprise.

In recent decades, scholars embarked on inquiries as to the quantitative importance of intangibles and their impact on the performance of the business enterprise. Four performance measures have received attention: (1) market value, as established in (public) capital markets; (2) gross margins; (3) patents; and (4) direct measures of innovation, such as innovation counts. The last is deeply imbued with judgmental assessment and is dealt with only in a cursory fashion here.

Stock Market Valuations

If the stock market is strongly efficient, the market value of a company is at all times equal to its fundamental value, where the fundamental value is defined as the expected present discounted value of future payments to shareholders. Assuming further the absence of market power, adjustment costs, and debt and taxes, then under the efficient market thesis, a company's value as determined by investors' pricing decisions equates to enterprise value, that is, the replacement cost of its assets. Put differently, the ratio of its market value to the replacement cost of capital, known as *Tobin's Q*, should equal 1.

An inference is that if the market value of the firm is greater than the replacement cost of its tangible assets, the difference must reflect the value of intangibles. Furthermore, since accounting standards require a very conservative treatment of intangibles, corporate balance sheets of publicly traded companies are believed, in the main, to capture tangible assets. Because intangibles are not properly reflected on balance sheets, researchers argue that the informativeness of financial information is compromised.

Nevertheless, the difference between market value and the replacement cost of tangible assets on the balance sheet has come to be used as a proxy for the value of intangibles. However, absent specification of what these intangibles are, it is very difficult to disaggregate and assign values to particular intangibles. Moreover, the inference that the difference between a firm's market value and the replacement cost of its physical assets represents the value of its intangibles requires the assumption of "strong form" market efficiency (where prices reflect all information, public as well as private), but this may be difficult to accept if investors lack good information about the firm's intangibles.

However, researchers have begun to explore the empirical relevance of (stock) market values. For instance, studies have established that investors regard R&D expenditures as a significant value-enhancing activity, presumably because they build (intangible) technological assets (Chan, Kesinger, and Martin 1992). Also, econometric studies that explore relationships between market-to-book ratios and R&D-to-sales ratios show positive, statistically significant associations (see Hirchez and Weygandt 1985). The evidence is clear that investors view R&D, on average, as value enhancing. Moreover, the magnitude of the contribution for the investing enterprise appears considerably higher than the cost of capital.

Gross Margins

Another approach utilizes accounting data, in particular gross margins (the difference between revenues and cost of goods sold), to assess how investment in intangibles affects performance. One basic approach, offered by Hand and Lev (2003), is to use econometric analysis and to regress the current-year dollar gross margin on the current and lagged R&D, advertising, and general and administrative expenses. Hand and Lev's analysis yielded several findings (p. 304): over the period 1980–2000, the mean yearly NPV (the present value of an investment's future net cash flows minus the initial investment) of $1.00 spent on R&D, advertising, and personnel were $0.35, $0.24, and $0.14, respectively. Scale also mattered, at least for R&D and advertising activities. Based on their findings, Hand concludes, "overall, my findings support the view that R&D and advertising intangibles have emerged over the past 20 years to become a critical means by which firms today create value and that one mechanism of value creation is that of increasingly profitable returns-to-scale" (Hand and Lev, p. 304).

Patent and Patent Citation Counts

The issuance of patents and the size of a firm's patent portfolio are also measures, albeit noisy ones, of innovative output. Because of the skewness in patent values— many patents are quite worthless but a few extremely valuable—it has turned out to be necessary to impose some at least crude measure of quality to make sense of the data. The most common measure of quality is the number of citations to a patent included in other subsequent patent applications. A number of studies demonstrated that quality-adjusted patents capture some element of the firm's R&D asset value. For instance, Hall, Jaffee, and Trajtenberg (2000) show that citation accepted patent counts help explain Tobin's Q values.

Innovation Counts

Another way to measure innovative output is directly, that is, to map significant technological innovations, then assign them to the particular firms responsible for their creation and commercialization. While this approach is superior at one level— it actually highlights innovation rather than say R&D expenditure (expenditure measures the cost of inputs into innovative activities)—it suffers from the lack of comparability; that is, there is no easy way to compare innovations and quantify their significance, except possibly through panels of experts who make qualitative judgments.[13]

Organizational Capital

The primary focus in this very short survey of measurement issues has been on technological assets. However, it is well recognized that organizational innovation is as significant (if not more so) than technological innovation in creating value. A. H. Cole asserted that, "if changes in business procedures and practices were patentable, the contribution of business change to the economic growth of the nation would be as widely recognized as the influence of mechanical inventions" (1968, pp. 61–62).

As an example, consider Henry Ford's invention of the moving assembly line. This was unquestionably one of the greatest innovations in the automobile industry, with ramifications for other industries, too. However, this invention was not technological,

---

[13] Very few studies of this kind have been done. The most notable study was done by Mansfield (1968), where he examined innovation in the petroleum industry. This study was extended and updated by Teece (1977b).

it was organizational. The Ford Motor Company's entire system of production had to be modified to accommodate it.

Another organizational innovation was the adaptation of the M-form structure. The transition from corporations organized in a unitary structure to corporations organized in a decentralized, profit-center-oriented multidivisional structure had a salutary effect on business performance. In a study of the adaptation of this new structure in the petroleum industry (Armour and Teece 1978), the innovation was shown to produce a statistically significant improvement in return on equity of approximately 2 percentage points during the diffusion period 1955–1968. A subsequent study (Teece 1981b) of the pairwise differential performance of the two leading firms in a number of industries yielded a similar finding. This study, which used a sample of the largest firms and most important U.S. industries, found that the M-form innovation displayed a statistically significant improvement in firm performance amounting to 2.37% and 1.22% for return on equity and return on assets, respectively. These results held while the innovation was being diffused. Both studies support the insights from Chandler (1966) and Williamson (1975) on the importance of organizational innovation and organizational design on economic performance.

Also, the diffusion path of the M-form innovation was not unlike diffusion paths associated with technological innovations. Teece (1980) argued that such similarities between the diffusion processes affecting technological and administration or organizational innovations indicates the broader potential of insights from the economics of technological change literature. Indeed, we may see more-recent work examining issues regarding the relationship between organizations and performance as contributors to this stream of ideas in the Mansfield/Teece tradition.

More recently, other (indirect) measures of the impact of organizational innovation have been attempted. Brynjolfsson and Yang, 1999, showed that a $1.00 investment in computers has about a $10.00 impact on market value. This has been interpreted to reflect positive results from new business processes the installation of enterprise software frequently requires. The authors' explanation is as follows: "our deduction is that the main portion of computer related intangible assets comes from the new business processes, new organizational structure and new market strategies—computer use is complementary to new workplace organization—Wal-Mart's main assets are not the computer software and hardware, but the intangible business processes they have built around those computer systems" (1999, p. 30).

Furthermore, recent evidence (Morck and Yeung 2003) supports earlier work (Teece 1982), indicating that know-how transfer inside firms (across jurisdictions and product space) enhances value. In the earlier study, internal technology transfer processes were seen as more efficient and effective than arm's-length transfers across organizational boundaries. Morck and Yeung's work supports this analysis by showing a positive contribution of diversification to value when it is aimed at scaling intangibles.

Conclusion

Knowledge and other intangible assets have emerged as key to business performance in the economic system. The development, ownership, and use of intellectual capital also helps explain wealth creation and levels of living around the globe. This is not just because of the importance of knowledge itself but because of expansion and competition in the goods and factor markets. These developments left intangible assets as the main basis for competitive differentiation in many sectors of the economy. There is implicit recognition of this, with the growing emphasis being placed by scholars on the importance of intangible assets, reputation, loyalty, and technological knowledge. Although many foundational insights were provided by classical economists (and some neoclassical economists), the Dosi/Mansfield/Nelson/Teece/Winter tradition provided key elements of the analytical and conceptual framework put forward here for analyzing and applying those early ideas to issues of knowledge and intellectual capital. Recent work further advances this tradition and lays an expanded foundation for the further understanding of the economics and management of intellectual capital.

References

Armour, H., and D. Teece. 1978. "Organizational Structure and Economic Performance: A Test of the Multidivisional Hypothesis." *Bell Journal of Economics* 9, no. 2: 106–122.

Abramovitz, M. 1962. "Economic Growth in the United Sates." *American Economic Review* 52: 762–782.

Arrow, K. 1962. "The Economic Implications of Learning by Doing." *Review of Economic Studies* 29: 155–173.

Becker, G. 1964. *Human Capital*. New York: Columbia University Press.

Brynjolfsson, E., and S. Yang. 1999. "The Intangible Costs and Benefits of Computer Investments: Evidence From Financial Markets." Working Paper, Sloan School, Massachusetts Institute of Technology, Cambridge, MA.

Chan, S., J. Kesinger, and J. Martin. 1992. "The Market Rewards Promising R&D." *Journal of Applied Corporate Finance* 5: 59–62.

Chandler, A. 1966. *Strategy and Structure*. Boston: Harvard Business School Press,.

Chesbrough, H. 2003. *Open Innovation: The New Imperative for Creating and Profiting from Technology*. Cambridge, MA: Harvard University Press.

Cole, A. H. 1968. "The Entrepreneur, Introductory Remarks." *American Economic Review* 58, no. 2: 60–63.

Cyert, R., and J. G. March. 1963. *A Behavioral Theory of the Firm*. Englewood Cliffs, NJ: Prentice-Hall.

David, P. 1993. "Path-Dependency and Predictability in Dynamic Systems with Local Network Externalities." In: *Technology and the Wealth of Nations*, ed. D. Forey and C. Freeman, London: Pinter.

Denison, E. G. 1962. *The Sources of Economic Growth in the United States and the Alternatives before Us*. New York: Committee on Economic Development.

Debreu. G. 1959. *Theory of Value*. New Haven, CT: Yale University Press.

Dosi, G. 1982. "Technological Paradigms and Technological Trajectories. A Suggested Interpretation of the Determinants and Directions of Technical Change." *Research Policy* 11: 147–162.

Drucker, P. 1993. *Post-Capitalist Society*. New York: HarperBusiness.

Evans, D. 2004. "The Antitrust Economics of Multi Sided Platform Markets." *Yale Journal of Regulation* forthcoming.

Freeman, C. 1982. *The Economics of Industrial Innovation*. London: Pinter Publishers.

Griliches, Z. 1963. "The Sources of Measured Productivity Growth: United States Agriculture, 1940–60." *Journal of Political Economy* 71: 331–346.

Grindley, P., and D. Teece. 1997. "Managing Intellectual Capital: Licensing and Cross-Licensing in Semiconductors and Electronics." *California Management Review* 39, no. 2: 8–41.

Hahn, F., and C. Matthews. 1964. "The Theory of Economic Growth: A Survey." *Economic Journal* 74: 779–902.

Hall, B., A. Jaffee, and M. Trajtenberg. 2000. "Market Value and Patent Citations: A First Look." Working Paper. National Bureau of Economic Research, Cambridge, MA.

Hand, J., and B. Lev. 2003. *Intangible Asset Values, Measures, Risks*. Oxford: Oxford University Press.

Hayek, F. A. 1945. "Economics and Knowledge," *Individualism and Economic Order*. Chicago: University of Chicago Press.

Hirschez, M., and J. Weygandt. 1985. "Amortization Policy for Advertising and R&D Expenditure." *Journal of Accounting Research* 23, no. 10: 326–335.

Jorgensen, D., and Z. Griliches. 1967. "The Explanation of Productivity Change." *Review of Economic Studies* 34: 249–283.

Kline, S., and N. Rosenberg. 1986. "An overview of innovation." In: *The Positive Sum Strategy*, ed. R. Landau and N. Rosenberg, pp. 275–305. Washington, DC: National Academy Press.

Knight, F. 1921. *Risk, Uncertainty and Profit*. Cambridge, UK: Riverside Press.

———. 1944. "Diminishing Returns from Investments." *Journal of Political Economy* 52: 26–47.

Krugman, P. 1998. "Two Cheers for Formalism." *Economic Journal* 108: 1829–1836.

Kuznets, S. 1967. *Toward a Theory of Economic Growth*. New York: Norton.

Levin, R., C. Klevorick, R. Nelson, and S. G. Winter. 1987. "Appropriating the Returns from Industrial Research and Development." *Brookings Papers on Economic Activity*, 1987, no. 3: 783–820.

Lippman, S., and R. Rumelt. 1982. "Uncertain Imitability: An Analysis of Interfirm Differences in Efficiency under Competition." *Bell Journal of Economics* 13: 418–438.

Mansfield, E. 1968. *The Economics of Technological Change*. New York: W. W. Norton.

———. 1988. "The Speed and Cost of Industrial Innovation in Japan and the United States External vs. Internal Technology." *Management Science*. 34, no. 10: 1157–1168.

———, R. John, R. Anthony, W. Samuel, and B. George. 1977. "Social and Private Rates of Return from Industrial Innovations." *Quarterly Journal of Economics* 91: 221–240.

———, M. Schwartz, and S. Wagner. 1981. "Imitation Costs and Patents: An Empirical Study." *The Economic Journal* 91: 907–918.

Loasby, B. 2004. "Evolution and the Human Mind." Paper Presented at the Schumpeter Society Conference, Milan, 2004.

Mansfield, E. 1986. "Patents and Innovation: An Empirical Study." *Management Science* 32: 173–181.

March, J. G. 1991. "Exploration and Exploitation in Organizational Learning." *Organization Science* 2: 71–87.

———, and H. A. Simon 1958. *Organizations*. New York: Wiley.

Marshall, A. 1890. *Principles of Economics*. London: MacMillan.

———. 1925. *Industry and Trade*. London: MacMillan.

Morck, R., and B. Yeung. 2003. "Why Firms Diversify: Internalization vs. Agency Behavior." Intangible Assets, SSRC Working Paper.

Nelson, R. R., and S. G. Winter. 1977. "Dynamic Competition and Technical Progress." In: *Economic Progress, Private Values, and Public Policy: Essays in Honor of William Fellner*, ed. B. Balassa and R. R. Nelson. Amsterdam: North-Holland.

Nelson, R., and S. G. Winter 1982. *An Evolutionary Theory of Economic Change*. Cambridge, MA: Belknap Press.

Nonaka, I. 1991. "The Knowledge-Creating Company." *Harvard Business Review* 69, no. 6: 96–104.

Patel, P., and K. Pavitt. (1998). "The Wide (and Increasing) Spread of Technological Competencies in the World's Largest Firms: A Challenge to Conventional Wisdom." In: *The Dynamic Firm: The Role of Technology, Strategy, Organization, and Regions*, ed. A. D. Chandler, P. Hagström, and Ö. Sölvell, pp. 192–212. Oxford: Oxford University, Press.

Penrose E. 1959. *The Theory of the Growth of the Firm*. Oxford: Blackwell.

Polyani, M. 1962. *The Tacit Dimension*. New Haven, CT: Yale University Press.

Rochet, J., and J. Tirole. 2004. "Multisided Markets: An Overview." Working Paper, MIT, Boston, MA.

Romer, P. 1986. "Increasing Returns and Long Run Growth." *Journal of Political Economy* 94: 1002–1037.

———. 1993. "Economic Growth." In: *The Fortune Encyclopedia of Economics*, ed. D. Henderson. New York: Time Warner Books.

———. 1990. "Endonenous Technological Change." *Journal of Political Economy* 98: 71–102.

Rosenberg, N., and W. E. Steinmuller. 1988. "Why Are Americans Such Poor Imitators?" *American Economic Review* 78, no. 2: 229–234.

Rumelt, R. 1984. "Towards a Strategic Theory of the Firm." In: *Competitive Strategic Management*, ed. R. B. Lamb. Englewood Cliffs, NJ: Prentice-Hall.

Schankerman, M. 1998. "How Valuable Is Patent Protection? Estimates by Technology Field." *Rand Journal of Economics* 29, no. 1: 77–107.

Schumpeter, J. 1934. *The Theory of Economic Development.* Cambridge, MA: Harvard University Press.

———. 1943. *Capitalism, Socialism, and Democracy.* New York: Harper and Brothers.

Shannon, C., and W. Weaver. 1949. *A Mathematical Theory of Communication.* Urbana: University of Illinois Press.

Simon, H. A. 1955. "A Behavioral Model of Rational Choice." *Quarterly Journal of Economics* 69: 99–118.

———. 1978. "Rationality as Process and as Product of Thought." *American Economic Review* 68, no. 2: 1–16.

Smith, A. 1776. *An Inquiry into the Nature and Causes of the Wealth of Nations.* London: Methuen and Co., Ltd.

Solow, R. 1956. "A Contribution to the Theory of Economic Growth." *Quarterly Journal of Economics* 70, no. 1: 65–94.

———. 1957. "Technical Change and the Aggregate Production Function." *Review of Economics and Statistics* 39: 312–320.

———. 1994. "Perspectives on Growth Theory." *Journal of Economic Perspectives.*

Teece, D. 1977a. "Technology Transfer by Multinational Firms: The Resource Cost of Transferring Technological Know-How." *The Economic Journal* 87: 242–261.

———. 1977b. *R&D in Energy: Implications of Petroleum Industry Reorganization.* Stanford, CA: Stanford University Institute for Energy Studies.

———. 1980. "The Diffusion of an Administrative Innovation." *Institute of Management Sciences* 26, no. 5: 464–470.

———. 1981a. "The Market for Know-How and the Efficient International Transfer of Technology." *Annals of the Academy of Political and Social Science*: 81–96.

———. 1981b. "Internal Organization and Economic Performance: An Empirical Analysis of the Profitability of Principal Firms." *Journal of Industrial Economics* 30, no. 2: 173–199.

———. 1982. "Towards an Economic Theory of the Multiproduct Firm." *Journal of Economic Behavior and Organization* 3: 39–63.

———. 1984. "Economic Analysis and Strategic Management." *California Management Review* 26, no. 3: 87–110.

———. 1986. "Profiting from Technological Innovation." *Research Policy* 15, no. 6: 285–305.

———. 1989. "Inter-Organizational Requirements of the Innovation Process." *Managerial and Decision Economics*, Special Issue: 35–42.

———. 1992. "Competition, Cooperation, and Innovation: Organizational Arrangements for Regimes of Rapid Technological Progress." *Journal of Economic Behavior and Organization* 18, no. 1: 1–25.

———. 1993. "The Dynamics of Industrial Capitalism: Perspectives on Alfred Chandler's Scale and Scope (1990)." *Journal of Economic Literature.*

———, and G. Pisano 1994. "The Dynamic Capabilities of Firms: An Introduction." *Industrial and Corporate Change* 3: 3.

———, C. Boerner, and J. Macher. 2001. "A Review and Assessment of Organizational Learning in Economic Theories." In: *Handbook of Organizational Learning and Knowledge.* ed. M. Dierkers, A. B. Antal, J. Child, and I. Nonaka. NY: Oxford University Press.

———, G. Pisano, and A. Shuen 1997. "Dynamic Capabilities and Strategic Management." *Strategic Management Journal* 18, no. 7: 509–533.

———, and S. G. Winter. 1984. "The Limits of Neoclassical Theory in Management Education." *American Economic Review* 74, no. 2: 116–121.

Williamson, O. E. 1975. *Markets and Hierarchies: Analysis and Antitrust Implications.* New York: The Free Press.

———. 1985. *The Economic Institutions of Capitalism.* New York: The Free Press.

Young, A. 1928. "Increasing Returns and Economic Progress." *Economic Journal* 38: 527–542.

A Strategy Perspective on Intellectual Capital

Bernard Marr
Cranfield School of Management

Göran Roos
Cranfield School of Management

Introduction

Kenneth Andrews (1971) defined *corporate strategy* as follows: "The pattern of decision making in a company that determines and reveals its objectives, purposes, or goals, produces the principal policies and plans for achieving those goals, it defines the range of business the company is to pursue, the kind of economic and human organisation it is or intends to be, and the nature of the economic and non-economic contribution it intends to make to its shareholders, employees, customers, and communities." The way strategy is approached changed significantly over the past 20 years, and with this change, the importance of understanding intellectual capital as essential value driver in firms increased. Strategic approaches have evolved from paradigms in which organizations were seen as "black boxes" that could be reconfigured to address any opportunities in the market to paradigms in which the internal resource configuration is critical.

Organizations perform well and create value when they implement strategies that respond to market opportunities by exploiting their internal resources and capabilities. Therefore, organizations need to understand what resources they possess and how to configure them to deliver value. Traditionally, those resources were of a physical nature, such as land and machines, or financial nature. With a shift from seller's markets to a buyer's markets and the development of the resource- and knowledge-based view of firms, intellectual capital has been identified as a key resource and driver of organizational performance and value creation (Itami 1987; Teece 2000; Nahapiet and Ghoshal 1998; McGaughey 2002; Delios and Beamish 2001).

In this chapter, we illustrate the increased strategic importance of intellectual capital by outlining the relevant developments in strategic thought. We then go on to define the concept of intellectual capital and distinguish between a static and dynamic view of intellectual capital. We next outline current practices of organizations in strategically managing their intellectual capital, before concluding with a look into the future.

Development of Strategy

A key question strategic management tries to answer is why some firms perform better than others. Here, we outline the development of strategic thought by discussing two differing views. The first view of strategy emphasizes the exploitation of market power, taking a primarily external perspective; the second view of strategy emphasizes efficiency, taking primarily an internal perspective (e.g., Teece, Pisano, and Shuen 1997).

The Market-Based Paradigm

These traditional paradigm models of strategy focus on the exploitation of market power, such as competitive forces (Porter 1980) and strategic conflict (Sharpiro 1989). In 1980, Michael Porter synthesized research on industrial organization into a basic paradigm that argues that it is possible to increase industry profitability by purposefully modifying industry structure. The basic strategic decisions here are entry/exit decisions and decisions that change the firm's ability to modify the industry structure. Porter defined industry profitability as the interaction of five forces: the power of the buyers, the availability of substitute products or services, the power of suppliers, the ease of entry into the industry, and the existing competition. The stronger these forces, the lower the industry profitability. This view was further developed with the strategic groups construct, which argues that the reason why firms in the same industry differ in their profitability is a set of forces, known as *mobility barriers*, that prevent some firms from imitating the strategy of the most successful firms in the industry (Caves and Porter 1977; Hatten and Hatten 1987; McGee and Thomas 1986).

The strategic conflict view was developed by Carl Shapiro (1989), who argues that business strategy can utilize approaches that find their origin in game theory. The idea is to analyze the competitive interactions in one industry and influence the behavior and actions of competitors by influencing the market environment with activities such as advertising.

Both Porter's competitive forces and Shapiro's strategic conflict approaches are about generating rents from privileged product market positions (Teece et al. 1997), which are difficult for others to enter. Erecting barriers to entry allows the extraction of *monopoly rents*, which arise when supply is artificially constrained to levels below demand and supply cannot be expanded. As a consequence, the market-based paradigm is about creating monopoly rents.

The Resource-Based Paradigm

In the resource-based paradigm, differences in profitability between firms are due to differences in the resource architecture of competing firms as well as the way these resources are deployed. If firm A possesses more valuable resources than firm B or if firm A more-effectively utilizes its resources, then firm A can achieve higher profitability. Increasingly today, organizations realize that when formulating a corporate strategy, it no longer is enough to identify the competitive forces, opportunities, and threats of the industry; in addition, organizations have to identify their corporate resources to evaluate opportunities. Different firms develop different distinctive resource architectures; the question firms have to ask themselves is this: Does the organization have the right resources (including, e.g., competence) to pursue certain opportunities? This view of competence-based competition was first sketched by Edith Penrose (1959), then later picked up by Birger Wernerfelt (1984) and Richard Rumelt

(1984), who are seen as developers of the modern resource-based view of the firm (Foss 1997). Resource-based theorists see firms as heterogeneous entities characterized by their unique resource base (Nelson and Winter 1982; Barney 1991); and in this resource base, intellectual capital is of increasing significance (Roos and Roos 1997; Lev 2001; Sveiby 1997; Marr and Schiuma 2001).

Wernerfelt (1984) defines *resources* as inputs into the firm's operations; examples of resources include intellectual property, plant and equipment, as well as capabilities and competent people. Grant (1991) and Schulze (1994) define a *capability* as the capacity to perform a task or activity that involves complex patterns of coordination and cooperation between people and other resources. Capabilities might include research and development, superior customer service, or high-quality manufacturing. Resources and capabilities, known as *strategic assets*, must be embedded in the end products or services that create value for the customers. Resources themselves never create value, instead, value is created from the services these resources can render (Penrose 1959, p. 25). It is, therefore, beneficial for companies to be able to apply their strategic assets to a wide range of products, services, and activities (Prahalad and Hamel 1990).

Resources contribute to a sustainable competitive advantage if they are valuable, rare, difficult to imitate, or hard to substitute (Barney 1991). This means that a competitive advantage of firms in today's economy does not result from market position but difficult-to-replicate knowledge-based assets and the manner they are developed (Teece 1998). This understanding led to the development of another concept in strategic management: the dynamic capability, which is the ability to achieve new forms of competitive advantage by appropriately adapting, integrating, and reconfiguring organizational skills, resources, and competencies to match the requirements of a changing environment (Teece et al. 1997). Another contribution to this field argues that the development or "evolution" of organizational resources and competencies is path dependent, that is, influenced by past decisions and actions. This evolutionary view tries to explain economic development using an evolutionary analogy. Nelson and Winter suggest that organizational routines (i.e., all regular and predictable patterns of behavior in firms) could be viewed as inherited competencies of firms.

The rarer a strategic asset, the greater is its probability of creating *scarcity rents*, which arise when demand exceeds supply and supply cannot be rapidly expanded. As a consequence, the resource-based paradigm is about creating scarcity rents. The development of the resource-based paradigm has increased the importance of intellectual capital as strategic value driver. Next, we outline the concept of strategic value drivers.

Static and Dynamic Value Drivers

According to the resource-based paradigm, value generated is a function of the way in which resources are managed. In the 1980s, Hiroyuki Itami introduced the concept of "invisible assets" and defined them as information-based assets, which include technology, consumer trust, brand image, corporate culture, as well as management skills. According to Itami, they are the most-important resources for long-term success, because only invisible assets can be used simultaneously in several areas. In 1989, David Aaker wrote that assets and skills are the basis of competition; in the same year, Richard Hall introduced the concept of intellectual assets, and later (1992) intangible assets, as critical value drivers. *Intangible assets* are defined as those assets whose essence is an idea or knowledge and whose nature can be defined and recorded in some way (Hall 1992). Hall split them into intellectual property (those assets for which the organization has property rights) and knowledge assets (those assets for which the organization has no property rights). Intangible assets drive capability differentials, which in turn drive sustainable competitive advantage, which is why organizations need to bring intangible resources and core competences into their strategic thinking (Hall 1993).

In his 1991 *Fortune* article, Tom Stewart wrote, "Every company depends increasingly on knowledge—patents, processes, management skills, technologies, information about customers and suppliers, and old-fashioned experience . . . Added together, this knowledge is intellectual capital." He defines *intellectual capital* as "the sum of everything everybody in your company knows that gives you a competitive edge in your marketplace." Quinn (1992) maintained that the majority of economic and production power of an organization lies in its intellectual capability. Hall (1992) used the classification of intangible resources and split them into assets and skills: Assets include trademarks, patents, copyrights, registered designs, contracts, trade secrets, reputations, networks (personal and commercial relationships); whereas skills comprise know-how or culture. In a survey of 95 firms, Hall identified company reputation, product reputation, and employee know-how as the most important contributors for overall success.

Following the pioneering work of these authors, other authors defined taxonomies for intellectual capital. Hudson (1993) defined intellectual capital as a personal asset of individuals, a combination of genetic inheritance, education, experience, and attitude about life and business. Nahapiet and Ghoshal (1998) moved away from a personal definition toward organizational intellectual capital; they use the term *intellectual capital* to refer to the knowledge and knowing capability of a social collective, such as an organization, intellectual community, or professional practice. Brooking (1996, 1997) went even broader and defined *intellectual capital* as market assets, human-centered assets, intellectual property assets, and infrastructure assets. Edvinsson (1997), former director of intellectual capital at the Swedish insurance company Skandia, defined intellectual capital as human capital plus structural capital. Skandia uses the reduction approach in their Value Scheme, which identifies intellectual capital by deducting financial capital from overall value, leaving intellectual capital; deducting human capital from intellectual capital leaves structural capital; deducting customer capital (customer relationships) leaves organizational capital; deducting the value of processes leaves innovation capital; deducting intellectual property (patents, trademarks) leaves intangible assets as balancing value. Roos and Roos (1997) defined *intellectual capital* in the broadest sense, as human capital (knowledge capital, skill capital, motivation capital, task capital), business process capital (flow of information, flow of products and services, cash flow, cooperation forms, strategic processes), business renewal and development capital (specialization, production processes, new concepts, sales and marketing, new cooperation form), and customer relationship capital (customer relationship capital, supplier relationship capital, network partner relationship capital, investor relationship capital).

Although the previously mentioned authors agree on the significance of intellectual capital as a resource underpinning organizational performance, there is considerable lack of consensus on the definition of *intellectual capital* (Marr and Chatzkel 2004).

To gain a common understanding of the terminology used in this chapter, we provide a taxonomy of organizational assets (see Figure 2.1). This taxonomy is the result of an extensive literature review on the subject (Marr, Schiuma, and Neely 2004), but we adopt the change recommended by Bainbridge, Jacobsen, and Roos (2001) to use

Figure 2.1

Taxonomy of organizational assets.

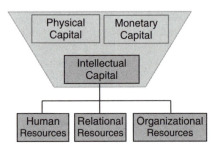

the term *resource* rather then *capital* to avoid confusion with the accounting language. The aim of this classification is to facilitate the identification of organizational resources in firms and provide a language to discuss the topic. However, we emphasize that from a strategy perspective, it is more important that organizations identify all their context-specific value drivers, disregarding differences in language or taxonomy. Resources are classified as monetary capital, physical capital, and intellectual capital; intellectual capital is divided into human resources, relational resources, and organizational resources. We now discuss these constructs in further detail.

- *Monetary capital.* Monetary capital has always been an important asset for any organization. Cash is needed by organizations to invest in other resources. Itami (1987) pointed out that money, as one of the invisible assets of an organization, is a necessary input as well as an output of operations in the form of cash flow.
- *Physical capital.* Penrose (1959) defined physical assets as tangible things, such as plant, equipment, land, and natural resources. Williamson (1975) emphasized the importance of physical assets to gain a competitive advantage. Here, physical assets comprise all tangible infrastructure assets, such as structural layout and information and communication technology. They include databases, servers, and physical networks like intranets.
- *Relational resources.* Relational resources are the relationships between an organization and its external stakeholders as well as the exchange of knowledge between them. Relationships can include official relationships, such as partnering, or distribution arrangements as well as nonformalized relationships, such as relationships with customers or suppliers. Roos and Roos (1997) mention relationships with customers, suppliers, network partners, as well as with investors. Itami (1987, p. 19) highlights the information or knowledge exchange between organizations and their external environment. Information flows from the firm to the external environment include corporate reputation, corporate image, and influence over the distribution channel and its suppliers.
- *Human resources.* Penrose explicitly distinguished human resources from other assets of the firm. Human assets were identified as a key asset of the firm. Becker (1964) and Schultz (1981) used the phrase *human capital* to define a core asset of an organization. Hall (1992) emphasized skills and know-how as important assets, and Roos (1998) defined *human resources* as the knowledge, skills, and experience of employees. Human resources, therefore, include

employees' skills, competences, commitment, motivation, and loyalty. Some of the key components are know-how, technical expertise, and problem-solving capability, creativity, education, and attitude. Roos also made explicit that any type of competence that can take on another form, such as written information, falls under the heading of organizational resources; therefore, *human resources* here is very similar to Nonaka and Takeuchi's (1995) concept of tacit knowledge.

- *Organizational resources.* Organizational resources include all intellectual assets that can be assigned to the company and usually stay with the organization even if people leave. This includes intellectual property, practices and routines, documented information, IT systems, as well as organizational culture.
- Patents and trade secrets have become a key element of competition (Grindley and Teece 1997). Here, we define *intellectual property* as the sum of assets such as patents, copyrights, trademarks, brands, registered design, trade secrets, and processes whose ownership is granted to company by law. They represent the tools and enablers that allow a company to gain a protected competitive advantage.
- Shared knowledge in organizations is expressed in routines and practices (Nelson and Winter 1982). Formalized routines include process manuals providing codified procedures and rules; informal routines would be tacit rules of behavior or work flows. Practices and routines determine how processes are handled and how work flows through the organization.
- Corporate culture gives each person in an organization a common, distinctive method for transmitting and processing information; it defines a common way of seeing things, sets the decision-making pattern, and establishes the value system (Itami 1987, p. 23). A critical part of this is a common language (von Krogh, Roos, and Slocum 1994). Nahapiet and Ghoshal (1998) refer to it as social capital and context. Culture assets embrace categories such as corporate culture, organizational values, and management philosophies.

The Dynamic Nature of Value Creation

The preceding taxonomy of organizational resources provides the static picture of the resource architecture. As discussed earlier, to create value, these resources must be transformed into products or services that deliver value. Intellectual capital resources are often referred to as *performance drivers*, which suggest causal relationships between these resources and organizational value creation. Intellectual capital resources such as employee skills and customer relationships often deliver customer satisfaction and loyalty, which in turn delivers shareholder value (Rucci, Kirn, and Quinn 1998; Ittner and Larcker 1998).

Management tools such as strategy maps (Kaplan and Norton 2000, 2004) and success maps (Neely, Adams, and Kennerley 2002) were developed to visualize the causal links between intangible value drivers and organizational performance outcome. Such maps contain outcome objectives and performance drivers, linked together in a cause-and-effect diagram. The balanced scorecard approach suggests human capital, information capital, and organizational capital as intangible value drivers (Kaplan and Norton 2004). Kaplan and Norton claim that by using these categories, organizations can understand the readiness of their intangible assets in the context of a set strategic objectives. The balanced scorecard strategy map template is depicted in Figure 2.2.

Figure 2.2

Strategy map (Source: Kaplan and Norton 2004).

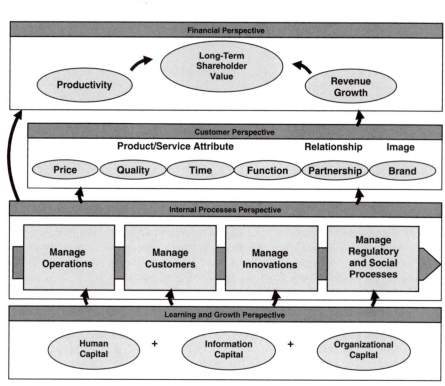

According to the resource-based paradigm, resources exist as a bundle and these resource bundles affect performance with causal ambiguity (Lippman and Rumelt 1982). It is therefore difficult to identify how individual resources contribute to success without taking into account the interdependencies with other assets (Lippman and Rumelt 1982; Dierickx and Cool 1989; King and Zeithaml 2001). For example, the latest technology is worth little without the right knowledge and competency in operating it. In turn, all the latest understanding and knowledge of how to operate technology is worthless if employees have no access to the technology (Marr et al. 2004). Following the same logic, corporate culture influences employee competencies and vice versa. Roos and Roos (1997) wrote that, a "balance sheet approach to intellectual capital is inherently a 'snapshot in time' and does not provide information on the transformation from one asset category into another" (p. 419). Baruch Lev (2001) noted that, "intangibles are frequently embedded in physical assets (for example, the technology and knowledge contained in an airplane) and in labor (the tacit knowledge of employees), leading to considerable interactions between tangible and intangible assets in the creation of value. . . . When such interactions are intense, the valuation of intangibles on a standalone basis becomes impossible" (Lev 2001, p. 7). In summary, this means organizations require a better understanding of how their resources, in particular their intangible assets, interact to create value and a competitive advantage.

Figure 2.3

Interdependence of resources.

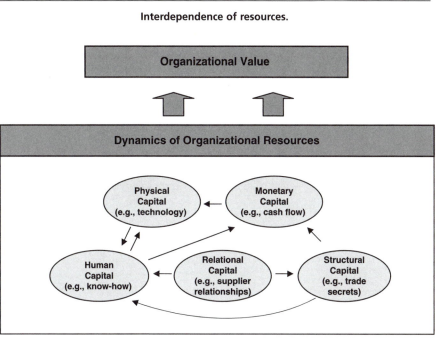

Figure 2.3, drawing on the IC navigator approach introduced by Roos, shows how organizational resources might be interrelated to create value. These resources are valuable only in the specific context of the firm's value creation. For example, knowledge of how to operate specialist technology in chip-manufacturing might be of little value to an agriculture firm; in turn, a good relationship with farmers would be of little value to a chip manufacturer. To understand these dynamics of value creation, tools were developed to help firms identify their key value drivers and understand their interactions or value creation pathways (Gupta and Roos 2001; Marr et al. 2004).

Identifying and Mapping Strategic Value Creation—The Status Quo

In this section, we discuss the practical application of tools designed to help organizations identify and map their strategic value creation. To understand the stock and flow of organizational resources, firms need to answer two questions:

- What are the most valuable resources that enable our firm to deliver value to our stakeholders?
- How do these resources depend on each other and dynamically interact to deliver this value?

Understanding the Resource Architecture

It is important to link internal competencies and resources to external opportunities. The question to ask would be this: What resources and capabilities are critical to deliver our value proposition? Kenneth Andrews brought the strategic importance of competencies to a head when he stated that "opportunism without competence is a path to fairyland" (Andrews 1971). One company that built its success on under-standing its intellectual capital is Wal-Mart, which transformed the company by build-ing on its knowledge of "cross-docking" (Stalk, Evans, and Shulman 1992). This innovative practice of supply management was one of the factors that enabled Wal-Mart to outperform its rival Kmart. Grindley and Teece (1997) identified, from their studies of the semiconductor industry, the increasing importance of patentable intellectual property. They state that patents and trade secrets have become a key ele-ment of competition in many high-tech organizations. Honda's superior knowledge in engine construction and its relationship management with its retailers enabled the firm to build on these knowledge assets and become a major competitor to many established manufactures. In Honda's case, this understanding led to vertical integra-tion in the key areas. Examples where companies have not understood their key com-petencies include Exxon, which tried to diversify into areas such as office equipment and computers, completely unrelated to its energy business (Javidan 1998). Collins and Montgomery (1995) identified companies such as Disney, Newell, Cooper, and Sharp as ones that demonstrate the power of resource-based strategies and the return they generate. Marr, Schiuma, and Neely (2002) documented how Lycos and Great Universal Stores identified their knowledge-based assets to influence their strategy formulation process.

The process Lycos went through was to first arrange a workshop with the senior managers to identify the resource stock of an organization (Marr and Schiuma 2001). In this workshop, participants identified the key value drivers. To cover all possible resources, a facilitator discussed each of the resources introduced in Figure 2.1 indivi-dually. This ensured that, especially, the different intangible resources were included. In a facilitated discussion, consensus was gained on the relative importance of key resources. The outcome of this was a map of key resources and their relative impor-tance. Figure 2.4 depicts an example of a resource stock map from an online retailer; the sizes of the resource bubbles indicate their relative importance to this company. In this example, organizational resources and human resources are the most important value drivers for this firm. In Lycos's case, the company identified brand management skills as a key knowledge-based asset (Marr and Schiuma 2001). As a result of identi-fying brand management as a key asset underpinning the firm's strategy, Lycos took various strategic initiatives, including outsourcing technology and consolidation of various brands.

Understanding the Dynamics of Value Creation

Going a step further is to understand how these key value drivers interact with each other to create value. No intangible resources can create value on their own; they need to interact with other resources. Therefore, understanding this interdependence allows managers to better reconfigure this resource deployment system (for a further discus-sion of this concept and its application see, e.g., Chatzkel 2002 and Fernström and Roos 2004). Companies such as 3M demonstrated this approach by understanding that they have shared competencies in just a few areas such as, in the case of 3M, sub-strates, coatings, and adhesives (Prahalad and Hamel 1990). Identifying the various ways to combine these core competencies has allowed that company to enter busi-nesses as diverse as sticky tape, photographic film, magnetic tape, and "Post-it" notes.

Gupta and Roos (2001) reported a case study in which two companies in a planned merger mapped their intellectual capital and the way the different assets interacted

Figure 2.4

Map of the resource stock.

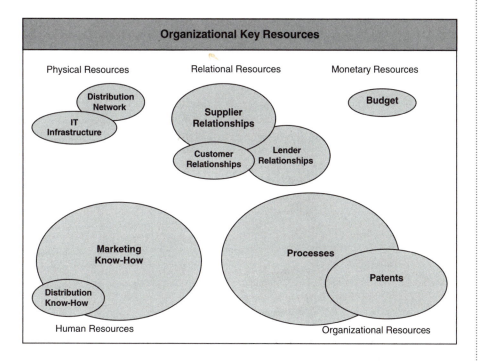

with each other. This analysis resulted in the discovery that the two businesses had a fundamentally different approach in the way they utilized their intellectual capital to create value. Similarly, Marr (2004) conducted a case study in two subsidiaries of a leading pharmaceutical company with the objective of transfering best practices between these two subsidiaries. The analysis of the stock of intellectual value drivers revealed that the resource architecture was identical; only after mapping the dynamic interactions of the assets did it became apparent that the two subsidiaries worked in significantly different ways, which resulted in a termination of the project to transfer best practices between them.

The pharmaceutical firm approached this by taking the key resources identified earlier and captured in a map of resource stock. The individual resources were then transferred into a matrix allowing managers to rate the influence of all resources on each other using a Lickert scale or a ratio scale. For example, managers have to rate how resource A influences resource B, and vice versa, until all resource combinations are assessed. The scale used for assessing the relationships could be between 0 and 5, 0 indicating no relationship and 5 indicating a very strong impact. The results from the individual matrixes allow the creation of a resource map of stocks and flows. Such a map is called an IC navigator (Gupta and Roos 2001; Neely et al. 2003), value creation path (Roos and Jacobsen 1999), or value creation map (Marr et al. 2004). Figure 2.5 depicts such a map.

Figure 2.5

Map of the resource stock and flows.

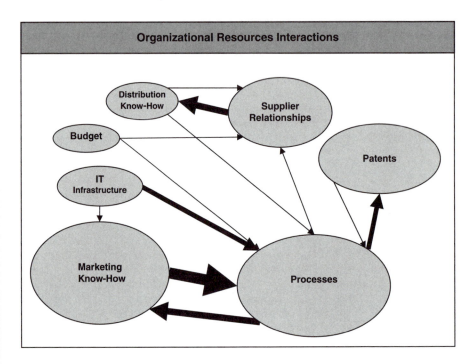

The map illustrates the key resources and how they dynamically interact with each other to deliver organizational performance. Analyzing the relative importance of both resources and their interactions allows managers to extract insight and understanding about how intellectual capital resources, physical resources, and monetary resources interact with each other. The final consolidated map can therefore be used to direct strategic management decisions about resource acquisition and allocation.

Look into the Future

With the development of the resource-based paradigm, intellectual capital has become of significant strategic importance in the strategic management of organizations. An increasing number of firms are trying to understand their resource structure, in particular their knowledge-based resources, to direct their strategy formulation and strategic decision making. In this chapter, we discussed the fundamental ideas and theories underlying this movement. We outlined examples in which companies used the ideas and applied them in strategic settings. However, these firms are pioneers and we believe that this is only the beginning of a much larger movement. To understand the role of intellectual capital, a wider application of the resource-based approach is necessary to counterbalance the prevailing finance-based paradigm. As many people point out, opportunities in the market have to be met with the right capabilities and resource base. Much work goes into the development of the resource-based theories, and refinements of this will provide future insight into how resources and their configurations contribute to a sustainable competitive advantage.

References

Aaker, D. A. 1989. "Managing Assets and Skills: The Key to a Sustainable Competitive Advantage." *California Management Review* 31, no. 2: 91–106.

Andrews, K. R. 1971. *The Concept of Corporate Strategy.* Homewood, IL: Dow Jones-Irwin.

Bainbridge, A., K. Jacobsen, and G. Roos. 2001. "Intellectual Capital Analysis as a Strategic Tool." *Strategy and Leadership Journal* (April 29): 21–26.

Barney, J. B. 1991. "Firm Resources and Sustained Competitive Advantage." *Journal of Management* 17, no. 1: 99–120.

Becker, G. S. 1964. *Human Capital.* New York: Columbia University Press.

Brooking, A. 1996. *Intellectual Capital: Core Assets for the Third Millennium Enterprise.* London: Thompson Business Press.

Brooking, A. 1997. "The Management of Intellectual Capital." *Long Range Planning* 30, no. 3: 364–365.

Caves, R. E., and M. E. Porter. 1977. "From Entry Barriers to Mobility Barriers: Conjectural Decisions and Contrived Deterrence to New Competitors." *Journal of Economics* 91, no. 421–434.

Chatzkel, J. 2002. A Conversation with Göran Roos. *Journal of Intellectual Capital* 3, no. 2: 96–117.

Collins, D. J., and C. A. Montgomery. 1995. "Competing on Resources: Strategy in the 1990s." *Harvard Business Review* (July–August): 118–128.

Delios, A., and P. W. Beamish. 2001. "Survival and Profitability: The Roles of Experience and Intangible Assets in Foreign Subsidiary Performance." *Academy of Management Journal* 44, no. 5 (October): 1028–1038.

Dierickx, I., and K. Cool. 1989. "Asset Stock Accumulation and Sustainability of Competitive Advantage." *Management Science* 35, no. 12: 1504–1511.

Edvinsson, L. 1997. "Developing Intellectual Capital at Skandia." *Long Range Planning* 30, no. 3, pp. 320–331.

Fernström, L., and G. Roos. 2004. "Differences in Value Creating Logics and Their Managerial Consequences—The Case of Authors, Publishers and Printers." *International Journal of the Book* 1: 493–506.

Foss, N. 1997. "Resources and Strategy: A Brief Overview of Themes and Contributions." In: *Resources Firms and Strategies: A Reader in the Resource-Based Perspective*, ed. N. Foss, pp. 3–18. Oxford: Oxford University Press.

Grant, R. M. 1991. *Contemporary Strategy Analysis.* Oxford: Blackwell.

Grindley, P. C., and D. J. Teece. 1997. "Managing Intellectual Capital: Licensing and Cross-Licensing in Semiconductors and Electronics." *California Management Review* 39, no. 2 (Winter): 8–41.

Gupta, O., and G. Roos. 2001. "Mergers and Acquisitions through an Intellectual Capital Perspective." *Journal of Intellectual Capital* 2, no. 3, pp. 297–309.

Hall, R. 1992. "The Strategic Analysis of Intangible Resources." *Strategic Management Journal* 13, no. 2: 135–144.

——. 1993. "A Framework Linking Intangible Resources and Capabilities to Sustainable Competitive Advantage." *Strategic Management Journal* 14: 607–618.

Hatten, K. J., and M. L. Hatten. 1987. "Strategic Groups, Assymetrical Mobility Barriers and Contestability." *Strategic Management Journal* 8: 329–342.

Hudson, W. J. 1993. *Intellectual Capital: How to Build It, Enhance It, Use It.* New York: Wiley.

Itami, H. 1987. *Mobilizing Invisible Assets.* Cambridge, MA: Harvard University Press.

Ittner, C. D., and D. F. Larcker. 1998. "Are Nonfinancial Measures Leading Indicators of Financial Performance? An Analysis of Customer Satisfaction." *Journal of Accounting Research* 36, supplement.

Javidan, M. 1998. "Core Competence: What Does It Mean in Practice?" *Long Range Planning* 31, no. 1: 60–71.

Kaplan, R. S., and D. P. Norton. 2000. "Having Trouble with Your Strategy? Then Map It." *Harvard Business Review* 78, no. 5 (September–October): pp. 167–176.

——. 2004. *Strategy Maps—Converting Intangible Assets into Tangible Outcomes.* Boston: Harvard Business School Press.

King, A. W., and C. P. Zeithaml. 2001. "Competencies and Firm Performance: Examining the Causal Ambiguity Paradox." *Strategic Management Journal* 22, no. 1: 75.

von Krogh, G., J. Roos, and K. Slocum. 1994. "An Essay on Corporate Epistemology." *Strategic Management Journal*, Special Issue on Rethinking Strategy (Summer).

Lev, B. 2001. *Intangibles: Management, Measurement, and Reporting.* Washington DC: The Brookings Institution.

Lippman, S. A., and R. P. Rumelt. 1982. "Uncertain Imitability: An Analysis of Interfirm Differences in Efficiency under Competition." *Bell Journal of Economics* 13, no. 2: 418–438.

Marr, B. 2004. "Measuring and Benchmarking Intellectual Capital." *Benchmarking—An International Journal* 11, no. 5–6.

Marr, B., and J. Chatzkel. 2004. "Intellectual Capital at the Crossroads—Managing, Measuring, and Reporting of IC." *Journal of Intellectual Capital* 5, no. 2: 224–229.

Marr, B., and G. Schiuma. 2001. "Measuring and Managing Intellectual Capital and Knowledge Assets in New Economy Organisations." In: *Handbook of Performance Measurement,* ed. M. Bourne. London: Gee.

Marr, B., G. Schiuma, and A. Neely. 2002. "Assessing Strategic Knowledge Assets in E-Business." *International Journal of Business Performance Management* 4, nos. 2–4: 279–295.

——. 2004. "The Dynamics of Value Creation—Mapping Your Intellectual Performance Drivers." *Journal of Intellectual Capital* 5, no. 2: 312–325.

McGaughey, S. L. 2002. "Strategic Interventions in Intellectual Assets Flows." *Academy of Management Review* 27, no. 2 (April): 248–274.

McGee, J., and H. Thomas. 1986. "Strategic Groups: Theory, Research and Taxonomy." *Strategic Management Journal* 7: 141–160.

Nahapiet, J., and S. Ghoshal. 1998. "Social Capital, Intellectual Capital, and the Organizational Advantage." *Academy of Management Review* 23, no. 2: 242–266.

Neely, A., C. Adams, and M. Kennerley. 2002. *The Performance Prism: The Scorecard for Measuring and Managing Business Success.* London: Financial Times Prentice-Hall.

Neely, A., B. Marr, G. Roos, S. Pike, and O. Gupta. 2003. "Towards the Third Generation of Performance Measurement." *Controlling* 3–4 (March–April): 61–67.

Nelson, R. R., and S. G. Winter. 1982. *An Evolutionary Theory of Economic Change.* Cambridge, MA: Harvard University Press.

Nonaka, I., and H. Takeuchi. 1995. *The Knowledge-Creating Company: How Japanese Companies Create the Dynamics of Innovation.* Oxford: Oxford University Press.

Penrose, E. T. 1959. *The Theory of the Growth of the Firm.* John Wiley, New York.

Porter, M. E. 1980. *Competitive Strategy.* New York: The Free Press.

Prahalad, C. K., and G. Hamel. 1990. "The Core Competence of the Corporation." *Harvard Business Review* 68, no. 3: 79–91.

Quinn, J. B. 1992. *Intelligent Enterprise: A Knowledge and Service Based Paradigm for Industry.* New York: The Free Press.

Roos, G., L. Fernström, and S. Pike. 2004. "Human Resource Management and Business Performance Measurement." *Measuring Business Excellence* 8, no. 1: 28–37.

Roos, G., and K. Jacobsen. 1999. "Management in a Complex Stakeholder Organisation." *Monash Mt. Eliza Business Review* (July): 82–93.

Roos, J. 1998. "Exploring the Concept of Intellectual Capital (IC)." *Long Range Planning* 31, no. 1: 150–153.

Roos, J., and G. Roos. 1997. "Measuring Your Company's Intellectual Performance." *Long Range Planning* 30, no. 3: 325.

Rucci, A. J., S. P. Kirn, and R. T. Quinn. 1998. "The Employee-Customer Profit Chain at Sears." *Harvard Business Review* 76, no. 1: 82–98.

Rumelt, R. P. 1984. "Towards a Strategic Theory of the Firm." In: *Competitive Strategic Management,* ed. R. B. Lamp. Englewood Cliffs, NJ: Prentice-Hall.

Schultz, T. W. 1981. *Investing in People: The Economics of Population Quality.* Berkeley: University of California.

Schulze, W. S. 1994. "The Two Schools of Thought in Resource-Based Theory: Definitions and Implications for Research." *Advances in Strategic Management* 10A: 127–151.

Sharpiro, C. 1989. "The Theory of Business Strategy." *Journal of Economics* 20, no. 1: 125–137.

Stalk, G., P. Evans, and L. E. Shulman. 1992. "Competing on Capabilities: The New Rules of Corporate Strategy." *Harvard Business Review* 70: 57–69.

Stewart, T. A. 1991. "Brainpower." *Fortune* (June 3): 44–60.

Sveiby, K. E. 1997. *The New Organizational Wealth: Managing and Measuring Knowledge-Based Assets*. San Francisco: Barrett-Kohler.

Teece, D. J. 1998. "Capturing Value from Knowledge Assets: The New Economy, Markets for Know-How, and Intangible Assets." *California Management Review* 40, no. 3: 55–79.

———. 2000. *Managing Intellectual Capital: Organizational, Strategic, and Policy Dimensions*. Oxford: University Press. Oxford.

———, G. Pisano, and A. Shuen. 1997. "Dynamic Capabilities and Strategic Management." *Strategic Management Journal* 18, no. 7: 509–533.

Wernerfelt, B. 1984. "A Resource Based View of the Firm." *Strategic Management Journal* 5, no. 3: 171–180.

Williamson, O. 1975. *Markets and Hierachies*. New York: The Free Press.

An Accounting Perspective on Intellectual Capital

Baruch Lev
New York University

Leandro Cañibano
Autonomous University of Madrid

Bernard Marr
Cranfield School of Management

Introduction

In this chapter, we provide an accounting perspective on intellectual capital. For this purpose, we first provide an overview of how the topic of intellectual capital has evolved in the field of accounting. We then discuss its definitions and the current regulatory standards as well as the latest scholarly thinking. In the concluding section, we discuss potential future developments of accounting standards.

In the developed economies, we have seen a shift from the industrial economy, in which tangible resources were dominant, to a knowledge economy, in which intellectual capital (IC) is a critical resource and a key determinant of competitive advantage, economic success, and value creation in firms. In the accounting field, the term *intangible assets* is more commonly used and refers, like IC,[1] to the nonphysical value drivers in organizations that represent claims to future benefits.

In an industrial economy, production facilities, physical location, and efficient manufacturing processes are the vital resources for a firm and sufficient to sustain a superior position in the marketplace (Chandler 1980, 1994; Nakamura 2001). The booms after the two World Wars created sellers' markets in most of the developed countries (Marr and Spender 2004). In such a world, traditional cost-focused reporting methods provided an adequate picture of firm performance. However, global trade has gradually changed this toward buyers' markets. Such markets, when they are saturated, do not absorb all goods produced. Consumers are better informed and more demanding, which leads to increasing innovation speed and decreasing product life cycles. Differentiation and innovation become critical; and capabilities and assets such as research and development (R&D), creativity, brand image, patents, and copyrights are essential to achieving a competitive advantage. This also means that traditional

---

[1] For the purpose of this chapter, we use the terms *intellectual capital* and *intangible assets* interchangeably.

cost-focused reporting tools cannot provide the adequate information on firm performance.

The objective of financial reporting is to provide useful information for making economic decisions on the financial position and performance of the firm, as stated by the Financial Accounting Standards Board (FASB 1978) *Statement of Financial Accounting Standards* (SFAS 1, par. 34) and the International Accounting Standards Board (IASB) framework for the preparation and presentation of financial statements (IASC, International Accounting Standards Commitee, 1989 par. 12). Even though it is generally accepted that investments in intangibles are important sources of future performance, restrictive accounting asset recognition rules mean that most intangible assets cannot be included in the balance sheet, especially if they are developed internally. Instead, all costs incurred to develop intangible assets usually must be directly charged as expenses in the income statement. For companies that invest in intangibles, this immediate expensing means that the current profit and financial position of an organization is reduced, while future reported profits are often overstated.

A key argument against the recognition of intangible assets in balance sheets is the uncertainty of future economic flows from such assets. As a consequence, current accounting systems are more likely to *"front-load the costs"* of investing into intangibles and *"delay the recognition"* of its benefits (Lev and Zarowin 1999). In the late 1980s, academics and practitioners started to raise their concerns about this practice, arguing that if accounting rules would not adapt to the increasing need to provide relevant information about investments in IC, accounting would loose its relevance (e.g., Johnson and Kaplan 1987). Both the views of professional organizations and academic research emphasized the need to adjust the existing accounting practices to provide users the *true and fair* view of the firm's financial position and performance.

One visible effect of a possible loss in relevance of accounting information was the increasing gap between the market value and the book value of equity during the 1980s and 1990s.[2] This could not be explained with the contemporary earnings growth rates but was partly because investors started to value the increasing level of investment in IC as potential sources of future profitability (Nakamura 1999). In fact, R&D investments in the U.S. economy doubled for the period of 1953–1997, while investment in tangible assets remained steady.[3] Even with this increase in investments in IC as future sources of value and profit, most of them have to be immediately expensed, thus decreasing current earnings and book value of equity. In fact, Lev and Sougiannis (1999) confirm Nakamura's (1999) assertions that "innovative capital" is a fundamental variable underlying the market-to-book value effect.

The American Institute of Certified Public Accountants (AICPA) and the Association for Investment Management and Research (AIMR) were among the first professional associations to express their concerns about the current financial reporting model. In 1991, the board of directors of the AICPA[4] established a special

---

[2] The loss of relevance of accounting information is also clear from Lev and Zarowin (1999), who show that R&D-intensive firms experience more changes than firms with no R&D and lose the informativeness of financial information quicker than no-R&D firms.

[3] Research and development expenditures as a proportion of nonfinancial corporate gross domestic product increased from 1.3 for the period 1953–1959 to 2.9 for 1990–1997. Conversely, tangible investment remained the same 12.6% over the total nonfinancial corporate gross domestic product.

[4] The AICPA had previously taken other initiatives to improve the information provided in the financial statements (Rimmerman 1990).

committee on financial reporting. After 2 years, the committee published a summary report (AICPA 1994) warning that the existing accounting system fails to meet the current needs of investors and creditors and a static business reporting model without the important non-financial information will have harmful consequences (Jenkins 1994; Upton 2001). The AICPA publication and a similar report published by the AIMR led the FASB to undertake a research project focused on improving business reporting in 1998. As a result, the FASB published several reports[5] emphasizing the importance of voluntary disclosure of information about intangible assets. In October 2001, the FASB started a new project on the voluntary disclosure of information on intangible assets but deactivated this project.

The concerns about the decreasing relevance of traditional accounting information quickly surpassed the U.S. boundaries. The Canadian Institute of Chartered Accountants (CICA), the Danish Agency for Development of Trade and Industry, the Netherlands Ministry of Economic Affairs, the Organization for Economic Cooperation and Development (OECD), the Institute of Chartered Accountants in England and Wales (ICAEW), and the Chartered Institute of Management Accountants (CIMA) all conducted studies addressing the need to identify, measure, and report information on intangibles that are the major value drivers in the knowledge economy (Starovic and Marr 2003; Upton 2001).

Not only professional and regulatory bodies but also academics discussed the erosion of relevance of published earnings information, and historical cost accounting in general, due to the fast changes in the environment and the delayed reaction of regulators. Ely and Waymire (1999) suggest, "Standard-setters may need to write new standards at an accelerating rate merely to maintain the overall relevance of accounting data at the existing level." Empirical findings of studies in the field support this view.[6] While Collins, Maydew, and Weiss (1997) and Francis and Shipper (1999) did not find clear evidence on the decline in the value relevance of accounting information, Lev and Zarowin (1999) reported a significant decline in the combined relevance of earnings and book values. Brown, Lo, and Lys (1999) showed that after controlling for the scale effects, the results in the Collins et al. (1997) and Francis and Shipper (1999) studies support the argument of a temporal decline in the value relevance of earnings. Lev and Zarowin (1999) clarified previous evidence showing that the decreasing relevance was not due to the increasing number of firms in the intangible-intensive or high-tech industrial sectors, but to the rate of business change and an increasing investment rate in R&D. This means that firms that are innovative, creative, and faced with quick changes are those for which the current historical-cost accounting system is least suitable.[7]

Together with evidence on the inadequacy of the reporting system for a business environment with an increasing degree of innovation and investment in intangibles

---

[5] The FASB published three reports as part of their project, including *Improving Business Reporting: Insights into Enhancing Voluntary Disclosures* and *Business and Financial Reporting, Challenges from the New Economy.* These reports are available online at http://www.fasb. org/brrp/BRRP2.PDF and http://accounting.rutgers.edu/raw/fasb/articles&reports/sr_new_economy.pdf.

[6] These studies follow the definition of *value relevance* as the ability of earnings to explain the cross-sectional variation in stock returns, measured mainly through the R^2 together with the coefficient estimates from the regression analysis.

[7] Evidence for Europe reports similar results for countries with an Anglo-American accounting system, while those with a continental-European reporting system do not seem to suffer a decline in the value relevance of earnings (Høegh-Krohn and Knivsflå 2000).

(Lev and Zarowin 1999), an extensive body of literature has documented the positive effects of intangibles on the firm's future profits and market values. Not only R&D but also advertising, patents, brands, trademarks, and human resources are important value drivers,[8] and investors need relevant and timely information on these value drivers to assess the economic conditions of the firm and its future potential. Cañibano, Garcia-Ayuso, and Sánchez (2000) assert, "in order to provide the users of financial statements with relevant information for investment and credit decisions, standard setting bodies should develop guidelines for the identification of intangible elements, and set criteria for their valuation and adequate standards for financial reporting."

There is no common definition of IC. Stolowy and Jeny-Cazavan (2001) found that most regulations provide a general conceptual definition of intangibles, then include a list of items or categories of intangible assets. Most regulatory accounting bodies include in their definition of intangibles (a) the promise of future benefits, (b) the lack of physical substance, and (c) the non-monetary nature. The International Accounting Standard (IAS 38) specifies that a company can recognize an asset only if it is identifiable, controlled, and probable that future benefits specifically attributable to the asset will flow to the enterprise; and cost can be reliably measured. These recognition criteria apply to both purchased and self-created assets. If any intangible asset does not meet these criteria, IAS 38 requires expensing this item. The uncertainty regarding future benefits from intangibles, their uniqueness in certain occasions (Hendriksen 1982), and the importance of reliability over relevance in current accounting systems narrow the list of items recognized as intangible assets. Regardless of the long list of intangible resources relevant to organizations, the categories recognized as assets in accounting are very limited; they mainly refer to acquired (not internally generated) intangibles: (a) goodwill, (b) research and development, and (c) other identifiable intangibles such as patents, software, licenses, copyrights, or brands. Goodwill is an all-inclusive asset category defined as the excess of the cost of an acquired company over the sum of the fair value of identifiable net assets. In many acquisitions, the purchase price is higher than the value of the net assets included in the balance sheet. Goodwill allows firms to account for the "unidentifiable assets and liabilities" that cannot be recognized in the firm's balance sheet using current accounting standards. Goodwill appears only in an acquisition transaction. Furthermore, while identifiable intangible assets may be recognized individually, as a part of a group of assets, or as part of an entire enterprise, unidentifiable assets cannot be recognized individually. Also, internally generated goodwill is not recognized in balance sheets, and together with other intangibles has to be expensed immediately, including investments in advertising, training programs, customer lists, and startup costs.[9]

Intangibles are sources of value and competitive advantage, but it is clear from the preceding list that much of what is commonly regarded as IC and intangible value drivers would not pass the accounting recognition test. Regulatory accounting bodies have not yet developed an adequate reporting system to provide investors and other users with the required information for making investment and credit decisions. This lack of information has harmful consequences for both firms and investors as they

---

[8] An analysis of the literature on the value relevance of different intangibles can be found in Cañibano et al. (2000).

[9] In certain regulatory regimes after an acquisition transaction, some of these intangible resources will be recognized as assets apart from goodwill in the acquirer's balance sheet if they comply with the recognition criteria for "identifiable" assets and liabilities.

might lead to higher cost of capital and interest rates, greater degree of uncertainty over earnings, greater errors in earnings forecasts, and larger information asymmetries between managers and stakeholders, leaving a greater degree of freedom for insider gains and earnings management (García-Ayuso 2003; Starovic and Marr 2003). However, firms seem to be reacting, and, guided by international research efforts, they are starting to provide voluntary information on their intangible resources to comply with the new needs and requirements for better information (e.g., Mouristen, Bukh, and Marr 2004).

Accounting for Intangible Assets: Current Techniques and Practices

Hendriksen (1982) proposes two approaches to account for intangible assets: (a) matching outlays with future revenues whenever possible, or (b) expensing the outlays in the years incurred if they cannot be easily matched with future revenues. In fact, current regulatory accounting frameworks are likely to apply both perspectives, depending on the ways a firm has acquired intangibles, whether they have been internally developed or purchased externally.

Applying the recognition and valuation rules to externally acquired intangible assets, such as brands or patents, is not a difficult task, since the determination of costs is similar to the approach used for tangible assets. However, identifying, measuring, and reporting internally generated intangibles and assets acquired in a business combination is causing a serious problem for accounting. Given the full adoption of International Accounting Standards (IAS/IFRS) for consolidated accounts of listed companies from January 2005 onward in Europe and other countries like Australia or New Zealand,[10] our analysis of current regulations of intangibles refers to the standards issued by the leading regulatory accounting bodies: IASB and FASB.

The general criteria for whether intangibles can currently be recorded on the balance sheet are these: (a) the assets can be identified, (b) their future economic benefits will flow to the enterprise, and (c) the cost can be measured reliably (IAS 38, in IASC 1998a, and SFAS No. 5, 1984). However, while these criteria hold true for most intangibles obtained by an acquisition transaction, the difficulty in recognizing internally generated intangibles has created a great degree of nonconformity among accounting regulators, revealing the difficulties in trying to settle accounting requirements for intangibles (Powell 2003).

Uncertainty over the control of future economic benefits coming from intangibles (Cañibano et al. 2000) together with the difficulties in reliably establishing the value of internally developed intangibles are the main arguments against the recognition of these resources on the balance sheet.[11] While acquired intangibles are measured at fair value[12] (SFAS No. 142, 2001, par. 9) or at cost (IAS 38, 1998, par. 22), most

---

[10] More than 90 countries in the world will adopt IAS/IFRS by the year 2007.

[11] Note that any balance sheet recognition has an important effect on the income statement, too. When a previously expended item (e.g., R&D) is recognized as an asset, income increases. However, the amortization of the recognized asset decreases future earnings.

[12] Fair value refers to the amount at which an asset (liability) could be bought (incurred) or sold (settled) in a current transaction between willing parties, that is, other than in a forced or liquidation sale. Quoted market prices in active markets are the best evidence of fair value and should be used as the basis for the measurement, if available. (FAS (Financial Accounting Standards) 133, par. 540, page 234)

of the costs of internally developed intangibles are immediately expensed (IAS 38, 1998; SFAS 2, 1984; APB (Accounting Principals Board) opinion No 17, 1970; SFAS 142, 2001). This means that the majority of investments in intangibles (e.g., advertising, research costs, training expenses, internally developed goodwill) are not recorded on the balance sheet.[13]

While acquired intangibles must be stated at fair value, APB no. 17 allows for capitalization of the costs incurred for internally developed intangibles, other than R&D, as long as the assets are identifiable, have a limited useful life span (i.e., the period of future benefits can be reasonably well determined), and is not part of a subdivision or the firm as a whole (par. 24). Otherwise, outlays related to internally developed intangibles must be expensed, as is the case with internally generated goodwill. Likewise, IAS 38 sets certain criteria linked to technical feasibility and the future economic benefits for internally generated intangibles. It requires capitalization when these conditions are met (par. 45). IAS 38 specifically prohibits the recognition of internally generated brands, mastheads, publishing titles, customer lists, and items similar in substance (par. 51).

Even though IAS 38 concurs with the conservative accounting treatment of internally developed intangibles in the United States, certain differences arise in the recognition of development costs (in contrast with the initial research). SFAS 2 (1974) requires all costs incurred for internally developed research and development activities to be expensed immediately, except those incurred for computer software to be sold, leased, or marketed, once technical feasibility has been achieved (SFAS 86, 1985). In addition, firms are required to disclose information on research and development expenditures in the income statement to provide investors with some information on the innovation activities of the firm. On the other hand, IAS 38 requires research costs to be expensed, while development costs must be capitalized under certain recognition criteria (par. 45).

The abolition of the pooling or uniting of the interest method of accounting for business combinations (after the issuance of SFAS No. 141, for fiscal years beginning after December 2001) provides users a more-truthful picture of these types of transactions. It means that all identified assets and liabilities of an acquired firm must be recorded in the acquirer's balance sheet (par. 35), along with the corresponding goodwill.[14] SFAS 141 allows recognition of an intangible asset by the acquirer when "it arises from contractual or legal rights" or "it is separable from the acquired entity" and includes an illustrative list of intangible assets that meet the recognition criteria to categorize them as *identified*. IAS 22 allows both uniting of interest and purchase methods to account for business combinations. Yet, the former is the exception since most business combinations are accounted for as a purchase in a way similar to SFAS 141, but this standard sets more general criteria for *identified* assets and liabilities and

---

[13] Australia is one of the few jurisdictions with a liberal accounting regulation on intangibles. A loose interpretation of AASB (Australian Accounting Standards Board) 1010 superseded by AASB 1041 "revaluation of non-current assets" allows capitalization of internally generated intangibles crediting an asset revaluation reserve (Wyatt 2002). In fact, this issue is creating a great controversy due to the future compliance of Australian firms with IFRS, since IAS 38 does not allow such a degree of recognition for internally generated intangible assets.

[14] Goodwill arises as the difference between the price paid for the acquired firm and the fair value of all identified assets and liabilities.

allows for the accounting of its fair value[15] (par. 26). Consequently, under both regulatory frameworks intangibles assets should be recorded separately in the acquirer's balance sheet after an acquisition transaction, while the value of all nonidentified intangible resources of the acquired firm are included in the *goodwill* category. Both IAS 22 and SFAS 141 consider the nature of goodwill as the payment made in anticipation of future economic benefits arising from both identified and nonidentified net assets, as well as from the synergies among them (SFAC 141, 2001, par. B201; and IAS 22, 1998, par. 42). Yet, differences in the recognition and valuation criteria of *identifiable* assets and liabilities may lead to divergences in the amount of goodwill as well as in the recognized assets and liabilities in the acquirer's balance sheet.[16]

Major differences between IAS/IFRS and U.S. GAAP (Generally Accepted Accounting Principles) arise in the accounting treatment of both goodwill and certain intangible assets. SFAS no. 142 abolished the amortization of goodwill and intangible assets with indefinite useful life and requires annual impairment tests for both categories of intangibles to account for possible value depletion. IAS 38 diverts from current U.S. regulation, since amortization of goodwill and intangible assets is required. However, in response to the FASB-IASB Norwalk Agreement on convergence between both regulatory bodies, the IASB recently issued Exposure Draft 3, "business combinations," which aligns with SFAS 141 and 142 requirements of goodwill and other intangible assets.[17] Among other differences in the accounting treatment for intangible assets, we highlight the revaluation alternative allowed under IAS 38 of intangible assets. Yet, as previously stated, there is a common objective of both regulatory bodies toward harmonization, which should erase differences in future regulatory developments.

The first steps toward this were taken in 2004: IFRS 3 (IABS 2004a), IAS 36 (IASB 2004b), and IAS 38 (IASB 2004c) introduce several changes to converge to U.S. GAAP. The main changes are related to the use of the fair value method to measure intangible assets and the abolition of amortization of goodwill and intangible assets with indefinite useful life; both categories of assets require an annual impairment test,[18] which makes it compulsory to write off potential losses.

---

[15] IAS 22 allows for two alternative treatments for the recognition of identifiable assets and liabilities. Under the benchmark treatment, assets and liabilities are measured as the sum of the fair value at the date of the exchange transaction proportional to the percentage of interest obtained in the transaction plus the minority's interest proportion of the preacquisition carrying amount of the assets and liabilities identifiable. On the other hand, the alternative treatment aligns to SFAS 141 and allows identifiable assets and liabilities to be accounted for at fair value regardless of the percentage of the firm acquired in the transaction. ED-3 (Exposure Draft) proposes eliminating the current benchmark treatment and aligns with the SFAS 141 recording of identifiable assets and liabilities at fair value.

[16] When the acquirer pays an amount lower than the net fair value of all identifiable assets and liabilities, it is assuming possible future losses, thus a negative goodwill arises from the transaction.

[17] As explained in Powell (2003), in spite of the changes included in ED-3 (2002), differences between the two standards will remain in the treatment of in-process research and development acquired in a business combination transaction. Under SFAS no. 141, the item must be directly expensed, while under the ED-3 requirements, it can be recorded apart from goodwill if it complies with the corresponding criteria. The FASB, however, is currently proposing capitalization of in-process R&D.

[18] IFRS 3 (2004a), IAS 36 (IASB 2004b), and IAS 38 (IASB 2004c) were issued on March 31, 2004, having starting the endorsement process at the European Union.

Irrespective of the accounting harmonization process worldwide and the increasing disclosure requirements, information on intangibles in annual accounts is scarce compared to the importance of intangible resources in most businesses. Increasingly, companies feel the need to improve transparency and communication with stakeholders, especially after the burst of the technology bubble and the latest accounting scandals, which negatively affected the confidence of investors (García-Ayuso 2003). Sánchez, Charminade, and Olea (2000) state that "there is a need for information on the intangible determinants of the value of companies that will help improve the decision making process of managers and stakeholders."

Several research projects developed alternative methodologies to report and measure intangible resources within organizations to complement current accounting standards. General measures such as the book-to-market ratio and Tobin's Q (a ratio of the stock market value of the firm divided by the replacement cost of its assets) were proposed to indicate a more reliable picture to investors (Stewart 1997). In the management accounting and general management literature, measurement and reporting frameworks were developed to incorporate intangibles. Examples include the Balanced Scorecard (Kaplan and Norton 1992), the Performance Prism (Neely, Adams, and Kennerley 2002), and guidelines for reporting on intangibles (e.g., Meritum 2002; Danish Agency of Trade and Industry 2000).[19] There are significant differences in the way information on IC is published in Europe and the United States as well as among different European countries (e.g., Ordóñez de Pablos 2002). Scandinavian firms together with some Spanish companies seem to be leading the way and are already publishing information on IC in their annual reports or in separate IC statements. Various Danish firms are producing IC statements, such as the consulting firm Carl Bro A/S[20] (e.g., Marr, Mouritsen, and Bukh, 2003). Companies such as Unión Fenosa or Telefónica in Spain also publish information about their intangibles.

However, from the investors' perspective, there is a serious drawback to these reports or any other voluntary information on intellectual capital: the lack of harmonization (comparability) among firms, industries, or different years for which the data are published. This significantly reduces the usefulness of the information. There is a tremendous call for homogenization on voluntarily disclosed information on intangibles (Ordóñez de Pablos 2002) that requires both the management and the accounting field to keep devoting research efforts to improve the efficiency of the current reporting model to both manage and communicate to outsiders on the intangible *value drivers* of firms.

A Look into the Future: How Will the Reporting of Intangibles Evolve?

Several studies have proposed different ways of reporting on intangibles so that financial statements reflect the increasing changes that affect the business environment. Together with the intellectual capital reports in the management field, accounting academics have suggested certain changes of the current accounting system so that the reporting model follows the pace of the modern economy.

---

[19] Upton (2001) provides a detailed explanation of most of these frameworks to report nonfinancial information on intellectual capital.

[20] A list of all Danish firms reporting intellectual capital reports is available at www.efs.dk/icaccounts.

According to Francis and Shipper (1999), recommendations of possible changes address both the relevance and timeliness of accounting information. Changes are suggested not only on what to report but also on frequency of reports. Criticism of current conservative accounting standards addresses the direct expensing of most of the intangible outlays and supports both capitalization and greater disclosure of information on intangibles (Roslender 2004).

The key arguments of the FASB, IASB, and other standard-setting bodies against recording intangibles on the balance sheet are (a) the uncertainty of future economic benefits, (b) the lack of reliability of monetary value, and (c) the greater degree of discretion given to mangers by the capitalization alternative compared to immediate expensing. Yet, the strong support toward capitalization is leading academics to propose alternatives that would offer investors more-relevant information without losing the required reliability of accounting measures. Authors such as Lev and Zarowin (1999), Høegh-Krohn and Knivsflå (2000), and Upton (2001) propose less-conservative alternatives to accounting for intangible assets, supporting either full-cost or fair value capitalization approaches.

Similar to IAS 38 (IASC 1998a) for development costs, or SFAS no. 86 for software development expenditures, Lev and Zarowin (1999) and Høegh-Krohn and Knivsflå (2000) support the condition-based cost capitalization approach to account for certain intangible assets, with attributable benefit streams, together with the corresponding amortization or impairment test to revise the asset's value. Lev and Sougiannis (1996), Aboody and Lev (1998), Barth and Clinch (1998), and Healy, Myers, and Howe (2002) provide evidence on the significant association between intangibles' capitalization and market values, thus supporting the argument that this approach provides more relevant information. Yet, conversely to the IAS 38 or SFAS no. 86 capitalization rules, these authors go beyond a simple cost capitalization approach. They propose adding all previous expenditures related to a project to the capitalized amount, thus recognizing the reversal of expenditures from previous years on current year earnings and recording the corresponding intangible asset in the balance sheet[21] (Høegh-Krohn and Knivsflå 2000).

Lev and Zarowin (1999) offer a second alternative and suggest accounting for all previous costs of developing intangibles before technical feasibility is achieved. As they explain, condition-based capitalization is easier to apply to certain intangibles investments with a clear development phase. However, other intangible "value drivers," such as restructuring, advertising, or employee training costs, are not directly linked to a product development, therefore the simple capitalization approach is more difficult to apply. In contrast to the Høegh-Krohn and Knivsflå (2000) alternative of reversing previous years expenses on current earnings, Lev and Zarowin (1999) propose the restatement of past financial reports, reversing previous years' expensing and recording an asset on the current balance sheet once the benefits of the intangible outlays start to flow into the firm.

There is a danger that the two capitalization methods of intangibles, either crediting to current profits or restating previous financial statements, offer organizations the possibility of *earnings management.* Myopic behavior and market pressure to meet certain earnings benchmarks may lead managers to use either the expense or capital-

---

[21] The recorded asset must equal the revenues recognized and amounts of expenditures incurred in previous years minus the corresponding accumulated depreciation since the intangible outlays started.

ization alternative to meet market expectations or smooth earnings irrespectively of the informativeness of accounting information.[22]

The restatement alternative (Lev and Zarowin 1999; Høegh-Krohn and Knivsflå 2000) partially constrains firms to delay capitalization, since managers have to capitalize all previous expenditures incurred in the corresponding project at some point in the future (Upton 2001). Notwithstanding this restatement, capitalization alternatives do not abolish the risk of earnings management, since they leave a certain degree of discretion to capitalize the outlays and the time in which capitalization must be accomplished. To avoid *creative accounting practices*, authors emphasize (Høegh-Krohn and Knivsflå 2000) the need to (a) clarify the amount of expenses to be capitalized and (b) settle on a clear condition-based criteria for capitalization. Regarding the first issue, they propose to publish annual information in the notes of the outlays devoted to potential intangible assets, so that future capitalization is allowed only if information has been previously reported. Second, they propose to create clear capitalization criteria for intangibles to guide firms in the capitalization process and avoid *creative accounting practices.*

Together with the arguments in favor of extending the capitalization approach to intangible outlays, other authors highlight the need for a greater emphasis on additional qualitative and quantitative disclosure of information on intangibles. In fact, the currently frozen FASB project on intangibles aims to increase the amount of information disclosed in the notes about internally generated intangibles not recognized in financial statements[23] (FASB 2001c). Authors such as Amir and Lev (2003) have shown that current accounting practices do not provide the relevant information for high-tech industries and highlight that other firm- or industry-specific intangibles are critical.

The importance of intangibles as key value drivers is widely accepted, but the lack of control over the future economic benefits of many intangible outlays and the difficulties in setting a monetary value supports the voluntary reporting of qualitative information on intangibles. This view was also supported by the Security and Exchange Commission task force report (2001), stating the need for developing a disclosure framework for information on intangibles and other measures of operating performance.

While these alternatives are based on historical-cost measurement of intangibles, other alternatives suggest a fair value recognition approach. Upton (2001) argues that cost-based capitalization of intangibles might not be suitable in certain situations; for instance, in interrelated intangibles projects, where separate outlays for each of the projects cannot be clearly identified. Other circumstances where the capitalization approach might not be appropriate are when the costs incurred in the development of a project are unrelated to the future reported revenues. Even though the lack of active markets for most intangibles constrains fair value measurements, special valuation techniques and new markets for certain intangibles such as patent and know-how

---

[22] Aboody and Lev (1998) show how the effects of either capitalizing or expensing software development costs have a different impact on earnings, depending on the life cycle of software firms. Firms choose to either capitalize or expense depending on its effect on future earnings.

[23] The FASB project aims to disclose information on those intangible assets that are not recognized in the financial statements but would have been recognized if acquired in an arms' length or acquisition transaction, including in process research and development. In addition, the FASB proposal comments on the possibility of extending the initial scope to the disclosure of other nonfinancial intangible information or the recognition of research and development.

licensing (Gu and Lev 2001) have arisen, widening the possibility of a fair value approach for valuing intangibles. Moreover, converse to the general belief that there is a lack of measurement reliability, a greater degree of discretion, and possible market inefficiencies, Wyatt's (2002) insight on the fair value accounting practices for intangibles in Australia shows how these concerns are exaggerated.

Accounting regulators are aware of the current reporting deficiencies for intangibles, but regulatory changes take place slowly. It seems that in the near future, the field of accounting for intangibles is going to evolve faster in the management domain, strengthening voluntary disclosure in financial statements and adopting less-conservative criteria to record internally generated intangibles in the balance sheet.

Conclusions

In this chapter, we outlined the evolution of accounting for intellectual capital, or intangible assets. We demonstrated that factors such as globalization and innovations created buyers' markets in most developed countries, which means that intangible resources, such as R&D, relationships, skills, or innovation capacity, increasingly represent the foundation of a competitive advantage of firms and superior business performance. This evolution means that investors and stakeholders require information on all relevant assets and productive resources of a firm to be able to assess its performance and future course. Traditional cost-based accounting information needs to be complemented with information on the intangible value drivers. However, the accounting principles and rules developed over the last century to ensure that information reported is accurate and reliable struggle to include information on many intangibles.

In particular, the uncertainty about future economic benefits, the lack of full control, and the absence of markets to measure and value of intangibles reliably have made accounting regulators reluctant to adopt more liberal measures. We discussed the current accounting standards for intangibles issued by the leading regulatory bodies, IASB and FASB. This discussion highlights the controversy about the recognition and disclosure of internally generated intangibles.

We then outlined various proposals of how to overcome the problem of accounting for intangibles. Academic research supports both the capitalization alternative and a fair value approach. Both approaches have advantages and disadvantages. However, at this stage, regulators are still cautious and prefer to devote efforts to harmonize current practices and develop a framework of voluntary disclosure for intangibles. Further research and experimentation is invaluable if we are to arrive at a point of convergence among the disparate approaches of accounting for intellectual capital.

Acknowledgment

We would like to acknowledge the help of Ana Gisbert, assistant professor at the Autonomous University of Madrid, in producing this chapter.

References

Aboody, D., and B. Lev, B. 1998. "The Value Relevance of Intangibles: The Case of Software Capitalization." *Journal of Accounting Research*. 36 (supplement): 161–191.

Accounting Principles Board (APB). 1970. "Intangible Assets." APB opinion no. 17. New York: APB.

American Institute of Certified Public Accountants (AIPCA). 1994. "Improving Business Reporting—A Customer Focus." New York. Available online at http://www.aicpa.org/

members/div/acctstd/ibr/index.htm   or   http://accounting.rutgers.edu/raw/aicpa/business/
main.htm.

Association for Investment Management and Research (AIMR). 1994. "Financial Reporting in the 1990s and Beyond." Charlottesville, VA: AMIR.

Amir, E., B. Lev, and T. Sougianns. 2003. "Do Financial Analgsts Get Intangibles?" *European Accounting Review* 12, no. 4, 635–659.

Barth, M., and G. Clinch. 1998. "Revalued Financial, Tangible, and Intangible Assets: Associations with Share Prices, and Non-Market Based Value Estimates." *Journal of Accounting Research*. 36 (supplement): 199–233.

Brown, S., K. Lo, and T. Lys. 1999. "Use Of R² In Accounting Research: Measuring Changes In Value Relevance Over The Last Four Decades." *Journal of Accounting and Economics*. 28: 83–115.

Cañibano, L., M. García-Ayuso, and P. Sánchez. 2000. "Accounting For Intangibles: A Literature Review." *Journal of Accounting Literature*. 19: 102–130.

Chandler, A. 1980. *The Visible Hand: The Managerial Revolution in American Business.* Cambridge, MA: Harvard University Press.

——. 1994. *Scale and Scope: The Dynamics of American Capitalism.* Cambridge, MA: Harvard University Press.

Collins, D. W., E. L. Maydew, and I. S. Weiss. 1997. "Changes in the Value-Relevance of Earnings and Book Values over the Past Forty Years." *Journal of Accounting and Economics* 24: 39–67.

Danish Agency of Trade and Industry (DATI). 2000. *A Guideline for Intellectual Capital Statements—A Key to Knowledge Mangement.* Copenhagen: Ministry of Trade and Industry.

Edvinson, L., and M. S. Malone. 1997. *Intellectual Capital.* New York: HarperCollins.

Ely, K., and G. Waymire. 1999. "Accounting Standards-Setting Organisations and Earnings Relevance: Longitudinal Evidence From NYSE Common Stocks, 1927–1993." *Journal of Accounting Research* 37, no. 2: 293–317.

Financial Accounting Standards Board (FASB). 1974. "Accounting for Research and Development Costs." Statement of financial accounting standard no. 2. CT: FASB.

——. 1978. "Objectives of Financial Reporting by Business Enterprises." Statement of financial accounting concepts no. 1. CT: FASB.

——. 1985. "Accounting for the Costs of Computer Software to Be Sold, Leased or Otherwise Marketed." Statement of financial accounting standard no. 86. CT: FASB.

——. 2001a. "Business Combinations." Statement of financial accounting standard no. 141. CT: FASB.

——. 2001b. "Goodwill and Intangible Assets." Statement of financial accounting standard no. 142. CT: FASB.

——. 2001c. "Proposal for a New Agenda Project: Disclosure of Information about Intangible Assets Not Recognized in Financial Statements." Available online at http://www.fasb.org/proposals/intangibles.pdf.

Francis, J., and K. Shipper. 1999. "Have Financial Statements Lost Their Relevance?" *Journal of Accounting Research* 37, no. 2: 319–352.

García-Ayuso, M. 2003. "Intangibles. Lessons from the past and a look into the future." *Journal of Intellectual Capital* 4, no. 4: 597–604.

Gu, F., and B. Lev. 2001. "Markets in Intangibles: Patent Licensing." Working Paper. Boston University and New York University.

Healy, P., D. Myers, and C. Howe. 2002. "R&D Accounting and the Tradeoff between Relevance and Objectivity." *Journal of Accounting Research* 40, no. 3: 677–710.

Hendriksen, E. S. 1982. *Accounting Theory*, 4th Edition. Burr Ridge, IL: Richard D. Irwin.

Høegh-Krohn, N. E., and K. H. Knivsflå. 2000. "Accounting for Intangible Assets in Scandinavia, the UK, the US, and by the IASC: Challenges and a Solution." *International Journal of Accounting* 35, no. 2: 243–265.

International Accounting Standards Board (IASB). 2002. "Business Combinations." Exposure draft no 3. London: IASB.

———. 2004a. "Business combinations." International financial reporting standard no. 3, London: IASB.

———. 2004b. "Impairment of Assets." International accounting standard no. 36 revised. London: IASB.

———. 2004c. "Intangible Assets." International accounting standard no. 38 revised, London: IASB.

IASC. 1989. "Framework for the Preparation and Presentation of Financial Statements." London: IASC.

———. 1998a. "Intangible Assets." International accounting standard no. 38. London: IASC.

———. 1998b. "Business Combinations." International accounting standard no. 22. London: IASC.

Jenkins, E. L. 1994. "An Information Highway in Need of Capital Improvements." *Journal of Accountancy* 177, no. 5: 77–82.

Johnson, T. H., and R. S. Kaplan. 1987. *Relevance Lost: The Rise and the Fall of Management Accounting.* Boston: Harvard Business School Press.

Kaplan, R. S., and D. P. Norton. 1992. "The Balanced Scorecard—Measures That Drive Performance," *Harvard Business Review* (Jan.–Feb.): 71–79.

Lev, B. 1989. "On the Usefulness of Earnings and Earnings Research: Lessons and Directions from Two Decades of Empirical Research." *Journal of Accounting Research* 27, no. 3: 153–192.

———, and T. Sougiannis. 1996. "The Capitalization, Amortization and Value-Relevance of R&D." *Journal of Accounting and Economics* 21: 107–138.

———, and T. Sougiannis. 1999. "Penetrating the Book-to-Market Black Box: The R&D Effect." *Journal of Business Finance and Accounting* 26, nos. 3 and 4: 419–449.

———, and P. Zarowin. 1999. "The Boundaries of Financial Reporting and How to Extend Them." *Journal of Accounting Research* 37, no. 2: 353–385.

Amir, E., B. Lev, and T. Sougianns. 2003. "Do Financial Analysts Get Intangibles?" *European Accounting Review* 12, no. 4: 635–659.

Marr, B., J. Mouritsen, and P. N. Bukh. 2003. "Perceived Wisdom." *Financial Management* (July–August): 32.

Marr, B., and J.-C. Spender. 2004. "Measuring Knowledge Assets: Implications of the Knowledge Economy for Performance Measurement." *Measuring Business Excellence* no. 1.

Meritum 2002. "Guidelines for Managing and Reporting Intangibles." Intellectual Capital Report. Madrid: Fundación Airtel Móvil.

Mouritsen, J., P. N. Bukh, and B. Marr. 2004. "Reporting on Intellectual Capital—Why, What, and How." *Measuring Business Excellence* no. 1.

Nakamura, L. 1999. "Intangibles: What Put the New in The New Economy?" *Federal Reserve Bank of Philadelphia Business Review* (July–August): 3–16.

———. 2001. "Education and Training in an Era of Creative Destruction." Working Paper no. 00–13R. Philadelphia: Federal Reserve Bank of Philadelphia.

Neely, A., C. Adams, and M. Kennerley. 2002. *The Performance Prism: The Scorecard for Measuring and Managing Business Success.* London: Financial Times Prentice Hall.

Ordóñez de Pablos, P. 2002. "Evidence of Intellectual Capital Measurement from Asia, Europe and the Middle East." *Journal of Intellectual Capital* 3, no. 3: 287–302.

Powell, S. 2003. "Accounting for Intangible Assets: Current Requirements, Key Players and Future Directions." *European Accounting Review* 12, no. 4: 797–811.

Roslender, R. 2004. "Accounting for Intellectual Capital: Rethinking Its Theoretical Underpinnings." *Measuring Business Excellence* 8, no. 1: 38–45.

Rimmerman, T. W. 1990. "The Changing Significance of Financial Statements." *Journal of Accountancy* 169, no. 4: 79–83.

Sánchez, P., C. Chaminade, and M. Olea. 2000. "Management of Intangibles. An Attempt to Build a Theory." *Journal of Intellectual Capital* 1, no. 4: 312.

Securities and Exchange Commission (SEC). 2001. "Strengthening Financial Markets: Do Investors Have the Information They Need?" Report of an SEC-Inspired Task Force. Washington, DC: SEC.

Starovic, D., and B. Marr. 2003. *Understanding Corporate Value—Measuring and Reporting Intellectual Capital.* London: Chartered Institute of Management Accountants.

Stewart, T. A. 1997. "Intellectual Capital: The New Wealth of Organizations." New York: Doubleday.

Stolowy, H., and A. Jeny-Cazavan. 2001. "International Accounting Disharmony: The Case of Intangibles." *Accounting, Auditing and Accountability Journal* 14, no. 4: 477–496.

Upton, W. 2001. "Financial Accounting Series: Special Report-Business and Reporting Challenges from the New Economy." Available online at http://accounting.rutgers.edu/raw/fasb/articles&reports/sr_new_economy.pdf.

Wyatt, A. 2002. "Towards a Financial Reporting Framework for Intangibles. Insights from the Australian Experience." *Journal of Intellectual Capital* 3, no. 1: 71–86.

A Finance Perspective on Intellectual Capital

Sudi Sudarsanam
Cranfield School of Management

Ghulam Sorwar
Cardiff Business School

Bernard Marr
Cranfield School of Management

Introduction

Intellectual capital is an increasingly major component of the total capital of firms as firms move from manufacturing and industrial activities toward services and more knowledge-based activities. Relative to the other components of a firm's capital, such as physical and monetary capital, intellectual capital is more difficult to define, measure, manage, and value in the traditional sense. Yet, given the profound importance of such assets to a firm's competitive advantage and value creation capabilities, serious attempts need to be, and increasingly are, made to establish clear definitions, measurement rules, and valuation principles. In this chapter, we discuss intellectual capital from a valuation perspective. We examine the nature of such capital and why traditional valuation methods fail to reflect the unique characteristics of intellectual capital. We review existing valuation approaches and develop a valuation perspective based on the real option models that have been extended from their origins in financial asset valuation to the valuation of firms' growth opportunities. Intellectual assets embody these opportunities, contributing to both their evolution over time and their realization in the future. This approach provides a richer framework to analyze the issues that confront the valuation of intellectual capital.

Paul Krugman argued that in the past, businesses invested primarily in the tangible means of production, such as buildings and machines. The value of a company was at least somewhat related to the value of its physical capital. But, now, businesses increasingly invest in intellectual capital. Once a chip is designed or a code for a new operating system written, no further investment is needed to ship the product to yet another customer. "The intangibility of a company's most important assets makes it extremely hard to figure out what that company is really worth. That may partly explain the nauseating volatility of stock prices" (Krugman 2000).

Krugman's observation reflects the phenomenal growth in the market values of some of knowledge-driven Internet companies in the second half of the 1990s and the subsequent crash of 1999–2000. The ascent of stock markets around the world driven by dot-com companies was as spectacular as the crash. This experience is a potent reminder of the perils of overvaluation of knowledge-rich companies. Biotechnology companies that sought to exploit new advances in biosciences to create new drugs and cures had been similarly overvalued, only to experience dramatic falls in their values.

The merger of AOL with a more mature media company, Time Warner, in 2001 provides a cautionary tale in valuing knowledge-based companies. When the friendly "merger of equals" was announced in January 2000, the combined market capitalization of the two entities was $288 billion. When the deal was consummated in January 2001, it was $205 billion. By the middle of 2003, the merged firm, AOL Time Warner, was valued at just $74 billion. Somehow, 74% of the value of the two firms had been wiped out. While part of the decline was due to the general decline of stock markets, given the size of the firm, the stock market decline itself was partly due to the value decline of AOLTW. An analysis of the valuation metrics used at the time of merger announcement and merger consummation shows that the firms' values were based on extraordinary and wildly exuberant optimism (Applegate 2002). It is starkly apparent from cases like the AOL Time Warner merger that tools for valuation of knowledge-based companies are woefully inadequate.

In this chapter, we briefly outline why intellectual capital is important for organizations. Subsequently, we describe and review various tools and approaches developed to value intellectual capital. We then focus attention on real option models for the valuation of intellectual capital and outline its benefits as well as it limitations.

Intellectual Assets,[1] Growth Opportunities, and the Value of a Firm

A firm's value is made up of contributions from the various components of its asset portfolio. Physical assets and monetary assets generate income, profits, and cash flows by enabling the firm to produce, market, and sell its goods and services. These are sold to identifiable customers in existing markets. On the other hand, certain types of assets have no immediate, measurable payoffs. Investments in these assets are aimed at enabling the firm to produce goods or services some time in the future, but the outcomes are subject to much uncertainty. These investments are intended to secure and exploit future growth opportunities. Therefore,

Firm value = value of assets in place + value of future growth opportunities from assets in place + value of future growth opportunities from new assets

An example of the second component is a patent that resulted from R&D investments already made. An example of the third component is a product that may be discovered or developed from future investments that may be made. Both the second and third components are largely path dependent and derive from the firm's accumulation of resources and capabilities from past investments, although occasionally a firm may

---

[1] For the purpose of this chapter, we use the term *intellectual asset* instead of *intellectual capital*, as the former is more frequently used in the finance literature.

chance upon these growth opportunities. Future growth opportunities allow a firm to create new knowledge leading to new products and services and new markets hitherto unknown. In the words of Hamel and Prahalad (1993), while assets in place and the growth opportunities they create enable a firm to compete in the world as it exists, future investment in assets that can generate growth opportunities enable a firm to compete in the future.

Research and development leading to innovations must be valued for their potential contribution to the generation of valuable growth opportunities. Investments in activities to generate future growth opportunities may lead to subsequent investments in intangibles as well as the tangible assets necessary to exploit the growth opportunities. Thus, research investment is the first stage of a sequence of investments. The first-stage investment is somewhat speculative, with no guarantee that it will successfully result in exploitable growth opportunities, such as a new design, drug, or process. In making the first stage investment, a firm merely buys an option. Valuation of the first stage investment cannot be completed without valuing the payoffs from the subsequent-stage investments. In valuing the initial investment as an option, we also have to allow for the possibility that in certain unfavorable states of nature, as when it is not worthwhile to continue to maintain the option, it may be abandoned.

Valuing Intellectual Assets

To value any asset, we need to specify an income stream clearly identified with that asset. Alternatively, the value of that asset may be determined through buy-and-sell transactions in a market. In the case of some of the intellectual assets, such as patents or licenses for know-how, such transactions often take place but the transaction prices may be negotiated by the buyer and seller. An active, competitive secondary market with numerous buyers and sellers may not exist for most intellectual assets. Apart from intellectual property, such as patents and brands, which are protected by law, intellectual assets may therefore have to be valued in other ways. Even in the case of traded assets such as patents, the buyer and seller need to value them before entering into the purchase or sale transaction.

Valuation models may be broadly divided into two kinds:

- Models that estimate the aggregate value of intellectual assets at a point in time. They thus estimate the value of the accumulated intellectual assets. These models do not differentiate the temporal differences in the accumulated intellectual assets or the differences among different categories of intangibles at the time of valuation. Lev's residual income model, Tobin's Q model, and the market value less book value model belong in this group. We call these *static models*.
- Models that value the investments in intangibles each at a time. Discounted cash-flow models and real option models belong in this group. We call these *dynamic models*.

Here, we outline a selection of static and dynamic approaches to value intellectual assets in firms.

Static Valuation Models

Technology Broker

The technology broker model proposed by Annie Brooking (1996) tries to calculate a dollar value for intellectual assets. It is based on an interpretation of intellectual assets as an amalgam of four components: market assets, human-centered assets, intellectual property assets, and infrastructure assets. Market assets are the market-related intangibles such as brands, contracts, customers, distribution channels, licensing agreements, and franchise contracts. Human-centered assets are the knowledge of the people within the organization and involve components such as expertise, problem solving capability, creativity, and entrepreneurial and managerial skills. Intellectual property assets are corporate assets for which it is possible to provide a financial evaluation. Examples of these assets are trade secrets, copyrights, patents, service marks, and design rights. Finally, infrastructure assets equal those technologies, methodologies, and processes that enable the organization to function.

From an operational point of view, the implementation of the technology broker starts with a test based on 20 questions. These questions are used to understand whether the organization needs to focus on the development of management practices to increase the strength of its intellectual assets. To examine the intellectual assets of a company, the technology broker model uses a number of specific audit questionnaires.

Once an organization completes its technology broker audit, Brooking offers three approaches to calculate a monetary value for its intellectual capital. These approaches are

1. The cost approach, which is based on the assessment of the replacement cost of assets.
2. The market approach, which uses market comparables to assess the value.
3. The income approach, which assesses the income-producing capability of the asset.

Market- or Value-Based Approach

An often-used but potentially misleading way of calculating the value of an organization's intellectual assets is to take the difference between its market value (i.e., the number of shares in issue multiplied by the market value of the share) and the net value of its assets. This can be carried out with a minimum of information, and the gap between the two figures, the market-to-book ratio, is often used as an indication that a company has a large amount of intellectual assets not reflected in its financial statements.

This method has several drawbacks. The most obvious flaw, of course, is that this method values IC as one asset and makes no attempt to separate the items that might constitute it. Furthermore, the market value of a company is subject to a number of external variables, including deregulation, media and political influences, and rumors. One has to look only at the overvaluation of some of the earliest dot-coms to go public and the subsequent and dramatic drop in their share values. In the case of lastminute.com, the share price fell by 90% in less than 18 months, yet there was little change in the company's intellectual assets.

In addition, the current financial accounting model does not attempt to value the firm in its entirety. Instead, it records each of its severable assets at an amount in accordance with extant legislation and the financial accounting standards. The market, however, would value the company in its entirety as a going concern. This means the figure for intellectual assets would differ simply by the adoption of different accounting policies across national boundaries.

Table 4.1

	Lev's Residual Income Model
Stage 1	Take average annual earnings for a company. Lev suggests using 3 years of past earnings and 3 years of earnings as provided by the consensus forecasts of analysts. For the sake of this example, assume these are $1 billion.
Stage 2	Look at what the company balance sheet has in the way of financial assets. Assume that they are $5 billion. Then, take the expected aftertax return on financial assets, which is approximately 4.5%. Therefore, the $5 billion worth of financial assets explains $225 million of the earnings.
Stage 3	Now turn to the physical assets of the company and assume they are worth $5 billion. Using the average aftertax return for physical assets, which is approximately 7%, $350 million of earnings can be credited to them.
Stage 4	This leaves a balance of $425 million that must have been produced by assets not on the balance sheet, which Lev calls *knowledge-capital earnings*. These earnings are then divided by an expected rate of return on knowledge assets, which has been worked out to be 10.5% (see note).
Stage 5	Using the formula *Earnings = Knowledge capital earnings/Knowledge capital discount rate* It can now be assessed that to produce $425 million in earnings, this imaginary company needs $4.06 billion in intangible assets.

Note: To calculate the intellectual asset discount rate Lev looked at whether cash flow, traditional earnings, or knowledge earnings correlates most with return on equity. He found just a 0.11 correlation between strong returns on equity and cash flows, a 0.29 correlation with traditional earnings, and a strong 0.53 correlation with knowledge earnings. This, therefore, would seem to justify a rate of 10.5% that compares with 4.5% for financial assets and 7% for physical assets.

Lev's Residual Income Model

A major problem with intellectual assets is their embedded nature, which disallows the development of secondary markets. They are part of a bundle of physical, financial, and intellectual assets. One approach is to value the bundle as a whole, then subtract the values of the physical and financial assets to arrive at the value of the intellectual assets. Baruch Lev (2001) adopts this approach by matching the earnings to assets that generate them. From the aftertax earnings of the firm as a whole, Lev subtracts aftertax earnings attributable to financial assets and aftertax earnings attributable to physical assets (see Table 4.1). The residual earnings are then attributed to intellectual or knowledge capital and capitalized at an appropriate discount rate, which Lev derives from correlation analysis of IC earnings and equity returns.

The value derived from this procedure represents the collective value of all the intangibles the firm possesses and does not identify the values of the individual components of intellectual assets. Further, it is not clear how, not just how much, intellectual assets contribute to firm value. The process by which intellectual assets create value is not delineated. The IC value is derived from a fairly static picture of the composition of a firm's assets.

Tobin's Q

Similar in spirit to the Lev model is the Tobin's Q model, developed by the economist James Tobin. This approach estimates the value of intellectual assets as the difference between the market value of a firm and the replacement cost of its tangible assets. If the replacement cost is lower than the market value, then the company concerned is making a higher than normal return on its investment. Technology and human capital assets were traditionally associated with high Q values. Apart from the difficulty of estimating the replacement cost of knowledge assets, in practice, this model suffers from the inability to separately value the individual components of the firm's intellectual assets. A more widely used proxy for the Q ratio is the excess of market value of a firm over the accounting book value of its tangible assets.

Dynamic Valuation Models

Discounted Cash-Flow Model

In contrast to the "residual income" approach to intellectual assets valuation by Lev, the discounted cash-flow (DCF) model, in corporate finance, projects the cash flows from investment in a particular asset throughout the economic life of that asset and discounts these cash flows at an appropriate rate. The present value of the investments in the assets are subtracted to give the net present value of that investment. In theory, this model can be used to value any type of asset: physical, financial, or intangible. It is also a dynamic model, in that cash flows from the asset are forecast into the future, thereby allowing for the future market conditions to determine the magnitude and timing of the cash flows and hence the value of the asset.

However, the DCF model is generally based on point estimates of future cash flows and does not explicitly account for the total riskiness of these cash flows but only for the systematic component of that risk in the form of a market-determined discount rate. Importantly, a model assumption is that the investment in the asset is irreversible; that is, the firm commits itself to the investment now whatever state of nature transpires later. There is no going back, no abandonment of the investment in unfavorable states of nature. In brief, the DCF does not accommodate the option like unforeseen circumstances and ignores managerial flexibility.

Moreover, in practice, estimating the future cash flows associated with some intangibles is difficult, not only because of their embedded nature but also because they are exploratory investments that allow for learning. Future cash flows are also subject to the impact of competitors' ability to develop similar options, such as investment in R&D to create generic or "me-too" drugs to compete with patented drugs. Such competitor reactions erode the value of the real options the firm has developed through investments in intangible assets.

DCF is thus a model that best captures the value of assets in place that generate relatively stable or predictable cash flows. The model may still capture the growth opportunities arising from these assets in place. It is a model for those corporate investments that facilitate "competing for the world" rather than "competing for the future." The DCF model does not altogether escape the need to consider the interactive nature of many intangible assets. In the resource-based view of competition, what gives firms competitive advantage and the ability to create value is not just the possession of certain resources but the capabilities that lever these resources in such a way as to give the firm a sustainable competitive advantage. Many of these resources and capabilities, as noted earlier, are in the form of IC. Therefore, DCF cash flows need to be incremental cash flows, that is, the cash flows with the intellectual asset being valued and the cash flows in the absence of that asset. In practice, this may be a tricky variable to estimate.

Real Option Models

Intellectual assets provide firms with a range of options that managements can exercise flexibly over time. Such flexibility itself is a source of value since it helps managers avoid decisions that lock into negative-value outcomes. Real option models provide a means of valuing these options. Extended from the financial markets, where option pricing models have been used to value options on financial assets such as stocks, bonds, and currencies, real option models can provide useful insights into corporate competitive strategies, the place of intellectual capital in such strategies, and how they affect corporate value.

There are two types of options on financial assets: call and put options. A call option gives the buyer of that option the right, but not the obligation, to buy the asset on which it is written at an agreed price (the exercise price) at maturity of the option contract (in the case of a European option) or any time before maturity (in the case of an American option). The price of the option is called the *option premium*. A put option gives the buyer the right, but not the obligation, to sell the asset at the agreed price at or before maturity. An investor buys a call option when she expects the asset to increase in value beyond the exercise price. An investor buys a put when he expects the asset to decline in value below the exercise price.

Next, we expand on the use of real options as an approach for valuing investments in intellectual assets.

Valuing Intellectual Assets Using Real Options Models

Since the parentage of real option models is the financial option pricing models (OPMs), it is useful to start with a description of the latter. The best known of the OPMs is the Black-Scholes OPM (BSOPM). The Black-Scholes model is one of the most outstanding models in financial economics. Myron Scholes and Robert Merton, who developed a similar model independently, received the Nobel Prize in economics for its development. The BSOPM is based on the following stochastic calculus. The value of a European call option, C, is

$$C = SN(d_1) - Ee^{-rt}N(d_2)$$

where $d_1 = [\ln(S/E) + (r + 1/2\sigma^2)t]/\sqrt{\sigma^2 t}$ and $d_2 = d_1 - \sqrt{\sigma^2 t}$. Here, S = current stock price; E = exercise price; r = annual risk free continuously compounded rate; σ^2 = annualized variance of the continuous return on the stock; and t = time to expiration of the option. The exponential term, e^{-rt}, discounts the exercise price to the present value.

$$\text{Call value} = SN(d_1) - \text{present value of } E \times N(d_2)$$

In this equation, $N(d_1)$ and $N(d_2)$ represent the probability distributions. Values of $N(d_1)$ and $N(d_2)$ are obtained from normal probability distribution tables. They give us the probability that S or E will be below d_1 and d_2. In the Black-Scholes model, they measure the risk associated with the volatility of the value of S. Software is available to calculate the Black-Scholes option prices for various parameter values.

Suppose Wild Goose Chase (WGC) Company stock is selling for $10 and a call option on the stock is available. The exercise price is $10. This European call has a maturity of 1 year. The risk-free rate (the government Treasury bill rate for 1 year) is 12%. The standard deviation (σ) of the annual returns on WGC is 10%. We need to use normal probability distribution tables to get $N(d_1)$ and $N(d_2)$. We get $N(d_1)$ of 89.4% and $N(d_2)$ of 87.5%. So the value of the call is $1.2. This value will change with the value of the various parameters in the Black-Scholes model.

The valuation of put options follows from the put-call parity theorem that establishes the following parity: Stock value + put value = call value + present value of exercise. Knowing the value of the call, we can value the put option.

An interpretation of the Black-Scholes model allows us to come up with the following statements:

- The underlying asset value (S). High S increases call value and reduces put value.
- The exercise price (X). High X reduces call value but increases put value.
- The volatility of the value of $S(\sigma)$. High σ increases both call and put values.
- The time to maturity (t). High t increases both call and put values.
- Any dividend payment. High dividend reduces call value and increases put value.
- The risk-free rate (r_f). High r_f increases call value and reduces put value.

One of the most intriguing relationships is that high volatility enhances the option value. Since an option restricts the downside loss to the option premium but does not restrict the upside potential, high volatility benefits the option. This perspective has particular relevance to real options, which we discuss next. Examples of such contingent investments are research and development, advertising, pilot marketing, license for oil exploration, geological testing for mineral reserves, and the like. In some cases, managers make an initial investment knowing well that they can exit or abandon that investment.

Real option describes an option to buy or sell an investment in physical or intangible assets rather than in financial assets. Thus, any corporate investment in plant, equipment, land, patent, brand name, or the like can be the assets on which real options are "written." Purchase of a brand is an option on the related product or service. A license to explore for oil is an option on oil. Many investment projects have call and put option features. Investment in R&D is a call option, since it may lead to "buying" (investing in) a second-stage production facility. Any exploratory investment in a growth opportunity such as the Internet or biotechnology is a call option. An investment that can be sold of if it does not meet the investor's expectations may be regarded as a put option, such as a mine that is abandoned when the price of gold falls and is unlikely to recover.

In addition to these examples of real options, we can identify many other types of real options. These are listed in Table 4.2. A compound option combines two or more of these options. Investment and financing decisions are replete with such options, if only managers do not miss the wood for the trees.

The BSOPM may be used to value real options (Luehrman 1998). We first show such a valuation application then discuss the limitations and caveats in valuing real options using the BSOPM. The variables in the BS model when applied to real options are as follows:

- C = the first-stage investment.
- S = the present value of the second-stage investment.

Table 4.2

Types of Real Options—Where Do They Exist?		
Option Type	Description	Typical Context
Growth	Early investment to open up future markets	Investments in multiple generation products; bolt-on acquisitions
Abandonment	Resale or exit from loss-making investment or one with no prospects	New product introduction; mineral licenses; brand names
Switch	Allows switch in output mix with same inputs or in/out mix for same outputs	Investments with scope economies in production, marketing, technology
Afterscale	Option to expand or contract output	In cyclical or fashion industries
Source: Trigeorgis 1998.		

- t = the time to making the second-stage investment (i.e., how long will that opportunity be open; how long can the second stage investment be deferred).
- X = the present value of the cost of the second-stage investment.
- Dividend = intermediate costs to keep the second-stage investment opportunity open, such as maintenance costs or rents.
- σ = the volatility of the value of the second-stage investment.

The risk-free rate has the same connotation as in the financial asset case. While waiting to make the second-stage investment, the company gathers information that flows from the first-stage investment, say, about feasibility of technology and from the outside world, such as the size of the potential market or the price of the output, say, gold or a drug or a regulatory change. This involves learning what the company's resources and capabilities are and how they can be adapted to the environmental changes (a process of self-discovery) as well as learning about the environment (intelligence gathering) (Bernardo and Chowdhry 2002; Kogut and Kulatilaka 2001).

What is the option value that a firm has acquired when there is competition? How soon will competitors acquire similar options? Real options may give rise to unique nonimitable claims on the underlying second-stage investment opportunity, or they can be replicated by competitors, in which case the opportunity is shared. This is a fundamental issue in competitive strategy and not peculiar to the real options framework (Luehrman 1998; Bowman and Moskowitz 2001; Smit 2001) However, the real options framework may be used to shed light on value implications of shared options.

Whether competitors enter and spoil the game for the first mover depends on whether the claims on the growth opportunities are shared as well as entry barriers and what the first option holder does to forestall such entry. The game theory framework can be used to figure out how the game will be played with shared opportunities and entry and pre-emptive strategies of different players. One way we can model the threat of entry is to incorporate an estimate of competitive erosion (proxied by "dividend" payment in the BSOPM). Where there is more than one competitor, this attrition can be increased to reflect this on the option value.

Intellectual Assets as Real Options

While not all intellectual assets share real option characteristics, many of them are, in essence, real options that firms create through their activities, organic investments, or acquisitions. Among these are

- Customer relationship arrangements, such as joint ventures and licensing agreements as well as informal relationships.
- Investment in human resources, such as education, training, and development; domain expertise; creativity; problem-solving capability; entrepreneurial spirit; and ability to work in teams.
- Investment in information technology for knowledge management and enhancement of the capability to exploit organizational learning, expertise, and resources.
- Investment in developing a unique culture that increases managerial flexibility, organizational learning, and creativity.
- Practices and routines that identify growth opportunities and facilitate exploitation of such opportunities.
- Intellectual property, such as patents, copyrights, trademarks, brands, and registered designs.
- Research and development.

Investments in intellectual assets do not generate immediate payoffs. Indeed, they are considered costs and often expensed in company accounts. But they are often small, exploratory, and speculative investments made in expectation that they will lead to new growth opportunities and unique competitive advantages. Some of them create switching options that allow the firm to switch existing resources to alternative uses, such as customer relationship information that allows the firm to switch its focus from low-value customer segments to high-value customer segments.

Table 4.3 lists the types of real options associated with some of the knowledge assets. Each knowledge asset may be a bundle of options rather than a single option. Thus, intangibles may be impregnated with substantial managerial flexibility.

Applying BSOPM to Valuing a Patent or R&D

We illustrate the application in the context of a firm that has acquired a patent, which is a real option to undertake production and marketing of the patented drug (see Damodaran 2001 for further discussion). Biogen is a biotechnology company with a patent on a drug called Avonex, which received FDA approval to treat multiple sclerosis. The patent gives the firm legal monopoly for 17 years. Biogen, however, is strapped for cash and wants to shop its patent and invest the proceeds in further research. Major Pharma (MP) is considering buying the firm because of its patent for the MS drug. There is no other drug with Biogen.

MP analyzed the situation as an acquisition opportunity. How much is Biogen worth? The following data are used to value Biogen as a real option, since the patent would give MP the opportunity to manufacture the drug if the market conditions are favorable in the next 17 years. If the drug is produced on a commercial scale and marketed today, the investment cost is £2.875 billion (X). The present value of cash flows from that project is $3.422 billion (S). Although immediate investment is a positive $547-million NPV (Net Present Value) decision, MP wants to know whether waiting until more marketing and other information is available will create more value. There is the risk that competitors may come up with alternative me-too drugs and erode

Table 4.3

Intangibles as Embedded Real Options	
Intangible Asset	**Types of Real Options That May Be Incorporated**
Research and development	Option to defer, option to abandon, growth option to invest in production
Patents	Option to defer, option to abandon, growth option to invest in production
Advertising (brand name)	Growth option to invest in production, marketing, and selling
Capital expenditures	Option to alter operating scale, multiple interacting options, option to switch process technology
Information systems	Time-to-build options, option to switch, option to expand
Technology acquisitions	Option to switch, growth option
Human resource practices, such as incentive-based compensation and employee training	Option to expand, option to switch, option to defer

MP's competitive advantage. The risk free, 17-year Treasury bond rate is 6.7%. Time to expiration of the option is 17 years (t). MP estimates the variability of the expected present value S as 22.4% (σ). With a single potential competitor, the option value is eroded evenly at $1/17$. This is the expected cost of delay. Estimation of σ is often taken from the volatility of the stock of a company similar to the follow-on project. It is the variability of the value of the follow-on manufacturing project. Analysts may be able to estimate this variability through simulation.

These data, used in the Black-Schioles model, give an option value of $907 million compared to a static NPV of $547 million. This suggests that MP will increase the value of its acquisition if it waits to exercise the second-stage investment option. If we assume that with more competitors, the attrition rate doubles to $2/17$, the option value is $255 million. In this case, MP is nearly $300 million better off by buying Biogen now and manufacturing straight away—unless it can think of other ways of challenging potential competitors and keep them at bay, such as erecting entry barriers or threat of nasty and expensive litigation.

We can apply the same model to the valuation of any investment, such as R&D, human resource training, brand development, software development, customer relations initiatives, joint ventures, or strategic alliances.

Limitations of Real Option Valuation Models

Extrapolation of the BSOPM model to real options and strategic options is fraught with problems. Many of the assumptions that underlie financial options do not hold in the real options context. Data such as volatility are difficult to estimate, since the underlying investment opportunities are not traded. By their very nature, many of these are exploratory, and historical data about them is not available. Many other differences between financial and real options make valuation of real options using BSOPM less reliable.

The Black-Scholes model ignores many of the complications associated with intangibles like R&D. A more-realistic approach to value the option to abandon would need to include

- The rate at which the patent-owning organization may invest.
- The total cost of completion. This is an unknown, it must be incorporated as a random process.
- The possibility of catastrophic future events that lead to the termination of the project. Such an event may include change in government regulation or a rival company developing a similar product in advance.
- Physical difficulties in completing the project.
- The completion date of the investment project, again modeled as a random event.
- Cash flow received from the investment.
- The salvage value of the project, which may be zero.

Amram and Kulatilaka (1999) maintain that the difficulties just highlighted with the Black-Scholes approach can be overcome using Monte Carlo simulation. Simulation models roll out thousands of possible paths of evolution of the underlying asset from the present to the option maturity or exercise date. The optimal investment strategy at the end of each path is determined and the payoff calculated. The current value of the option is found by averaging the payoffs and then discounting the average back to the present. The Monte Carlo method can handle many aspects of real-world applications, including complicated decision rules and complex relationships between the option value and the underlying asset.

Simulation models can also solve path-dependent options, where the value of the option depends not only on the value of the underlying asset but also on the particular path followed by the asset. For example, investments in further customer relations initiatives depend on the profitability of past customer relations.

Similarities between some of the knowledge assets and real options may not be readily apparent. Further, identifying the option parameters, such as exercise price or time to maturity, is not easy. Perhaps, the most difficult part of the application process is the estimation of volatility for use in models such as the BSOPM. However, some of these problems may be handled by alternative models such as Monte Carlo simulation.

Summary and Conclusions

In this chapter, we explore how the intellectual assets that have come to dominate the valuation of many firms can be valued. We focus special attention on valuing intellectual assets using advances in real option valuation. The context of the paper is the rising proportion of intangibles in the overall value of firms; problems in identifying, measuring, and valuing such intangibles; and the inadequacies of traditional valuation tools. We argue that intangibles, in general, contribute to firms' competitive advantage and value creation as they give rise to growth opportunities. Exploitation of these growth opportunities requires investments, and whether such investments will be made depends on the result of initial investments to develop the intellectual assets. Thus, intellectual assets represent an option to pursue growth or abandon such opportunities. Given this fundamental similarity, we set out alternative real option valuation models and illustrate how some of the intellectual assets may be valued.

While it is conceptually easy to regard some, if not all, intangibles as real options, in practical application, estimating some of the model parameters may be difficult. We point to alternative estimation procedures, such as Monte Carlo simulation, to make these problems more tractable. Even though the real options framework may not provide easy solutions to the problem of intellectual capital valuation, it still provides a challenging way of thinking about intellectual capital, its nature, and how it contributes to value creation.

References

Amram, M., and N. Kulatilaka. 1999. *Real Options: Managing Strategic Investment in an Uncertain World*. Financial Management Association Survey & Synthesis Series. Cambridge, MA: Oxford University Press.

Applegate, L. 2002. "Valuing the AOL Time Warner Merger." Harvard Business Review case 9-802-098, Boston, MA.

Bernardo, A. E., and B. Chowdhry. 2002. "Resources, Real Options, and Corporate Strategy." *Journal of Financial Economics* 63: 211–234.

Bowman, E. H., and G. T. Moskowitz. 2001. "Real Options Analysis and Strategic Decision Making." *Organization Science* 12, no. 6 (November–December): 772–777.

Brooking, A. 1996. *Intellectual Capital: Core Assets for the Third Millennium Enterprise*. London: Thompson Business Press.

Damodaran, A. 2001. *Applied Corporate Finance*. New York: John Wiley & Sons.

Hamel, G., and C. K. Prahalad. 1993. "Strategic Intent." *International Review of Strategic Management* 4: 63–86.

Kogut, B., and N. Kulatilaka. 2001. "Capabilities as Real Options." *Organization Science* 12, no. 6 (November–December): 744–758.

Krugman, P. 2000. "Reckonings: Unsound Bytes?" *New York Times*, October 22, 2000.

Lev, B. 2001. *Intangibles: Management, Measurement, and Reporting*. Washington, DC: The Brookings Institution.

Luehrman, T. A. 1998. "Strategy as a Portfolio of Real Options." *Harvard Business Review*, September–October.

Miller, K. D., and H. G. Waller. 2003. "Scenarios, Real Options and Integrated Risk Management." *Long Range Planning* 36, no. 1: 93–107.

Smit H. T. J. 2001. "Acquisitions Strategies as Option Games." *Journal of Applied Corporate Finance*, (Summer), pp. 79–89.

Trigeorgis, L. 1998. *Real Options*, Cambridge, MA: The MIT Press.

A Reporting Perspective on Intellectual Capital

Jan Mourtisen
Copenhagen Business School

Per Nikolaj Bukh
Aarhus School of Business

Bernard Marr
Cranfield School of Management

Introduction

Increased attention to intangibles and knowledge resources to create value has called for new frameworks to report organizational performance (Bukh 2003; Marr and Spender 2004; Meritum 2002; PRISM 2003). The advent of the knowledge economy has increased the importance of knowledge-based resources. However, the majority of these resources are not reported in traditional balance sheets. This has created an information gap in the market, and more firms and organizations are calling for voluntary disclosure of these knowledge-based resources and intangible assets to close the gap. There have been considerable efforts in Europe, where governments, trade organizations, and the European Commission have invested in developing guidelines and best practices on how to report on intellectual capital. In some countries, most notably Scandinavia, firms have experimented with voluntary reporting and produced and published intellectual capital statements.

Much of the effort in Europe has tried to address the dynamic nature of intangible assets and, therefore, tried go beyond the static reporting of separable assets, such as patents or R&D investments, in balance sheets. The aim is to move away from the static reporting of "assets on hold" toward a more organic view, in which these knowledge assets are seen as interconnected in organizational processes (Mouritsen 2003). Understanding the interconnectedness of resources has increased the interest of companies in reporting on, for example, the effectiveness of business processes, investments in human competencies, and development of relationships with customers.

Some companies include information on their intangibles in the narrative part of their annual report, and others produce more elaborate separate supplement reports. The example for the former is the leading financial firm UBS, which writes in its latest annual review, "To the Outside world, our strength is often perceived as being derived from the financial success of our business. Yet, at the same time, we also believe our strength is projected through other more intangible factors—factors such as the values we share, our culture, our client relationships and our brands. We have distilled these factors into the five key elements of Client Focus, Innovation and Learning, Talent and Culture, Brand and Identity and Financial Intelligence. They are the value drivers of our business." The report then moves on to provide further information on each of these value drivers. One of the first companies to produce a supplement report on their intellectual capital was the Swedish insurance company Skandia in 1995. Even though Skandia separates human capital and structural capital, it is the relationship and interaction between these components that is important (Edvinsson and Malone 1997). To address the increasing importance of knowledge-based assets and their dynamic interaction (Marr et al. 2004; Mouritsen and Larsen 2004), both companies and capital markets call for "integrated" performance management systems (Kaplan and Norton 2001, 2004; Amir and Lev 1996) that address these issues and improve our understanding of organizational performance.

Understanding the competitive position of firms no longer concerns positioning the firm vis-à-vis its competitors with regard to opportunities in the market. Increasingly, it concerns the internal resource architecture, capabilities, and competencies. A competitive advantage can be gained by possessing resources that are rare and difficult to imitate (Barney 1991), and, often, knowledge-based assets fulfill these criteria. Firms, therefore, need to understand and report their knowledge-based resources, such as know-how of employees, relationships with customers or suppliers, brand and image, and information technology (Marr, Schiuma, and Neely 2002; Mouritsen 1998). The extent of this problem is highlighted by the fact that firms such as Microsoft or Coca-Cola report only their traditional assets in their balance sheets, which account for a very small fraction of their market value. Even for manufacturing firms, such as Honda or BP, the assets in the balance sheet represent less than 30% of the market value. Even if such measures are debatable, they indicate that there is more to corporate growth than is currently recognized in financial statements.

In this chapter, we provide a European perspective on the voluntary reporting of intellectual capital. Intellectual capital reports are influenced by management accounting and are responses to the relevance loss of traditional accounting. In the following sections, we outline the reasons why extended reporting on intellectual capital is crucial. We then discuss what firms should include in these reports, before we discuss the two major movements on reporting on intellectual capital in Europe: the Meritum and the Danish guidelines. We then provide a practical case example of intellectual capital reporting, before we take a look into the future of intellectual capital reports.

Why Is There a Need for Intellectual Capital Reporting?

The value relevance of traditional annual reports appears to be declining (e.g., Lev and Zarowin 1999). Even though the extent of this erosion of relevance is debated (Collins, Maydew, and Weiss 1997; Core, Guay, and van Buskirke 2003; Francis and Schipper 1999; AAA Financial Accounting Standard Committee 2003), most authors agree that nonfinancial information like market size and market penetration are significantly related to market value (Amir and Lev 1996). There is widespread and growing frustration with traditional financial reporting as is expressed in, for example, the "Jenkins Report" (American Institute of Certified Public Accountants 1994), the work of the former commissioner of the Securities and Exchange Commission (SEC), Steven Wallman (1996, 1997), and more recently, the Accounting Standard Board (2002) and Canadian Institute of Chartered Accountants (2001). They all argue that the financial reporting system is incapable of explaining "new" resources, for example, internally generated intangibles such as relationships or knowledge. Disclosing information on such factors is likely to lower the cost of equity capital because it decreases uncertainty about future prospects of a company and facilitates a more-precise valuation of the company (Botosan 1997). Others argue that it also enhances stock market liquidity and increases demand for companies' securities (Healy and Palepu 2001).

Various studies of information demands of investors and analysts indicate a substantial difference between the types of information found in companies' annual reports and the types of information demanded by the market (Beattie and Pratt 2002a, 2002b; Beattie, McInnes, and Fearnley 2002; Eccles et al. 2001; Eccles and Mavrinac 1995). This information gap is partly due to an increased demand for non-financial information, that is, concerning the company's strategy and competencies and its ability to motivate the staff, increase customer satisfaction, and so forth. However, this information gap may also be due to lack of understanding of business models and lack of proper communication between company management and the capital market (Bukh 2003).

Here, we summarize some of the main reasons why there is an increasing need for externally reporting information on intellectual capital. It has been suggested that the capital market may be at a disadvantage in several ways if information on intellectual capital is not reported:

1. Smaller shareholders may be disadvantaged, as they usually have no access to information on intangibles often shared in private meetings with larger investors (Holland 2001).
2. Insider trading might occur if managers exploit internally produced information on intangibles unknown to other investors (Aboody and Lev 2000).
3. Stock market liquidity and increased demand for companies' securities is enhanced by greater disclosure on intangibles (Diamond & Verrecchia, 1991).
4. Volatility and the danger of incorrect valuations of firms is increased, which leads to investors and banks placing a higher risk level on organizations.
5. Cost of capital is increased, due to, say, higher risk levels placed on companies (Lev 2001).

Reporting of intellectual capital is important for capital markets and external stakeholders to improve their understanding of the firms' competitive positions. However, reports on intellectual capital can also be used to improve internal communication and therefore the internal understanding of organizational value drivers (Marr et al. 2004). The challenges many firms face are (1) identifying critical intellectual resources and (2) finding the right means to manage them in order to improve the competitive position of the firm. A management tool is required that can help managers answer managerial questions such as these: Are the firm's intellectual resources increasing or decreasing? What knowledge does it possess? How is it developed? Reports on intellectual capital can help organizations to better understand their intellectual resources and the way they are managed.

What Intellectual Capital Should Companies Report?

Intellectual resources are often context specific, idiosyncratic, and interconnected (Marr et al. 2004). Resources that might be extremely valuable for one organization might be of no value to another. Amazon, the online book retailer, might possess knowledge about book retailing and have good relationships with book suppliers; however, these are probably of no value to, say, a pharmaceutical company. Furthermore, it is difficult to understand the value of individual intellectual resources without taking into account the interdependencies with other assets (Lippman and Rumelt 1982; Dierickx and Cool 1989; King and Zeithaml 2001). For example, the latest technology is worth little without the right knowledge and competencies of how to operate it. In turn, all the latest understanding and knowledge of how to operate technology is worthless if employees lack access to the technology (Marr, Schiuma, and Neely 2004). This means that organizations need to provide more context and information about what intellectual resources are important and how they are combined to deliver organizational performance. The implication for intellectual capital reporting is that it is impossible to precisely define the different assets. It is possible only to provide examples or classifications of intellectual assets that might help organizations make sense of their intellectual resources. This is a key reason why traditional balance sheet approaches are unsuccessful, as they fail to provide the context or information about interconnectivity of assets. Taking into account the preceding outlined limitations of any taxonomy, we provide examples of possible knowledge-based assets companies might want to report (see also Starovic and Marr 2003):

- Human resource assets such as skills, competence, commitment, motivation, and loyalty of employees. Some key components are know-how, technical expertise, problem-solving capability, creativity, education, attitude, and entrepreneurial spirit.
- Relations to partners such as customers and suppliers. These relationships could be licensing agreements, partnering agreements, contracts, and distribution arrangements.
- (Virtual) infrastructure assets that embrace organizational capabilities found in routines and practices, as well as intellectual property, such as patents, copyrights, trademarks, brands, registered design, trade secrets, and processes whose ownership is granted the company by law.
- Technologies refer to the technological support of the other three knowledge resources. Focus is usually on the company's IT systems (software and hardware) such as the intranet, IT infrastructure, databases, or physical networks.

A company intellectual capital strategy is therefore about these knowledge resources and *their interaction*. When the interaction among these knowledge resources is understood, the firm's knowledge management *strategy* is clear (Marr and Schiuma, 2001, Mouritsen, Bukh, et al. 2003).

Intellectual Capital Reporting in Europe

Various initiatives are under way in Europe to address the shortcomings in corporate reporting. One project is the combined E*Know Net and Meritum project funded by the European Commission to create a network across Europe for research into the management and reporting of intangibles (Meritum 2002). Another large pan-European project is the PRISM project, organized to bring together researchers and practitioners around research and development work in relation to intangibles (PRISM 2003). A third large project was sponsored by the Danish government to design guidelines for firms to prepare intellectual capital statements. The guidelines were then tested with about 100 firms and public organizations, which experimented with producing intellectual capital statements (Mouritsen et al. 2003).

The Danish guidelines focus on the links between the various resources in their narrative, which is an open-ended interpretation of how the elements of intellectual capital cohere in dynamic interactions. The Meritum guidelines emphasize the identification of the different components (human capital, organizational capital, and relational capital) and attempt to justify their existence as organizational value drivers. The difference is in how rigid the guidelines define the elements of intellectual capital. The Danish guidelines focus on the translation of knowledge into knowledge assets. The aim is to highlight the relationships between a narrative understanding of knowledge, a business model of how knowledge works in the firm, a set of knowledge-management activities, and a reporting system that can monitor the development and use of knowledge resources. It is a process model of how knowledge translates into organizational performance. The Meritum model differs slightly, as it starts with the strategic objectives and then aims to identify the knowledge-based performance drivers. These are classified into human, organizational, and customer capital, and performance indicators are developed for these components. This approach is more of a structural model of knowledge elements in organizations. The PRISM model is slightly different again, as it differentiates tangibles assets from three types of intangibles assets: intangible goods, intangible competencies, and latent capabilities.

The difference between these guidelines is that the Danish guidelines emphasize the procedural nature of the management of knowledge, whereas the Meritum guidelines view is more structural. The Danish guidelines encourage organizations to produce reports that contain the following three main elements:

1. Knowledge narrative.
2. Management challenges and initiatives.
3. Set of indicators.

The knowledge narrative concerns the achievements of the firm relative to its customer value proposition and related resource position. Being a narrative, it must contain a story line involving a connected set or network of resources and ambitions that must be in place for the firm to understand its required intangibles. The story line conveys how the products and services of a firm add value to its customers and identifies the critical knowledge resources that will help the organization deliver the value. By using words such as *because, therefore,* and *in order to*, organizations can describe how knowledge assets drive organizational performance and deliver value to stakeholders. Therefore, the knowledge narrative establishes the link between value perceived by customers and the company's knowledge resources.

Management challenges are derived from the knowledge narratives, which concern the management of the organizational knowledge resources in connection with customers, employees, processes, and technologies. Translating the knowledge narratives into well-defined challenges involves explaining which knowledge resources need to be strengthened or acquired to address the challenges and achieve the strategic objective. Management challenges are further broken down into activities, initiatives, and processes that need to be put in place to address the challenges and attain competitiveness. In this part of the intellectual capital statement, organizations can clarify their resource allocation and set priories on activities and managerial actions.

To measure the successful management of the organizational challenges, the firm puts in place a set of indicators. These indicators quantify the success of the actions corresponding to individual management challenges. Indicators make it possible for an organization to visualize its performance in terms of its intellectual capital management. Organizations must ensure that the set of indicators makes it possible to monitor whether the initiatives have been successful and the management challenges met. There is no predefined set of measures; organizations must choose the most-appropriate set for their unique positions and contexts. The set can include indicators that measure effects, activities, or the resource mix.

This outlined approach differs from other approaches, which often focus on the value relevance of specific intellectual assets, such as patents or R&D expenses (Lev and Sougiannis 1996; Lev and Zarowin 1999), without taking into account their interconnectedness. These "bottom-line" approaches are often influenced by the more "traditional" accounting perspective; they often focus on how various categories of intangible assets relate to financial performance. These quantitative studies consider intangible assets recognized in balance sheets, such as goodwill, brand names or patents, and deferred charges, such as advertising, research and development, or training costs (Cañibano, García, and Sánchez 2000). Even though these approaches might give us some interesting insights into the value of individual assets, the difficulty is that they do not address the interconnectedness of such assets and address only those assets for which information is publicly available in quantitative formats.

Intellectual Capital Statements in Practice

In practice, intellectual capital statements contain various financial and nonfinancial metrics, such as staff turnover, job satisfaction, training, turnover split on customers, customer satisfaction, or precision of supply (Bukh, Larsen, and Mourtisen 2001; Mouritsen, Larsen, and Bukh 2001a) as well as a substantial narrative part positioning the indicators within the context and strategic framework of the firm. The formats, lengths, and contents of intellectual capital statements vary. In this section, we refer to the Danish guidelines.

The guidelines recommend that a firm report on its value creation potential and its strategy for knowledge management, including a specification of which knowledge resources are vital value drivers. Thus, the purpose of an intellectual capital statement is to communicate the value propositon, the key knowledge resources, the related management challenges the company is facing, as well as a set of indicators to track the initiatives (see Figure 5.1).

The value propostion is outlined in a narrative including the aim of the company's knowledge management. It accounts for present performance and formulates a strategy for the company's know-how in the future. Three elements should be addressed in the knowledge narrative: (1) How do the products or services produced by the firm create value to its users? (2) Which knowledge resources are critical to delivering the described value proposition? (3) What is the particular nature of the product or service?

The management challenges are a series of concrete activities in relation to the management of the knowledge resources. These activities concern the intellecutal capital (e.g., employees, customers, processes, and technologies), most often a combination of these. To verify that the appropriate actions have been implemented, specific indicators are linked to each action. This allows measuring to what extent each has been implemented and documenting the realization status of its management challenges.

Together, the four elements represent an overview of the company's intellectual capital. The elements are interrelated, and their relevance becomes clear when put into context. The indicators report on initiatives. The initiatives formalize the problems identified as management challenges. The challenges single out what has to be done if

Figure 5.1

Intellectual capital statement template.

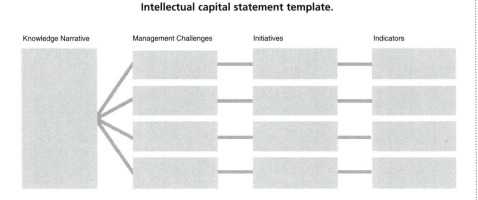

Knowledge Narrative   Management Challenges   Initiatives   Indicators

knowledge resources are to be developed. The knowledge narrative also sums up, communicates, and reorients what the company's skills and capacity do or must do for its users, and what knowledge resources are needed within the company.

The Case of Maxon Telecom

One example of how to use the Danish guidelines is the company Maxon Telecom A/S (Mouristen, Bukh, and Marr 2004; see Table 5.1). The Danish company designs and develops cutting-edge mobile telephones for its Korean parent company, which then manufactures the phones. Maxon Telecom is given the basic specification for mobile phones and takes part in an active dialogue on technical specifications and designs. Further, the firm provides insights into technological competencies, necessary for its Korean parent company to supply "communication, anytime, everywhere" to its customers.

Therefore, Maxon Telecom must be able to compile and exploit the necessary knowledge resources. This can be achieved in many ways, and the knowledge narrative specifies which knowledge resources Maxon Telecom considers necessary to creating value. Highly skilled employees are seen as particularly important, because they have the ability to "play" with technology and make new technologies work. These employees must also be motivated to become involved in the company's business; only then will customers' and users' needs be met. This requires an understanding of the needs of mobile phone users, manufacturers, and operators. Maxon Telecom is a development house and therefore has to be at the cutting edge of technology and requires knowledge of existing as well as future technologies.

The mobile phone market demands that new developments be quickly brought to the market. If this is not achieved, communication is weakened, which affects the product's value. As development work is organized into independent projects, the company must be able to run projects so that they finish on time, on budget, and at the required quality level. These are the knowledge resources that Maxon Telecom must strengthen through initiatives.

Some of the management challenges are about developing existing knowledge resources, such as personal knowledge and project management skills, which deliver on-time products. Others are about acquiring knowledge that is not found within the

Table 5.1

Extract of Maxon Telecom's Intellectual Capital Statement 2002

Knowledge Narrative	Management Challenges	Initiatives	Indicators
• Product or service: Maxon Telecom develops and designs mobile phones based on cutting edge tehnology	• Product development • Improvement of personal skills	• Check users' expectations and satisfaction • Conduct employee performance reviews	• Number of satisfaction studies (and market surveys) conducted • Customer satisfaction with quality • Number of projects ordered in the year • Absence • Rate of completion of training needs outlined in the MUS conclusions
• Use value: Provision of insights into technological competencies		• Establish and implement competency development plans • Implement tutor schemes • Implement management training	• Employee satisfaction with course or training initiatives • Number of performance reviews held on schedule
• Knowledge resources: Employees' specialist knowledge and competencies, insight in users' and customers' needs, insight in existing and future technologies and the capacity to run projects		• Implement CASE training • Implement leadership coaching	• Employee satisfaction • Employees' assessment of their colleagues' interpersonal skills and competencies • Staff turnover • Number of employees with competency development plans • Number of employees on job rotation, promoted, or posted abroad • Number of employees who believe they can develop in Maxon, both professionally and personally • Number of employees who see their immediate superiors as being capable of motivating them satisfactorily

Knowledge Narrative	Management Challenges	Initiatives	Indicators
	• Ensuring products are on time	• Launch Microsoft Projects training • Implement project organization • Implement team-building process	• Number of new employees in proportion to number of tutor schemes • Number of projects implemented on time • Number of projects kept within the agreed budget • Number of junior project managers recruited in-house • Number of employees approved to work as project managers • Satisfaction with distribution of responsibilities between and within departments • Employees' satisfaction with the ability to act with speed • Number of project groups with under 16 members • Number of project groups without own project room
	• Creating knowledge of and competencies within current and future technologies	• Train people in new technologies • Introduce roadmap • Participate in conferences • Being a part of operators' and development houses' networks	• Participation in CEBIT (World Center for Office, Information and Communications Technology) and Cannes • Number of coordinating meetings a year • Number of departmental managers/technology scouts in operators' networks • Number of developers in external networks

company, such as monitoring technology development and product development with respect to customers' and users' needs.

The challenges are addressed in the initiatives launched by Maxon Telecom. The initiatives are designed to establish contact with external parties through communication with end users and through networking and conferences. Initiatives also address the systematic development of the competencies identified as necessary to supply use value; which includes, in this case, personal and specialist competencies and project management competencies.

The indicators give the company the ability to follow up on how initiatives develop, their effects, and ultimately whether Maxon Telecom is able to supply the use value they are working for.

A Look into the Future

Although most academic studies conclude that more information in the marketplace lowers the cost of capital, "academic studies are not really necessary to reach this conclusion," as the former FASB (Financial Accounting Standards Board) board member John Foster stated in his reflections on the FASB and the capital market, because "[m]ore information always equates to less uncertainty, and it is clear that people pay more for certainty" (Foster 2003). It is not sufficient, however, that credible, reliable, and neutral information is conveyed to the capital market. The information should also be relevant in relation to assessing aspects of the firm's current and future performance, and the investors and analysts should be able to comprehend this information.

Traditional accounting rules have changed over the past decade in acknowledgment of the increasing importance of intellectual resources. In 2005, when the international reporting standards replace national rules (for companies listed on regulated markets within the European Union), IAS (International Accounting Standards) 38 will be the proposed international standard for reporting intangible assets. IAS 38 specifies that a company can recognize an asset only if it is identifiable, controlled, it is probable that future benefits specifically attributable to the asset will flow to the enterprise, and costs can be reliably measured. If the item does not meet these criteria, IAS 38 requires the expenditure on this item to be recognized as expense when it is incurred. It also requires the following items to be expensed: internally generated goodwill; startup, preopening, and preoperating costs; training costs; advertising costs; and relocation costs. It is clear from this list that much of what is commonly regarded as intellectual capital would not pass the recognition test. Even if we accept that, for the time being, intangibles are unlikely to appear in published balance sheets, we are still left with a problem of how to report, measure, and manage what are undoubtedly important value drivers in today's businesses.

Experience suggests that intellectual capital statements can be used as a tool for conceptualizing the important role and value contribution of intellectual capital. The purpose of the intellectual capital statement is often twofold, as it functions as a *management tool* used internally in the firm and as a *communication tool* used to communicate how the firm works to develop its knowledge resources to generate value. Developing such statements improves the internal understanding of which resources are important and how they can be combined and managed to create value. It might therefore help to develop a resources-based or knowledge-based strategy and monitor the implementation of such a strategy. Furthermore, any external communication of intellectual capital will help close the current information gap. Any company producing intellectual capital reports today is an innovator and early mover. The reasons for reporting might be to gain an advantage for being recognized as an innovator, and therefore these reports might act more as a marketing tool than a serious reporting tool. Intellectual capital statements may help communicate the importance of employees and partners, which in turn might attract new employees or partners, and in some cases it may even attract customers. However, this advantage will last only as long as a small group of companies produce such reports.

We currently face an information gap with serious implications, and it seems that traditional accounting does not currently offer any light at the end of the tunnel. Intellectual capital statements are one way to overcome this gap. However, intellectual capital statements are complex ideas that require a good deal of investment to be understood, and it is obvious that, at this stage, the idea is fragile. Firms may think they publish meaningful reports, but if readers do not see this meaning because they lack understanding, then it is not clear that the firm will be motivated to continue. And if managers cannot craft a knowledge management strategy that can survive in times of turbulence, then it is not clear that relations are necessarily taken seriously.

Therefore, for intellectual capital reports to have a future, two things have to be in place:

1. The audience of intellectual capital statements have to appreciate them, such as through training and an assurance that the reports are not "mere marketing."
2. Managers have to be able to formulate a knowledge-based strategy and communicate and "prove" the value relevance of such a strategy. Organizations need to be serious about their long-term value creation, even when it is necessary for economic reasons to postpone investments or reallocate intangible resources. The financial strategies and the knowledge strategies have to be integrated even though their time horizons differ.

In its current format, intellectual capital statements offer a way to address the complexities of commercial reality; however, only experimentation with these tools will allow us to improve them, identify best practices, and maybe arrive at a point of convergence among the disparate approaches. At the moment, intellectual capital statements are fragile and have to be supported if they are not to become extinct.

References

AAA Financial Accounting Standard Committee. 2003. "Implications of Accounting Research for the FASB's Initiatives on Disclosure of Information about Intangible Assets." *Accounting Horizons* 17, no. 2: 175–185.

Aboody, D., and Lev, B. 2000. "Information Asymmetry, R&D, and Insider Gains." *Journal of Finance* 55, no. 6: 2747–2766.

Accounting Standard Board. 2002. *Operating and Financial Review, Revision to Guidance, Exposure Draft*. London: Accounting Standard Board.

American Institute of Certified Public Accountants (AICPA). 1994. *Improving Business Reporting—A Customer Focus: Meeting the Information Needs of Investors and Creditors; and Comprehensive Report of the Special Committee on Financial Reporting*. New York: AICPA.

Amir, E., and B. Lev. 1996. "Value-Relevance of Nonfinancial Information: The Wireless Communication Industry." *Journal of Accounting and Economics* 22: 3–30.

Barney, J. B. 1991. "Firm Resources and Sustained Competitive Advantage." *Journal of Management* 17, no. 1: 99.

Beattie, V. 1999. *Business Reporting: The Inevitable Change*. The Institute of Chartered Accountants of Scotland, Glasgow.

——, B. McInnes, and S. Fearnley. 2002. *Through the Eyes of Management: A Study of Narrative Disclosures*. Institute of Chartered Accountants in England and Wales, London.

——, and K. Pratt. 2002a. *Voluntary Annual Report Disclosures: What Users Want.* Institute of Chartered Accountants of Scotland, Glasgow.

——, and K. Pratt. 2002b. "Disclosure items in a comprehensive model of business reporting: an empirical evaluation." Working paper. University of Sterling, Glasgow.

Blair, M., and S. Wallman. 2000. *Unseen Wealth.* Washington, DC: The Brookings Institution.

Botosan, C. A. 1997. "Disclosure Level and the Cost of Equity Capital." *The Accounting Review* 72, no. 3 (July): 323–349.

Bukh, P. N. 2003. "The Relevance of Intellectual Capital Disclosure: A Paradox?" *Accounting, Auditing and Accountability Journal* 16, no. 1: 49–56.

——, M. Johansen, and J. Mouritsen. 2002. "Multiple Integrated Performance Management Systems: IC and BSC in a Software Company." *Singapore Management Review* 24, no. 3: 21–33.

——, H. Larsen, and J. Mouritsen. 2001. "Constructing Intellectual Capital Statements." *Scandinavian Journal of Management* 17, no. 1: 87–108.

Canadian Institute of Chartered Accountants. 2001. "Management's Discussion and Analysis: Guidance on Preparation and Disclosure, Review Draft." Canadian Institute of Chartered Accountants, Toronto, Canada.

Cañibano, L., M. García-Ayuso, and M. P. Sánchez 2000. "Accounting for Intangibles: A Literature Review." *Journal of Accounting Literature* 19: 102–130.

Collier, Paul M. 2001. "Valuing Intellectual Capital in the Police." *Accounting, Auditing and Accountability Journal* 14, no. 4: 437–455.

Collins, D. W., E. L. Maydew, and I. S. Weiss 1997. "Changes in the Value-Relevance of Earnings and Book Values over the Past Forty Years." *Journal of Accounting and Economics* 24: 39–67.

Core, J. E., W. R. Guay, and A. van Buskirke. 2003. "Market Valuation in the New Economy: An Investigation of What Has Changed." *Journal of Accounting and Economics* 34: 43–67.

Diamond, D., and R. Verrecchia. 1991. "Disclosure, Liquidity and the Cost of Equity Capital." *Journal of Finance* (September): 1325–1360.

Dierickx, I., and K. Cool. 1989. "Asset Stock Accumulation And Sustainability Of Competitive Advantage." *Management Science* 35, no. 12 (December): 1504.

Eccles, R. G., R. H. Herz, E. M. Keegan, and D. M. Phillips. 2001. *The Value Reporting Revolution: Moving beyond the Earnings Game.* New York: John Wiley & Sons.

Eccles, R., and S. Mavrinac. 1995. "Improving the Corporate Disclosure Process." *Sloan Management Review* (Summer): 11–25.

Edvinsson, L., and M. S. Malone. 1997. *Intellectual Capital.* London: Piatkus.

Foster, John M. 2003. "The FSB and the Capital Market." *FASB Report* (June).

Francis, J., and K. Schipper. 1999. "Have Financial Statements Lost Their Relevance?" *Journal of Accounting Research* 37, no. 2: 319–352.

Gu, F., and B. Lev. 2001. "Intangible Assets: Measurement, Drivers, Usefulness." Working paper. Boston University, Boston.

Healy, P. M., and K. G. Palelu. 2001." Information Asymmetry, Corporate Disclosure, and the capital Market: A review of the Empirical Disclosure Literature." *Journal of Accounting and Economics* 31: 405–440.

Holland, J. 2001. "Financial Institutions, Intangibles and Corporate Governance." *Accounting, Auditing & Accountability Journal* 14, no. 4: 479–529.

Hussi, T., and G. Ahonen. 2002. "Managing Intangible Assets—A Question of Integration and Delicate Balance." *Journal of Intellectual Capital* 3, no. 3: 277–286.

Kaplan, R. S., and D. P. Norton. 2000. *The Strategy-focused Organization.* Boston: Harvard Business School Press.

——. 2004. *Strategy Maps: Converting Intangible Assets into Tangible Outcomes.* Boston: Harvard Business School Press.

King, A. W., and C. P. Zeithaml. 2001. "Competencies and Firm Performance: Examining the Causal Ambiguity Paradox." *Strategic Management Journal* 22, no. 1 (January): 75.

Lev, B. 2001. *Intangibles—Management, Measuring and Reporting.* Washington, DC: The Brookings Institution Press.

——, and T. Sougiannis. 1996. "The Capitalization, Amortization, and Value-Relevance of R&D." *Journal of Accounting Research* 21: 107–138.

——, and P. Zarowin. 1999. "The Boundaries of Financial Reporting and How to Extend Them." *Journal of Accounting Research* 37: 353–386.

Lippman, S. A., and R. P. Rumelt. 1982. "Uncertain Imitability: an Analysis of Interfirm Differences in Efficiency Under Competition." *Bell Journal of Economics* 13, no. 2 (Autumn): 418.

Marr, B., D. Gray, and A. Neely. 2003. "Why Do Firms Measure Their Intellectual Capital." *Journal of Intellectual Capital* 4, no. 4: 441–464.

Marr, B., O. Gupta, G. Roos, and S. Pike. 2003. "Intellectual Capital and Knowledge Management Effectiveness." *Management Decision* 41, no. 8: 771–781.

Marr, B., and G. Schiuma. 2001. "Measuring and Managing Intellectual Capital and Knowledge Assets in New Economy Organisations." In: *Handbook of Performance Measurement*, ed. M. Bourne. London: Gee.

Marr, B., G. Schiuma, and A. Neely. 2002. "Assessing Strategic Knowledge Assets in e-Business." *International Journal of Business Performance Management* 4, nos. 2–4: 279–295.

Marr, B., G. Schiuma, and A. Neely. 2004. "The Dynamics of Value Creation—Mapping Your Intellectual Performance Drivers." *Journal of Intellectual Capital* 5, no 2.

Marr, B., and J.-C. Spender. 2004. "Measuring Knowledge Assets—Implications of the Knowledge Economy for Performance Measurement." *Measuring Business Excellence* 8, no. 1: 18–27.

Meritum. 2002. *Guidelines for Managing and Reporting on Intangibles*, ed. L. Cañibano, M. P. Sánchez, M. García-Ayuso, and C. Chaminade. Fundación Airtel Móvil, Madrid.

Mouritsen, J. 1998. "Driving Growth: Economic Value Added versus Intellectual Capital." *Management Accounting Reserach* 9: 461–482.

——. 2003. "Intellectual Capital and the Capital Market." *Accounting, Auditing and Accountability Journal* 16, no. 1: 18–30.

——, P. N. Bukh, et al. 2003. *Intellectual Capital Statements—The New Guideline Danish Ministry of Sciences Technology and Innovation.* Copenhagen: Ministry of Science Technology and Innovation.

——, P. N. Bukh, and B. Marr. 2004. "Reporting on Intellectual Capital—Why, What, and How?" *Measuring Business Excellence* 8, no. 1: 46–54.

——, and H. T. Larsen. 2004. "The Second Wave of Knowledge Management: Re-centering Knowledge Management through Intellectual Capital." *British Accounting Review* (forthcoming).

——, H. Larsen, and P. N. Bukh. 2001a. "Intellectual Capital and the 'Capable Firm': Narrating, Visualising and Numbering for Managing Knowledge." *Accounting, Organisations and Society* 26, no. 7: 735–762.

——, H. Larsen, P. N. Bukh, and M. Johansen. 2001b. "Reading an Intellectual Capital Statement: Describing and Prescribing Knowledge Management Strategies." *Journal of Intellectual Capital* 2, no. 4: 359–383.

PRISM. 2003. *The PRISM Report*, ed. Clark Eustace. Information Society Technologies Program, Report no. 2. European Commission, London.

Starovic, D., and B. Marr. 2003. *Understanding Corporate Value—Measuring and Reporting Intellectual Capital.* London: CIMA.

Wallman, S. 1996. "The Future of Accounting and Financial Reporting, Part II: The Colorized Approach." *Accounting Horizons* 10, no. 2: 138–148.

——. 1997. "The Future of Accounting and financial reporting, Part IV: 'Access' Accounting." *Accounting Horizons* 11, no. 2: 103–116.

A Marketing Perspective on Intellectual Capital

Lisa Fernström
Intellectual Capital Services Ltd.

Introduction

Marketing as a discipline has a long history, and the more recent thinking around "intellectual capital" (IC) is rarely used within the marketing field. Even though marketing people may not include intellectual capital in their most used terminology, they do constantly talk about and manage intellectual capital resources, brands being the most obvious example. Brands today make up large proportions of the value of many companies, who in turn invest huge amounts of resources in building these brands. A number of other marketing resources and capabilities fall under intellectual capital resources, however, such as customer relationships and their management, creative skills, and negotiation skills of the sales force.

At the same time, marketing practitioners frequently express their frustration about not being considered as important or taken as seriously by the top management as, say, the Finance or Operations Departments, because of the lack of appropriate ways of measuring the outcome of marketing. In this context, a more holistic view of the firm's resources can help visualize the importance of marketing and the value it generates.

This chapter provides a marketing perspective on intellectual capital. It begins with an overview of the development of modern marketing. Then, it discusses marketing-based intellectual capital resources under the following three classifications: human, organizational, and relational resources. Finally, potential future developments of the marketing field related to IC are discussed.

The Origin of Modern Marketing

This section revisits the theoretic foundations of marketing and gives an overview of the development from the Four Ps to relationship marketing.

The Four Ps model (McCarthy 1960) and the marketing mix approach (Borden 1964) date back to the 1960s and undeniably are the main, conventional theoretic foundation of marketing. The concept of the marketing mix and the Four Ps—product, price, place, and promotion—entered the marketing textbooks at that time. It has been criticized in more recent years, however, for being too simplistic (e.g., Grönroos 1997). The marketing mix perhaps is not so much of a model as a list of categories of marketing variables, and it is contested whether this way of describing a phenomenon can be considered a valid one (ibid.). Grönroos also goes on to question whether the marketing mix and the Four Ps approach actually serve the core purpose of the marketing concept, that is, the notion that the firm is best off by organizing its activities to fulfill the needs of customers in chosen target markets. In practice, marketing has focused primarily on managing the toolbox that is the Four Ps instead of actually exploring the nature of the firm's market relationships and fulfilling the needs of the market.

There is reason to criticize the Four Ps model, but one also has to put it in context. The model was coined for a market with very different preconditions than today's business environment. The market in the 1960s was characterized by tangible product offers and a pure transaction focus, much unlike the largely service-based market we see today. Therefore, even if the Four Ps model always has been simplistic, it worked well under the conditions for which it was created.

When the service sector began to gain importance, services became the subject of research in academia. In the early 1970s, the marketing of services emerged as a separate area of marketing, with concepts and models of its own, developed for the specific characteristics of services. Grönroos (1979, 1982) introduced the concept of the interactive marketing function, to cover the marketing impact on the customer during the consumption of usage process, where the consumer of a service typically interacts with systems, physical resources, and employees of the service provider. Langeard and Eiglier (1987) called this system of interactions *servuction* (the result of compressing the words *service* and *production*), describing the interactions that occur between the customer and employees in the production of a service. By identifying all the stakeholders involved in the servuction in advance, it is easier to control the production process of the service.

The fact that services are delivered in interaction between the seller and the customer puts the relationship issue in the limelight. The service dimension, in both pure service providers and product companies, which now also need to provide services around their product offerings, forces companies to excel on customer relationship management. The pure product companies of yesterday did not have the same requirement. Parallel to the development of the service sector was the development of information technology. In essence, the service revolution and the information revolution are two sides of the same coin. Information technology gives the company the ability to learn and store more information about the customer, which in turn gives the company more ability to customize its services and develop customer relationships (Rust 2004). Hence, the rise of the service industry, spurred on by information technology developments, triggered research into relationships. This notion of relationships is discussed in more detail in the section "Relationship Marketing and Relational Resources."

Marketing, the Resource-Based View, and Intellectual Capital

The IC perspective is based on the resource-based view (RBV) of the firm (e.g., Penrose 1959; Wernerfeldt 1984; Barney 1991), which considers the firm as a set of resources that determines the firm's ability to obtain a competitive advantage. For this, the resources need to be durable, rare, and difficult to imitate and substitute (Barney 1991). They should also be valuable, and the company must be able to appropriate some of the value they create (Collis and Montgomery 1995). With these attributes, the resources have the potential to generate economic rent above and beyond normal profit (Amit and Schoemaker 1993). The RBV has been applied within the field of marketing as well (Bharadwaj, Varadarajan, and Fahy 1993; Hooley, Broderick, and Moller 1998; Capron and Hulland 1999; Day 2001; Hunt 1997; Hunt and Morgan 1995) but not to any great extent. This section presents some of the research to integrate the RBV with various marketing approaches.

Srivastava, Fahey, and Christensen (2001) attempted to incorporate the RBV with marketing. Their framework is built on marketing-specific resources that may, if properly developed and maintained, constitute a basis for competitive advantage. The cornerstones of their approach comprise market-based assets, processes, and capabilities. They make a further distinction between relational and intellectual assets. The definition of *relational assets* correlates with that of relational resources of IC thinking, in that they are relationships with external stakeholders (e.g., customers, channels, strategic partners, suppliers, and networks) and constitute resources not owned by the firm (ibid.; Fernström, Pike, and Roos 2004; relational resources are discussed in more detail later). Intellectual assets, on the other hand, as defined by Srivastava et al. (2001), are owned by the firm and include knowledge and know-how embedded in individuals and processes. This reasoning does not correspond with IC thinking, however, where knowledge is always a human resource, not owned by the firm (see later for details).

To create value, Srivastava et al. (ibid.) point out that these assets have to be transformed into various processes (customer connecting or non-customer connecting), and the market-based capabilities capture how well the firm performs each of the customer-connecting processes. This resource transformation reasoning is the essence of value creation in IC thinking as well (e.g., Roos in Chatzkel 2002).

Hooley et al. (1998) examined the combination of the RBV and the market orientation stream, two seemingly contradictory approaches, to form a concept of competitive positioning. As mentioned already, the RBV looks at the existence and development of internal resources to determine a firm's competitiveness, while market orientation suggests that an external view is needed to reach that goal (ibid.). Hooley et al. state that the most important marketing assets are often intangible, referred to as *customer-based assets* (Hooley and Saunders 1993), including relationships, brands, reputation (Aaker 1991), and customer loyalty (Payne et al. 1995).

In their framework, Hooley et al. (1998) divide resources into assets and capabilities on several levels and identify the following range of marketing specific resources (similar to Srivastava's et al. 2001):

- *Strategic-marketing capabilities*: market-sensing capability and market-targeting and -positioning capabilities.
- *Functional-marketing capabilities*: customer-relationship management, customer-access capabilities, product-management capabilities, and new-product-development capabilities.
- *Operational- or task-marketing capabilities*: implementation capabilities, including implementing promotions, PR, offers, packaging redesign, and the like.

Hooley et al. (1998) then used this framework to support their argument that competitive positioning is about finding a fit between the chosen market targets and the internal resources at the company's disposal for serving those chosen targets more effectively than competitors. To do this, companies have six basic positioning strategies to choose from, as identified by Hooley et al. (ibid.). They are outlined in Table 6.1 together with their main resource requirements (ibid., p. 107).

Table 6.1

Basic Positioning Strategies and Their Resource Needs		
Position	**Strategic Focus**	**Resources**
Low price	Internal efficiency	Cost-control systems, processes, procurement and information systems
Superior quality	Superior quality and image management	Market sensing, quality control and assurance, brand reputation, supply-chain management
Rapid innovation	First to market	New product/service development, R&D, technical skills, creative skills
Superior service	Relationship building	Market sensing, customer linking, service systems, skilled staff, feedback systems, continuous monitoring
Differentiated benefits	Focused targeting	Market sensing, NP/SD, creativity in segmentation
Tailored offering	Tailoring to individual customer wants and needs	Market sensing, customer bonding, operations flexibility
Source: Hooley et al. (1998).		

In the marketing literature, a more widely accepted approach to competition was created by Hunt (e.g., 1997) and Hunt and Morgan (e.g., 1995), called the *resource-advantage theory* (R-A), to explain certain deficiencies in the dominant theory of competition. The R-A theory draws on a number of theories, including the RBV as explained previously. It also draws on the heterogeneous demand theory (Alderson 1957, 1965; Chamberlain 1933) and the competitive advantage theory (Alderson 1957, 1965; Clark 1961; Porter 1985). For the R-A theory, Hunt and Morgan (1995) define the *resources* of the firm as "tangible and intangible entities available to the firm that enable it to produce efficiently and/or effectively a market offering that has value to some market segment(s)." A central assumption within the writing on intellectual capital is captured in Hunt's definition of *resources*, namely, that value-creating resources are not only found in the ownership of a company, some may be external to the company, such as relational resources (see later for details), which are both owned and controlled by the other party (Fernström et al. 2004). Hunt (2000) divides the resources into seven categories: financial, physical, legal, human, organizational, informational, and relational. These categories are very similar to those prevailing in IC literature, that is, human, organizational, and relational (Roos and Roos 1997) on the intangible side; and financial and physical on the tangible side. The informational and legal resources identified by Hunt (2000) typically fall under the organizational resource category in IC language.

Many of the resources identified by the marketing scholars cited here comprise marketing capabilities of the employees. All these capabilities belong to the human resource category of IC, which is discussed next.

Human Resources

Capabilities as described previously by Srivastava et al. (2001), Hooley et al. (1998), and Hunt (e.g., 2000) are most often inherent in what, in IC terms, would be called *human resources*. These resources include, for example, the knowledge, competence, intellectual agility, relationship ability, and attitude of the employees. Competence or capabilities refer to the skills and knowledge of the employees that are used to create value for the company. Human resources, by definition, are not owned by the company, although it may well control them (Fernström et al. 2004). Human resources behave according to the law of increasing returns (Lev 2001; Romer 1986; Hand 2003); the more you know, the easier it is to learn. For example, the more languages you know the easier it is to learn a new one.

Looking specifically at what can be categorized as marketing skills and capabilities, thus belonging to human resources, we find competences such as communication skills, negotiation skills, creative skills, and relationship abilities, among many others. These human resources may be particularly valuable within the marketing department. However, given the increasingly interconnected network of customers, suppliers, competitors, and others, the relationship ability becomes even more important and not solely among sales and marketing people. Gummesson (1994) refers to "part-time marketers," when describing all employees in the company outside the Sales and Marketing Departments, who interact with customers on different levels. In an IT service company, these part-time marketers range, for example, from corporate management to call center employees to service engineers. Companies, especially service companies, depend on these human resources to be up to date and continually developed. In the case of the IT service company, the engineers have to be up to date with the products and services offered and the problems and issues surrounding them, as well as being able to offer friendly and patient advice to customers.

Relationship Marketing and Relational Resources

As marketing research evolved into services marketing and the relationships between the firm and its customers, attention was given to the length of these relationships. Grönroos (1980, 1982) developed the customer relationship life-cycle model to cover the long-term nature of the formation and evolution of the relationship between a product or service provider and its customers. Managing this life cycle is a relationship-marketing task, although the term itself was not used at that time (Grönroos 1997).

This research developed into relationship economics. Heskett (1987) introduced the concept of market economies, which means achieving results by understanding the customers and their needs as opposed to concentrating on developing scale economies. Numerous pieces of research have shown that retaining existing customers has a major positive impact on the profitability of a firm and acquiring new customers is most often much more expensive (e.g., Reichheld 1993; Grant and Schlesinger 1995; Heskett, Sasser, and Schlesinger 1997; Wilton 1998). Long-term relationships in which both parties learn over time how to best interact with each other lead to decreasing relationship costs for the customer as well as the supplier or service provider, as shown in Grönroos's relationship cost theory, based on the quality cost literature (Crosby 1979) and transaction costs (Williamson 1975). A mutually satisfying relationship makes it possible for customers to avoid significant transaction costs involved in shifting supplier or service provider and for suppliers to avoid suffering unnecessary quality costs.

Over time, the research around relationships grew and broadened to include more than just the basic business relationship between a firm and its customers, resulting in the emergence of the concept of *relationship marketing*. The term was first used by Berry (1983) in a services marketing context, but the research of the Nordic School of services marketing (e.g., Grönroos and Gummesson 1985) has played a more prominent role in the development of relationship marketing. Some industrial marketing and most modern service marketing approaches view marketing as an interactive process in a social context, where relationship building and management are vital.

Relationship marketing (RM) can be defined as follows (Grönroos 1990, p. 138): "Marketing is to establish, maintain, and enhance relationships with customers and other partners, at a profit, so that the objectives of the parties involved are met. This is achieved by a mutual exchange and fulfilment of promises." Gummesson gives a more condense definition, which has been reworked from "RM is marketing seen as relationships, networks and interaction" (Gummesson 1995) to "RM is marketing based on interaction within networks of relationships" (Gummesson 2003). Hunt (2000) uses the R-A theory to underpin relationship marketing theory, in which "co-operate-to-compete," that is, the interaction element, is a necessary thesis.

Relationship marketing has established itself as a cornerstone paradigm in modern marketing, given the need for companies to move away from a short-term transaction-oriented goal to a long-term relationship-building goal (Kotler 1992; Webster 1992). In an interview in the early 1990s, Kotler (1991) described the shift from a marketing mix focus to a relationship focus and stated that there is a movement away from a focus on exchange, in the narrow sense of transaction, toward one on building and retaining valuable relationships and marketing networks. In the mid-1990s, the notion of one-to-one marketing was coined (Peppers and Rogers 1993) and CRM (customer relationship management) thereafter emerged as the number one business buzzword at the start of the millennium (Storbacka and Lehtinen 2000). One-to-one marketing and CRM are essentially the same, although there may be some differences in emphasis and procedures (Gummesson 2004).

Gummesson's research in services marketing and relationship marketing (e.g., 1994, 1995, 1997) resulted in the 30R approach, identifying and defining 30 different relationships of a business and examining their consequences. The 30 relationships have different properties and can be divided into (1) *market relationships*, involving direct contact with the customers; (2) *nano relationships*, meaning internally directed relationships offering support to the market relationships; (3) *mega relationships*, existing on a level above the actual market (e.g., media relationships). In addition, the 30Rs cover organizational issues (e.g., the owner and financial relationship and non-commercial relationships) and form and content relationships, which include, for example, the green relationship and the knowledge relationship. Relationship marketing is hence a step toward considering marketing in a broader management perspective rather than as an isolated function in a company.

By identifying the knowledge relationship, Gummesson takes a first step toward incorporating the early thinking of knowledge management and IC. He is one of very few marketing scholars who used the term *intellectual capital* (e.g., Gummesson 1998, 2004), relating it to Edvinsson and Malone (1997), the early IC experiences of Skandia (ibid.), and the balanced scorecard (Kaplan and Norton 1996) as a potential way of measuring return on relationships. The balanced scorecard has since proven more effective as an internal communication tool than a means for measuring intangible resources (Pike and Roos 2003).

Using the IC lens, the relationships just discussed are grouped in the relational resources of the firm. As mentioned, they are external to the firm and, hence, not owned nor controlled by the firm (Fernström et al. 2004).

Relationship Value

Initiatives have been taken to put a value on the relationships of a company. Most recently, Gummesson (2002, 2004) developed the thinking around return on relationships (ROR), which he defines as follows (Gummesson 2002, p. 228): "Return on relationships (ROR) is the long-term net financial outcome caused by the establishment and maintenance of an organization's network of relationships." This definition implies that firms have valuable relationships other than merely those with its customers. However, in organizations today, relationship metrics are often limited to this latter relationship (e.g., customer retention and loyalty metrics). Gummesson, therefore, gives this narrower definition in order to operationalize ROR (Gummesson, 2004, p. 141): "ROR in a narrow sense is the long-term net financial outcome caused by the establishment and maintenance of individual customer relationships."

Gummesson outlines the types of potential revenue streams from various relationships of a firm, both present and future, their nature, and how they behave in interaction. Moreover, he describes the need for integrating ROR goals in the marketing planning process and the importance of transforming relational resources into organizational resources, which are owned and controlled by the company, such as making sure that a business relationship of an individual employee is anchored in the organization as well as, say, by entering the customer's contact details and purchase history into a CRM system.

Gummesson concludes that (ibid., p. 147) "ROR should ideally help a company to determine whether it should act at the zero relationship end of the scale (the occasional transaction based solely on a price and customer convenience relationship) or move along the scale towards closer and more enduring relationships. Moving along the scale calls for more comprehensive ROR indicators, thus raising accounting from historical, financial measurement to broader forms of future-oriented, knowledge generation." These future-oriented measures are found in the many models for measuring and disclosing IC (e.g., Roos et al. 1997; Edvinsson and Malone 1997; Kaplan and Norton 1996; and as described in Bukh and Johansson 2003).

Brands and Organizational Resources

Thus far, two categories of intangible resources have been examined in marketing language: human resources (marketing capabilities, knowledge, skills) and relational resources. The third resource category referred to in the IC literature is organizational resources, sometimes referred to as *organizational* or *structural capital*. Organizational resources are owned and controlled by the firm (Fernström et al. 2004) and include all the structures, systems, and processes the company uses to support its operations, also items such as brands and trademarks, which to a large extent are the result of marketing activities, and culture, prototypes, documented information, and intellectual property. Organizational resources follow network economic behavior (Lev 2001). For example, the more people in a firm use the same database and the more data they enter and use, the more valuable the database becomes. However, when the database is created, it lacks content, meaning that a lot of effort has to be expended for a very low return. Similarly, as the database gets very large, a lot of effort has to be put in again for a relatively low return.

An issue of great interest, in both marketing and the wider business community and academia, is the value of brands (organizational resource). Brands may be developed into very valuable resources, but how is this value achieved? Looking at value creation and brands, Doyle (2001) shows that four factors are required for a brand to create value. First and foremost, an attractive consumer value proposition is needed for a brand to be successful. This, however, must be supported by other factors. The brand has to be effectively integrated with the firm's other tangible and intangible resources, constituting the foundations for its core business processes. Moreover, the market economics in which the brand operates must permit earning returns above the cost of capital. The final requirement is that management pursue brand strategies directly linked to shareholder (or stakeholder) value creation.

When studying the brand in its context, Doyle (2001) applies the RBV to support his statement about the need for the brand to be integrated with the other value creating resources of the firm and point out that they are not independent from one another. To illustrate the point, Doyle explains (ibid., p. 257): "if a company's marketing strategy is based on achieving superior customer relationships through individualized solutions, it will also need the product development and supply chain management processes in order to design and deliver the tailored responses efficiently. Without the combination of effective processes it will not be able to execute the strategy." These processes need to be managed by the company, but they may well be outsourced to specialists. Dell and American Express are examples of companies that concentrate on product development and customer relationship management and outsource most of their supply chain management activities.

If revisiting the issue of brands and value creation, the RBV just described offers a range of insights into the role of brands and the creation of shareholder value. Doyle (2001) warns marketers about exaggerating the importance of brands, since in many industries, the more important drivers of value are other intangible resources, such as skills and motivation, systems and patents, and customer and supplier relationships. Table 6.2 shows the relative importance of brands against other tangible and intangible resources. Only in luxury consumer goods are brands the dominant source of

Table 6.2

Relative Importance of Brands and Other Resources (in percent)			
	Tangibles	Brands	Other Intangibles
Utilities	70	0	30
Industrial	70	5	25
Pharmaceutical	40	10	50
Retail	70	15	15
Information technology	30	20	50
Automotive	50	30	20
Financial services	20	30	50
Food and drink	40	55	5
Luxury goods	25	70	5
Source: Interbrand in Doyle (2001).			

value, while brands play a much smaller role in many of the newer, fast-growing industries, such as information technology, pharmaceuticals, and financial services. The caveat is really about the risk of overinvesting in traditional branding activities and underinvesting in other tangible and intangible resources, thereby losing the competitive edge. The decline of strong brands such as Procter & Gamble and Heinz may be partly explained by their insufficient investment in new technology and lack of genuine innovation (Berthon, Hulbert, and Pitt 1999).

Merely having a resource, such as a strong brand, is not sufficient for it to create value (Gupta and Roos 2001). Value creation is a dynamic process, in which the interaction between resources plays an essential role. One resource is often useless without another; for example, a market intelligence database (organizational resource) does not create value for the company unless it is used by the employees (human resource) in their work. Therefore, resources have to be used and transformed into other resources for value to be created. Notably, as a consequence, value is not merely generated in the transaction between the firm and its customers but through the many other transformations of resources into other resources. This reasoning is demonstrated in Doyle's (2001) outline of how brands interact with other intangible resources. Brands have an impact on the customer-relationship-management process through enhancing or destroying the confidence and satisfaction customers gain from the product. Effective brand management, however, also engages with the product-development and supply-chain-management processes (Jaworski and Kohli 1993). In the past, brands such as Jaguar, MG, and Schlitz Brewing have seen their financial values eroded by the companies' inability to provide the quality, delivery, and performance for making a reality of the desired images. Doyle (2001), therefore, concludes that brand management must be seen as an integral part of the total management process rather than a specialist marketing activity (see also Urde 1999). It becomes a core capability of the firm only when it is effectively coordinated with the firm's other resources and capabilities to enhance all the core business processes.

Brand Measurement

An issue of great interest and concern is that of measurement. How do we measure marketing-related intangible resources? Measurement initiatives within the marketing community have addressed issues such as the value of brands (Aaker 1996), customers, and (customer) relationships. Measurement is not the focus of this chapter, so only a brief comment on brand measurement models is given here.

As a pioneer of brand management and measurement, Aaker (e.g., 1991, 1996) identifies a set of measures to be used when measuring the value of brand equity,[1] which fall into the following categories (Aaker 1996, p. 105):

- *Loyalty measures*: price premium, satisfaction, loyalty.
- *Perceived quality and leadership measures*: perceived quality, leadership.
- *Association and differentiation measures*: perceived value, brand personality, organizational association.
- *Awareness measures*: brand awareness.
- *Market behavior measures*: market share, price, and distribution indices.

---

[1] *Brand equity* is defined as the brand assets or liabilities linked to a brand's name and symbol that add or subtract from a product or service. Brand equity assets can be grouped into brand awareness, brand quality, brand associations, and brand loyalty (Aaker and Joachimstahler 2000).

A number of commercial companies apply much of Aaker's work for brand valuation, Interbrand being the most prominent, along with Young & Rubicam (with their BrandAsset Valuator), Brand Finance, and BrandEconomics, to name but a few. It should be noted, however, that models for brand valuation have received little credibility in stock markets and investor communities (Plender 2003).

What Is Next?

This chapter has shown that the marketing field is converging with IC thinking, relationship marketing and brand management being the most important drivers. Further evidence of this direction is given in Vargo and Lusch's (2004) recent article, which was commented on by a number of prominent scholars (e.g., Day, Gummesson, Hunt, and Prahalad). They propose a service-centered dominant logic of marketing, implying that marketing should play a central and integrative role in the company. In turn, the company should proactively involve consumers in the value-creation process, and marketing communications should be characterized by dialogue with, not messages directed toward, consumers. The authors identify a shift in focus away from *operand* resources (i.e., resources that are relatively static, captured, and acted on) toward a focus on *operant* resources (i.e., resources that are dynamic and capable of changing and creating other resources). This dynamic view of resources has been expressed in the writing on intellectual capital (Chatzkel 2002; Marr, Schiuma, and Neely 2004). In their article, Vargo and Lusch (2004) urge marketing academics to rethink the terminology of marketing, subordinating many of the dominant, traditional goods-centered concepts to revised service-centered concepts.

At the core of Vargo and Lusch's article (ibid.) are a number of propositions underpinning their service-centered model. Among these are (1) service provision is the fundamental unit of exchange; (2) knowledge is the fundamental source of competitive advantage; (3) goods are appliances that serve as a distribution mechanism for services; (4) the consumer is always a coproducer of value; (5) the enterprise can make only value propositions; and (6) a service-centered model of exchange is inherently customer oriented and relational. These propositions are easily interpreted with an IC lens, and it should therefore be possible to beneficially incorporate some of them in IC thinking.

With the increasing insight in the business community about the need to focus on the customers and their needs and wants, marketing has already gained a more prominent position in firms than a decade or two ago. Day (2004) comments on the argument of the aforementioned Vargo and Lusch article's statements that marketing should be at the center of the integration and coordination of the cross-functional processes of a service-centered business model and that this depends on what is meant by *marketing*. Day (2004) elaborates that it will probably not be the marketing function as it is in most companies today; instead, marketing as a general management responsibility of the top team will have the crucial tasks of navigating through effective market sensing and articulating the new value proposition. This broadened role is most effective in a market-driven organization that has superior skills in understanding, attracting, and keeping valuable customers (Day 1999). Should marketing progress this way, being a more general responsibility of top management, then it might make powerful use of the IC thinking and the strategic use of resources. Much of the IC literature takes a top-down strategic perspective to managing, measuring, and disclosing intangible resources and their value in one way or another. In contrast, marketing has more of a bottom-up, practical approach to how to deploy the resources. The advantage with the IC approach is that it is holistic, meaning that it views marketing in its context of the entire company.

Another indication that marketing is moving toward a more-holistic approach is the relationship marketing approach described previously, which emphasizes that marketing is embedded in the whole management process (Gummesson 1994). By taking this more holistic view, all parties benefit, as the nature of intangible resources is such that their value-creating potential increases the more they are integrated with other resources (e.g., Doyle 2001).

The IC perspective could gain significant insights about how to develop resources if referring to the marketing stream on relationships (relational resource), brands (organizational resource), and specific marketing capabilities (human resource). IC may also benefit from developing the thinking around customer resources and a customer focus. In accordance with this, Srivastava et al. (2001) argue that a marketing perspective focusing on improving and sustaining customer value leads to an increased understanding of the key RBV resource attributes, which are rarity, durability, inimitability, and nonsubstitutability.

On a final note, this chapter has been a first attempt to look at the potential synergies between the fields of marketing and IC. The research agenda to take this further is vast. For marketing academics, there should be substantial benefits in grasping the methodologies developed within the IC field for measurement and management of intangible resources and applying them in, say, relationship marketing. An item for the IC scholars is to integrate marketing thinking about resources into the IC imperative of developing resources. The list can be expanded indefinitely.

References

Aaker, D. 1991. *Managing Brand Equity.* New York: The Free Press.
——. 1996. "Measuring Brand Equity across Products and Markets." *California Management Review* 38, no. 3: 102–120.
——, and E. Joachimstaler. 2000. *Brand Leadership.* New York: The Free Press.
Alderson, W. 1957. *Marketing Behavior and Executive Action.* Homewood, IL: Richard D. Irwin.
——. 1965. *Dynamic Marketing Behavior.* Homewood, IL: Richard D. Irwin.
Amit, R., and P. J. H. Schoemaker. 1993. "Strategic Assets and Organisational Rent." *Strategic Management Journal* 14: 33–46.
Ballantyne, D, M. Christopher, and A. Payne. 2003. "Relationship Marketing: Looking back—Looking Forward." *Marketing Theory* 3, no. 1: 159–166.
Barney, J. B. 1991. "Firm resources and sustained competitive advantage." *Journal of Management* 17, no. 1: 99-120.
——, P. M. Wright, and D. J. Ketchen. 2001. "The Resource-Based View of the Firm: Ten Years after 1991." *Journal of Management* 27, no. 6: 625–641.
Berry, L. L. 1983. "Relationship Marketing." In: *Emerging Perspectives of Services Marketing,* ed. L. L. Berry, G. L. Shostack, and G. D. Upah, p. 25. Chicago: American Marketing Association.
——, and A. Parasuraman. 1991. *Marketing Services. Competing through Quality.* Lexington, MA: The Free Press/Lexington Books.
Berthon, P., J. M. Hulbert, and L. R. Pitt. 1999. "To Serve or Create? Strategic Orientations towards Customers and Innovation." *California Management Review* 42, no. 1: 37–58.
Bharadwaj, S. G., P. R. Varadarajan, and J. Fahy. 1993. "Sustainable Competitive Advantage in Service Industries: A Conceptual Model and Research Propositions." *Journal of Marketing* 57: 83–99.
Borden, N. H. 1964. "The Concept of the Marketing Mix." *Journal of Advertising Research* 4 (June): 2–7.

Bukh, P. N., and U. Johanson. 2003. "Research and Knowledge Interaction: Guidelines for Intellectual Capital Reporting." *Journal of Intellectual Capital* 4, no. 4: 576–587.

Capron, L., and J. Hulland. 1999. "Redeployment of Brands, Sales Forces, and General Marketing Management Expertise Following Horizontal Acquisitions: A Resource-Based View." *Journal of Marketing* 63: 2.

Chamberlain, E. 1933. *The Theory of Monopolistic Competition.* Boston: Harvard University Press.

Chandon, P. 2004. "Note on Brand Audit: How to Measure Brand Awareness, Brand Image, Brand Equity and Brand Value." Class discussion note, INSEAD, France.

Chatzkel, J. B. 2002. "Conversation with Göran Roos." *Journal of Intellectual Capital* 3: 2.

Clark, J. M. 1961. *Competition as a Dynamic Process.* Washington, DC: the Brookings Institution.

Collis, D., and Montgomery, C. 1995. "Competing on Resources: Strategy in the 1990s." *Harvard Business Review* (July–August): 119–28.

Crosby, P. B. 1979. *Quality Is Free.* New York: McGraw-Hill.

Day, G. S. 1999. *The Market-Driven Organization.* New York: The Free Press.

———. 2001. "Capabilities for forging customer relationships." Unpublished manuscript. The Wharton School, University of Pennsylvania, Philadelphia.

———. 2004. "Achieving Advantage with a New Dominant Logic." Invited commentary on "Evolving to a New Dominant Logic for Marketing." *Journal of Marketing* 68 (January): 18–19.

Doyle, P. 2001. "Building Value-Based Branding Strategies." *Journal of Strategic Marketing* 9: 255–268.

Edvinsson, L., and M. S. Malone. 1997. *Intellectual Capital.* New York: HarperCollins.

Fernström, L., S. Pike, and G. Roos. 2004. "Understanding the Truly Value Creating Resources— The Case of a Pharmaceutical Company." *International Journal of Learning and Intellectual Capital* 1, no. 1: 105–120.

Grant, Alan W. H., and Leonard A. Schlesinger. 1995. "Realize Your Customers' Full Profit Potential." *Harvard Business Review* (September–October): 59–72.

Grönroos, C. 1979. "Marknadsforing av Tjanster. En Studie av Marknadsforingsfunktionen i Tjansteforetag" [Marketing of Services. A Study of the Marketing Function of Service Firms], with an English summary. Dissertation, Swedish School of Economics and Business Administration, Finland. Stockholm: Akademilitteratur/Marketing Technique Center.

———. 1980. "Designing a Long-Range Marketing Strategy for Services." *Long Range Planning* 13 (April): 36–42.

———. 1982. *Strategic Management and Marketing in the Service Sector.* Swedish School of Economics and Business Administration, Helsinki, Finland. Published in 1983 in the United States by the Marketing Science Institute and in the United Kingdom by Studentlitteratur/Chartwell-Bratt.

———. 1990. *Service Management and Marketing. Managing the Moments of Truth in Service Competition.* Lexington, MA: The Free Press/Lexington Books.

———. 1997. "From Marketing Mix to Relationship Marketing—Towards a Paradigm Shift in Marketing." *Management Decision* 35, no. 4: 132–148.

———, and E. Gummesson. 1985. "The Nordic School of Service Marketing." In: *Service Marketing—Nordic School Perspectives,* ed. C. Grönroos and E. Gummesson, pp. 6–11. Stockholm: Stockholm University.

Gummesson, E. 1994. "Making Relationship Marketing Operational." *International Journal of Service Industry Management* 5, no. 5: 5–20.

———. 1995. *Relationsarkandsföring: Från 4P till 30R.* Liber-Hermods, Malmö.

———. 1997. "Relationship Marketing as a Paradigm Shift: Some Conclusions Form the 30R Approach." *Management Decision* 35, no. 4: 267.

———. 1998. "Productivity, Quality and Relationship Management In Service Operations." *International Journal of Contemporary Hospitality Management* 10, no. 1: 4–15.

———. 2002. *Total Relationship Marketing.* 2nd edition. Oxford: Butterworth-Heinemann/ Chartered Institute of Marketing.

———. 2003. "Relationship Marketing: It All Happens Here and Now!" *Marketing Theory* 3, no. 1.

———. 2004. "Return on Relationships (ROR): The Value of Relationship Marketing and CRM in Business-to-Business Contexts." *Journal of Business and Industrial Marketing* 19, no. 2: 136–148.

Gupta, O., and G. Roos. 2001. "Using the Intellectual Capital Perspective to Analyse the Value Creation Potential of Mergers and Acquisitions." *Journal of Intellectual Capital* 2: 3.

Hand, J. R. M. 2003. "The Increasing Returns-to-Scale of Intangibles." In: *Intangible Assets: Values, Measures and Risks*, ed. J. R. M. Hand and B. Lev, Oxford: Oxford University Press.

Heskett, J. L. 1987. "Lessons in the Service Sector." *Harvard Business Review* 65 (March–April): 118–126.

———, W. E. Sasser Jr., and L. A. Schlesinger. 1997. *The Service Profit Chain: How Leading Companies Link Profit and Growth to Loyalty, Satisfaction and Value*. New York: The Free Press.

Hooley, G., A. Broderick, and K. Moller. 1998. "Competitive Positioning and the Resources-Based View of the Firm." *Journal of Strategic Management* 6: 97–115.

Hooley, S. D., and J. A. Saunders. 1993. *Competitive Positioning: The Key to Market Success*. London: Prentice-Hall International.

Hunt, S. 1997. "Competing through Relationships: Grounding Relationship Management in Resource-Advantage Theory." *Journal of Marketing Management* 13: 431–445.

———. 2000. *A General Theory of Competition*. Thousands Oaks, CA: Sage Publications.

———, and R. M. Morgan. 1995. "The Comparative Advantage Theory of Competition." *Journal of Marketing* 59: 1–15.

Jaworski, B. J., and A. K. Kohli. 1993. "Market Orientation: Antecedents and Consequences." *Journal of Marketing* 57: 53–70.

Kaplan, R., and D. Norton D. 1996. *The Balanced Scorecard: Translating Strategy into Action*. Boston: Harvard Business School Press.

Kohli, C., and L. Leuthesser. 2001. "Brand Equity: Capitalizing on Intellectual Capital." *Ivey Business Journal* (March–April).

Kotler, P. 1991. "Philip Kotler Explores the New Marketing Paradigm." *Marketing Science Institute Review* (Spring): 1, 4–5.

———. 1992. "It's Time for Total Marketing." *Business Week ADVANCE Executive Brief* 2.

Langeard, E., and P. Eiglier. 1987. *Servuction. Le Marketing des Services*. Paris: Wiley.

Lev, B. 2001. *Intangibles: Management, Measurement, and Reporting*. Washington, D.C.: The Brookings Institution Press.

Levitt, T. 1960. "Marketing Myopia." *Harvard Business Review* (July–August): 24–47.

Marr, B., G. Schiuma, and A. Neely. 2004. "The Dynamics of Value Creation." *Journal of Intellectual Capital* 5, no 2.

McCarthy, E. J. (1960) *Basic Marketing*. Homewood, IL: Richard D. Irwin.

Payne, A., M. Christopher; M. Clark, and H. Peck. 1995. *Relationship Marketing for Competitive Advantage*. London: Butterworth-Heinemann.

Penrose, E. T. 1959. *The Theory of the Growth of the Firm*. New York: Wiley.

Peppers, D., and M. Rogers. 1993. *The One to One Future: Building Relationships One Customer at a Time*. New York: Doubleday.

Peteraf, M. A. 1993. "The Cornerstones of Competitive Advantage: A Resource-Based View." *Strategic Management Journal* 14, no. 3: 179–191.

Pike, S., and G. Roos. 2004. "Mathematics and Modern Business Management." *Journal of Intellectual Capital* 5, no. 2: 243–256.

Plender, J. 2003. "Casting a Shadow on Capitalism." *Financial Times* (January 28).

Porter, M. E. 1985. *Competitive Advantage: Creating and Sustaining Superior Performance*. New York: The Free Press.

Reichheld, F. E. 1993. "Loyalty-based management." *Harvard Business Review* 71 (March–April): 64–73.

Romer, P. M. 1986. "Increasing Returns and Long-Run Growth." *Journal of Political Economy* 94, no. 5.

Roos, G., and J. Roos. 1997. "Measuring Your Company's Intellectual Performance." *Long Range Planning* 30, no. 3.

Roos, J., G. Roos, N. Dragonetti, and L. Edvinsson. 1997. *Intellectual Capital: Navigating the New Business Landscape.* London: Macmillan Press.

Rust, R. 2004. "If Everything Is Service, Why Is It Happening Now, and What Difference Does It Make?" Invited commentary on Evolving to a New Dominant Logic for Marketing. *Journal of Marketing* 68 (January): 23–24.

Srivastava, R. K., L. Fahey, and K. Christensen. 2001. "The Resource-Based View and Marketing: The Role of Market-Based Assets in Gaining Competitive Advantage." *Journal of Management* 27: 777–802.

Storbacka, K., and J. Lehtinen. 2000. *CRM.* Malmo, Sweden: Liber.

Teece, D. J. 1998. Capturing Value from Knowledge Assets: The New Economy, Markets for Know-How and Intangible Assets. *California Management Review* 40, no. 3: 55–79.

Urde, M. 1999. "Brands Orientation: A Mindset for Building Brands into Strategic Resources." *Journal of Marketing Management* 15: 117–133.

Vargo, S. L., and R. F. Lusch. 2004. "Evolving to a New Dominant Logic for Marketing." *Journal of Marketing* 68 (January): 1–17.

Webster, F. E. Jr. 1992. "The Changing Role of Marketing in the Corporations." *Journal of Marketing* 56 (October): 1–17.

Wernerfelt, B. 1984. "A Resource-Based View of the Firm." *Strategic Management Journal* 5, no. 2: 171–180.

Williamson, O. 1975. *Markets and Hierarchies: Analysis and Antitrust Implications.* New York: The Free Press.

Wilton, P. 1998. "Building Customer Franchise—A Paradigm for Customer Partnering." *Monash Mt Eliza Business Review* 1, no. 2: 72–81.

A Human Resource Perspective on Intellectual Capital

Ulf Johanson

Mälardalen University and Uppsala University

Introduction

Resources and capabilities related to people are often referred to in the managerial context as *human capital* (HC), and HC has always been at the center of organizational performance. As the primary source of production in our economy shifted from physical to intellectual capital (IC), the interest of how HC as a part of IC contributes to the value creation of organizations gradually increased over the last 40 years.

The fact that under current accounting rules, investments in traditional physical assets are depreciated over time and most investments in HC are expensed immediately makes it difficult for firms, which are under pressure to deliver short-term financial success, to justify investments in human capital. These pressures led many firms to take a short-term view and downsize. However, research has shown that this often has detrimental effects in the long run (Morris, Cascio, and Young 1999).

Various attempts have been made to improve our understanding of how HC contributes to organizational performance. This chapter discusses the various approaches introduced to improve our understanding of HC. First, a brief section discusses the meaning of HC, and then the development of tools such as human resource accounting and HR scorecards are outlined. Subsequently, two problems are raised: the measurement trap and the conflicting interests. Then, practical examples are provided about how companies addressed the issue of managing their HC. The chapter concludes with a look into the future.

What Do We Mean by Human Capital?

Human capital is often defined as part of intellectual capital (IC) or intangible resources of firms. Skandia, for example, divided intellectual capital into human capital and all other intangible values. The latter were subdivided into structural capital, composed of customer capital and organizational capital. A frequently used method to classify intellectual capital is to split it into human capital, structural capital, and relational capital. However, many believe that HC is the most-important intangible resource of firms. Guy Ahonen (2000) emphasizes that human capital is, in fact, the only generative intangible and, therefore, the central element of IC.

The importance of HC as an IC category is also emphasized elsewhere. For example when testing the Meritum[1] guidelines on managing and reporting IC in Europe, HC was found to be one of the two key reasons for measuring and reporting IC (Meritum 2002). Furthermore, almost 90 percent of Danish public organizations that produced IC reports stated that the main reason for working with IC statements was to demonstrate the importance of their human assets (Thorbjörnsen et al. 2003). Roslender and Fincham (2003) also argue that HC is the most-important category of IC, as people provide business with their competence, deliver customer relations, and are the source of intellectual property.

However, IC is more than HC or the sum of the human, structural, and relational resources of the firm. IC is about how to let the knowledge of a firm work for it and have it create value (Chaminade and Roberts 2003). This can be achieved by creating the right connectivity between human, structural, and relational resources through the appropriate activities. The productivity of one resource may be influenced by the investment into another resource. From experience with the IC concept in Danish firms, Bukh (2003) concludes that IC is about the complement among different IC categories.

Most commentators agree on the definition of *human capital* (Roslender and Fincham 2004). It is usually related to competence of employees, which includes the knowledge, skills, experiences, and abilities of people (Meritum 2002, p. 63). Some HC can be unique to the individual, whereas other HC (Human Capital) may be generic. Examples include innovation capacity, creativity, know-how and previous experience, teamwork capacity, employee flexibility, tolerance for ambiguity, motivation, satisfaction, learning capacity, loyalty, and formal training and education. One interesting addition to HC is the health of individuals (Ahonen 2000). The proposal originates from Finland, where (as in Sweden) health issues and working environment are sometimes linked to the IC concept (Hussi 2003).

Human Capital in Organizations

One way of dealing with human capital in organizations is to include it in the balance sheet or improve the specification of HC costs in the profit and loss account. One rationale behind this is that firms are driven by routines (Johanson, Mårtenson, and Skoog 2001a, 2001b; Nelson and Winter 1982) and accounting approaches constitute an important routine in most companies. This also means that traditional accounting procedures influence habits and behavior in organizations. In this respect, accounting rituals can be powerful enablers or barriers of change. The fact that accounting figures are normally discussed as the first point on the agenda at many management meetings means that traditional financial performance is perceived to be the top, if not the only, priority. At the same time, people have argued that putting HC measures onto the balance sheet or in the profit and loss account provides an opportunity to influence what is discussed in organizations.

The Swedish Work Environment Commission picked up on this at the end of the 1980s and suggested a legal requirement for organizations to disclose human resource costing and accounting information in their profit and loss account. The general idea

---

[1] Meritum was a European research project in 1998–2001. Nine universities addressed different management control and capital market issues related to intangibles. At the end of the project, IC guidelines for managing and reporting intangibles were proposed to the European Commission.

was to increase the awareness of the importance of HC and improve the working environment. Also, in Finland, the government encourages organizations to publish human resource reports to improve working conditions. The European Commission provides another example. It proposed in 1995 that training investments be put on the balance sheet to promote training and education in member countries (European Commission 1995).

In most organizations, money is the common unifying and integrating language. To obtain change, the old language of accounting and money needs be filled with new content. The objective of concepts such as human resource accounting was to address these issues and quantify the economic value of people to the organization (Sackmann, Flamholz, and Bullen 1989). Human resource accounting (HRA) was introduced in the 1960s (e.g., Hermansson 1964; Brummet, Flamholtz, and Pyle 1968) and triggered an ongoing debate on how and whether to value humans and their contribution to organizational performance. At the same time, utility analysis (UA) models for estimating the financial value of employees were developed (e.g., Cronbach and Glaser 1965; Naylor and Shine 1965). Many other concepts have been suggested since then, including human resource costing and accounting (HRCA), which brings together HRA, UA, and cost-benefit analysis of human resources (Gröjer and Johanson 1996).

In the 1980s, at the height of interest and experimentation with HRCA in Sweden, a group of practitioners wrote a book, *The Invisible Balance Sheet* (Sveiby et al. 1989). They borrowed the balance sheet as a metaphor but argued for nonfinancial measures of human, structure, and market capital. Karl Erik Sveiby later proposed "the intangible assets monitor," which suggests indicators reflecting growth and renewal, efficiency and stability in the areas of customers (external structure), organization (internal structure), and employees (competence) (Sveiby 1997). In 1986, the newly appointed managing director of the Swedish insurance company Skandia initiated a process to develop tools for visualizing, measuring, and managing intangible values (Roy 2003). In 1991, he appointed Leif Edvinsson director of intellectual capital, who subsequently, inspired by the balanced scorecard concept (Kaplan and Norton 1992), launched the Skandia Navigator. This model takes its structure from the balanced scorecard but emphasizes the importance of HC, placing it at the center of organizational performance.

In 2001, Becker, Huselid, and Ulrich introduced the HR scorecard. Using the four perspectives of the balanced scorecard (finance, customers, internal processes, and learning and growth), the HR scorecard is a tool to link people with strategy and performance. The authors write that the most potent action HR managers can take to ensure their strategic contribution is to develop a measurement system that convincingly showcases the impact of human resources on business performance (Becker et al. 2001, p. 4). The authors claim that causally linking people and their activities to strategic objectives enables us to understand how HC creates value.

Over the past 20 years, numerous projects and experiments have taken place in private and public organizations. Some of these were inspired by HRCA, whereas others were influenced by the balanced scorecard, the Skandia Navigator, or the invisible balance sheet. Many firms started their work without necessarily following any of the proposed approaches but with the same objective: to develop tools for measuring and managing HC in accordance with the organization's strategy.

The Measurement Trap

Cristina Chaminade and Hanno Roberts (2003) proposed that the original discussion about IC as the difference between market and book value (Stewart 1997; Roy

2003) reinforced a conceptual ownership by the finance and accounting function. They hold that the links between IC and accounting might lead to an excessive focus on measurement issues instead of management processes. Roslender and Fincham argue that IC is often about equipping accountancy with a new kind of language, thereby responding to an occupational crisis of perceived irrelevance (Roslender and Fincham 2003). Pfeffer (1997) also attacked the focus on accounting and measurement in "Pitfalls on the Road to Measurement: The Dangerous Liaison of Human Resources with the Ideas of Accounting and Finance." He argues that the low-status of Human Resources Departments makes the measurement task so attractive.

HRA has been criticized (e.g., Scarpello and Theeke 1989) for the lacking efforts to develop valid, reliable measures. HRA has also been criticized for not focusing on the real concern of HRA, outcomes and values. In general, the HRA and UA literature is very measurement oriented. However, Flamholtz (1985) argues that HRA has been misunderstood. HRA is not just a technique for putting people on the balance sheet or demonstrating the costs of human resources. The aim of HRA is to obtain a change in behavior (Flamholtz 1985). Flamholtz suggests that HRA represents both a paradigm (a way of looking at human resource decisions and issues) and a set of measures for quantifying the effects of human resource management strategies on the cost and value of people as organizational resources (Flamholtz 1999). Grounded in behavioral accounting, Gröjer and Johanson (1996) argue that there is a conflict between a focus on measurement and influencing behavior. If the purpose of HRCA is to influence change, then the emphasis should be on affecting behavior. This is to say that, in spite of an original idea that affecting behavior exceeds the importance of measurement preciseness, HRCA seems to have fallen into the measurement trap.

Conflicting Interests

In spite of initial enthusiasm, there is significant hesitation to implement concepts such as HRCA (Johanson 1999). Even after decades of experience, these concepts are far from accepted (Gröjer and Johanson 1998). In addition, there are different suggestions on how to use concepts such as HRA. Some people advocate using the concepts internally within the firm, whereas others propose external publication. The reason for this may be in the conflicting agendas of those interested in the subject. Some may have a management control interest (affecting behavior from a company board perspective) or a capital market interest (valuing the firm from a shareholder perspective), others may have an accounting interest (a precise reproduction of the firm), and still others, a quality of working life interest (obtaining change from a workers perspective).

Ethical considerations may also cause hesitation to apply HRCA. There is a risk that putting a price on people may make human beings substitutable to other forms of capital. Consequently, many investigators argue against the use of HRCA on ethical grounds. Paradoxically, other investigators express approval of HRCA for the very same reasons. Schuller (1997, p. 5) states that the human capital concept is an immensely powerful analytical notion, "but it is time to ask whether it may have achieved, at least implicitly, a dominance which partially undermines its contemporary utility." Furthermore, he argues that the more the language of human capital is accepted, the more difficult it will be to justify, say, learning activities, which fail to show a visible return. Roslender and Fincham (2004) hold that talking about human capital is to misdesignate human beings.

In a number of Swedish case studies, Hällsten (1997) investigated whether the implementation of a HRCA way of thinking improved working conditions from an ethical standpoint. Although single examples could be found, the author warns that if the utility assumption underlying HRCA is strained, organizations might become even more instrumental and hence come into conflict with ethical values. Is there any future for a concept aspiring to reveal the importance of humans for the firm's value creation if humans are looked upon as just another form of capital, interchangeable with other forms of capital? As Holmgren (1998) points out, this controversy mirrors two ethical standpoints: Those arguing against HRCA take a deontological viewpoint, while those in favor of HRCA take a teleological position. These two points of view can never reach a settlement. In spite of what different proponents might argue, HRCA has often been interpreted as a model that looks upon the firm as a profit-maximizing organization acting on a foundation of rational decision making for the sake of its owners.

One basic conflict could be identified with respect to whether the HC project concerns discovering an objective reality or constructing reality. Those in favor of the former approach hold that a true representation of HC is an important, urgent task. Valid and reliable measures are needed. However, advocates of the latter view argue that most of the HC issues can never be interpreted in any other way than as constructs of reality. Closely linked to these conflicting standpoints is the issue of whether HC project are concerned primarily with determining value (mostly financial) or mobilizing change.

People interested in HC include researchers (within different areas, such as accounting, strategy, human resource management), consultants, senior executives, Human Resource Departments, Accounting Departments, business policy representatives, investors, banks, financial analysts, auditors, and labor unions. When organizations attempt to construct HC reports, they often think of using the statement for communication with a variety of stakeholders (Thorbjörnsen et al. 2003). Will it ever be possible to develop models that can fulfill the demands of all these conflicting parties?

State of the Art: Case Study Examples

Many firms, especially in Scandinavia, experimented with approaches for measuring and reporting HC. The following three examples are outlines of organizations managing their HC.

NCC, a Swedish construction firm with about 20,000 employees in northern Europe started its work on measuring and managing HC almost 15 years ago (Johanson et al. 2001a, 2001b) when the company developed its human capital index. This index is not reported externally but used as an internal communication tool. The external communication is a small section in their annual report. Internally, the communication of the human capital index takes place using a number of Power Point slides together with verbal dissemination.

The basic source of information is an annual human capital questionnaire, which is distributed to all employees. The insights gained from the data are then used for continuous internal reporting, performing evaluations, creating attention and motivation, encouraging commitment, as well as accomplishing follow-ups. Johanson et al. (2001b) conclude that the HC index routine is well integrated in the management control process. Statistical analysis, benchmarking activities, dialogue among managers, and salary bonuses and contracts support this integration, all or part of which is closely aligned with the HC index. The salary bonus for the managers depends not only on profitability but also on the HC index. Every single HC indicator has its owner

Figure 7.1

Causal link between HC and performance or profitability at NCC.

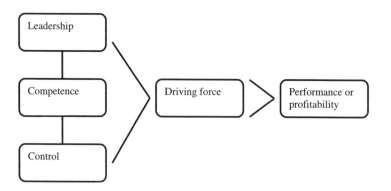

and is evaluated in a dialogue between each manager and his or her superior or sub-ordinates. This evaluation results in a performance contract, which is then followed up and assessed in regular intervals. The use of the HC questionnaire in itself is also subject to a follow-up. Response rates on the attitude survey vary between different years and different departments (normally between 80 and 90%). Follow-up studies have shown that the response rate correlates with the management actions based in the HC index. This indicates that people are more happy to complete the HC index if they feel it is used to take action.

The general aim of the HC system is to support management and, as a result, increase profitability. The picture often used to portray how top management believes that the individual employee's construction of leadership, competence, and control is linked to company performance is depicted in Figure 7.1. This picture reveals casual thinking of HC as an input and performance or profitability as an outcome.

In this firm, the enabling of HC includes leadership, competence, and control. These enablers affect the driving force or "energy of employees at work." This active force is a part of the employee performance, which also comprises quality, customer sensibility, and recommending the enterprise as an employer. The diagram reveals not only an order among the different categories of intangibles but also a logic of action. Almost every year, this hypothesis of correlation among different items in the diagram is subject to a statistical test. The firm holds that the correlation among different items is extremely high. However, the exact measures are not what is important. This frequently used picture rather tells a story to the managers about what is important to address to mobilize the individuals' driving force and, as a result, the performance and profitability of the company (Johanson et al. 2001a).

Another example is Nokian Tyres in Finland (Nordic Industrial Fund 2001, pp. 60–61). This company publishes an annual human resource report with the following structure: introduction, human resource income statement, personnel structure, knowledge and work ability, internal relations, and external relations (see Table 7.1).

Innovation and growth are important for this company, and it believes that good internal relations are a key driver for this. Internal relations include the satisfaction levels of employees, trust, and culture. To measure internal relations, Nokian Tyres plc (Public Company) implemented a so-called daily weather report, a kind of exit poll

Table 7.1

Human Resource Report, Nokian Tyres	
Section	**Items and Indicators**
Introduction	Business and personnel strategy
Human resource income statement	Personnel cost structure, including training and development, sickness and accidents, turnover and vacation Sustainable development overview
Personnel structure	Number of employees Permanent and temporary employed Employee turnover Demography Seniority
Knowledge and work ability	Life-long learning Teams Education level The management Occupational health and safety
Internal relations	Employee satisfaction Internal customership Compensation and reward system Employee participation Process and product initiatives Development projects and experiments
External relations	Customer satisfaction University and institutional cooperation

indicating daily employee satisfaction with the company. Management is responsible for keeping up an atmosphere of trust and creativity, which is a precondition for innovation.

By revealing this information, together with the financial information, Nokian Tyres plc wants to focus its management and other personnel on the issues that sustain profit development. The public human resource supplement is used for both informing shareholders and investors about the human assets of the company and as an internal tool for strategic management. The report indicates what is considered important for sustainable success and what the management believes are the critical drivers for success: the welfare of committed and innovative employees.

Another case example is from a Swedish management consulting firm with about 100 employees. In this firm, a balance sheet valuation of competence investments is used to emphasize that continuous competence development is as important as earning money in the short term (Johanson et al. 2001a). This firm included human capital investments, such as training programs, development of new products, software development, and recruitment, in its balance sheet for more than a decade. The managing director estimates the value of the various HC elements. Valuing intangible investments on the balance sheet is a symbol that reveals the significant importance of investing for the future. The aim is not to "objectively" measure something, since the preciseness in this balance sheet valuation is not the critical issue; rather, the message is that the owner appreciates intangible investments for the future as much as he appreciates tangible investments. This message filters down to the employees through the balance sheet valuation routine and external documents. The process of controlling intangibles is completely integrated in the management control process.

Look into the Future

Approaches to manage and measure HC have been very successful in raising awareness, however, as stated in the E*Know-Net report (E*Know-Net 2004), creating action is far more demanding than raising attention.

Approaches such as HRA and HRCA were quickly seen as technical measurement instruments and interpreted as a complex technical control instrument in spite of the original idea as tools to influence peoples behavior (e.g., Flamholtz 1985; Likert 1967; Gröjer and Johanson 1996; and Johanson and Johrén 1993). There has been strong demand for HC measures that are in compliance with the rigid rules of accounting and more precise prescriptions of how to measure aspects of HC. However, too detailed standards prescribing how to measure human behavior always are rejected sooner or later. This is probably what happened to HRA and HRCA. The original idea was forgotten. HRA, UA, HRCA—all fell into the measurement trap. Exact measures of human behavior are impossible, because human behavior, to a great extent, is tacit and not measurable. Roslender and Fincham (2001) question the very idea of HC metrics. They hold that identifying the best portfolio of metrics to uncover reality is naive because reality is socially constructed and, further, "the measurements developed by management, and their accounting cadres, are generally consistent with their interests" (ibid., p. 393). This leads us to the next dilemma. Who is actually interested in HC reports?

The demands from different and conflicting interests are high. Some propose that HC and IC models should provide detailed information, such as a set of well-defined indicators, whereas others believe that there is no need for such detailed information. The conflicting interests and ethical tensions are more demanding and need further elaboration. Roslender and Fincham (2004) propose human capital accounts to be separate from accounting for intellectual assets. The two forms of accounts are suggested to be interlocking but not totally integrated. The IC self-accounts (i.e., personal accounts from employees) are supposed to express how the employees experience the process of value creation. However, Roslender and Fincham suggest narratives as the format for these reports rather than a statement revealing numbers, trends, costs, or targets. Another possible trajectory to overcome the conflicting interests could be to develop HC and IC models based on a position analysis, that is, considering the different stakeholder interests and their power positions. Söderbaum (2004) states that "position analysis" is a way of illuminating an issue from different perspectives instead of trying to solve an issue using a one-dimensional numerical model.

The conflicting interest and the measurement traps might be overcome by the emancipation of Human Resource Departments and HR research. In many organizations, HR fulfills an operational and mainly administrative function, as opposed to playing a role as a strategic partner that understands and enables value creation based on human resources (Becker et al. 2001). What we need is an integrated view of organizational resources and how they interact to create value. At the same time, we need a better understanding of the audience for measures and reports concerning HC. It is hoped that future research will address the issues raised in this chapter. There is a need for an alternative to traditional accounting, at least with respect to the human factor.

References

Ahonen, G. 2000. Generative and Commercially Exploitable Intangible Assets. In: *Classification of intangibles*, ed. J. E. Gröjer and H. Stolowy, pp. 206–214. Paris: HEC School of Management.

Becker, B. E., M. A. Huselid, and D. Ulrich. 2001. *The HR Scorecard*. Boston: Harvard Business School Press.

Brummet, R. L., E. G. Flamholtz, and W. C. Pyle. 1968. "Human Resource Measurement: A Challenge for Accountants." *The Accounting Review* 43: 217–224.

Bukh, P. N. 2003. "The Relevance of Intellectual Capital: A Paradox?" *Accounting, Auditing and Accountability Journal* 16, no 1.

Chaminade, C., and H. Roberts. 2003. "What It Means Is What It Does: A Comparative Analysis of implementing Intellectual Capital in Norway and Spain." *European Accounting Review* 12, no 4.

Cronbach, L. J., and G. C. Glaser. 1965. *Psychological Tests and Personnel Decisions*, 2nd ed. Urbana: University of Illinois Press.

Danish Ministry of Science, Technology and Innovation. 2003. *Intellectual Capital Statements— The New Guidelines*. Copenhagen: Danish Ministry of Science, Technology and Innovation (www.vtu.dk/icaccounts).

E*Know-Net. 2004. *Towards a European Research Agenda on Intangibles, Report to the European Commission*. Brussels: E*Know-Net.

European Commission. 1995. *Teaching and Learning. Towards the Learning Society*. City Luxembourg, Luxembourg: Office for Official Publications of the European Communities.

Flamholtz, E. 1985. *Human Resource Accounting*. Los Angeles: Jossey-Bass Publishers.

———. 1999. *Human Resource Accounting. Advances in Concepts, Methods and Applications*, 3rd ed. London: Kluwer Academic Publishers.

Gröjer, J. E., and U. Johanson. 1996. *Human Resource Costing and Accounting*. Stockholm: Joint Industrial Safety Council.

———. 1998. "Current Development in Human Resource Costing and Accounting: Reality Present—Researchers Absent?" *Accounting, Auditing and Accountability Journal* 11, no 4.

Hällsten, F. 1997. *Personalekonomi och det goda*. [Human Resource Costing and Accounting and the Good Work Place]. BAS, School of Business, Gothenburg University, Gothenburg, Germany.

Hermansson, R. 1964. "Accounting for Human Assets." Occasional paper no 14. Michigan State University, East Lansing.

Holmgren, M. 1998. "HRCA and Ethics." Working paper. Stockholm University, School of Business, Stockholm.

Hussi, T. 2003. "Intellectual Capital and Maintenance of Work Ablity—The Wellbeing Perspective." Discussion paper no. 858. ETLA, Helsinki.

Johanson, U. (1999) "Why the Concept of Human Resource Costing and Accounting Does Not Work." *Personnel Review* 28, no. 1–2.

Johanson, U., and A. Johrén. 1993. *Personalekonomi* [Human Resource Costing and Accounting]. Stockholm: TBV.

Johanson, U., M. Mårtensson, and M. Skoog. 2001a. "Mobilising change by means of the management control of intangibles." *Accounting, Organisation and Society* 26, nos. 7–8: 715–733.

———. 2001b. Measuring to Understand Intangible Performance Drivers. *European Accounting Review* 10, no. 3: 1–31.

Kaplan, R. S., and D. P. Norton. 1992. "The Balanced Scorecard—Measures That Drive Performance." *Harvard Business Review* 70, no. 1: 71–79.

Likert, R. 1967. *The Human Organisation: Its Management and Value*. New York: McGraw-Hill.

Meritum. 2002. *Guidelines for Managing and Reporting on Intangibles*, ed. L. Cañibano, P. Sanchez, M. Garcia-Ayuso, and C. Chaminade. Madrid: Fundación Airtel Móvil. (www.euknow.net).

Morris, J. R., W. F. Cascio, and C. E. Young. 1999. "Downsizing After All These Years: Questions and Answers about Who Did It, How Many Did It, and Who Benefited from It." *Organizational Dynamics* 27, no. 3 (Winter): 78–87.

Naylor, J. C., and L. C. Shine. 1965. "A Table for Determining the Increase in Mean Criterion Score Obtained by Using a Selection Device." *Journal of Industrial Psychology* 3: 33–42.

Nelson, R. R., and S. G. Winter. 1982. *An Evolutionary Theory of Economic Change.* Cambridge, MA: Harvard University Press.

Nordic Industrial Fund. 2001. *Intellectual Capital. Managing and Reporting.* Oslo: Nordic Industrial Fund.

Pfeffer, J. 1997. "Pitfalls on the Road to Measurement: The Dangerous Liaison of Human Resources with the Ideas of Accounting and Finance." *Human Resource Management* 36, no. 3: 357–365.

Roslender, R., and R. Fincham. 2001. "Thinking Critically about Intellectual Capital Accounting." *Accounting, Auditing and Accountability Journal* 14, no 4: 383–398.

———. 2003. "Intellectual Capital as Management Fashion: A Review and Critique." *European Accounting Review* 12, no. 4.

———. 2004. "Intellectual Capital Accounting in the UK: A Field Study Perspective." *Accounting, Auditing and Accountability Journal* 17, no. 2: 178–209.

Roy, S. 2003. *Navigating in the Knowledge Era. Metaphors and Stories in the Construction of Skandia's Navigator.* School of Business, Stockholm University, Stockholm.

Sackmann, S., E. Flamholz, and M. Bullen. 1989. "Human Resource Accounting: A State of the Art Review." *Journal of Accounting Literature* 8: 235–264.

Scarpello, V., and H. Theeke. 1989. "Human Resource Accounting: A Measured Critique." *Journal of Accounting Literature* 8: 265–280.

Schuller, T. 1997. "Social Capital: A Necessary Environment for Human Capital." Paper presented at the OECD seminar on The Role of Comparative International Indicators of Human Capital Investment in Public Policy.

Söderbaum, P. 2004. "Decision Processes and Decision-Making in Relation to Sustainable Development and Democracy—Where Do We Stand?" *The Journal of Interdisciplinary Economics* 14: 41–60.

Stewart, T. A. 1997. *Intellectual Capital: The New Wealth of Organizations.* New York: Doubleday/Currency.

Sveiby, K. E. 1997. *The New Organizational Wealth. Managing and Measuring Knowledge-Based Assets.* San Francisco: Berret-Koehler Publishers.

——— et al. 1989. *Den osynliga balansräkningen* [The Invisible Balance Sheet]. Affärsvärlden/ Ledarskap, Stockholm.

Thorbjörnsen, S., and J. Mouritsen. 2003. "Accounting for the Employee in the Intellectual Capital Statement." *Journal of Intellectual Capital* 4, no 4: 559–575.

Thorbjörnsen, S., M. R. Johanson, P. N. Bukh, and J. Mouritsen. 2003. "Nye erfaringer med videnregnskaber" [New Experience with Intellectual Capital Statements]. *Offentlig ekonomistyring.* Denmark (June): Internethåndbogen.

An Information Systems Perspective on Intellectual Capital

Joe Peppard
Loughborough University

Introduction

As we have seen in this book, the origins of the intellectual capital (IC) movement can be found in the quest to understand, mobilize, and measure the intangible or "invisible" aspects of organizations. In today's knowledge-based economy, these are seen as the main drivers of value creation. The genesis of this movement can be traced to a number of parallel developments that have, until recently, evolved with seemingly little awareness or recognition of each other. First is the work of economists, particularly Penrose, Coarse, Rumelt, Wernerfelt, and Teece. Fundamental to this stream of research is the proposition of resource heterogeneity across organizations, with marketplace advantage seen as flowing from the creation, ownership, protection, and use of difficult-to-imitate resources, both tangible and intangible. From this work, new theories of the firm have emerged, including resource-based theories (Barney 1991; Wernerfelt 1984) and knowledge-based theories of the firm (Grant 1996b; Spender 1996). A parallel development within this genre has been a focus on intellectual property (IP) and the commercialization of the intellectual endeavors of employees (Teece 1998, 2000b).

However, perhaps the workings of the Konrad group in Sweden, in particular the efforts of Sveiby, led to the birth of today's IC movement. Sveiby recognized the need to measure human capital (endeavor), and he pioneered accounting practices for these intangible assets. In 1989, he reported on the results of the Konrad working group in the book *The Invisible Balance Sheet* (Sveiby 1989), proposing a theory for measuring what he referred to as *knowledge capital* by dividing it into three categories: customer capital, individual capital, and structural capital. The approach was adopted by a large number of Swedish-listed companies, and in 1993, the Swedish Council of Service Industries adopted it as their standard recommendation for annual reports. Edvinsson and Malone (1997) went on to relabel these intangible assets *intellectual capital*, when Edvinsson produced Skandia's first annual report supplement on intellectual capital in 1995.[1] Since then, considerable effort has been exerted within the IC movement on

---

[1] For a detailed description of Skandia AFS, see Marchand, Roos, and Oliver (1995).

designing methods for valuing intangibles (Andriessen 2004; Lev 2001; Roos and Roos 1997). Even the financial markets have recognized the need for financial reporting and disclosure to reflect the value inherent in intangibles and expose their value-creating potential (Blair and Wallman 2001; Mouritsen et al. 2002; Rylander, Jacobsen, and Roos 2000). Yet, researchers such as Roos and Roos (1997) and Peppard and Rylander (2001) have emphasized the importance of not just measurement but also in visualizing the value-creation processes of these intangibles. This quest received added impetus with knowledge management (KM) emerging as an organizational practice during the 1990s.

Since the turn of the century, scholarly writings on intangibles have begun to recognize the existence of other perspectives and now readily draw on the cumulative research base for inspiration. This convergence has been a positive step in the attempt to understand, manage, and report these intangible aspects of organizations. In considering intangibles from different perspectives, a richer appreciation and consideration of the issues may be achieved. Yet, if there is a weakness of the research to date, it is the inadequate understanding it has provided of "resources in action" (Black and Boal 1994; Bowman and Ambrosini 2000; Haanes and Feldstad 2000; Majumdar 1998; Peppard and Rylander 2001): both understanding the process of creating IC and illuminating how IC creates value.

The current chapter focuses on the management of information systems (IS) through the adoption of an IC perspective, seeking particularly to address these latter aspects. References to IS[2] have appeared fleetingly in the IC literature, but it is little discussed or actively considered. Although portrayed as an intangible asset, *how* IS contributes to value creation in an organization has not been explored. IS typically appears in taxonomies of IC, usually under the heading of "organizational" or "structural capital." Yet, beyond this recognition, little attempt has been made to delve into its nature or the process of creating, developing, or deploying this "capital." It should equally be acknowledged that the IS literature makes little reference to developments within the IC movement nor looks to apply findings from the IC perspective to IS management. In this chapter, we integrate both literatures in an attempt to develop insights and suggest how to improve the value that organizations achieve through IS investments.

In adopting an IC perspective and considering IS as IC, the preceding resume of the IC movement points toward three core themes to explore. First is the theme of examining IS as an asset, essentially reflecting on whether IS is an asset and, if so, what makes it so. Second is the theme of considering the valuation of IS assets: If IS is indeed an asset, it should be possible to place a value on it. Third is the theme of viewing IS management as an asset and understanding how IS management practice is embedded in an organization. These three themes provide the structure for this chapter.

To begin, the chapter seeks to establish clarity in the language encountered in the discourse around IS, as this helps highlight the issues to be considered and expose where the IC perspective can provide additional insights. It examines the relationships between information, information systems, technology, and knowledge, as all are central to any dialogue. The chapter then looks at approaches to valuing information and IS. The relationship between human capital and organizational capital and the transformation from human capital to organizational is then developed. The chapter

---

[2] IS is used both as singular and plural.

concludes by considering what insight an IC perspective provides in improving the management of IS and the achievement of business value.

A Context for Intellectual Capital: Information, Systems, and Technology in Organizations

Intellectual capital represents the intangible aspects of an organization. However, this invisibility of IC makes it notoriously difficult to manage. How can something that cannot be seen, touched, or perhaps even "owned" by an organization be managed? While information systems are intangible, through their research IS scholars have shed considerable light on their management; similarly, the IC perspective suggests an alternative lens for exploring IS and IS management than can be found in the contemporary IS literature. Together, both literatures offer the opportunity to advance our understanding of how value is created through IS, how organizations can appropriate this value, and how the realization of this value can be sustained over time.

However, to bring clarity to the discussion, it is important at the outset to make a distinction between the concepts of IS and information technology (IT).[3] Many find difficulty in distinguishing between IS and IT, as technology seems to overwhelm their thinking about the fundamental information system that the technology is to support (Checkland and Holwell 1998). Indeed, systems have always existed in organizations, and only relatively recently have they been automated through the deployment of IT. Because the technology that underpins IS has a visibility—the hardware, servers, cables, routers, data centers, and so forth—generally, this is the aspect that is managed. Indeed, these tangible components can even appear on an organization's balance sheet; this is ironic, as IT has no inherent value.[4] Outside of the technology, IS are not visible to the human eye yet can be fundamental for the performance of organizations.

Essentially, information systems exist in the organization to serve, help, or support people taking action in the real world (Checkland 1981). This "action" is the outcome of decision-making processes. Sometimes, decision making is automated and embedded in an IT-based system, for example, automatically triggering reordering of raw materials when their quantity falls below a specified level or the automatic processing of customers' orders placed via an Internet website. On other occasions, decision making is supported by information provided by the IS: Information is seen as reducing uncertainty (Simon 1960). Therefore, to create a system that effectively supports the organization, it is first necessary to conceptualize that which *is* to be supported (the IS), since the way it is described dictates what would be necessary to serve or support it (the IT) (Checkland 1981). IT is effectively a tool, providing the ability to handle information (capture, process, manipulate, communicate, store, etc.); humans (i.e., employees) must decide on the information-handling facilities they require to support

---

[3] The domain of study of IS involves the investigation of theories and practices related to the social and technological phenomena, which determine the development, use, and effects of information systems in organizations and society (UK Academy of Information Systems, www.ukais.org). Although technology is the immediate enabler of IS, "IS actually is part of the much wider domain of human language and communication . . . [and] IS will remain in a state of continual development and change in response both to technological innovation and to its mutual interaction with human society as a whole" (Mingers 1995).

[4] A substantial body of research suggests little, if any, positive relationship between investment in IT and overall financial performance (Berndt and Malone 1995; Brynjolfsson 1993; David 1990; Markus and Robey 1988; Roach 1987).

the organization both operationally and strategically. Through the IS strategy process, an organization determines the investments that it should make in IS and IT.

This ability of technology to handle information provides organizations novel options for strategy and operations. For example, rethinking information flows in an organization can increase efficiency through reducing transaction costs. New work practices can be established, spans of control increased, and empowerment extended while similarly maintaining control. New organizational forms, such as virtual organizations, are facilitated by IS. Business networks and supply chains can be reconfigured, often leading to the establishment of a virtual value chain, with disintermediation affecting traditional business relationships. The digitization of products and services has seen the deployment of new business models defined entirely by information. Technologies like the Internet can extend the scope of an organization's operations.

This central role of information has long been recognized, such that it has been portrayed as a corporate asset (Glazer 1998; KPMG/IMPACT 1994; Oppenheim, Stenson, and Wilson 2003; Porter and Miller 1985) with the practice of information resource management (IRM) or information asset management (IAM) emerging in organizations over the years. This practice is typically concerned with the stewardship of an organization's information resources, focusing on their accuracy, accessibility, protection, and security. The IS/IT strategy determines *how* the information is to be used and the IT deployed.

In deploying IT-based systems, the universal adoption of technical standards by was vendors and manufacturers and the very significant reduction in price-performance has reduced barriers to access to technology and ensured that that the same technology resource is available to all competing firms in an industry. As already noted, the value of IT is not in its possession; if it was, all that would be required is for an organization to purchase it. Yet, the wide experience that organizations have with IT and the high failure rate of IT implementations[5] serves only to highlight that some companies are better able to leverage it than others. Keen (1993) suggests this is due to a "management difference," drawing attention to the fact that some management teams are better able to leverage IT than others. This assertion has been supported by Mata et al. (1995) who concluded that "[o]nly IT management skills are likely to be the a source of sustainable competitive advantage (SCA)." More recently, Weill and Ross (2004) concluded that "[a]n effective IT governance structure is the single most important predictor of getting value from IT."

This "management difference" thesis and the more recent focus on IT governance highlights the criticality of decision making in IS success; perhaps more significantly, it illustrates that success has little to do with "technical wizardry" (Dvorak et al. 1997). It is widely acknowledged that many decisions that may have traditionally fallen within the remit of IT management must become the responsibility of non-IT managers (Ross and Weill 2002). Governance structures provide a framework for coherence in decision making—management is the making of decisions—and are a direct requirement of the devolution of IS decision making out of a central IS function to local IT units and indeed out of the remit of IT altogether.

---

[5] It is worth pointing out that the overwhelming body of evidence suggests that implementations fail not for technological reasons but organizational, managerial, and people-related reasons (Clegg et al. 1997; McDonagh, 2001).

Decision making is the "thinking" aspect of IS management. Decisions that are made can initiate activities, such as building systems; determining user requirements; purchasing hardware, software, and services; and running computer operations and data centers. These activities represent the "doing" aspect of IS management; this is traditionally where much of the IS research is to be found. A third dimension to consider is that, in addition to investing and building IT-based systems, organizations must excel in "collecting, organizing and maintaining information, and with getting their people to embrace the right behaviors and values for working with information" (Marchand et al. 2000). This "using" aspect signifies that if information, the raison d'être of IS, is not used, then no value flows to the organization. This triumvirate of thinking, doing, and using are interdependent and central to the effective management of IS.

Thinking, doing, and using all require the application of the knowledge and skills of employees. Many aspects of "doing" are predetermined by "thinking" that previously took place in the organization. For example, policies, such as those governing IT security or software development, represent the outcomes of decisions already made; "doing" involves the execution of these decisions. "Using" information effectively similarly requires the application of knowledge, both domain knowledge and knowledge of how to use the information.

Therefore, the ability to manage IS is a knowledge-based activity, having little to do with technology. This capability is to be found in the very fabric of the organization. This is its intellectual capital. The manifestation of this capability is crucially dependent on people and their ability to deploy their knowledge and skills. Therefore, to successfully deliver business value from IT investments, the challenge for organizations is to harness knowledge. This knowledge is dispersed throughout the organization and not solely located in the IS function—this points to the folly of attempting to manage IS from within a box on an organization chart.[6] Often, IT and non-IT specialists must come together and apply their knowledge. Hence, success with IS depends on integrating and coordinating knowledge from across the organization. As no one person has responsibility for all the required knowledge and thus the people providing the knowledge, this becomes the key challenge in IS management. It also provides an explanation as to why organizations are very poor at delivering business value from IT investments. In the language of IC, the organization requires the capacity to convert human capital into organizational capital. This is its IS capability, and we address this requirement later in the chapter.

Information, Knowledge, and Information Systems

The relationship between data, information, and knowledge has been widely debated, particularly in recent years with the emergence of knowledge management as a managerial practice. In an organizational context, data are most usefully described as "structured records of transactions" (Davenport and Prusak 1998 and can be defined as a set of discrete, objective facts about events. While information is based on data, it is not based on data alone. "Information is a message, usually in the form of a document or an audible or visible communication" (Davenport and Prusak 1998). Information

---

[6] In fact, this analysis suggest that the concept of an IS function as currently portrayed in the research literature needs to be reconceptualized. See Peppard (2004) for a detailed assessment of this point.

that is communicated takes into account both the *intention* of the sender and the *expectations* of the receiver.[7] As such, it cannot be viewed as an independent entity. While knowledge and information can be equally difficult to distinguish, both involve more human participation than the raw data on which they are partly based. If information is data that has been given structure, knowledge is information that has been given meaning. In essence, knowledge is information interpreted by individuals and given a context. Thus, knowledge is the result of a dynamic human process, in which humans justify personal information produced or sustain beliefs as part of an aspiration for the "truth" (Nonaka 1994; Seely Brown and Duguid 2000) and can be portrayed as information combined with experience, content, interpretation, and reflection (Davenport, DeLong, and Beers 1998). The interpretation of information a person receives is relative to what he or she already knows (Nonaka 1994); knowledge is intensely personal, embodied in people (Blackler 1995) and can be tacit (Polanyi 1966). It is suggested that a person cannot grasp the meaning of information about his or her environment without some frame of value judgment. So, for knowledge to be created from information, a belief system is necessary, as is a process of converting and interpreting information to produce knowledge.

As organizations increasingly look to proactively manage knowledge, Davenport and Marchand (2000) pose the question as to whether *knowledge management* (KM) is "just good information management." They argue that KM contains a large component of information management and much of what passes for the former is actually the latter. Nonaka, Toyama, and Konno (2000) contend that the "knowledge management" academics and business people talk about often means just "information management," although Teece (2000a) notes that the latter can certainly assist the former. However, true KM goes well beyond information management.

Additionally, one argument calls KM (i.e., actively managing knowledge) a contradiction in terms, being a hangover from an industrial era when control modes of thinking were dominant (Denning 2000). If knowledge is information combined with experience, context, interpretation, and reflection, the use of the term *KM*, suggesting that knowledge can be managed, is to misunderstand the very personal and often tacit nature of knowledge. Therefore, formalized approaches may not mirror the realities of knowledge in organizations where knowledge is distributed among people and artifacts and socially embedded in ongoing practice (Cook and Seeley Brown 1999; Lave and Wenger 1991; Orlikowski 2002). There is a suggestion that *only* the "context" and conditions surrounding knowledge can be managed (Lave and Wenger 1991; Wenger and Snyder 2000). This is essentially the rationale behind the concept of communities of practice (COPs). Some practitioners have even suggested that knowledge *sharing* is a better description than knowledge *managing*, while others prefer *learning*, as a key challenge in implementing KM is making sense and interpretation.

If knowledge is personal and embodied in people, it cannot be transferred or imitated by transmitting information—we already argued that knowledge is distinct from information. The technology used by organizations to manage knowledge (e.g., intranets, extranets, portals, document management systems) therefore contains codified "knowledge," not knowledge as articulated previously but really information (Zack 1999). As McDermott (1999) cautions, the "great trap in knowledge management is using information management tools to design knowledge management

---

[7] This analysis is drawn from the work of Shannon and Weaver (1949), who developed a mathematical theory of communication.

systems" (p. 104). This is why IT can never be the answer to knowledge management. Walsham (2001) argues that IT-based systems used to support KM can be of benefit only if used to support the development and communication of meaning. *Knowing* is a human act, whereas knowledge is the residue of thinking. To *know* a topic or a discipline is not just to possess information about it, it is the very human ability to *use* that information.

Thus, while information plays a role in knowing, it is worth highlighting that many organizations are plagued by poor-quality information, which can have a negative impact on knowledge-based activities. Research (Redman 1995, 1998) indicates that

- Many managers are unaware of the quality of information they use and often mistakenly assume that because it is "on the computer," it is accurate.
- At an operational level, poor information leads directly to customer dissatisfaction and increased cost. Costs are increased as time and other resources are spent detecting and correcting errors.
- Poor information quality can result in subtle and indirect effects. For example, significant mistrust can ensue when the information that is entered from one part of the business, say, order entry, and used by another, perhaps customer billing, is unreliable.
- Inaccurate information makes just-in-time manufacturing and self-managed work teams infeasible. The right information needs to be at the right place at the right time. To illustrate the severity of this problem, one manufacturer was still allowing customers, via its website, to purchase products it no longer produced.
- Poor information in financial and other management systems means that managers cannot effectively implement business strategies. Decisions are no better than the information on which they are based.
- The Internet has seen an explosion in the volume of information available to employees. This information is of varying quality, and a challenge that organizations face today is assessing this quality. Information from the Net is not subject to any review standards, policies, or quality-control procedures.

Figure 8.1 illustrates the relationships among data, information, knowledge, action, and business results and provides a way to view two contrasting perspectives of knowledge, its management and the use of IT. Viewed from the left, it draws on an information theoretic perspective, where knowledge is conceptualized in organizations as something "out there" to be created, stored, retrieved, and reused. Managing knowledge is portrayed as processing data and the provision of information. Such codified knowledge is captured in corporate databases and other knowledge repositories. This perspective usually results in the codification and transfer of "best practice" in organizations: IT has a key role to play. There is a relationship between the codification of knowledge and the costs of transfer. The more knowledge and experience has been codified, the more economically it can be transferred.

Viewing the model from right to left provides an alternative view. Knowledge is seen as being inherently "personal" and very often tacit and socially embedded in organizational practices. It views knowledge sharing and creation as a social process and notes that knowledge can never be managed directly, particularly the creation of knowledge. Information plays a role, but within a wider social context. The focus of KM is on business results and the actions and knowledge required to achieve these results. Key questions to address include these: What knowledge do you want to work with? Where is it? What do you want to do with it? What would you gain if you did this? It may be that no IT-based system will result from the analysis.

Figure 8.1

Information, knowledge, and action: two contrasting perspectives.

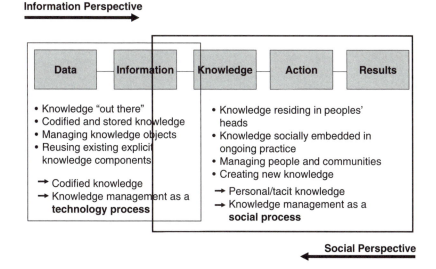

Information Perspective

| Data | Information | Knowledge | Action | Results |

- Knowledge "out there"
- Codified and stored knowledge
- Managing knowledge objects
- Reusing existing explicit knowledge components

→ Codified knowledge
→ Knowledge management as a **technology process**

- Knowledge residing in peoples' heads
- Knowledge socially embedded in ongoing practice
- Managing people and communities
- Creating new knowledge

→ Personal/tacit knowledge
→ Knowledge management as a **social process**

Social Perspective

Valuing Information, Information Systems, and IS Management

As noted in the introduction, the origins of today's IC movement can be found in the quest to value intangible assets. If, as has been suggested, information and information systems are corporate assets, it should be possible to place some value on them. However, given their intangible nature, this has proven a challenging task, with a complex set of issue to address. In accounting, the definition of an *asset* is "rights or other access to future economic benefits controlled by an entity as a result of past transactions or events" (Financial Accounting Board 2001 Goodwill and Intangible Assets, Statement of financial accounting standard, no 141, CT: FASB). Using this definition, an information system could be recognized as an asset because it gives "rights or other access to future economic benefits," for example, in licensing agreements for software that has been developed. While this may be obvious for such agreements, in other situations, it may not be so obvious. Information can also be recognized as an asset in accounting terms, even if it is not owned by the organization, if it can be shown to give future benefits (Davis, Paterson, and Wilson 1998).

Focusing first on information, its characteristics are unlike other assets an organization has at its disposal. Its properties are different, it behaves differently from physical assets, and it does not conform to the economic principles on which the accounting framework is based. Consequently, accounting rules and regulations are inadequate in dealing with information. For example, information is considered too volatile and its value too difficult to determine for it to be recognized as an asset in accounting terms; therefore, it appears in financial statements only if it is acquired, and even then it is shown merely as a cost. In determining the value of information, the following variables are particularly important:

- *Specificity of time.* Information can have a time dimension to it, either in its acquisition or the need to use it within a certain time frame to be of value. For example, information about a customer's first impression of a product or the magnitude of an earthquake has to be captured when it occurs or the opportunity to register the information is lost forever. This information is thus time specific *in acquisition*. Information that loses its value if it is not used directly after it is available is time specific *in use* (Sampler 1998). Just consider how economic and political information can influence a company's share prices. Time specificity is also relevant for other types of information that organizations use, such as sales statistics for seasonal or fashion-sensitive goods.

- *Specificity of knowledge.* Information can require a certain degree of knowledge from the person that is to acquire or put the information to some use. For example, many market research organizations employ students to collect survey information. They are equipped with questionnaires and prompts and given some basic training. A certain level of knowledge is therefore required *to acquire* this information. However, additional knowledge is generally required *to use* this information (Sampler 1998). To analyze and interpret the survey information, knowledge possessed only by statisticians and sociologists is required. Similarly, many technical help desks are staffed by employees who are not engineers but answer customer calls and record information about faults reported; scripts are often used to guide them through the questions to ask customers who phone in. Engineering knowledge, however, is usually required to assess and evaluate this information and determine possible solutions as well as ensure that these problems are recognized and corrected in later versions of the product.

- *Situation of use.* The situation, or context, of the user when the information is perceived, processed, and assimilated significantly affects the understanding and appreciation of the information product. The environment within which information is used has significant importance for the value of information to the user. This includes everything from the user's state of mind when the information is received to the physical environment and the device used to access or display the information. Returning to the example of share prices for trading, which is highly time specific information, it does not necessarily follow that the information lacks value when it is "old." In another situation or with different objectives, 10-year-old information could be of greater value than information from today, for example, a researcher studying long-term stock price trends.

Information also has a multiplicative quality. That is, combining one type of information with another can increase the value of both. For example, information about market and industry trends and specific information about a company are often crucial complements to examining share price trends to make investment decisions.

Yet information in isolation can have little value outside of a specific organizational context. The value of information to an organization is ultimately reflected in how it is used in the organization, the "using" dimension referred to earlier, for example, using customer information to generate additional revenue by attracting new customers; to reduce customer defections; to generate additional revenue from new customers; to reduce advertising, marketing, and sales force costs through better targeting; or to generate additional revenues by customizing products and services to better meet individual customer needs. However, this ability to use information, even similar information, can vary across organizations.

For example, Knox et al. (2003) report on two building societies that implemented a customer relationship management solution from the same software vendor. However, their experiences could not have been more contrasting. In a survey shortly after implementation was complete, the staff at one of the societies considered that the systems had been implemented to get customers out of the branch quicker. Prompts and scripts generated by the system were ignored by frontline staff members, as they did not have confidence in the information provided by the CRM (Customer Relationship Management) system. At the other, the ability to work with information has seen it increase not only customer retention rates but also the average number of products held by customers from 1.2 to over 2. This is startling, considering that they have over 2 million customers and the impact on the bottom line is easy to see. At this society, one in four customer interactions in a branch results in a sale. The ability of their marketing staff to work with information has seen it develop a new customer segmentation strategy, and they continue to refine their propensity to purchase models. A consequence has been that the cost income ratio of marketing campaigns has reduced from 90 pence to less than 20 pence.

An organization's capacity to use information has been referred to as its "information culture" (Marchand 1995). An information culture can be defined as the values, attitudes, and behaviors that influence the way employees at all levels in the organization sense, collect, organize, process, communicate, and use information. Marchand (1995) identified four common information cultures that can be found in organizations today:

- *Functional culture.* Managers use information as a means of exercising influence or power over others.
- *Sharing culture.* Managers and employees trust each other to use information (especially about problems and failures) to improve their performance.
- *Inquiring culture.* Managers and employees search for better information to understand the future and ways of changing what they do to align themselves with future trends and directions.
- *Discovery culture.* Managers and employees are open to new insights about crisis and radical changes and seek ways to create competitive opportunities.

Each type of culture influences the way employees use information (their information behavior) and reflects the importance senior management attributes to the use of information in achieving success or avoiding failure. However, establishing an effective information culture can be a challenge. Davenport (1994) captured this point succinctly when he noted that it "must begin by thinking about how people use information—not with how people use machines." Changing a company's information culture requires altering the basic behaviors, attitudes, values, management expectations, and incentives that relate to information. "Changing the technology only reinforces the behaviors that already exist."

Haeckel and Nolan (1993) use the analogy of the airplane pilot "flying by wire" when considering information usage. When pilots fly by wire, they fly informational representations of airplanes. In a similar way, managing by wire is the capacity to run a business by managing its informational representation. Davenport et al. (2001) note that most organizations have not developed the capacity to aggregate, analyze, and use data to make informed decisions that lead to action and generate real business value. From their research, they propose a model that consists of three major elements: context, transformation, and outcomes. *Context* includes the strategic, skill-related, organizational, cultural, technological, and data factors that must be present for an analytic effort to succeed. The *transformation* element is where the data are actually analyzed and used to support a business decision. *Outcomes* are the changes that result from the analysis and decision making.

An additional aspect to consider is that, today, many companies trade information products. Digitization has seen the emergence of products and services defined by information. Examples include software, music, and reports. Bespoke developed software can be "productized" and licensed to other organizations for a fee; therefore, it has a value. This is essentially what software companies, such as Microsoft, Oracle, Software AG, and SAP do, as it represents the intellectual endeavors of employees. However, particular issues affect the valuation of information products:

- *Experience good.* The product or service has to be experienced before value can be assessed.
- *Nonrivalry.* Information can be deployed at the same time in multiple locations and for multiple users. Thus, the law of diminishing returns does not apply to information.
- *Perfect fiduciary.* Information can be perfectly copied and this does not diminish its value.
- *Exchange relationships.* Information exchange does not necessarily equate with traditional models of value exchange; if I pass on information to someone else, the receiver may gain value but I do not necessarily lose value.
- *Movement.* Information can travel almost instantaneously and at trivial cost.
- *Production costs.* Information has large fixed costs but minimal marginal costs.
- *Requirement for complementary assets.* Complementary assets can sometimes be a critical requirement to release the value of some information. This includes everything from other information assets to physical assets (e.g., an MP3 player and software is required to play MP3 files or an Adobe Acrobat Reader is required to read Acrobat files).

Assessing the value of information systems that the organization has no intention of selling is even more problematic. Calculating the replacement cost of any underlying hardware and software is a relatively straightforward procedure. But, this does not capture the *value* they represent to the organization. For example, many financial services institutions depend on systems that were developed in the 1960s and 1970s and fully depreciated. Looking at this issue another way, a starker observation can be made: If these systems were to fail, their business would be severely affected.

Finally, an organization's ability to manage IS, the management difference thesis, also has a value. This ability helps an organization continuously deliver business value through IT. It requires that the organization have the capacity to "think," "do," and "use." These interdependent requirements are fundamental to the expression of the organization's ability to deliver business value through IT. This is its IS capability (Bharadwaj 2000; Peppard and Ward 2004). Calculating the value of this capability is extremely difficult, as it is to be found in the very fabric of the organization and we have little understanding as to its components. Indeed, it is probably easier to recognize if it is *not* present in an organization. In the following section, we explore the IS capability in more detail and examine research attempting to shed some light on its core underpinnings.

Human Capital and Structural Capital: Transforming Knowledge into Action and Value

We already argued that the ability to successfully manage IS is to be found in the very fabric of the organization and represents an aspect of its intellectual capital. The

Figure 8.2

Converting human capital into organizational capital.

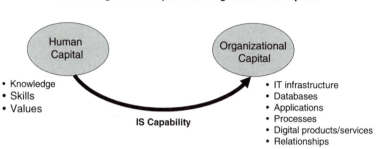

databases, information products and services, IT infrastructure, applications, data centers, and the like that result from building IS are also a component of its intellectual capital. Information itself, the ingredient of IS, is a further part of the organization's intellectual capital. However, the latter two aspects are directly related to the former: Both are created through the deployment of knowledge. For example, architecting the IT infrastructure requires the application of knowledge, and the resulting technical infrastructure represents the embodiment of knowledge.

If, as we argued, IS management is a knowledge-based activity, mobilizing this knowledge becomes the key challenge. It is about having the right people with the right knowledge, then ensuring the integration and coordination of this knowledge. This knowledge is not just technical knowledge but also knowledge from the business; crucially, all this knowledge does not reside solely in the IT function. The fact that this entails individuals from different disciplines and backgrounds, with varied experiences and expectations and who are located in different parts of the organization, coming together and working with each other indicates why research over the years has highlighted the importance of a strong relationship between IS employees and non-IS employees (Peppard and Ward 1999). Knowledge integration demands a close partnership between the IS staff and the business staff at all levels, both in formal processes and informal working relationships.

Figure 8.2 illustrates the relationship between human capital and organizational capital that can be found in the contemporary IC discourse. It shows that through the IS capability, human capital creates organizational capital. Organizational capital can be seen as representing the fruits of the intellectual endeavors of employees. If we consider what may happen if employees leave, the information and information system remains, but the personal knowledge, skills, and relationships are lost. The IS management capacity is thus diminished. Even hiring new employees with the same knowledge and skill base does not guarantee the same results. Successfully managing IS is an intellectual exercise, not a technical endeavor. Given the dependence on people and their knowledge in the creation of organization capital, this aspect proves very difficult to capture and retain in an organization.

We noted that the IS capability represents an organization's ability to continuously achieve business value through IT. Figure 8.3 presents a model describing the IS capability, indicating that it has three components, corresponding to the thinking, doing, and using dimensions introduced earlier: fusing business knowledge and IS knowledge; a flexible, reusable IT platform; and an effective use process.

Figure 8.3

Achieving business value through IS: the IS capability.

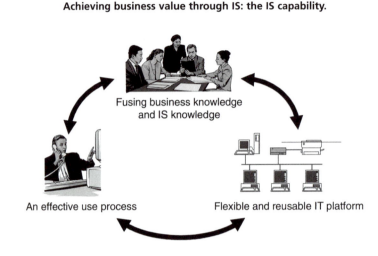

Fusing business knowledge
and IS knowledge

An effective use process   Flexible and reusable IT platform

Fusing IS knowledge and business knowledge is paramount to ensure the conception of strategies involving technological innovation to make appropriate choices from the opportunities available and to implement these strategies quickly and effectively, including managing change. It also requires knowing the extent of change the business can absorb.

A flexible and reusable IT platform provides the technical platform, services, and specialist resources needed to respond quickly to required business changes as well as the capacity to develop innovative IS applications to support new process designs or business initiatives. This infrastructure is the supply-side component of the IS capability. Through the deployment of technical knowledge and skills, some of which may be brought in from third party providers the organization "creates" an IT platform that influences future options and the speed of response but has a degree of permanence attached to it. The IT platform can be viewed as the embodiment of knowledge and skill.

An effective use process links IS/IT assets with value realization through the application of the technology as well as creating an environment conducive to collecting, organizing, and maintaining information, together with embracing the right behaviors for working with information. The use process has two aspects: using the technology and working with information.

Figure 8.4 develops the link between human capital (knowledge and skills resident in people) and the ultimate manifestation of the IS capability (organizational capital). The model has three levels: the resource level (essentially employees), the organizing level (how these resources are organized and structured, incentive schemes and management practices), and the enterprise level (where the capability is ultimately exhibited).[8]

---

[8] The intellectual inheritance of this model is to be found in resource-based theory (RBT) (Barney 1991; Wernerfelt 1984). A fuller description and background to this model can be found in Peppard and Ward (2004).

Figure 8.4

IS management: linking human capital and organizational capital.

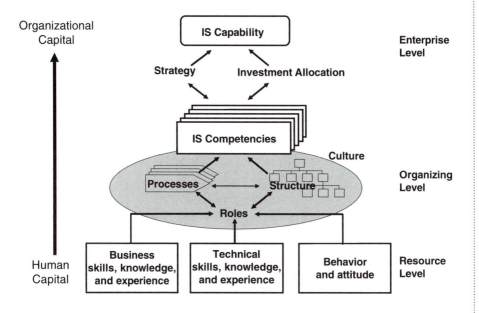

The model suggests that the IS capability is underpinned by a set of competencies, with each contributing toward the manifestation of the IS capability. These competencies fall into six domains: strategy development, defining the IS contribution, defining the IT capability, exploitation of information and IT services, delivering solutions, and supplying human and technical resources (Peppard et al. 2000). These competence domains are defined in Table 8.1.

The competencies[9] in each of these domains represent the integration and coordination of knowledge and skills from individuals located right across the organization. This integration and coordination takes place in organizational processes as employees "work" together through interaction and dialogue. One way of viewing this is to recognize that people play a variety of different roles in an organization. In performing these roles, they bring to bear their knowledge, skills, and experiences. Behaviors and attitudes are equally important in this process as knowledge creation and sharing is a social process.

At an organizing level, the proper structures, incentives, and management can help in the deployment and use of knowledge. While knowledge assets are grounded in the experience and expertise of individuals, organizations provide the physical, social, and resource allocation structure so that knowledge can be shaped into these competencies. How these competences are configured and deployed dramatically shapes the outcomes.

---

[9] Research by Peppard et al. (2000) identified 26 IS competencies.

Table 8.1

Domains of IS Strategy Development	
Strategy development	The ability to identify and evaluate the implications of IT-based opportunities as an integral part of business strategy formulation and define the role of IS/IT in the organization
Defining the IS contribution	The ability to translate the business strategy into processes, information, and systems investments and change plans that match the business priorities
Defining the IT capability	The ability to translate the business strategy into long-term information architectures, technology infrastructure, and resource plans that enable the implementation of the strategy
Exploitation of information and IT services	The ability to maximize the benefits realized from the implementation of IS/IT investments through effective use of information, applications, and IT services
Delivering solutions	The ability to deploy resources to develop, implement, and operate IS/IT business solutions that exploit the capabilities of the technology
Supplying human and technical resources	The ability to create and maintain an appropriate and adaptable information technology and application supply chain and resource capacity

IS competencies are intangible; in fact they can be seen as the emergent properties of business processes. They are typically supported by routines, not dependent on a single individual, and generally do not reside inside any one particular business function. Competencies cannot be bought and sold but must be developed. Even understanding all the relevant routines that support a particular competence may not be transparent. Many routines are tacit (Nelson and Winter 1982).

Organizational culture also plays a prominent role.[10] It facilitates the integration of knowledge from different areas of the business; indeed, the "cultural gap" between IT professionals and the rest of the organization has long been recognized (Ward and Peppard 1996). If, for example, the relationship between business management and IT management is strained, it is likely to be very difficult to achieve the synergies necessary to deploy their respective knowledge bases in creating a competence. If the culture is such that decisions about IS, which should be made by business management, are delegated to the IS professionals, then the outcome is likely to be suboptimal. The culture represents the unique environment that knowledge integration takes place in, what has been referred to as its *ba* (Nonaka and Konna 1998).

Conclusion

The IC perspective provides an emerging viewpoint in the quest to understand, mobilize, and measure the intangible aspects of an organization. An organization's IS

---

[10] Barney (1986) suggests that culture is a resource. The logic of this paper suggests that it is an enabling layer in the manifestation of competencies.

are invisible, and in adopting an IC perspective, an alternative lens with which to view IS is provided. In guiding the discourse conducted in this chapter, we draw on three core themes from the IC perspective: considering IS as an asset (including information, information products, and IS management itself), valuing IS, and the mobilization and creation of IS assets. While the former two aspects are well rehearsed in the IC literature, although there are still many issues to address, the latter is less developed.

With this in mind, the concept of an organizational IS capability was introduced and described. This capability is central to both the mobilization and creation of IS assets and represents an organization's ability to continuously deliver business value from its IT investments. It is built around the triumvirate of thinking, doing, and using developed in the chapter. This capability itself is intangible, found in the very fabric of the organization. A model is proposed, linking organizational resources, essentially people and their knowledge, to the ultimate manifestation of this capability. The model indicates that the IS capability is itself underpinned by a set of competencies. These competencies represent the emergent properties of organizational practice, with employees coming together to deploy their knowledge and skills. The proper structures, incentives, and management can help the deployment of organizational knowledge. While knowledge is grounded in the experience and expertise of individuals, the organization provides the physical, social, and resource allocation structure so that knowledge can be shaped into competences. Organizations cannot hope to purchase these IS competencies; they must be developed.

From the analysis, we argue that continuously delivering business value through IT is a knowledge-based activity and has little to do with technology, although technology solutions can represent the embodiment of organizational knowledge. What is crucial is that the knowledge and skills necessary for successfully leveraging value through IT are not located solely in the IS function of an organization. This provides a key reason as to why many organization are disappointed with the value they achieve from their IS investments. The challenge for management is to mobilize the knowledge and skills of employees from across the organization as each of the competencies requires the integration and coordination of knowledge from diverse locations. This has been articulated in the IS literature as the need for a close relationship between IS and business employees. But, this "relationship" merely provides a context in which knowledge integration and coordination can occur.

Given the dependence on IT today and the central role that it can play in competitiveness, all organizations require an IS capability. Although this capability is embedded in the organization, its effects are all too obvious. Poor capability will see disappointment in the return from investments made in IT. The strength or otherwise of the capability must be judged relative to the role of IT in the business and its competitive strategy. The challenge is to build this capability as it represents the transformation of human capital into structural capital.

Acknowledgments

I would like to thank Anna Rylander for her helpful comments on an earlier draft of this chapter.

References

Andriessen, D. 2004. *Making Sense of Intellectual Capital: Designing a Method for the Valuation of Intangibles.* Oxford: Elsevier Butterworth-Heinemann.

Barney, J. B. 1986. "Organisational Culture: Can It Be a Source of Sustained Competitive Advantage?" *Academy of Management Review* 11: 656–665.

———. 1991. "Firm Resources and Sustained Competitive Advantage." *Journal of Management* 17: 99–120.

Berndt, E. R., and T. W. Malone. 1995. "Information Technology and the productivity Paradox: Getting the Question Right." *Economics of Innovation and New Technology* 3: 77–182.

Bharadwaj, A. 2000. "A resource-based perspective on information technology and firm performance: an empirical investigation." *MIS Quarterly* 24 no. 1: 169–196.

Black, J. A., and K. B. Boal. 1994. "Strategic Resources: Traits, Configurations, and Paths to Sustainable Competitive Advantage." *Strategic Management Journal* 15 (Summer special issue): 131–148.

Blackler, F. 1995. "Knowledge, Knowledge Work and Organizations: An Overview and interpretations." *Organization Studies* 16, no. 6: 1021–1046.

Blair, M. M., and S. M. Wallman. 2001. *Unseen Wealth*. New York: The Brookings Institution.

Bowman, C., and V. Ambrosini. 2000. "Value Creation versus Value Capture: Towards a Coherent Definition of Value in Strategy." *British Journal of Management* 11: 1–15.

Brynjolfsson, E. 1993. "The Productivity Paradox of Information Technology: Review and Assessment." *Communications of the ACM* 36, no. 12: 67–77.

Checkland, P. 1981. *Systems Thinking Systems Practice*. Chichester, England: Wiley.

———, and S. Holwell. 1998. *Information, Systems and Information Systems: Making Sense of the Field*. Chichester, England: John Wiley & Sons.

Clegg, C., C. Axtell, L. Damadoran, B. Farbey, R. Wull, R. Lloydosones, S. Nicholls, R. Sell, and C. Tomlinson. 1997. "Information technology: a study of performance and the rule of human and organizational factors," *Ergonumics* 40, no. 9: 851–871.

Cook, S. D., and J. Seeley Brown. 1999. "Bridging Epistemologies: The Generative Dance between Organizational Knowledge and Organizational Knowing." *Organization Science* 10, no. 4: 381–400.

Davenport, T. H. 1994. "Saving IT's Soul: Human-Centred Information Management." *Harvard Business Review* (March–April): 119–131.

———, D. DeLong, and M. Beers. 1998. "Successful Knowledge Management Projects." *Sloan Management Review* (Winter): 43–57.

———, J. G. Harris, D. W. DeLong, and A. L. Jacobson. 2001. "Data to Knowledge to Results: Building an Analytical Capability." *California Management Review* 43, no. 2 (Winter): 117–138.

———, and D. A. Marchand. 2000. "Is KM Just Good Information Management?" In: *Mastering Information Management*, ed. D. A. Marchand, T. H. Davenport, and T. H. Dickson, pp. 165–169. London: Financial Times, Prentice-Hall.

———, and L. Prusak. 1998. *Working Knowledge: How Organizations Manage What They Know*. Boston: Harvard Business School Press.

David, P. A. 1990. "The Dynamo and the Computer: A Historical Perspective on the Modern Productivity Paradox." *American Economic Review Papers and Proceedings* 1, no. 2: 355–361.

Davis, M., R. Paterson, and A. Wilson. 1998. *UKGAPP: Generally Accepted Accounting Principles in the United Kingdom*. London: Macmillan.

Denning, S. 2000. *The Springboard: How Storytelling Ignites Action in Knowledge-Era Organizations*. Boston: Butterworth-Heinemann.

Dhillon, G., and J. Backhouse. 2000. "Information System Security Management in the New Millennium." *Communications of the ACM* 43, no. 7: 125–128.

Dvorak, R. E., E. Holen, D. Mark, and W. F. Meehan. 1997. "Six principles of high-performance IT." *The McKinsey Quarterly* Issue 3: 164–177.

Edvinsson, L., and M. S. Malone. 1997. *Intellectual Capital: Realizing Your Company's True Value by Finding Its Hidden Brainpower*. New York: Harper Business.

Glazer, R. 1998. "Measuring the Knower: Towards a Theory of Knowledge Equity." *California Management Review* 40: 175–194.

Grant, R. M. 1996a. "Prospering in Dynamically-Competitive Environments: Organizational Capability as Knowledge Integration." *Organization Science* 7: 375–387.

———. 1996b. "Towards a Knowledge-Based Theory of the Firm." *Strategic Management Journal* (Winter special issue): 109–122.

Haanes, K., and O. Fjeldstad. 2000. "Linking Intangible Resources and Competition." *European Management Journal* 18, no. 1: 52–62.

Haeckel, S. H., and R. L. Nolan. 1993. "Managing by Wire." *Harvard Business Review* (September–October): 122–132.

Keen, P. G. W. 1993. "Information technology and the management difference: a fusion map." *IBM Systems Journal* 32 no. 1: 17–39.

Knox, S., S. Maklan, A. Payne, J. Peppard, and L. Ryals. 2003. *Customer Relationship Management: Perspectives from the Marketplace.* London: Butterworth-Heinemann.

KPMG/IMPACT. 1994. *Information as an Asset: The Board Agenda.* London: KPMG IMPACT.

Lave, J., and E. Wenger. 1991. *Situated Learning.* Cambridge: Cambridge University Press.

Lev, B. 2001. *Intangibles: Management, Measurement and Reporting.* Washington, DC: The Brookings Institute.

Majumdar, S. K. 1998. "On the Utilisation of Resources: Perspectives from the US Telecommunications Industry." *Strategic Management Journal* 19, no. 9: 809–831.

Marchand, D. A. 1995. "'What Is Your Company's Information Culture?' Mastering Management." *Financial Times* (December 8): 10–11.

——, W. Kettinger, and J. D. Rollins. 2000. "Information orientation: people, technology and bottom line". *Sloan Management Review* (Summer): 69–80.

——, J. Roos, and D. Oliver. 1995. *Skandia Assurance and Financial Services: Measuring and Visualising Intellectual Capital.* IMD case study, reference number: 396-116-1. Lausanne, Switzerland: IMD.

Markus, M. L., and D. Robey. 1988. "Information Technology and Organizational Change: Casual Structure in Theory and research." *Management Science* 34, no. 5: 583–598.

Mata, F. J., W. L. Fuerst, and J. Barney. 1995. "Information technology and sustained competitive advantage: a resource-based analysis." *MIS Quarterly* 19: 487–505.

McDermott, R. 1999. "Why Information Technology Inspired but Cannot Deliver Knowledge Management." *Sloan Management Review* 41, no. 4: 103–117.

McDonagh, J. 2001. "Not for the Faint-Hearted: Social and Organizational Challenges in IT-Enabled Change." *Organization Development Journal* 19: 11–20.

Mingers, J. C. 1995. "What Is the Distinctive Nature and Value of IS as A Discipline." *Systemist* 17, no. 1: 18–22.

Mouritsen, J., P. N. Bukh, H. T. Larsen, and M. R. Johansen. 2002. "Developing and Managing Knowledge through Intellectual Capital Statements." *Journal of Intellectual Capital* 3, no. 1: 10–29.

Nelson, R., and R. G. Winter. 1982. *An Evolutionary Theory of Economic Change.* Cambridge, MA: Belknap.

Nonaka, I. 1994. "A Dynamic Theory of Organizational Knowledge Creation." *Organization Science* 5: 14–37.

——, and N. Konna. 1998. "The Concept of 'Ba': Building a Foundation for Knowledge Creation." *California Management Review* 30, no. 3: 40–54.

——, R. Toyama, and N. Konno. 2000. "SECI, Ba, and leadership: A Unified Model of Dynamic Knowledge Creation." *Long Range Planning* 33, no. 1: 5–34.

Oppenheim, C., J. Stenson, and R. M. Wilson. 2003. "Studies on Information as an Asset. I. Definitions." *Journal of Information Science* 29, no. 3: 159–166.

Orlikowski, W. J. 2002. "Knowing in Practice: Enacting a Collective Capability in Distributed Organizing." *Organization Science* 13, no. 3: 249–273.

——, and C. S. Iacono. 2001. "Research Commentary: Desperately Seeking the 'IT' in IT Research—A Call to Theorizing the IT Artefact." *Information Systems Research* 12, no. 2: 121–134.

Peppard, J. 2004. "Rethinking the Concept of the IS Organisation: An Analysis of the Dependent Variable." Paper presented at 20th European Group for Organizational Studies (EGOS) Colloquium, Ljubljana, Slovenia (July).

——, R. Lambert, and C. E. Edwards. 2000. "Whose Job Is It Anyway? Organizational Information Competencies for Value Creation." *Information Systems Journal* 10, no. 4: 291–323.

——, and A. Rylander. 2001. "Using an Intellectual Capital Perspective to Design and Implement a Growth Strategy: The Case of APiON." *European Management Journal* 19, no. 5: 510–525.

——, and J. Ward. 1999. "'Mind the Gap': Diagnosing the Relationship between the IT Organisation and the Rest of the business." *Journal of Strategic Information Systems* 8: 29–60.

——, and J. M. Ward. 2004. "Beyond Strategic Information Systems: Towards an IS Capability." *Journal of Strategic Information Systems* 13: 167–194.

Polanyi, M. 1966. *The Tacit Dimension*. New York: Doubleday.

Porter, M., and V. Miller 1985. "How information changes the way you compete." *Harvard Business Review* (July–August): 149–160.

Redman, T. C. 1995. "Improve Data Quality for competitive Advantage." *Sloan Management Review* (Winter): 99–107.

——. 1998. "The Impact of Poor Data Quality on the Typical Enterprise." *Communications of the ACM* 41, no. 2: 79–82.

Roach, S. 1987. *America's Technology Dilemma: A Profile of the Information Economy*. Special economic study. Morgan Stanley, New York.

Roos, J., and G. Roos. 1997. "Measuring Your Company's Intellectual Performance." *Long Range Planning* 30, no. 3: 413–426.

Ross, J., and P. Weill. 2002. "Six decisions your IT people shouldn't make." *Harvard Business Review* (November): 85–91.

Rylander, A., K. Jacobsen, and G. Roos. 2000. "Towards Improved Information Disclosure on Intellectual Capital." *International Journal of Technology Management* 20, nos. 5–8: 715–741.

Sampler, J. 1998. "Redefining Industry Structure for the Information Age." *Strategic Management Journal* 19: 343–355.

Seely Brown, J., and P. Duguid. 2000. *The Social Life of Information*. Boston: Harvard Business School Press.

Shannon, C. E., and W. Weaver. 1949. *The Mathematical Theory of Communication*. Urbana: University of Illinois Press.

Simon, H. A. 1960. *The New Science of Management Decision*. New York: Harper and Row.

Spender, J. C. 1996. "Making Knowledge the Basis of a Dynamic Theory of the firm." *Strategic Management Journal* 11: 45–62.

Sveiby, K.-E. 1989. *Den Osynliga Balansräkningen* [The Invisible Balance Sheet]. Stockholm: Affärsvärlden Förlag AB.

Teece, D. J. 1998. "Capturing Value from Knowledge Assets: The New Economy, Markets for Know-How, and Intangible Assets." *California Management Review* 40, no. 3: 55–79.

——. 2000a. "Strategies for Managing Knowledge Assets: The Role of Firm Structure and Industrial Context." *Long Range Planning* 33: 35–54.

——. 2000b. *Managing Intellectual Capital: Organizational, Strategic and Policy Dimensions*. Oxford: Oxford University Press.

Walsham, G. 2001. "Knowledge Management: The Benefits and Limitations of Computer Systems." *European Management Journal* 19, no. 6: 599–608.

Ward, J., and J. Peppard. 1996. "Reconciling the IT/Business Relationship: A Troubled Marriage in Need of Guidance." *Journal of Strategic Information Systems* 5, no. 1: 37–65.

Wenger, E., and W. M. Snyder. 2000. "Communities of Practice: The Organizational Frontier." *Harvard Business Review* (January–February): 139–145.

Weill, P. and G. Ross. 2004. It Governance: How Top Performers Manage IT Decision Rights for super for Results, Harvard Business School Press, Boston, MA.

Wernerfelt, B. 1984. "A Resource-Based View of the Firm." *Strategic Management Journal* 5: 171–180.

Zack, M. H. 1999. "Managing Codified Knowledge." *Sloan Management Review* (Summer): 45–57.

Zander, U., and B. Kogut. 1995. "Knowledge and the Speed of the Transfer and Imitation of Organizational Capabilities: An Empirical Test." *Organisational Science* 6, no. 1: 76–92.

A Legal Perspective on Intellectual Capital

L. Martin Cloutier
University of Quebec at Montreal

E. Richard Gold
McGill University

Introduction

It is one thing to create or use intellectual capital; it is another to manage it in such a way as to profit from it. Properly managing intellectual capital involves understanding the tools available to control access to it and exploit it. These instruments are legal in nature but nevertheless have important implications for management. In this chapter, we aim to elucidate the understanding of these tools and their management.

Law possesses no inherent definition of "intellectual capital." Instead, the law divides the world into tangible goods and intangible goods. Tangible goods include houses and cars, while intangible goods include accounts receivable and shares in a corporation. The dividing line between tangible and intangible goods is whether the good has a physical presence. While intellectual capital falls within the category of intangible goods, it is a special sort of intangible, one in which its information content is most valuable.

For our analysis, we take intellectual capital to mean the sum of all ideas, information, and knowledge over which individuals or organizations may wish to exercise some form of control. There are two components to this definition. First, like all intangibles, intellectual capital is composed of assets that bear information. Second and more important, the information that they bear is something individuals wish to keep others from knowing or using. That is, the information provides a competitive advantage that is worth protecting.

The definition of *intellectual capital* (IC) bears some similarities to the concept of intangible assets used in accounting. In some ways, intellectual capital is less broad than intangible assets; while it certainly includes intellectual property, such as patents, trademarks, and copyrights, it does not extend to permits and regulatory licenses. On the other hand, intellectual capital is broader than intangible assets, as it includes information relating to or created through particular relationships, such as joint ventures or research agreements.

The law offers both formal and informal mechanisms through which to manage intellectual capital. The formal mechanisms include the statutory intellectual property regimes: patents, copyrights, trademarks, plant variety protection, integrated topography protection, and so on. Other formal mechanisms include corporate law and securities law, both of which control the flow of information about corporations and their business. Among the many informal mechanisms that law offers we can include license agreements, research agreements, contractual joint ventures, and trade secret law.

It is important to note that the particular manner and scope of legal enforcement depends on jurisdictional issues. Laws are national in nature (and in some cases, as with the European Community, regional as well) or regulated by particular states or provinces within a country. Thus, a great diversity of laws can be applicable to the management of intellectual capital, although most countries follow one or two common variants.

The Legal Management of IC

To properly appreciate intellectual capital and its management, one needs to understand the legal instruments that both turn it into a protectable asset and permit its management. In this section, we outline the legal instruments available to manage intellectual capital, both formal and informal, before discussing management techniques that rely on those instruments.

The law plays a critical role in determining what constitutes intellectual capital and how we use it. Formal legal rules set what can be protected, against whom, and for how long. Other rules tell us how to transfer intellectual capital from one person to another, how to combine it to build products, and how to construct value chains. Both these formal instruments of creating intellectual capital and informal mechanisms of trading in them are essential to the smooth functioning of the market. We examine both here.

Formal Instruments

The law provides several different approaches to protecting intellectual capital. These approaches differ in terms of the subject matter being protected, the length of time that protection lasts, and what rights the protection offers. We describe these various regimes in terms of the intellectual capital they create. Starting with reputation in the marketplace, we move on to applied ideas and end up with expressive works, such as written works, film, and databases.

Reputation

The legal system permits market actors to prevent others from using their reputations in a way that may confuse customers. It does so by permitting these actors to control the use of names, symbols, phrases, designs, packaging, and even, in certain circumstances, color and sound the public associates with the actor. Thus, everything from the Nike swoosh to the McDonald arches to the Coca-Cola name are forms of intellectual capital protected by law. Through this protection, the law encourages companies to invest in building their reputations and distinctive natures in the marketplace without fear that others will have a free ride on that reputation.

Trademarks provide the chief mode of protecting reputation, although in common law countries such as England and the United States, a second level of protection is offered through the law of passing off. A main difference between these two regimes is that trademarks must be registered with the relevant national authorities, whereas a right to protect a name or symbol through passing off arises from mere use.

Reputation can also be shared by particular groups of market actors. For example, producers from a particular region can share a symbol indicating the geographical origin of the product. Similarly, producers of products meeting defined quality standards can also share the use of a symbol or name.

To obtain a trademark, one must demonstrate to the relevant national authorities that the particular name, symbol, design, or the like (called a *mark*) that one claims distinguishes one's goods and services from those of competitors. This means that an average customer for the type of goods or services in question would recognize the mark as indicating that the good or service comes from a source previously encountered in the market (although that customer need not know the actual name or location of the source). In general, to demonstrate that one's mark distinguishes one's goods or services from those offered by others, one must already be using the mark in the marketplace. While this is the general rule, the law usually permits actors to register a mark prior to use as long as that actor puts the mark into use fairly soon.

Once the relevant national authority (each country has its own authority giving out trademarks good only in that country) issues the trademark, the trademark holder can use it as long as the trademark remains distinctive and the holder renews the trademark and pays the required fees. A trademark can lose its distinctiveness if, for example, an average customer comes to associate the mark with the general type of product (e.g., linoleum) rather than a particular source for that product.

In those countries that recognize passing off, no registration is required. Rather, should someone use the mark without the holder's consent, the holder can bring an action in passing off by alleging that the mark was distinctive, that the unauthorized infringer used the mark in such a way as to confuse the public, and that the holder suffered a loss as a result of this unauthorized use. Once again, distinctiveness of the mark is crucial for success.

A trademark holder or a person claiming protection under the law of passing off receives protection not only against others that use the exact same mark but marks that can be confused with the holder's actual mark. That is, third parties cannot escape liability for infringement by making slight changes to the mark. How big the changes need to be to escape liability depends on how unique the mark is, how well known it is, and whether customers would normally carefully scrutinize the mark in making purchases.

Trademark law also gives trademark holders the right to prevent others from a free ride on their marks. For example, in many jurisdictions, a trademark holder can prevent others from saying that their products are as good as a trademarked good. Negative comparisons are normally accepted since they do not ride on the reputation of the trademarked good; in fact, they seek to show that that reputation is undeserved.

Both trademarks and passing off apply to commercial uses of marks. Someone who merely invokes a mark without attempting to sell a product or service associated with the mark does nothing wrong. Therefore, a writer may use a trademarked name (we have already done so for Nike and Coca-Cola, for example) or an artist may normally paint a painting in which the mark may appear. In neither case is the mark being used to show the source of the product and is thus outside the scope of the holder's rights.

A person who uses a mark without authority may suffer anything from monetary damages (in the amount earned by the infringer or the amount lost by the mark's holder) to confiscation of material containing the mark to injunctions against using the mark again. It is to be noted that these remedies are cumulative; therefore, the holder can obtain monetary and injunctive relief where appropriate.

Applied Ideas

One of the most valuable aspects of a company's intellectual capital are ways of doing things, making things, or the things being made themselves. This means that a company that invests in applied ideas, whether in manufacturing, service provision, pharmaceuticals, information technology, or biotechnology, to name but a few, can prevent others from using those ideas without consent. The principal reason for providing this protection is to permit companies to gain the full economic value of their ideas so that they devote sufficient resources to innovation. While this economic reasoning is open to criticism, it is the one that underlies the law.

The law offers two ways to protect applied ideas: trade secrets and patents. As was the case in the distinction between trademarks and passing off, one of these systems (patents) requires registration whereas the other (trade secrecy) arises solely from the actions of the party claiming protection.

Trade secrecy protection is relatively straightforward to obtain provided one is careful. All one must do to claim control over an idea is to either not disclose it to anyone else—seldom a realistic option—or to disclose it only to persons who understand that they must keep it confidential. These obligations of confidentiality normally come about through the entry into confidentiality or nondisclosure agreements, although they can arise from the nature of the relationship (attorney-client, for example) or the circumstances (e.g., everyone in the industry would understand that the disclosure is confidential).

As indicated already, someone wishing to obtain a patent over an applied idea must register it with the relevant national authorities. These authorities carefully examine the idea to make sure it qualifies as an "invention." No single, universally accepted definition of *invention* exists, but it generally refers to things, ways of doing things, or compositions of things that would not exist in the form claimed without human intervention. Even so, different countries define inventions differently, particularly in the areas of information technology, medicine, and biotechnology. Once satisfied that the applied idea is an invention, the patent office makes sure that the applied idea is also new, involved some creativity (technically, that the invention had an inventive step or was not obvious), and was useful (also known as having an industrial application). As with the definition of *invention*, different countries give different meanings to the terms *new*, *inventive step*, and *industrial application*. Generally, however, the patent office grants a patent over an invention if it has never been previously disclosed in writing (or otherwise, depending on the country), the invention did not simply involve ordinary trial and error, and it works sufficiently well (but not necessarily better than other products or ways of doing things) that industry may wish to use it.

An interesting difference between trade secrets and patents is their contribution to publicly available information. By their nature, trade secrets must be kept confidential, out of the public domain. Patent law requires, on the other hand, applicants to fully disclose their inventions, putting the ideas behind those inventions into the public domain. This means that one cannot protect the exact same applied idea through both trade secrets and patents simultaneously.

A second difference between trade secrets and patents is the term of protection. Patents last for 20 years (subject to a few years extension in the case of pharmaceutical products in many countries), while trade secrets last as long as the idea is actually kept secret.

Unlike trademarks and passing off, which provide protection over marks that may deviate in important ways from the protected mark, both trade secrecy protection and patents are more literal when it comes to infringement. Both aim at protecting the actual applied idea developed by the rights holder rather than mere similar objects.

Trade secrets provide protection against disclosures and uses of the applied idea only by those actually bound by confidentiality obligations. Thus, the holder of an applied idea can sue someone to whom it disclosed an idea for using it but cannot prevent a third party who independently developed the same idea or used reverse engineering to discover the idea. That is, to succeed, the holder must show that the third party obtained the idea through the holder or someone to whom the idea was disclosed in a confidential manner.

Given this limitation, trade secrecy protection is effective in only those industries in which it is practical to keep the idea secret and in which the costs of reverse engineering are significant. The food industry, for example, relies heavily on trade secrecy, whereas the pharmaceutical industry relies more on patents.

Trade secrecy protection ends once the idea is generally known. A holder cannot enforce an obligation to keep an idea secret if that idea is generally known in the field. Once this happens, the idea becomes free to use by anyone.

Patents, on the other hand, are effective against everyone acting in the particular country. The patent holder can bring suit against any person who makes, uses, sells, or imports the invention within the country, regardless of whether that other person came by the knowledge legitimately or illegitimately. Thus, patent protection is much stronger than trade secret protection, since it permits its holders to enforce the right against those who independently created the same idea or used reversed engineering to discover the idea.

While aiming to protect the narrow idea identified by the patent holder, patent law does not interpret the invention in an absolutely literal fashion. Patent laws generally admit to some degree of flexibility in the way that one is to understand what constitutes the invention, although national laws differ significantly in this respect. Suffice it to note that patent holders can generally succeed in infringement actions over goods or processes that differ in technically insignificant ways from the invention as described by the patent holder.

Certain uses of a patented invention fall outside the scope of patent rights. In most countries, research conducted on the invention to discover its properties and uses is permitted. The United States differs, however, since it categorizes research activity at universities as being technically infringing. While most companies would not sue researchers for patent infringement, since whatever is discovered will increase the value of the patent holder's intellectual capital, the lack of a research exemption in the United States has worried some.

A person who wrongfully uses or discloses a trade secret is liable to pay damages to the trade secret holder and be prevented, by injunction, from using the applied idea. How far down the chain of disclosures the trade secret holder can go depends on the law of the particular jurisdiction. Some countries are quite generous, permitting trade secret holders to prevent the use of ideas made using the protected idea; others are more narrow.

A patent holder can recover both monetary damages (in the amount earned by the infringer or the amount lost by the patent holder) to injunctions against using the invention. It is to be noted that these remedies are cumulative; therefore, the patent holder can obtain monetary and injunctive relief where appropriate.

Expressive Works

The family of expressive works constitutes an important category of intellectual capital. Works ranging from books and computer manuals to computer programs and databases to works of fine art and performances all have important economic (as well as cultural) value. As this list makes clear, the variety and uses of these works differ significantly from one to another. Yet they all share a common element: They protect ways of expressing ideas. All are also protected through the law of copyright.

While there is no need to apply for copyright protection, it attaches automatically on creation, not all works are protected. As in patent law, initial hurdles exist, although for copyright these requirements are very minimal. The two principal hurdles are fixation and originality. The fixation requirement means simply that at some point in the work's life, it must be captured in material form, such as a canvass or an electric recording. In fact, what must be fixed is the gist of the expression and not the entire content itself, as notes may be sufficient. The originality standard is universally low but requires at least some nominal degree of intellectual effort.

The term of copyright protection varies from country to country but is generally in the range of the life of the author plus 50 to 70 years. While copyright arises automatically, some procedural advantages accrue from registering the copyright with the relevant national authorities when contemplating an infringement action.

Copyright provides its holder with the ability to prevent others from copying, in whole or in a significant manner, the expressive component of works. The concentration here is on the expression of ideas, not the ideas themselves. This vital distinction between ideas and expressions of ideas means that copyright protects only the form of a work and not its underlying content. For example, the holder of the copyright in a recording of Dr. King's "I Have a Dream" speech would be entitled to prevent others from reproducing or broadcasting it but would not have a monopoly in the ideal of racial harmony. Similarly, as bare facts are not themselves susceptible to copyright protection, any copyright in a database or a compilation of facts extends only to the particular expression, the arrangement and presentation of the information, and not to the underlying information itself. (Some jurisdictions, such as the European Community, offer protection over databases themselves and the extraction of information from them.)

Copyright provides protection for not only the literal expression used but works that are similar in nature. This means that a copyright holder can prevent others from using the same story, even if the names and some other elements are changed. What is important is that the basic expression was copying, not the literal words or symbols used. While the demarcation between what is permitted to be used and what is not is not always clear, copyright law attempts to find the balance between the interests of the copyright holder and others wishing to use the ideas and thoughts embodied in the work.

Copyright does not prevent the use by another who independently creates the same work even if the expression is the same. Nevertheless, the copyright holder can prevent others from using reverse engineering to create another copy of the work. Generally, the alleged infringer must demonstrate that he or she created the work without copying or using reverse engineering.

Certain uses of expressive works fall outside the scope of copyright. Whether referred to as *fair use* or *fair dealing*, copyright law sees these uses as providing a balance between the interests of the creator and those who use the works. Typical examples of these uses include copying a work for private study, copying the work to criticize it, and some archival uses.

A copyright holder can recover both monetary damages (in the amount earned by the infringer or the amount lost by the copyright holder) to injunctions against using the work. As was the case with trademarks and patents, these remedies are cumulative, thus the patent holder can obtain monetary and injunctive relief where appropriate.

Informal Instruments

In addition to the formal intellectual property regimes, the law provides several other instruments through which to control and manage intellectual capital and its value. These include contractual arrangements, through which access to and use of intellectual capital can be controlled, and the creation of joint venture corporations.

Contractual Relationships

Contracts provide a flexible tool through which actors can create, control, and exploit intellectual capital. Unlike the formal legal regimes just described, they apply only to the particular parties who agree to the arrangement. That is, while they provide a maximum of flexibility between the parties, unlike the formal regimes they cannot be used to create rights against third parties.

Contracts provide the basis for three important transactions: licenses, research agreements, and joint ventures.

Licenses

Licenses provide the means through which an actor holding intellectual capital permits another to use it, usually for a fee. By permitting the intellectual capital holder to set out the terms and conditions under which the user is to use and deal with the intellectual capital, licenses provide a flexible means through which to disseminate intellectual capital while protecting the economic interests of the holder.

Essentially, a license works in the following way. The licensor possesses intellectual capital of some value to which the licensee desires access. Generally, the licensor can prevent the licensee from using the intellectual capital because it is protected under one of the formal legal instruments described earlier. In return for giving up the right to sue the licensee for infringement, the licensor demands payment and financial and reporting requirements of the licensee. As long as the licensee abides by these requirements, the licensor cannot sue for infringement. Should the licensee breach its obligations, the license normally comes to an end and the licensor can once again enforce its rights.

Licenses control the transfer of intellectual capital both within related companies and between companies. They can be simple, such as the license that applies to the use of a standard word processor, to complicated, as in the case of exclusive licenses.

Research Agreements

One way to generate intellectual capital is to create it. Since not all actors have the ability to single-handedly provide financing, researchers, and time in the development of intellectual capital, they must contract among themselves to create it. Research agreements provide one means of doing so.

Research agreements normally include license terms but go beyond them. They set out the entirety of the agreement related to the production of new intellectual capital. Essentially, a research agreement involves two or more parties, where one party provides either or both of financing and material (and potentially intellectual capital) to the other while the other performs research services. The agreement sets out which party ends up with the produced intellectual capital, what uses the other party can make of that intellectual capital, and financial terms.

Contractual Joint Ventures

Often, simply creating new intellectual capital is not enough: Means need to be developed to exploit that intellectual capital in the marketplace. Here, contracts show their true flexibility. Contracts permit two or more parties to act in concert to both develop and exploit intellectual capital without having to create separate corporations or other entities.

Essentially, through contractual means, parties can set out their respective contributions of intellectual capital, their respective rights to use joint intellectual capital, the manner in which intellectual capital is to be used, how they provide goods or services, and the sharing of revenues (and liability for debts). As contractual arrangements depend only on the parties, they are extremely flexible and can be ended by simple agreement.

Contractual joint ventures provide an important tool in developing and exploiting a niche technology that requires the participation of several actors. They provide a means to ensure that intellectual capital is used for the benefit of all participants.

Corporate Joint Ventures

Corporate law provides another means through which to control and exploit intellectual capital. Where contractual joint ventures are flexible, corporate joint ventures facilitate financing by outsiders and the eventual independence of the venture from its parent corporations.

Just as contract law provides one mechanism to address issues relating to intellectual capital development and exploitation, so does corporate law. By licensing or assigning intellectual capital to a corporation jointly held by the participating actors, companies can join forces and intellectual capital to develop and sell products and services. While the corporate structure is more restrictive than simple contracts, it nevertheless provides significant flexibility to meet the needs of the participants.

Uses of Legal Instruments

Formal and informal legal instruments offer an array of opportunities for firms and organizations in the legal management of IC. In addition, these instruments can be embedded, whole or in part, in the business practice that a firm or an organization chooses to adopt. The topic and scope of the subject includes more academic discussions as well as plain advice for managers on alternative uses of legal instruments for intellectual capital (see, for example, Nermien 2003). Simple trends in the business environment make the legal management of IC increasingly complex and challenging for individuals, firms, and organizations that produce IC.

Clearly, CEOs and managers are concerned with the choice of legal instruments in their portfolio, an information management value-generating mechanism for products they are creating and services they provide. Some factors under consideration for determining appropriate means of legal management include, but may not be limited to, (1) pressures for time compression in R&D, production, and commercialization cycles; (2) the blurring of boundaries between firms and organizations; (3) the emergence of new coordination mechanisms between organizations, vertical linkages in supply chains and horizontal oligopolies; (4) the nature of products; (5) the practice and traditions in a given industry; and (6) legal jurisdictions.

Increasingly, firms generate quasi-rents from knowledge stocks and intangible asset management.[1] How these stocks of knowledge come to existence and are managed over time can also influence the use of alternative means of IC legal management. For example, upfront requirements in knowledge stocks required in the life sciences industry are quite different than in software development, and this may help explain, in part, alternative means of legal management. The product life cycle and shelf life and the nature of the information content may also influence the appropriate use of legal instruments. The tools employed to protect the IC thus vary among firms and across industries.

Patents are the strongest mean of legal protection and often are perceived as a necessary and sufficient mean of legal management and control of IC. Because patents offer much stronger legal protection than other formal and informal instruments, the assumption may not be that it is also what is best for invention management within the firm. This perception is evolving as firms and organizations discover new ways to embed both formal and informal legal instruments of IC management into business practice and design.

Means of legal protection other than patents are needed because of the shortcomings associated with patents. Patents may not be a preferred means of intellectual protection for many reasons. First, it is a costly process to demonstrate novelty. Even if a patent is granted, there is no telling whether considerable resources are needed to capture expected rents. Second, other trade-offs may interfere with the decision to seek a patent or employ other complementary instruments. Often, to maintain vertical business linkages, a firm must abandon the urge to enforce the economic potential of its patent because of a membership in a network organization; a membership that may secure market access for another product line. The structural dimensions are thus key to understanding the legal management of IC and the complementarity of many factors. Third, questions as to when and how to patent also are important. Patents are not always used properly and can be overused or underused. Practices such as patent fencing, poorly negotiated licensing practices, and co-ownership lead to negotiation problems and may affect firm performance.

Perhaps, it is appropriate to focus on aspects of the legal management of IC related to what firms and organizations actually do, that is, how they integrate in practice the formal and informal instruments available (Winter 2000). In many industries, patents are not considered effective or an exclusive means of legal management. In particular, the use of trade secrets, lead time, and complementary assets management in joint venture manufacturing and service integrate many formal and informal legal instruments, help generate value and quasi-rents from transactions, and are more effective. The use of legal instruments may best be understood by examining the many dimensions that may influence the business process. Some of these dimensions include the type of technology, industry structure, individual firm strategic purpose, perceived

---

[1] The term *quasi-rent* is employed to emphasize the temporary nature of economic rents and assumes the economic process eventually, with some time delay, dissipates rents.

value, technology cycle, jurisdictions, and legal and business traditions in certain locations and industries.

In particular, the technology cycle of the firm may require the alternative use of formal and informal legal instruments because of the intended use of the invention. For example, in some jurisdictions, it is typical for a biotechnology startup to seek patents to coordinate between inventors and investors. Over time, however, the limited value chain network of a biotechnology startup firm must be further enhanced. Typically, the firm may look for partnerships and more informal legal tools, such as licenses, contractual joint ventures, or business joint ventures, to secure access to manufacturing resources. Possibly, more-mature firms may help finance activities in startup companies to replenish their product pipeline, using an alternative business design with complementary asset management for consumer access; and the innovation of new products from R&D requires some form of contracting. Thus, the complementary management of assets plays a key role in IC management, and more-informal means, such as licensing, may be a more-appropriate form of legal instrument to consider.

At the societal level, a large number of issues stem from the use of patents, in particular whether they lead to more innovation or even greater disclosure and help support technology diffusion and transfer. Each of these issues sheds some light on some underlying trade-offs. Do patents lead to more innovation or raise barriers to entry (Barton 1998)? Do patents foster anticompetitive behavior (Anderson and Gallini 1998)? Are they value free (Gold et al. 2002)?

The integration of legal instruments is important for understanding IC and the legal management dimensions that relate to value creation in knowledge management. In particular, these means include (1) measuring and auditing IC portfolios (patent valuation, alternative use and value of patents for other parties, nonusable patents); (2) valuation methods of IC (benchmarking, rules of thumb, rating, discounted cash flow, option pricing), also complementary asset management (choice of partners in alliances, joint ventures, "carve-out" organizations); (3) IC asset management (importance of licensing, which bundles patents, trade secrets, copyrights, technology office, also in universities, intellectual capital model, intellectual asset management); (4) accounting aspects; and (5) financial management aspects of IC.

The appropriate combination of legal instruments influences firm performance and heterogeneity over time. The impact of legal means of IC management is illustrated in Figure 9.1 with a simple influence diagram.[2] Firms and other actors have many formal and informal instruments at their disposal and can choose the combination that provides the best outcome in line with business practice. These instruments can help actors manage the quasi-rent-generation potential required to compete with alternative information contents of products, services, and product lines. In turn, this affects firms in many alternative ways in terms of setting the stage for capturing future economic gains. These gains, or lack thereof, influence future innovation potential, economic performance, and knowledge management—all key ingredients in IC management. The optimistic perspective is that an appropriate portfolio of formal and

---

[2] The polarity + indicates a supporting relationship between variables, influences, or cause and effect, while the polarity − indicates an opposing relationship. An even number of + signs in an influence diagram depicts a reinforcing structure, while an odd number of − relationships indicates a balancing structure, a trend towards equilibrium, or in this case, inertia in the feedback loop. The letter *R* means reinforcing feedback loop, and the letter *B* denotes a balancing feedback loop.

Figure 9.1

Formal and informal use of legal instruments and its influence on performance (Source: Adapted from Cloutier and Saives 2003).

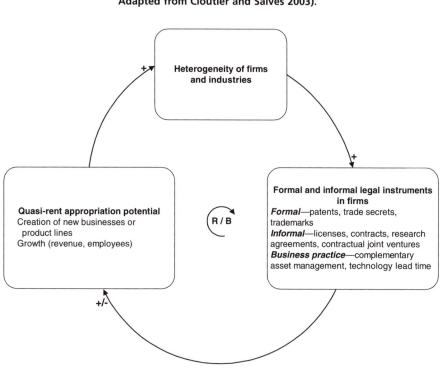

legal instruments may help reinforce the creation of new innovation and the growth of firms. If the right balance is not struck in the legal management of IC, then the quasi-rent appropriation potential may be more limited. This would be a hypothesis worth pursuing in future research.

Conclusion

In this paper, we provided a short introduction and overview to formal and informal legal instruments that individuals and market actors can use in IC management. These legal instruments include stronger and weaker means for ensuring the innovation benefits its inventor and user, and society as whole, through better and improved products and services available on the market. However, the use of these legal instruments involves complex processes embedded in business practice and requires many considerations, ranging from firm strategic objectives to planning.

References

Anderson, R. D., and N. Gallini (eds.). 1998. *Competition Policy and Intellectual Property Rights in the Knowledge-Based Economy.* Industry Canada Research Series. Calgary, AB: University of Calgary.

Barton, J. 1998. "Competition and Competitive Uses of Intellectual Property." Stanford Workshop on Intellectual Property and Industry Competitive Standards. Available at stlr.stanford.edu/STRL/Symposia/Antitrust/index.htm.

Cloutier, L. M., and A.-L. Saives. 2003. "Propriété Intellectuelle et Hétérogénéité des Capacités d'Innovation des Firmes du Système Bioalimentaire qui Exploitent la Biotechnologie au Québec." *Revue Gestion* 28: 64–74.

Gold, R. E., D. Castle, L. M. Cloutier, A. S. Daar, and P. J. Smith. 2002. "Needed: Models of Biotechnology Intellectual Property Rights." *Trends in Biotechnology* 20, no. 8: 327–329.

Nermien, A.-A. 2003. *Comprehensive Intellectual Capital Management.* New York: JohnWiley & Sons.

Winter, S. G. 2000. "Appropriating the Gains from Innovation." In: *Wharton on Managing Technology*, ed. G. S. Day and P. J. H. Schoemaker, pp. 242–265. New York: John Wiley & Sons.

An Intellectual Property Perspective on Intellectual Capital

Patrick H. Sullivan, Sr.
ICM Group, LLC

Introduction

Since the early 1990s, intellectual property (IP) has assumed increasing importance in business activity around the world. Intellectual property represents the legally protected and codified knowledge of its owners. Yet, it is only one of many forms of intangibles that together constitute an organization's intellectual capital (IC). This chapter briefly explains the relationship between intellectual capital and intellectual property and discusses current approaches to and methods for managing intellectual property, from an IC perspective.

While many tactical uses of intellectual property are available to a firm, some concerned with legal issues (e.g., protection, design freedom, and litigation), more and more companies are also using their IP offensively (e.g., to generate revenue, block competitors, or position themselves strategically). In this chapter, we focus on the strategic aspect of IP and its usefulness to the firm.

There is no single accepted definition of the term *intellectual capital*. All of the several definitions are different, all are correct, yet all are incomplete. They are incomplete because each appropriately defines IC in terms that are helpful to the issues and concerns being addressed by the persons using the definition (Sullivan 2000). The several perspectives from which definitions of IC have arisen include the knowledge perspective, the innovation perspective, the IP perspective, and the financial measurement and reporting perspective. Each perspective is developed from the point of view of persons trained and interested in that paradigm (e.g., knowledge, R&D, law, business, and accounting). And each definition of IC arising from these paradigms is helpful for those who use it.

In January 1995, representatives of seven large international corporations, all sophisticated about managing and extracting value from their intellectual property, gathered in Berkeley, California, to discuss what each of them called *intellectual capital*. The group comprised IP attorneys, licensing officers, and managers of intellectual assets. In the course of that meeting, the group arrived at a robust definition of IC that served their purposes. The collective interest of the participants in that and subsequent meetings of what came to be known as "the gathering" was to extract the most value possible from their firms' intellectual capital. In this context, they defined *intellectual*

Exhibit 10.1

Two components of the IP perspective on intellectual capital.

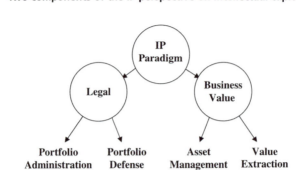

capital as "knowledge that can be converted into profits."[1] For their purposes, the two most important components of intellectual capital were "tacit knowledge" and "codified knowledge." Codified knowledge itself has a subset, intellectual property.

The IP Paradigm

Two very different perspectives are contained within the IP paradigm (see Exhibit 10.1). The first is the legal view, seen through an attorney's lens, IP qua IP. This view defines IP as a set of rights, largely used in a defensive manner. The IP legal perspective seeks to protect the legal interests of the owner of the rights to the company's IP and minimize any attacks or claims of others against the firm based on these rights.[2]

The complementary view is held by those within the IP paradigm who view IP as business assets that can be exploited in support of the business needs of their owners. People with this view are usually concerned with maximizing the value of these assets to the corporation.

Background and Development of IP

Broadly speaking, intellectual property defines the legal rights resulting from intellectual activity in industrial, scientific, literary, and artistic fields. From the legal perspective, intellectual property, sometimes referred to as IPR (intellectual property rights), is traditionally divided into two branches, industrial property and copyright. The generally accepted international authority for all matters relating to intellectual property is the World Intellectual Property Organization (WIPO). WIPO is a specialized agency of the United Nations system of organizations. The convention establishing the World Intellectual Property Organization was signed at Stockholm in 1967 and entered into force in 1970. Although the convention establishing WIPO was held in 1967, the roots of international treaties on intellectual property go back to 1883 and 1886, with the adoption of the Paris convention and the Berne convention, respec-

---

[1] This working definition of *intellectual capital* is an economic one. It appears in many publications as a basic definition of IC; see Sullivan (1998, p. 5).

[2] For information on best practices recommended for company IP attorneys, see Davis and Harrison (2001, Chapters 2 and 3).

tively. These conventions established basic definitions and methods related to industrial property and copyright matters, which were subsequently updated and incorporated under the WIPO umbrella in 1967. The international agreement on intellectual property is divided into two categories: (1) Industrial property includes inventions (patents), trademarks, industrial designs, and geographic indications of source; and (2) copyright includes literary and artistic works such as novels, poems, plays, films, musical works, artistic works such as drawings, paintings, photographs and sculptures, and architectural designs. Rights related to copyright include those of performing artists in their performances, producers of phonograms in their recordings, and those of broadcasters in their radio and television programs. The fields of intellectual property protection identified by WIPO are patents, copyright and related rights, trademarks, industrial designs and integrated circuits, geographical indications, and protection against unfair competition.[3]

Current Practices in Managing IP

What are the current practices regarding the management of the IP portion of the firm's IC, from both the business perspective and the legal perspective?

IP Legal Activities

IP legal activities usually fall under the purview of the company IP attorney and relate to the creation and maintenance of IP rights, typically in the form of legal documents, such as patents, copyrights, trademarks, and trade secrets. IP legal activities may be grouped under two major headings: portfolio administration and IP defensive activities.

Portfolio administration consists of maintaining the currency and accuracy of documents in the IP portfolio, including those that specify the author, content, and significant dates and developments for each piece of IP. Portfolio administration implies ensuring that the documentation of the property is properly maintained. (This contrasts with portfolio management, which ensures that the content of intellectual property is properly managed.) Portfolio administration includes such tasks as maintaining a complete inventory of intellectual property, ensuring that patent maintenance fees are paid, routinely culling the portfolio, and docketing and monitoring patent generation and prosecution activities.

The "best practices" recommended by the IC management "gathering" companies for portfolio administration include[4]

- Taking stock of the IP owned. Maintain a current inventory of the firm's IP, both active and former.
- Maintaining currency of IP. Make sure that the firm's IP is current; ensure that all maintenance fees are paid.
- Developing and improving processes for generating and maintaining IP.
- Establishing an IP committee to ensure and oversee IP as a business investment.
- Developing and implementing criteria for screening potential IP.

---

[3] WIPO (2001, pp. 3–4). The "geographic indications" and "protection against unfair competition" items relate to prior treaties or international agreements on intellectual property. They do not appear to be forms of protection. They appear to contain precedent information that expands on the agreement reached in Stockholm.

[4] Extracted from Davis and Harrison (2001).

- Routinely pruning the portfolio of IP that no longer supports the company's business.

IP defensive activities are those associated with the use of the company's IP to defend it against actions by others. These include the creation and prosecution of new IP as required (for protection, design freedom, and litigation avoidance), cross-licensing to avoid litigation, and the search for and deterrence of infringers.

Activities in the IP defensive space are generally not well codified, and best practices are neither well known nor widely shared among companies.

IP Business Value Activities

IP business value activities are those that create or extract value from the company's IP. They usually relate to the active use of IP in a business or "offensive" environment to generate company profits. Two overarching IP business value activities are of interest: the management of IP for business value and IP valuation.

Managing IP for Business Value

The IC management "gathering" developed a set of best practices for managing the company's IP for business value. These build on the best practices for legal portfolio administration, which typically are created early in a firm's IP development. The best practices listed here are designed for companies that want to maximize the business value of their intellectual property.

Best Practice 1. Define the Relationship between the IP Portfolio and the Company's Business

In most companies, the relationship between the portfolio and the business is unclear. This means that the company has not specified or determined what kind of value it wishes to obtain from its IP assets. Lacking such definition, the IP functions of these companies also lack focus and direction. For examples of all of the different ways in which intangibles such as IP can provide value to their owner, see Exhibit 10.2.

Companies assign roles to their IP in accordance with the kind of value they wish it to provide in support of the business strategy. For example, during the 1990s Hewlett-Packard's (HP's) business strategy was to provide solutions to the problems of current customers within the next 2 to 5 years. As a result, virtually all the innovations HP patented was related to product technologies, each with a specific product or market in mind. This was because the company wanted the patented technologies in its portfolio to generate product revenue within 2 to 5 years. In contrast, Xerox's business strategy was to reinvent the concept of "document" through technology development. The company intended to market a range of products around a newly defined "document" once its development was completed. As a result, Xerox conducted a range of small research projects in the fields of light, inks, papers, and mechanics, seeking to develop technologies that would allow a redefinition of the concept of "document." Technologies resulting from these research projects were patented and placed in the company IP portfolio. The company did not intend to immediately convert them into revenue but to use them as stepping stones on the way to creating a new suite of products. Two large and successful companies in the 1990s, HP and Xerox, demonstrate two very different kinds of relationships between the IP portfolio and the company's business strategy.

Exhibit 10.2

	Patents	Trademarks	Know-How	Relationships
Defensive Conflict avoidance, resolution	Protection (exclude others) Design freedom Cross-licensing (defensive) Litigation bargaining power	Protection (exclude others)	Protection (trade secret)	N/A
Offensive Revenue generation	Products and services: sales, licensing, joint venture, strategic alliance, optimization of core technology, value extraction from noncore technology, integration, donations Patents: sales, licenses, donations, infringement policing Increased bargaining power (e.g., suppliers, consumers, affiliates, joint venture, alliance partners) Market penetration Increased speed to market	Products and services: sales, joint ventures, strategic alliance Trademark: sales, licenses, cobranding, infringement policing	Sales Licenses Joint venture Strategic alliance Integration Increased speed to market	Products and services: sales
Cost reduction	Litigation avoidance Access to technology of others Improved knowledge transfer Reduced knowledge gaps	Litigation avoidance Access to technology of others	Litigation avoidance Improved knowledge transfer	Reduced marketing costs
Strategic position	Reputation, image Competition blocking (exclusivity) Barriers to competition Supplier control Consumer control Optimization of core technology	Name recognition Consumer loyalty Barriers to competition Joint venture Strategic alliance	Reputation, image Barriers to entry	Reputation, image Consumer loyalty Barrier to entry

IBM, the company receiving the most U.S. patents in 2003,[5] used its IP portfolio to produce licensing revenue of just under $2 billion. In major part, the business role for patents at IBM is to be used as the basis for licensing revenue.

Sony and NEC are examples of companies, also high on the list of those receiving the most U.S. patents in 2003, proud of their large portfolios of patents and also of their ability to generate large numbers of new patents per year. They position themselves in the marketplace as technology leaders, with their patent prowess as evidence of that leadership position. Certainly for companies such as these, patents play a role in the company's strategic positioning in the marketplace.

Best Practice 2. Maintain an Inventory of IP

Fewer than 20% of the companies holding intellectual property have an accurate, up-to-date knowledge of the contents of their portfolio. Even fewer companies are able to relate the contents of their portfolio to their company's business or its strategy. In fact, very few companies can describe the business relationship between their IP and company strategic or tactical activities. Most companies keep track of their patented intellectual property with a docketing system, an information system used to shepherd potential patents through the pre-, current-, and post-prosecution process. Docketing systems, however, do not identify each piece of IP with its business purpose(s) or the kinds of value the company expects to extract from it.

Most companies do not have accurate inventories of their current IP. In part, that is due to the costs of maintaining currency, in terms of personnel and resources. Other factors contribute to this problem as well. In some cases, where outside counsel is involved with writing or prosecuting patents, these records may not be currently available to the client company. In other cases, business divisions may be the source of the patent prosecutions, and there is no central repository for intellectual property. In still other cases, companies may have acquired other patents and not changed the ownership of the patent to reflect the current situation. A range of factors such as these may account for a firm's lack of awareness of the current contents of its portfolio of IP.

IP inventories may be simple or complex. They may simply contain a listing of the company's intellectual property, organized in some commonsense manner. Simple inventories typically contain a title for the piece of IP, any identifying numbers associated with it, the author(s), and the dates associated with the inception of the IP rights. Complex inventories may contain significantly more information. They may contain information about the use of the patent in company business, the products or services with which the property is concerned, and the roles it is assigned to fill in support of the company's business strategy.

Best Practice 3. Develop Screening Criteria

Screening criteria are used in determining which innovations are to become legally protected. There are two levels of screening criteria. At the simplest level are those criteria developed by the legal department to determine the patentability of an innovation and its need for legal protection. Advanced screening criteria should supplement those developed under the legal perspective and usually deal mostly with the alignment of an innovation with the company's business strategy.

---

[5] "2003 Top Patent Owners," IPO Statistical Series, www.IPO.org.

For example, HP has historically created a fairly tight set of screening criteria for its patent portfolio. It focused on identifying inventions that could be commercialized within the next 5 years. For HP, time to market is a critical factor, as the technology life cycle is continually shrinking. In subsequent years, HP added criteria that defined which types of patents it wished to encourage. Its advanced criteria also allowed the company to identify which patents to eliminate from the portfolio.

Best Practice 4. Organize to Extract Value from the Firm's IP

As firms build their competence in creating and extracting business value from intellectual property, they often move the value extraction function (i.e., the business function) out of the IP Department. This allows firms to review all of the business activity required to create and extract IP value and helps them ensure that organizational IP management functions are clearly delineated, responsibilities assigned, and authority identified.

The IC management "gathering" identified two areas of concern when companies ask themselves how to organize to extract value from their IP. The first concerns the functions that need to be performed in managing the firm's IP. The second involves the degree to which the activity should be centralized or decentralized, as well as to whom the activity should report.

The IC management "gathering" has identified the following functions as necessary for extracting value from intellectual property:

- IP generation, protection, maintenance, and enforcement.
- Portfolio inventory, management, and administration.
- Portfolio mining and opportunity identification.
- IP training, education, and process design.
- Brand management.
- IP transactions.
- Competitive assessment.
- Innovation.
- Relationship management (customers, suppliers, others).
- Marketing.

Concerning the question of centralization of IP management activity vs. decentralization, two major factors must be considered: Where should the IP management functions be performed (the "activity") and where should authority for decision making about IP reside ("authority"). Exhibit 10.3 identifies nine different possibilities for centralizing or decentralizing IP management activity and authority within the firm. Exhibit 10.4 contains judgments of where companies within the IC management "gathering" might fit on the matrix. Exhibit 10.5 highlights the very central cell in the matrix, because its "mixed" approach is arguably the most frequently occurring situation. The exhibit highlights the functions that are centralized as well as those that are decentralized in this popular organizational mode.

Best Practice 5. Focus on Strategic Value Creation through IP

In the early stages of company growth, IP is important to protect company products and services. But as the company matures and IP becomes recognized as a strategic asset (in addition to retaining its tactical uses), it becomes important to begin creating value through IP that transcends the company's current products and services.

Exhibit 10.3

Matrix of IAM Authority and Activity Centralization Possibilities

Authority	Activity		
	Decentralized	Mixed	Centralized
Centralized	Value extraction may or may not be strategic to the firm. IP activity dispersed throughout the BUs (Business Unit). All value extraction efforts are approved centrally.	Value extraction is not entirely strategic to the firm. Value activities are shared: legal and licensing tend to be centralized, other functions are decentralized.	Value extraction important to corporate strategy. All IP activities under one roof (business and legal). All value extraction efforts are approved centrally.
Mixed		Value extraction is not entirely strategic to the firm. Value activities are shared: legal and licensing tend to be centralized, other functions are decentralized. Some Activity given to BUs, others reside with corporate staff.	Value extraction is not entirely strategic to the firm. All IP activities under one roof (business and legal). Some authority given to BUs, others reside with corporate staff.
Decentralized		Value extraction is not entirely strategic to the firm. Value activities are shared: legal and licensing tend to be centralized, other functions are decentralized. Value extraction is controlled and approved by BUs.	Value extraction may or may not be strategic to the firm. All IP activities under one roof (business and legal). Value extraction is controlled and approved by BUs.

Source: Davis and Harrison 2001, p. 88.

Exhibit 10.4

Gathering Company Positioning on Centralization Possibility Matrix			
Authority	Activity		
	Decentralized	Mixed	Centralized
Centralized	(No "gathering" company in this category) *Minimize central staff*	Xerox Roche *Shared decision making*	IBM FGTI (Ford Global Technologies, Inc.) Litton *Efficiency and rapid response*
Mixed	Skandia *Minimize central staff Shared resources*	Boeing HP Eastman SAIC *Shared decision making Shared resources*	Fortran *Efficiency and moderate-speed response*
Decentralized	(No "gathering" company in this category)	Dow Dupont *BU (Business Unit)—centric decision making*	Lockheed *Efficiency but slow response*
	Value Extraction Mechanisms (few/many)		

Increased Speed of Response →

Source: Davis and Harrison 2001, p. 89.

Companies may create strategic value through their IP. This is accomplished by creating IP that supports the company's strategic objectives. For example,

1. Companies in a highly competitive tactical business environment should patent in areas that are of interest to *competitors* in addition to areas that protect its own products, services, and processes.
2. Companies whose competitors are preparing to make new strategic thrusts should create IP that can counter or blunt the thrusts.
3. Companies about to make their own strategic thrusts or initiatives should create patents to pave the way.
4. Companies in industries where competitors hold patents of interest should create a portfolio containing patents desired by competitors. As bargaining chips, patents are worth more than cash when one is negotiating for access to someone else's patents.
5. Companies should seek merger or acquisition candidates whose patent portfolio is complementary to its own or whose patents expand the coverage of its own. Companies whose portfolio duplicates its own provide no strategic IP value.

Best Practice 6. Focus on Strategic Value Extraction

As a firm becomes more sophisticated in its business use of IP, it will realize that its assets have strategic uses. It must develop ways to use those assets strategically as well

Exhibit 10.5

Detail of Mixed Authority and Activity Cell in Possibility Matrix			
Authority	**Activity**		
	Decentralized	**Mixed**	**Centralized**
Centralized		*Centralize*: Legal—IP protection and maintenance Inventory review IP portfolio management Patent portfolio management IP training IP audit Licensing/IP business development IP decision processes (best practices) Brand management	*Decentralize*: IP value extraction activity Invention capture Competitive assessment (technology and business) Product innovation Customer relationships Marketing
Mixed			
Decentralized			
	Value Extraction Mechanisms (few/many)		

Increased Speed of Response

Source: Davis and Harrison 2001, p. 90.

as tactically. In general, value extraction opportunities that require both IP and some associated complementary business assets tend to provide more value to the company than those involving IP by itself. For example,

1. A company can make the revenue generated through IP sufficient to be of strategic interest to the firm. Some companies (IBM is a good example) have made the licensing of IP a strategic activity within the firm. IBM generates sufficient revenue from its IP licensing arm to make that a significant portion of the firm's total revenue.
2. Some companies use their IP strategically to obtain access to business assets they would otherwise have to pay for out of cash. A joint venture where one party contributes IP and another contributes hard assets (e.g., laboratory facilities, test sites) is a way to leverage the company's IP strategically.
3. Other companies may create strategic value through their investments in spin-offs, in particular where the new company is in a different strategic market than the parent. A spin-off, where the parent company contributes IP (and the associated know-how) along with people and facilities resources has considerably better odds of business success than a spin-off without the IP or the know-how (3Com, Adobe, and SynOptics are three examples of very successful spin-offs where IP was a significant part of the package).
4. Still other companies find that research conducted for a strategic business reason may become moot as markets and customer needs change. Rather than discarding the resulting IP, it may be more useful to retain it and explore ways of converting it into value through licensing or sale to someone else.

Best Practice 7. Develop a Competitive Assessment Capability

As the firm's intellectual properties become strategic assets, so too does it become important to ensure that the firm maintains those strategic assets in relation to its IP competitors. The firm must incorporate an IP competitive assessment capability into its strategic thinking and planning. Competitive IP assessment involves the capability of analyzing a competitor's portfolio *in one's own context.*

Typically IP competitive assessment involves two levels of detail. At the first level, demographics, the analysis deals with the numbers of patents in a competitor's portfolio. Issues of interest in a demographic comparison of portfolios are questions such as these: How many patents does the competitor have in technology areas of concern to this company? What is the remaining life on those patents? What is the pace of patenting (in total and also in those technology areas of interest to this company)?

The second level of detail involves assessing the content of the competitor's portfolio. Of interest at the content level are questions such as these: In what ways does the competitor portfolio align with the company's business strategy? How does the competitor use its portfolio to support its business strategy? What is the distribution of technologies across the competitor's portfolio? What "coverage" do the competitor's patents provide to the company's products or services? Where are there holes in coverage that might be exploited?

Valuation of IP

Current approaches for measuring the current or potential value of intellectual property to the corporation are widely agreed to be inadequate. This may be largely due to the attempt to develop one universal valuation method that satisfies the needs of the stock market *and* financial reporting *and* management decision making. Attempts to accomplish this through the framework of accounting have produced a lot of heat but little illumination. Virtually all the proposed solutions conducted using the accounting framework focus on reporting IP to meet the needs of the stock market for value information or the requirements of financial reporting. These valuation methods do not provide company managers with the valuation information they need to support business decision making. In particular, they do not support decision making related to finding new sources of top-line revenues or bottom-line profits from intangibles.

The fundamental inadequacy of the accounting framework regarding intangibles is that it measures only transactions, which means, by definition, that accounting can measure something only after the fact. This obviously is not helpful for most management decision-making purposes, when we are trying to anticipate future outcomes and select the best current course of action. To the extent that accounting measures intangibles as assets, the focus is on comparing book value (based on past transactions) against an estimate of the fair market value. But fair market value, by definition, is the value an asset would have to a *buyer* not the value to the owner. It does not matter to accounting whether an intangible has the potential to generate value in more than one context and what those contexts are. What matters to accounting is simply, what transactions has the intangible generated lately?

Member companies of the IC management "gathering" recognized these valuation inadequacies some years ago and evolved methods for IP valuation that focus on measuring the value potential in a firm's intangibles from at least two key perspectives: optimizing the future value from an intangible based on current decisions and mea-

Exhibit 10.6

The typical fair market value calculation process.

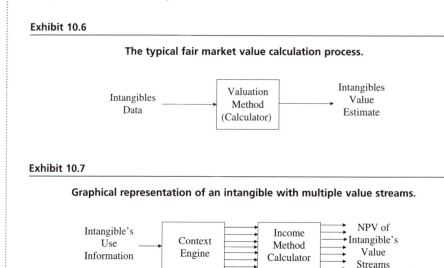

Exhibit 10.7

Graphical representation of an intangible with multiple value streams.

suring intangible "value to owner" rather than fair market value (FMV) or book value. These perspectives on IP valuation are based on three important principles:

1. The value of intangibles depends on the context within which they are used.
2. Intangibles may have *multiple simultaneous* value streams.
3. The value of intangibles resides in these multiple streams of value stretching into the future.

The valuation calculation itself is quite straightforward. The IP valuation challenge lies in defining each of the potential multiple value streams that IP may provide and, for each value stream, its context. Only by defining the context for each value stream is it possible to identify the appropriate data and information for use in the valuation calculation. The calculation process associated with fair market value, typically accomplished through the use of accounting information, may be graphically depicted as shown in Exhibit 10.6.

But, the process for determining the value of an intangible with multiple simultaneous value streams involves first identifying the value streams and their context, then calculating the net present value (NPV) of each value stream. The sum of these value-stream net present value calculations provides the best estimate of the full value of an intangible. The process for valuing an intangible such as IP using a multiple-context "engine" to identify each value stream before it is calculated is graphically represented in Exhibit 10.7.

The process for defining the context(s) for company intangibles' value streams, as well as the current and potential value streams available, involves several straightforward steps:

1. Taking an inventory of the company's intangibles.
2. Identifying the kinds of value the company seeks from its intangibles.
3. Matching each intangible with the kind of value it provides to the company.
4. Identifying current and potential applications for each intangible.
5. Providing information describing the context for each application:

- In what market segments could it create value?
- What mechanisms could be used to convert it into cash?
- For whom are the value streams to be calculated?
- Which value calculation approach is to be used?
- What is the business decision to be made with the value stream information?
6. Calculating the value streams for each context.
7. Summing the NPV of the value streams to obtain an estimate of the value of the intangible to the corporation.

Within the IC management "gathering," it has long been acknowledged that it is not possible to value IP through the use of the accounting framework. Although accounting serves many business valuation needs, it is incapable of comprehensively valuing intangibles. Valuing IP for the purposes of management decision making involves using standard financial and economic concepts and methods that specifically exclude the inadequacies of accounting and focus on the context dependency of intangibles.

Whereas accounting methodologies are useful for measuring and reporting, in particular for doing so where information is to be provided to the capital markets, it is misleading when applied to intangibles such as IP. And, it is not a valid method of valuing intangibles for most company decision-making purposes. For the latter, the methods and processes must be context sensitive and deal with all of the value streams that intangibles may simultaneously provide their owners.

Valuation Methods, Tools, and Techniques

As noted previously, there are several accounting-based methods of valuation, which focus primarily on valuations for reporting to the capital markets. These include fair market valuation methods and generally accepted accounting principles (GAAP). In recent years, an emerging *accounting* literature has criticized the ability of GAAP to accurately report the value of intangibles to the firm. This criticism is persuasive, yet it still deals only with the value of intangibles in capital markets, not the operational value of IP to the owning firm.

The U.S. Federal Accounting Standards Board (FASB) defines *fair market value* as "the amount at which an asset (or a liability) could be bought (or incurred) or sold (or settled) in a current transaction between willing parties: that is, other than in a forced or liquidation sale." Accounting standard setters in other countries use similar definitions. What are the implications of this definition for using fair market value as a way to value intangibles? Again, as noted already, intangibles have value only in context. By definition, the concept of FMV implies that the definitive context for measuring value is that of the *purchaser*. Using FMV as a value concept tells us what an intangible asset is worth *to someone else*.

However, FMV says nothing about what an intangible asset is worth *to its owner, in the owner's context*. In the world of tangible assets, one does not generally need to differentiate between value to owner and value to others. The value of a building is roughly the same to its owner as it is to potential purchasers. The same is largely true for a machine, a desk, or a corporate bond. But this is not true for an intangible asset.

At best, FMV provides only half of the information necessary for an owner to decide whether to sell or keep its drinks-dispensing patent (for example). In reality, however, FMV as used in typical practice is usually calculated in a way *insensitive to context*. What relevance do other nominally "comparable" transactions involving similar intangibles have to the owner's particular intangible in the owner's context? Most valuators do not fully recognize the ability of some intangibles to generate *multiple simultaneous* value streams. As normally used, FMV has little more economic relevance to a firm's business decision than book value.

Over the years, accountants and valuators developed tools and techniques to measure the value of tangible assets in accordance with the traditional concepts of book value and FMV. It would be natural to assume that one could use the same value concepts, tools, and techniques to measure intangibles. But this assumption would be wrong.

Calculating the value potential of intangibles requires a new set of concepts and methods that incorporate the notion of context dependency, distinguish between tradable and nontradable intangibles, and recognize the potential for multiple simultaneous value streams. We need a different value paradigm that reflects these unique characteristics of intangibles.

Value to Owner

Accountants have long distinguished between "value in exchange" and "value in use." An owner (a firm) needs to think about the value of an intangible to *it* in *its* context. Value to owner (VTO) recognizes that intangibles may have multiple simultaneous uses and contexts. The different uses and contexts represent separate, distinct value streams. Under the VTO approach to valuation, the uses for each intangible are identified, as are the potential multiple value streams arising from each use. The value streams are then quantified using standard valuation methods. The sum of the multiple context value streams is the total value of the intangible to its owner.

Value to Buyer

Equally, when considering selling or extracting value from an intangible through a third party, the owner wants to quantify the value of the intangible to the buyer, in the buyer's context. The process for determining and valuing the multiple contexts to the buyer are the same as those used for VTO.

A Look into the Future

The legal protections IP affords are likely to continue to be of value to its owners in the future just as they have in the past. Further, the value of IP as a strategic and tactical asset will likely increase over time, as firms discover more ways to create and extract value through their IP. Firms discovering how to do so most likely will take steps to improve their use and management of IP strategically.

Issues surrounding valuation will become ever more important as their impact on the strategic use of IP increases. Issues surrounding the management of and value extraction from IP will also continue to increase in importance.

We can expect to see companies become more aware of the current and potential business value of their IP and take steps to create value extraction capabilities like those found in sophisticated companies, such as the companies in the IC management "gathering." Further, understanding the true value of intangibles such as IP or IC requires shifts in thinking, away from a traditional accounting framework that is transaction based and backward looking toward one that is context sensitive and future oriented.

As the importance of intellectual capital, such as IP, to corporations rises, firms will develop methods, processes, and techniques to better utilize this valuable resource. In the very near future, we can expect CEOs to take a personal interest in the value created by IP for the firm as well as in the nature and kind of value the firm can extract from it.

References

Davis, J., and S. Harrison. 2001. *Edison in the Boardroom.* New York: John Wiley & Sons.
Sullivan, P. H. Sr. 1998. *Profiting from Intellectual Capital.* New York: John Wiley & Sons.
Sullivan, P. H. Sr. 2000. *Value-Driven Intellectual Capital.* New York: John Wiley & Sons.
World Intellectual Property Organization. 2001. *WIPO Intellectual Property Handbook: Policy, Law and Use.* WIPO Publication No. 489 (E) Geneva: WIPO.

Part II
Interdisciplinary Views

An Interfirm Perspective on Intellectual Capital

Giovanni Schiuma
University of Basilicata

Antonio Lerro
University of Basilicata

Daniela Carlucci
University of Basilicata

Introduction

In today's economy, characterized by phenomena such as globalization, higher degrees of complexity, fast evolution of new technology, client demands, and economic and political structures, knowledge resources are recognized as a fundamental strategic lever to manage business performance (Amit and Schoemaker 1993; Grant 1996; Sanchez, Heene, and Thomas 1996; Teece, Pisano, and Shuen 1997) as well as the productivity and competitiveness of nations as a whole (Edvinsson and Bounfour 2004). As a result, some new concepts have been introduced in the management literature to deal with knowledge resources. In particular, intellectual capital has emerged as a key concept to analyze and evaluate the knowledge dimensions of organizations (Prahalad and Hamel 1990; Senge 1990; Stalk, Evans, and Shulman 1992; Drucker 1993; Nonaka and Takeuchi 1995).

In this chapter, we focus our attention on the intellectual capital within firm clusters. Much focus to date has been on the individual firm; however, intellectual capital is an important factor for the economic and industrial development of regions as well as countries (Dierickx and Cool 1989; Tallman et al. 2004). Various scholars have highlighted the importance of knowledge and intangible assets for the competition of firm clusters (Doeringer and Terkla 1995; Jacobs and De Man 1996; Rosenfeld 1996, 1997; Saxenian 1994). Particular attention has been paid to competitive factors, such as the local values and their diffusion, individual and social behaviours, interpersonal and interfirm relationships, skills and know-how, social and institutional actors, and more generally, all the positive externalities provided by the development of a network of stakeholders in a cluster of firms. Therefore, policy makers as well as managers involved in driving the development of local and national networks of firms need approaches and tools to identify, classify, evaluate, and manage the knowledge resources at the basis of competitive development of firm clusters.

This chapter aims to analyze the role and the facets of intellectual capital within firm clusters to provide an interpretative framework to understand their knowledge foundations. First, we discuss what we mean by firm clusters and provide an interpretation of clusters and the competitive factors at the basis of their development. We then outline the role of knowledge assets as a strategic resource in these clusters. Afterward, we provide a framework, the Knoware Tree, for supporting the identification, evaluation, and management of intellectual capital within clusters. We conclude with some final remarks and a look into the future.

Clusters of Firms and Knowledge

Clusters of firms are a relatively recent phenomenon to be addressed in the management literature. Alfred Marshall (1920) already observed that a localized system of small- and medium-size firms vertically integrated and sharing knowledge tend to be very competitive. Other authors have studied the phenomenon of clusters (Hirschman 1958; Losh 1954), but only in the last decades has attention been focused on the system of firms with integrated, coordinated supply chains. Porter (1990) provided one of the first relevant contributions when he addressed the question of why only certain countries generate many companies that become successful international competitors in one or more industries. The analytical lens used by Porter brings into focus the individual company and its place in the structure of a particular cluster of firms in the same industry.

Clusters of firms have been addressed from a wide range of research streams, and it seems that each cluster has specific features in terms of its geographic and economic context (Jacobs and De Man 1996; Jacobs and De Jong 1992; Rosenfeld 1996, 1997). Porter (1990) distinguished between vertical and horizontal clusters. Firms in vertical clusters are linked through buyer-seller relationships. Horizontal clusters include firms that might share a common market for the end products, use a common technology or labour force skills, or require similar natural resources. More recently, Porter (2000) defined a regional cluster as a geographically proximate group of interconnected companies and associated institutions in a particular field, linked by commonalities and complementaries. Similarly, Doeringer and Terkla (1995) defined clusters as geographical concentrations of industries that gain performance advantages through colocation. According to Rosenfeld (1997), an industry cluster is a geographically bounded concentration of similar, related, or complementary businesses, with active channels for business transactions, communications, and dialogue, that share a specialized infrastructure, labor markets, and services; and they are faced with common opportunities and threats. On the base of a review of the economic literature on clusters of firms, it is possible to adopt the following working definition for the analysis of clusters: A cluster of firms is a system of firms, mainly of small or medium size, integrated through a network of interfirm relationships.

Today, the literature includes numerous important contributions on different complementary dimensions of clusters, such as agglomeration economies (Fujita and Thisse 1996); economic geography studies (Krugman 1995; Storper 1997); regional economies (Scott 1998; Saxenian 1994; Braczyk, Cooke, and Heidenreich 1998); industrial districts (Piore and Sabel 1984; Pyke, forse Becattini, and Sengenberger 1990); social networks (Granovetter 1985; Fukuyama 1995; Burt 1997); and cluster competitiveness factors (Porter 1998, 2000; Barnes 1999). Moreover, clusters of firms are important for the competitive success of many industries; examples include semiconductors (Saxenian 1994), biotechnology (Zucker, Darby, and Armstrong 1998), car production (Jenkins and Floyd 2001; Pinch and Henry 1999), information technology (Bresnahan, Gambardella, and Saxenian 2001), motion pictures (Miller and Shamsie 1996), wine making, leather fashions, and many others (Porter 1998).

Value Factors at the Basis of the Development of Firm Clusters

The development of firm clusters, as a particular economic and industrial production model, can be recognized in the 1970s, in concomitance with the crises of the mass production paradigm, based on vertical integration and large hierarchical firms that standardized products and processes. While there is consensus that the firms cluster because they receive some type of benefits, the factors that create those benefits are debated. Porter (1990) argues that competition is a driving force behind cluster development. Clustering is a dynamic process, and as one or more competitive firms grow within a cluster, they generate the demand for the development of the supply chain and other related industries. As the cluster develops, it becomes a mutually reinforcing system where benefits flow backward and forward throughout the industries in the cluster. Porter states that the competition between rival firms in the cluster drives the growth, because it forces firms to be innovative and improve and create new technology. This, in turn, leads to new business spin-off, stimulates R&D, and forces the development of new skills and the introduction of new services. Such growth can lead to either increasing vertical integration or horizontal integration of the sector. Increased vertical integration is realized when the division of labor gets more specialized, and new firms are able to fill new niche markets. Horizontal clustering means that new technology and labor skills are applied to related industries in different sectors.

Clustering often increases productivity and efficiency, due to more-efficient acquisition of production factors, such as work in process and end products, services, knowledge resources, labor skill, and information. Moreover, firms operating within a cluster can rely on a dense network of relationships with suppliers. This allows better interfirms coordination, facilitates the diffusion of best practices, and stimulates the creation of a mix of competitive and collaborative relationships, which spurs firms to continuously improve their business performance (Doeringer and Terkla 1995; Porter 1990).

Clusters stimulate innovation dynamics. It is easier for firms operating within clusters to pursue innovation processes. Clustering of firms specialized in the same or complementary industries enables both systemic and autonomous innovation. The circulation of information and knowledge allows imitation processes, which, combined with continuous improvement, determine the development of new products and process solutions. Moreover, the cooperation between firms specialized in diverse production stages of the same supply chain allows an integration of different know-how with a cross-fertilization in terms of innovation.

The creation of positive externalities related to the formation of economies of agglomeration represents another important factor leading to cluster development. Several authors also identify socialization mechanisms, based on face-to-face interaction and knowledge transfer processes, as a critical factor for cluster development (Doeringer and Terkla 1995; Rosenfeld 1997). This means that the social infrastructure within the cluster facilitates technology and knowledge transfer (Saxenian 1994).

In summary, cluster development is attributable to several key factors, including technology and knowledge transfer, development of a skilled labor force in related industries, and the benefits of agglomeration economies and a social infrastructure.

These factors promote cluster growth on the base of two interrelated and complementary mechanisms: competition and collaboration among the firms in a cluster.

The Role of Knowledge in Clusters of Firms

Knowledge represents a fundamental resource and a key success factor in clusters of firms. In fact, at the basis of the development of clusters is always the use and exploitation of specific individual and collective knowledge, which affects the development of agglomeration economies, flexible specialization, growth of an intensive networking activity among firms, widespread innovation capability, and a capability to operate in international markets.

It has always been possible to recognize the growth and diffusion of practical and technical know-how at the basis of the development of firm clusters (Albino and Schiuma 2003). For many clusters, the availability of a historic heritage of social-cultural values and technical-operative knowledge is of fundamental importance. This often creates a base for the development of specialized production competencies as well as of an entrepreneurial atmosphere of the cluster (Becattini 1987, 1990; Marshall 1920, Camagni 1991).

To stress the knowledge-based nature of clusters, we propose an interpretative metaphor outlining the cluster model as a "cognitive system"; that is, as a social-productive system in which productive, organizational, and social experiences are generated and accumulated over time and integrated with tangible infrastructures. In the remaining part of this chapter, we outline the cognitive nature of firm clusters and propose a framework for the identification, mapping, and evaluation of the intellectual capital dimensions of clusters.

Knoware Tree: Intellectual Capital Dimensions of Firm Clusters

In recent years, research on intellectual capital has emerged to address how to manage the knowledge dimensions organization system. It reflects the belief that knowledge is a new resource of corporate development and intellectual capital is a critical value driver for a company's competitiveness. There is no doubt that successful companies of today tend to be those that continuously innovate, take advantage of new technologies, and utilize the skills and know-how of their employees. At the same time, traditional tangible assets seem to become increasingly transient and rarely provide a long-term competitive advantage. Intellectual capital includes those assets that are intangible in nature, such as human resources, relationships, culture, routines, and practices, as well as those that represent an intellectual property, such as brands, patents, trademarks, and copyrights.

The wide literature about clusters focuses on knowledge as the critical driver for cluster development. To investigate the intellectual capital dimensions of clusters, we stress the knowledge nature of intellectual capital (Marr and Schiuma 2001; Marr, Gray, and Schiuma 2004) and adopt the following definition: Intellectual capital is the group of knowledge assets attributed to an organization system, that is, the firm as well as a cluster of firms, and most significantly contributes to an improvement of its competitive position by generating value to the stakeholders of the organization system.

Various approaches, frameworks, and tools have been proposed for measuring and managing intellectual capital in organizations (e.g., Brooking 1996; Lev 2001; Marr and Schiuma 2001; Roos et al. 1997; Sveiby 1997). These approaches were designed for the analysis of intellectual capital within firms and not for the identification, clas-

Figure 11.1

Knoware Tree, mapping and evaluating intellectual capital within clusters of firms.

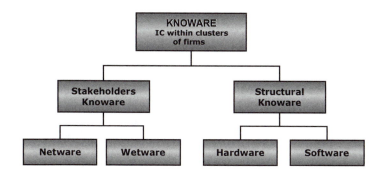

sification, and evaluation of knowledge assets within clusters of firms. The analysis of intellectual capital within firm clusters requires a wide approach that takes into account the systemic nature of clusters (i.e., the cluster's stakeholders and their relationships) as well as the soft and hard structural characteristics of a cluster. To provide managers, policy makers, and all the stakeholders of a cluster with a broader framework for the identification, evaluation, and management of knowledge assets within a cluster, we propose the *Knoware Tree* as a mapping and evaluation model. It is based on the logic of the knowledge asset map (Marr and Schiuma 2001) and assumes that knowledge is the foundation of each systemic component of a cluster; consequently, any dimension of a cluster can be interpreted, analyzed, evaluated, and managed in accordance with a knowledge-based viewpoint.

The intention of the Knoware Tree is to provide a framework that supports the understanding of the structure of knowledge assets in clusters. It allows the identification and definition of knowledge areas of a cluster and drives the design of indicators and metrics to assess the intellectual capital of a cluster of firms. It assumes that the knowledge assets of a cluster of firms can be grouped in two main categories: the Stakeholders Knoware and the Structural Knoware. This distinction reflects two key components of any cluster of firms: its actors and its constituent parts, the infrastructure items (see also Marr et al. 2003). Both categories are further divided into subcategories of knowledge assets. The Stakeholders Knoware can be divided in Netware and Wetware. The Structural Knoware can be split into Hardware and Software (see Figure 11.1). In the following, each dimension of the Knoware Tree is outlined.

Stakeholder Knoware: Wetware versus Netware

Wetware

We define *wetware* as the knowledge owned by human resources (Romer 2003), knowledge assets embodied in people. Wetware includes both know-how, which is unique to the individual, and knowledge, which is more generic. Examples of wetware are innovation capability, creativity, experiences, teamwork capability, leadership, flexibility, tolerance for ambiguity, motivation, satisfaction, learning capability, loyalty, formal training and education, commitment, technical expertise, problem-solving ability, and so on. To classify the nature of the knowledge, a distinction between tacit and codified knowledge can be adopted. Tacit knowledge is knowledge rooted in an individual's ability and difficult to articulate in a way that is meaningful and complete (Nelson and Winter 1982; Nonaka and Takeuchi 1995; Polanyi 1966). This knowledge can be transferred between individuals only by face-to-face interaction, while explicit or codified knowledge is incorporated into information code and can be transferred effectively by information processing. The nature of knowledge affects the efficiency of both interpersonal and interfirm relationships within clusters (Bohn 1994; Leplat 1990; Nonaka and Takeuchi 1995). When the knowledge to be transferred is not codified, ambiguities in the communication process can result, which can be overcome only by face-to-face interaction. In fact, the socialization process based on person-to-person interaction allows interpretation errors to be corrected by prompt feedback. This is a critical aspect of performance within clusters of firms that are strongly characterized by tacit knowledge embodied in individuals who design, produce, and manage the production processes and products. This requires that, to integrate and coordinate the activities within the cluster, face-to-face mechanisms are necessary. Instead, when the knowledge to be transferred is codified (i.e., knowledge translated into procedures, rules, and specifications), the transfer process can be performed by impersonal means, such as computer, intranet, Internet, or technical manuals.

Netware

We define *netware* as intangible assets of firm clusters related to the network of relationships created by the actors of a cluster. We group them in two main categories: the firms of the cluster and the social system of the cluster. The latter includes stakeholders within the cluster, such as the community, the institutions, the regulators, and the consumers; the former includes the stakeholders external to the cluster (Figure 11.2). The analysis of the network of relationships can be performed by adopting a cognitive approach, which is consistent with the resource-based and knowledge-based view. The knowledge-based approach to the theory of the firm, rejecting the pure contractual interpretation of the nature of the firm and the interfirm relationships (Foss 1996), interprets the relationships within a cluster as cognitive interaction between different actors (Grant and Baden-Fuller 1995; Kogut and Zander 1996).

The *internal network* involves all stakeholder relationships created within the cluster. We distinguish two main categories: interfirms relationships and relationships of firms with the social system of the cluster.

Figure 11.2

Netware, the relationships created by cluster's stakeholders within and outside the cluster.

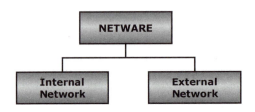

The interfirm relationships involve all interfirm networking processes developed within clusters. These are mainly due to the decomposition of the production process into operative subprocesses, in which groups of firms specialize. Although the reasons for the forming of interfirm relationships are numerous, ranging from the need to spread production and investment costs among different firms to the aim of acquiring new technical skills or technological capabilities from partner firms (Hamel 1991), every interfirm relationship involves a knowledge exchange and in such a way that the relationship in itself can be considered a knowledge asset. The specialization of a cluster's firms on specific stages of the production process involves the development of interfirm relational learning processes. In fact, the specialization with the integration of different competencies fosters an intensive networking activity by the firms aiming to coordinate their operations (Inkpen 1996; Powell, Koput, and Smith-Doerr 1996). The networking processes of the cluster firms involve an exchange of operation experiences that leads to the generation of new knowledge by the development of cognitive cross-fertilization processes (Nevis, oi Bella, and Gould 1995; Tsoukas, 1996). Furthermore, the cognitive growth of the cluster's firms is linked to the content of the interfirm relationships, involving numerous technical, economic, commercial, social, and personal aspects (Hakansson 1987). The networking processes within a cluster enable the firms to develop relational abilities. These abilities allow firms to reduce their coordination costs, thanks to sharing a set of tacit and explicit behavioral and interpretative rules, which reduce the uncertainty and the ambiguity of the informative-cognitive exchanges related to the interfirm relationships.

The relationships of firms with the social system of the cluster involve all the networking processes developed by firms with all the other stakeholders of the cluster. Different conceptual frameworks have been proposed in the literature to analyze the integration between the cluster production system, the cluster's firms, and the social system of a cluster. However, two main interpretative metaphors can be identified: the "district atmosphere" and the "milieu innovateur" (Camagni 1991). Both allow an analysis of the relationships linking the cluster's firms and the social system of the cluster. Moreover, they allow an understanding of the external economies that support the development of firm clusters. From a knowledge point of view, the cluster relationships network involves the formation of a "cognitive context" that allows collective learning processes to take place. The cluster's firms operate in an economic environment characterized by multiple social relationships, which appear mainly informal in nature. These are based on the spread of interpersonal relationships within the geographically local area. These relationships allow knowledge diffusion that supports both collective learning processes and the formation of an innovative context. The collective learning processes involve knowledge-creation processes, based either on learning by imitation or on local benchmarking processes. At a local level, the learning processes, based on the imitation of the products as well as of the behavior of successful cluster's of firms, represent one of the most important internal boosters for the extensive growth of clusters. In fact, emulation processes involve the growth of an entrepreneurial structure characterized by cooperation and competition at the same time.

The *external network* involves all the relationships between stakeholders of a cluster and the external environment. It can take different forms and has diverse characteristics. The relationships can range from institutional network relationships, such as the relationships between regulators and the cluster, to market relationships (i.e., all kinds of relationships with customers, investors, and companies). However, one of the most important relationships is the commercial one. This can be interpreted as the process of acquiring information from the market. The information flow can be based on an adaptive or pro-active approach. Thus, the firms, interacting with the outside environment, can identify signals of the market demands and either respond to the market requests or generate new market outlets opportunities. A cluster interacting with the external environment does not develop only commercial and business-oriented relationships, it also creates relationships with stakeholders that can affect the future growth of the cluster. Particularly important are relationships aimed to support the acquisition or the creation of new knowledge (Spender 1996; Powell et al. 1996). These include relationships with universities and research centers as well as with other clusters, which can spur the learning capability of the cluster (Hamel 1991; Powell et al. 1996; Hassen-Bauer and Snow 1996).

Structural Knoware: Hardware versus Software

Hardware

The hardware dimension of the structural knoware includes all assets important for knowledge development, acquisition, management, and application that are tangible in nature. Their importance is linked to the fact that tangible infrastructure incorporates and provides knowledge. As enablers, their importance is related to the influence they can have on the efficiency and effectiveness of using, implementing, and exploiting knowledge assets. Two subdimensions can be considered in this category: physical infrastructure, which includes transport infrastructures and territory infrastructures; and technological infrastructure, which includes operations technologies and the information and communication technologies (ICT) (Figure 11.3).

The *physical infrastructure* encompasses the technical sublayers that allow a cluster of firms to operate and grow. It involves two main categories of assets: the transport infrastructures and the territory infrastructures.

Transport infrastructure embraces road, railway, air, and harbor links; logistic systems; and the utilities networks. Transport infrastructure networks contribute to creating positive externalities and facilitate material, information, and knowledge transfer to and from the cluster. In particular, for firms based in local clusters, the spatial distribution of the production processes makes the transport infrastructure networks an integrated part of the production processes.

Territory infrastructure is linked mainly to the urban structure of a cluster area. It involves both the characteristics of the geographic context in which the cluster of firms

Figure 11.3

Hardware, the tangible infrastructure affecting the intellectual capital of clusters of firms.

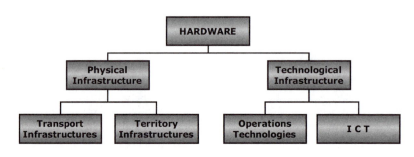

is located and the urban features, such as the size of towns involved in the cluster and the features of the urban development, that is, the use of the territory as well as the area environment. The territory infrastructure affects the culture, the attitudes, and behavior of people operating within a cluster of firms. Moreover, it affects the size of the population, the population density and the demographic trends, the structure and the typology of the families, the social stratification, the education levels, the activity and inactivity rate of the population, as well as the employment rate.

The *technological infrastructure* represents technical assets at the base of all internal processes of the firms and the whole cluster. It can be subdivided into operations technologies and ICT.

Operations technologies include all equipment and machinery that are needed for the productive processes. Their level of importance is related strictly to the nature of the cluster industry, capital vs. labor intensive.

ICT includes all the technological infrastructure, such as Internet, intranet, digital communication systems, and so on, which support the information and knowledge transfer processes within the cluster of firms and between the cluster and the external environment (i.e., other clusters of firms, companies, and generally other stakeholders). ICT is a strategic resource for clusters of firms, since it supports the integration and coordination of the activities within the firm as well as along the supply chains of the cluster.

Software

The software dimension of the structural knoware includes all widespread knowledge, routines, and practices that are the basis of the daily activities of clusters of firms. The software dimension involves two main categories of knowledge assets: the organizational/interorganizational routines and practices, and the sociocultural values (Figure 11.4).

The *organizational and interorganizational routines and practices* within a cluster of firms involve all the knowledge of an interpersonal nature developed by individual face-to-face relationships within an organization (Nelson and Winter 1982) as well as the interorganizational knowledge developed in the relationships along the supply chain of a cluster of firms (Albino and Schiuma 2003). The organization routines demonstrate mainly the form of nonformalized organizational rules and procedures as well as relationships between individuals within a firm in the cluster, while the interorganizational routines correspond to the overall knowledge developed by firms in their networking processes. These are mainly of a tacit nature, grounded in the firm's ability

Figure 11.4

Software, the intangible infrastructure affecting the intellectual capital of clusters of firms.

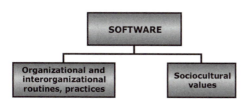

to establish flexible relationships. The interorganizational routines can be interpreted as the result of an interfirm socialization process, which takes the form of direct relationships between both entrepreneurs and workers operating in different firms integrated along the supply chains.

The *sociocultural values* involve a wide range of aspects related to the psychological and sociological features of a cluster. These are the result of the integration of the firms with the context in which the cluster is located. This context involves an extension of interpersonal networks, characterizing the cluster's firms, outside organizational borders, with the involvement of the overall social system of the cluster (i.e., all the cluster's stakeholders). The sociocultural values present a form of shared cognitive maps that give stakeholders operating within a cluster similar interpretative and behavioral frameworks. It includes the shared beliefs, cultural and political background, behavioral codes, life styles, and work ethics. Work ethics have been recognized by many authors as a fundamental viewpoint for interpreting the success of locally based clusters, that is, industrial districts (Becattini 1987). In fact, the high productivity of district firms, as well as the extensive startup of small firms within a district area, can be linked to the interpretation of the work, not only as a mean of subsistence but mainly as a social means of identification. The value of the work for the individuals operating in district firms involves the strong commitment of workers to the production processes, which contributes to support an entrepreneurial atmosphere. Traditionally, the literature investigated mainly the links between the sociocultural values and the relationship mechanism within clusters of firms. The sociocultural values have been interpreted as drivers of individual and organizational behavior in terms of attitudes and approaches to the relationships (Bourdieu and Wacquant 1992). Concepts like "cluster social capital" (Gabbay and Leenders 1999) were introduced to stress the relevance of sociocultural values within clusters of firms. They have been identified as the factors, within a cluster, that enable the access to information and opportunities (Burt 1992, 1997; Campbell, Marsden, and Hurlbert 1986; Coleman 1990; Granovetter 1973, 1985) and facilitate the creation of an atmosphere of trust among the different stakeholders, minimizing the uncertainties of change and maximizing the potential for the cooperation (Burt and Knez 1995; Gargiulo 1993; Gulati 1995).

Closing Remarks

For the analysis of intellectual capital within clusters of firms, we propose a cognitive approach. In accordance with this approach, a cluster of firms can be considered a "cognitive system," that is, an organism whose distinctive nature is represented by its ability to generate and accumulate knowledge.

This means that knowledge assets are at the center of clusters and can take the form of netware, wetware, hardware, and software. These knowledge assets, as "repositories" or "vectors" of knowledge (Krogh and Vicari 1992), evolve over time by knowledge management processes, specifically by knowledge creation and diffusion processes. Therefore, the success of clusters of firms is not only linked to the stock of intellectual capital owned by the cluster but mainly to the knowledge management processes, which represent the main "engine" of the cluster's growth.

To analyze the knowledge management processes within a cluster of firms, it is important to distinguish two cognitive spheres: one "internal" in nature and the other "external." The first corresponds to the cognitive heritage of a cluster; the second is the overall knowledge identifiable in the external environment of a cluster in the form of both "public knowledge," such as scientific-technological knowledge, and "private knowledge," such as knowledge linked to the know-how of the firms operating outside the cluster.

Consistent with this distinction of cognitive spheres, it is possible to identify two cognitive dynamics of clusters of firms. The first, the internal cognitive dynamic, is linked to the capabilities of a cluster to generate and diffuse knowledge, sometimes also by the acquisition of information from the external environment and its elaboration within the cluster. The second, the external cognitive dynamic, is related to the capabilities of a cluster to acquire knowledge from the external environment or to generate knowledge through relationships established with cognitive systems external to the cluster. For example, this can be performed by setting up collaborative relationships between a cluster's firms and other firms operating outside the cluster.

Knowledge-creation processes are related strictly to the characteristics of the actors operating within a cluster. Using the Knoware Tree, it is possible to analyze the cognitive dynamics in a cluster, taking into account two main aspects: the stakeholders involved in the knowledge-management processes and the relationships between them. We distinguish two main categories of stakeholders: the firms in the cluster and the social system of the cluster. Particularly important is the role of firms in the development of knowledge-creation processes within a cluster. It seems possible to identify two main classes of learning mechanisms: the "individual-learning" processes related to each firm and the "relational-learning" processes associated with cognitive relationships of cluster firms. In particular, the "individual-learning" processes involve all the knowledge-creation processes of individuals working in the cluster firms and directly involved in the firm's business processes. This is coherent with the main results of the studies on the characteristics of the learning organization, which stress that an organization learns through its individuals (Huber 1991; Kim 1993). These processes are performed mainly via two cognitive dynamics: those of a trial-and-error nature, based mainly on learning-by-doing and learning-by-using mechanisms, and those of asocial nature, based mainly on learning through social processes, which take the form of face-to-face relationships between individuals operating within the organisational context. The individual-learning mechanisms are based on the high specialization level of a cluster's firms. The specialization allows the development of specific core competences in cluster firms, involving the growth of learning based on learning by specialization.

It is important to stress that all the knowledge management processes of clusters of firms appear strongly related to the context in which they take place. This means that the knowledge developed within clusters is mainly context specific; that is, it is linked strictly to the context characteristics of the cluster. So, generally, the knowledge generated within a cluster appears strictly and inseparably linked to the firms and the social structure of the cluster. This feature points out that each cluster is unique. Although it is possible to identify a set of similar factors at the basis of growth, each cluster presents specific, distinctive features that appear based mainly on the specific intellectual capital and cognitive dynamics of the cluster.

Finally, to conclude this chapter, we believe that more attention should be paid to the development of operative tools to measure and report the intellectual capital within clusters of firms. For this reason, the Knoware Tree represents a first attempt to provide an interpretative framework to drive managers and policy makers toward the evaluation of the knowledge dimensions of the intellectual capital of clusters of firms. Moreover, it seems important to develop research aimed at disclosing the cause-effect chain that links the development of intellectual capital with the capabilities of a cluster of firms to generate and accumulate value.

References

Albino, V., and G. Schiuma. 2003. "New Forms of Knowledge Creation and Diffusion in the Industrial District of Matera-Bari." In: *The Net-Evolution of Local Systems—Knowledge Creation, Collective Learning and Variety of Institutional Arrangements*, ed. F. Belussi, G. Gottardi, and E. Rullani. Dordrecht, the Netherlands: Kluwer.

Amit, A., and P. J. H. Schoemaker. 1993. "Strategic Assets and Organizational Rent." *Strategic Management Journal* 14.

Barnes, J. B. 1999. "Industrial Geography, Institutional Economics and Innis." In: *The New Industrial Geography: Regions, Regulation, and Institutions*, ed. T. J. Barnes and M. Gertler. London: Routledge.

Becattini, G. 1987. *Mercato e forze locali: il distretto industriale.* Bologna, Italy: Il Mulino.

———. 1990. "The Marshallian Industrial District as a Socio-Economic Notion." In: *Industrial Districts and Inter-Firm Co-operation in Italy*, ed. F. Pyke, G. Becattini, and W. Sengenberger. Geneva: International Institute for Labor Studies.

Bohn, R. E. 1994. "Measuring and Managing Technological Knowledge." *Sloan Management Review* (Fall).

Bourdieu, P., and J. J. D. Wacquant. 1992. *An Invitation to Reflexive Sociology.* Chicago: University of Chicago Press.

Braczyk, H., P. Cooke, and M. Heidenreich. 1998. *Regional Innovation Systems.* London: UCL Press.

Bresnahan, T., A. Gambardella, and A. Saxenian. 2001. " 'Old Economy' Inputs for 'New Economy' Outcomes: Cluster Formation in the New Silicon Valleys." *Industrial and Corporate Change* 10.

Brooking, A. 1996. *Intellectual Capital: Core Assets for the Third Millenium Enterprise.* London: Thompson Business Press.

Burt, R. S. 1992. *Structural Holes. The Social Structure of Competition.* Cambridge, MA: Harvard University Press.

———. 1997. "The Contingent Value of Social Capital." *Administrative Science Quaterly* 42.

———, and M. Knez. 1996. "Trust and Third Party Gossip." In: *Trust in Organizations*, ed. R. Kramer and T. Tyler. Thousand Oaks, CA: Sage.

Camagni, R. P. 1991. *Innovation Networks. Spatial Perspectives.* London: Belhaven Press.

Campbell, K., P. Marsden, and J. S. Hurlbert. 1986. "Social Resources and Socioeconomic Status." *Social Network* 8.

Carlucci, D., B. Marr, and G. Schiuma. 2004. "The Knowledge Value Chain—How Intellectual Capital Impacts Business Performance." *International Journal of Technology Management* 27, nos. 6–7: 572–590.

Coleman, J. 1990. *Foundations of Social Theory.* Cambridge, MA: Harvard University Press.

Dierickx, I., and K. Cool. 1989. "Asset Stock Accumulation and Competitive Advantage." *Management Science*: 12.

Doeringer, P. B., and D. G. Terkla. 1995. "Business Strategy and Cross-Industry Clusters." *Economic Development Quarterly* 9: 225–237.

Drucker, P. F. 1993. *Post-Capitalist Society.* Oxford: Butterworth Heinemann.

Edvinsson, L., and A. Bounfour. 2004. "Assessing National and Regional Value Creation." *Measuring Business Excellence* 8, no. 1.

Edvinsson, L., and M. S. Malone, M. S. 1997. *Intellectual Capital: The Proven Way to Establish Your Company's Real Value by Measuring Its Hidden Values.* London: Piatkus.

Foss, N. J. 1996. "Knowledge-Based Approaches to the Theory of the Firm: Some Critical Comments." *Organization Science* 7, no. 5: 470–476.

Fujita, M., and J. F. Thisse. 1996. "Economics of Agglomeration." *Journal of the Japanese and International Economies* 10, no. 4.

Fukuyama, F. 1995. *Trust: The Social Virtues and the Creation of Prosperity.* New York: Free Press.

Gabbay, S. M., and R. T. A. J. Leenders. 1999. "CSC: The Structure of Advantage and Disavantage." In: *Corporate Social Capital and Liability,* ed. R. T. A. J. Leenders and S. M. Gabbay. Boston: Kluwer, pp. 1–14.

Gargiulo, M. 1993. "Two step Leverage: Managing Constraint in Organizational Politics." *Administative Science Quarterly 39.*

Granovetter, M. S. 1973. "The Strenght of Weak Ties." *American Journal of Sociology 78.*

———. 1985. "Economic Action and Social Structure: The Problem of Embeddedness." *American Journal of Sociology 91,* no. 3.

Grant, R. M. 1996. "Toward a Knowledge-Based Theory of the Firm." *Strategic Management Journal 17.*

———, and C. Baden-Fuller. 1995. "A Knowledge-Based Theory of Inter-Firm Collaboration." *Best Paper Proceedings Academy of Management:* 17–21.

Gulati, R. 1995. "Social Structure and Alliance Formation Patterns: A Longitudinal Analysis." *Administrative Science Quarterly 40.*

Hakansson, H. 1987. *Industrial Technological Development—A Network Approach.* London: Croom Helm.

Hamel, G. 1991. "Competition for Competence and Inter-Partner Learning within International Strategic Alliances." *Strategic Management Journal 12.*

Hassen-Bauer, J., and C. C. Snow. 1996. "Responding to Hypercompetition: The Structure and Processes of a Regional Learning Network Organization." *Organization Science 7,* no. 4.

Hirschman, A. 1958. *The Strategy of Economic Development.* New Haven, CT: Yale University Press.

Huber, G. 1991. "Organizational Learning: The Contribution Processes and the Literatures." *Organization Sciences 1,* no. 2.

Inkpen, A. C. 1996. "Creating Knowledge through Collaboration." *California Management Review 39,* no. 1.

Jacobs, D., and M. W. de Jong. 1992. "Industrial Clusters and the Competitiveness of the Netherlands." *De Economist* 140: 233–252.

Jacobs, D., and A. P. de Man. 1996. "Clusters, Industrial Policy and Firm Strategy: A Menu Approach." *Technology Analysis and Strategic Management 8,* no. 4: 425–437.

Jenkins, M., and S. W. Floyd. 2001. "Trajectories in the Evolution of Technology: A Multi-Level Study of Competition in Formula One Racing." *Organization Studies 22.*

Kim, H. 1993. "The Link between Individual and Organizational Learning." *Sloan Management Review* (Fall).

Kogut, B., and U. Zander. 1996. "What Firms Do? Coordination, Identity and Learning." *Organization Science 7,* no. 5: 502–518.

Krogh, G., and S. Vicari. 1992. "L'approccio autopoietico all'apprendimento strategico sperimentale." *Economia e Politica Industriale* 74–76.

Krugman, P. 1995. *Development, Geography, and Economic Theory.* Cambridge, MA: MIT Press.

Leplat, J. 1990. "Skills and Tacit Skills: A Psychological Perspective." *Applied Psychology: An International Review 39,* no. 2.

Lev, B. 2001. *Intangibles: Management, Measurement, and Reporting.* Washington, DC: The Brookings Institution.

Losch, A. 1954. *The Economics of Location.* New Haven, CT: Yale University Press.

Marr, B., D. Grey, and A. Neely. 2003. "Why Do Firms Measure Their Intellectual Capital." *Journal of Intellectual Capital 4,* no. 4.

Marr, B., Grey, D., Schiuma, G. (2004) *Measuring Intellectual Capital—What, why, and how?* In: *Handbook of Performance Measurement,* 3rd edition, ed. B. Bourne, pp. 369–412. London: Gee.

Marr, B., and G. Schiuma. 2001. "Measuring and Managing Intellectual Capital and Knowledge Assets in New Economy Organizations." In: *Performance Measurement Handbook,* ed. B. Bourne. London: Gee.

Marr, B., and G. Schiuma. 2003. "Intangible Assets—Defining Key Performance Indicators for Organisational Knowledge Assets." *Business Process Management Journal* 10, no. 4.

Marr, B., G. Schiuma, and A. Neely. 2002. "Assessing Strategic Knowledge Assets in eBusiness." *International Journal of Business Performance Management* 4, no. 2–4.

Marshall, A. 1920. *Principles of Economics*, 8th ed. London: Macmillan.

Miller, D., and J. Shamsie. 1996. "The Resource-Based View of the Firm in Two Enviroments: The Hollywood Film Studios from 1936–1965." *Academy of Management Journal* 39.

Nelson, R. R., and S. G. Winter. 1982. *An Evolutionary Theory of Economic Change*. Cambridge, MA: Belknap.

Nevis, E. C., A. J. di Bella, and J. M. Gould. 1995. "Understanding Organizations as learning Systems." *Sloan Management Review* (Winter).

Nonaka, I., and H. Takeuchi. 1995. *The Knowledge-Creating Company*. Oxford: Oxford University Press.

Norman, R., and R. Ramirez. 1993. "Designing Interactive Strategy. From Value Chain to Value Constellation." *Harvard Business Review* (July–August).

Ouchi, W. G. 1980. "Markets, Bureaucracies and Clans." *Administrative Science Quarterly* 25.

Pennings, J. M., K. Lee, and A. van Witteloostuijn. 1998. "Human Capital, Social Capital and Firm Dissolution." *Academy of Management Journal* 41.

Pinch, S., and N. Henry. 1999. "Paul Krugman's Geographical Economics, Industrial Clustering and the British Motor Sport Industry." *Regional Studies* 33.

Piore, M. J., and C. Sabel. 1984. *The Second Industrial Divide*. New York: Basic Books.

Polanyi, M. 1966. *The Tacit Dimension*. Garden City, NY: Doubleday.

Porter, M. E. 1990. *The Competitive Advantage of Nations*. New York: The Free Press.

——. 1998. *On Competition.* Boston: Harvard Business Review Book.

——. 2000. "Location, Competition, and Economic Development: Local Clusters in a Global Economy." *Economic Development Quarterly* (February):15–34.

——. 2003. "The Economic Performance of Regions." *Regional Studies* 37.

——, and O. Solvell. 1998. "The Role of Geography in the Process of Innovation and the Sustinaible Competitive Advantage of Firms." In: *The Dynamic Firm: The Role of Technology, Strategy, Organization, and Regions*, ed. A. D. Chandler, Jr., O. Solvell, and P. Hangstrom. Cambridge, MA: Oxford University Press.

Powell, W. W., K. W. Koput, and L. Smith-Doerr. 1996. "Interorganizational Collaboration and the Locus of Innovation: Networks of Learning in Biotechnology." *Administrative Science Quarterly* 41.

Prahalad, C. K., and G. Hamel. 1990. "The Core Competence of the Corporation." *Harvard Business Review* 68: 79–91.

Pyke, F., G. Becattini, and W. Sengenberger, eds. 1990. *Industrial Districts and Inter-Firm Cooperation in Italy*. Geneva: International Institute for Labor Studies.

Ring, P. S., and A. H. van de Ven. 1992. "Structuring Cooperative Relationships between Organizations." *Strategic Management Journal* 13.

Romer P. 2003. "The Soft Revolution: Achiving Growth by Managing Intangibles." In: *Intangible Assets*, ed. J. Hand, and B. Lev. Oxford: Oxford University Press.

Roos, J., G. Roos, N. C. Dragonetti, and L. Edvinsson. 1997. *Intellectual Capital: Navigating the New Business Landscape*. London: Macmillan.

Rosenfeld, S. A. 1996. *Overachievers, Business Clusters That Work: Prospects for Regional Development*. Chapel Hill, NC: Regional Technology Strategies, Inc.

——. 1997. "Bringing Business Clusters into the Mainstream of Economic Development." *European Planning Studies* 5, no. 1: 3–23.

Sanchez, R., A. Heene, and H. Thomas. 1996. "Toward a Theory of Competence-Based Competition." In: *Dynamics of competence-based competition*, ed. R. Sanchez, A. Heene, and H. Thomas. Oxford: Elsevier Pergamon.

Saxenian, A. L. 1994. *Regional Advantage. Culture and Competition in Silicon Valley and Route 128*. Cambridge, MA: Harvard University Press.

Scott, A. J. 1998. "The Geographic Foundations of Industrial Performance." In: *The Dynamic Firm: The Role of Technology, Strategy, Organization, and Regions*, ed. A. D. Chandler, Jr., O. Solvell, and P. Hangstrom. Cambridge, MA: Oxford University Press.

Senge, P. M. 1990. *The Fifth Discipline: The Art and Practice of the Learning Organization.* London: Random House, Business Books.

Sheppard, B. H., and D. M. Sherman. 1998. "The Grammars of Trust: A Model and General Implications." *Academy of Management Review* 23.

Sheppard, B. H., and M. Tuchinskj. 1996. "Micro OB in the Network Organization." In: *Trust in organizations*, ed. R. M. Kramer and T. R. Tyler. Thousand Oaks, CA: Sage.

Spender, J. C. 1996. "Making Knowledge the Basis of a Dynamic Theory of the Firm." *Strategic Management Journal* 17 (special issue).

Stalk, G., P. Evans, and L. E. Shulman. 1992. "Competing on Capabilities: The New Rules of Corporate Strategy." *Harvard Business Review* 70: 57–69.

Storper, M. 1997. "Territories, Flows, and Hierarchies in the Global Economy." In: *Spaces of Globalization: Reasserting the Power of the Local*, ed. K. R. Cox. New York: Guilford.

Sveiby, K. E. 1997. "The Intangible Assets Monitor." *Journal of Human Resource Costing and Accounting* 2, no.1.

Tallman, S., M. Jenkins, N. Henry, and S. Pinch. 2004. "Knowledge, Clusters, and Competitive Advantage." *Academy of Management Review* 2.

Teece, D. J. 1998. "Capturing Value from Knowledge Assets: The New Economy, Markets for Know-How and Intangible Assets." *California Management Review* 40, no. 3.

———. 2000. *Managing Intellectual Capital: Organizationa, Strategic, and Policy Dimensions.* Oxford: Oxford University Press.

———, G. Pisano, and A. Shuen. 1997. "Dynamic Capabilities and Strategic Management." *Strategic Management Journal* 18.

Tsai, W., and S. Ghoshal. 1998. "Social Capital and Value Creation: The Role of Intrafirm Networks." *Academy of Management Journal* 41.

Tsoukas, H. 1996. "The Firm as a Distributed Knowledge System: A Constructionist Approach." *Strategic Management Journal* 17.

Uzzi, B. 1997. "Social Structure and Competition in Interfirm Networks: The Paradox of Embedddedness." *Administrative Science Quarterly* 42: 35–67.

van der Linde, C. 2003. "The Demography of Clusters—Findings from the Cluster Meta-Study." In: *Innovation Clusters and Interregional Competition*, ed. J. Brocker, D. Dohse, and R. Soltwedel, pp. 130–149. Berlin, Heidelberg, New York: Springer-Verlag.

Walken, G., B. Kogut, and W. Shan. 1997. "Social Capital, Structural Holes, and the Formation of an Industry Network." *Organization Science* 8.

Zucker, L. G., M. R. Darby, and J. Armstrong. 1998. "Geographically Localized Knowledge: Spillovers or Markets?" *Economic Inquiry* 26.

A Public Policy Perspective on Intellectual Capital

Ahmed Bounfour
University of Marne La Vallee

Leif Edvinsson
Lund University and UNIC

Introduction

Traditionally, the concept of intellectual capital (IC) has been analyzed on an individual firm level. However, in the knowledge economy, the value of countries, regions, organizations, and individuals is directly related to their knowledge and IC.

The OECD claims in the report *Scoreboard 2001—Towards a Knowledge-Based Economy* that countries, to succeed in the future, need to provide support for the development of a knowledge-based economy. In that report, 30 member countries are scored according to their investment in IC, such as R&D, education, patents, and information and communication technology (ICT). Some countries have already started to include IC in their policy to position themselves for the knowledge economy:

- Denmark set up a National Competence Council for collaboration between the government and the business community and to map the knowledge competitiveness of Denmark. This led, among other things, to the establishment of guidelines for reporting intellectual capital, published by the Ministry of Trade and Industry.
- In Norway, several initiatives have begun. The local municipality of Larvik is prototyping both annual IC reports and IC ratings for its activities. The Norwegian cabinet is working on an initiative on the IC aspects of the public sector, and the Norwegian Association of Financial Analysts launched guidelines for reporting on knowledge capital in 2002.
- In Italy, the AIAF (Italian Association of Financial Analysts) explored a prototype to model intangible assets, and in 2005, financial analysts plan to classify companies on the basis of their level of IC disclosure.
- In Austria, the government passed a law that makes it compulsory for all universities and colleges to publish an annual knowledge capital report.
- In Finland, the parliament issued a report on the importance of managing its own knowledge, that is, the knowledge of its elected members and administrators (Suurla, Markkula, and Mustajärvi 2002).
- So-called knowledge cities are emerging (e.g., Barcelona) that shape the urban design for the knowledge economy and its knowledge workers. Barcelona, with

its transformational regional project called 22@, had already appointed a Chief Knowledge Officer for the city in 1999. In 2003, Dubai was formally inaugurated as leading knowledge village.

- Taxation of intangibles is another area in progress, not only related to brands or intellectual property rights but also as an attraction factor for knowledge investments and knowledge-worker migration. The first book on the subject was published in 2003 (Rosembuj 2003).
- Researchers conducted studies in this area, including the assessment of IC performance of countries (Edvinsson and Malone 1997; Bounfour 2003a, 2003b; Bontis 2002), the value creation of regions (Pulic 2003), and the benchmarking of IC in cities (Viedma 2004). In addition, the concept of knowledge zones is emerging (Amidon 2003).

These examples highlight that some cities, regions, or countries already value the importance of IC as a critical success factor. During the 1990s, research by Paul Romer of Stanford University highlighted the exponential value of multiplying knowledge as an exponential value curve, called *the law of increasing marginal utility*. In other words, the more connections, relationships, and interactions in a network society, the higher is its potential value. It might also be described as 1 + 1 = 11. The Club of Rome[1] argues: "the emergence of a networked knowledge society in the next twenty to thirty years is a major paradigm-shift from the industrial model of the nineteenth and twentieth century. It can be part of the solutions to our problems, or part of the problem. The hope that the dynamics of information and communication technology development within globalizing markets alone will contribute to general wealth and reduce poverty is too simplistic" (Club of Rome 2002, p. 9). This argument indicates that we need better understanding of the knowledge assets of regions and nations and we have to go beyond the traditional agricultural and industrial plans so often found in regional and national planning offices. Today, there is a quest for what makes regions, communities, and cities intelligent and knowledgable.

In this chapter, we discuss the emerging issue of IC in public policy. With this aim, we first discuss why IC is a public policy issue today. We then discuss the need for new models of cultivating and managing IC (e.g., knowledge zone design) and subsequently discuss the state of the art, especially comparing Europe with the United States. Finally, we take a look into the future and report on preliminary findings of applying a new approach to measuring and managing IC for cities, regions, and countries.

Why Is Intellectual Capital a Public Policy Issue Today?

The issue of IC or intangible resources can be discussed from two viewpoints: First, it can be discussed from an entrepreneurship perspective (the creation of "value" by a company); second, from a macroeconomic perspective (the creation of wealth by a community). These two viewpoints are different facets of the same problem: the emergence of a new model of competitiveness, in which IC occupies a critical place. Next, we outline some arguments of why IC is a political issue today.

---

[1] The Club of Rome is a global think tank and center of innovation and initiative. As a nonprofit, nongovernmental organization (NGO), it brings together scientists, economists, businesspeople, international high civil servants, heads of state, and former heads of state from five continents who are convinced that the future of humankind is not determined once and for all and that each human being can contribute to the improvement of our societies.

- *The rapid growth of service (and intangible) activities*, which now contributes more than 75% of the GDP in most of the developed economies. According to research (Jensen 1999), we are about to progress further on into edutainment and dreamsocieties, such as Celebration in Florida.
- *The dematerialization of manufacturing activities*, as most industries currently invest more money in developing, distributing and marketing, and managing products than in manufacturing them.
- *The industrialization of services*. These services register a deep change in their mode of production and valorization, which can be summarized briefly as the need to continuously create value for clients and the equal need to enhance internal resources. In organizational terms, such a requirement attests to the necessity in these organizations to shift from the "profession libérale" mode of production to a real "industrialized" one.
- *The recognition of knowledge as the main source of competitive advantage.* With this point we stress the great interest of managers in maximizing the value of knowledge within organizations, be it "in the head of individuals" or stored somewhere. And, at the same time, they seek to minimize organizational dependence on individual knowledge. From an analytical point of view, the evolutionary theory (Nelson and Winter 1982) or the knowledge-creation perspective (Nonaka 1994; Nonaka and Takeuchi 1995) contributed to a new understanding of knowledge in organizations. In addition, new information and communication technologies are naturally coming to be regarded as an important basis for new approaches in development and implementation.
- *The problem of understanding value creation/efficiency and distribution at both the microeconomic and macroeconomic levels.* Traditionally, the world economy has had a strong financial focus, partly due to the dominance of shareholder value as the alpha and the omega for judging performance. However, the recent crisis in the financial markets increased interest in putting more emphasis on other perspectives, such as stakeholder value. Here, value is assessed within a given socioeconomic system and cannot be maximized if the system does not take into account all the key stakeholders within and around organizations. This perspective forces firms, regions, and nations to consider governance as a policy theme as well as a quest for intelligent cities (Komninos 2002).
- *IC as driver for competitive advantage.* Surveys have demonstrated the role of IC in corporate competitiveness (PIMS Associates 1994; Research on Competitive Strategies 2000)[2] at the level of individual companies and concerning cooperative programs, such as those carried out at a national level. Several scholars stressed the importance of IC in building competitive advantage and economic growth, in Europe as well as in the United States. Some recent studies focus on the importance of intangible factors in output growth at the corporate and industry level (O'Mahony and Vecchi 2000), as well as at the cluster level (Peneder 2000). A recent study presents the quest for the creativity class and its clustering in various nations and regions (Floridaand Tanagli 2004).
- *The emergence of strong analytical issues.* Due to their intrinsic specificities, notably their inseparability and combinatory nature and the uncertainty surrounding their revenue generation, intangibles pose important analytical issues,

---

[2] See also papers presented at the Louvain La Neuve conference on intangibles.

especially with regards to the definition of stabilized taxonomies and the measurement and comparability of the defined items.

Intellectual Capital and New Models of Public Policy

If we admit that we face a big transition toward a system where knowledge is the preeminent resource, then we need to discuss—and challenge—the existing theories and models. As far as the IC theme is concerned, we do not lack new models. From a macroeconomic perspective, long established theories claim that IC is at the basis of nations' economic growth. The concept of human capital stresses the importance of investment in education, whereas the technical change and innovation theory put forward the importance of innovation as a cumulative and incremental process. For R&D specifically, several econometric studies tried to explain the growth residual factor following the seminal work of Moe Abramovitz (1956), starting with Robert Solow's (1957) formal growth, which concludes that technical change was responsible for nearly 50% of growth in the United States in the first half of the twentieth century. New growth theories demonstrated the importance of knowledge as the main source of growth, by considering items such as human capital and organizational capital. The evolutionary approach emphasizes learning in organizations and the importance of routines. Other approaches include the intellectual investment approach and the analytical approach, the latest focusing mainly on the importance of intangible investment and its impact on the GDP (Nakamura 2001; OECD 1992 and different national statistical offices, especially from Europe, INSEE in France 1992, among others). All these studies support the thesis that investments in IC are powerful drivers to improve the wealth of nations.

As outlined, the development of IC resources is an essential issue for public policy, and not only because of its direct impact on growth and employment. Public organizations must develop innovative approaches in fields such as research and development, systems of education, fiscal policies, and public procurement policies.

Understanding IC as an important resource allows us to challenge several dimensions of policy and decision making at the national, regional, and even local level. It allows us to ask questions such as these: Are we as a nation developing the right IC? Does the design of the city support knowledge work? Considering intangibles from the policy agenda perspective can be legitimated by the strong presence of public power in a corporate environment and business policy building. The debate on the future of the Minitel system in France, whose existence is considered to constitute an obstacle to the development of the Internet, well illustrates a problem that is at the same time entrepreneurial (a program managed by a commercial operator, France Telecom, in association with editors and service firms) and collective (it concerns the whole of France). Looking at the achievements of the program, one can state that the Minitel made way for an interesting set of knowledge and routines, which gave France a unanimously recognized advantage. But this advantage could turn into a stumbling block if innovations are not made that would make it possible for France to continue to be competitive from the point of view of the best practices of the moment (the Internet). Here, one finds the necessary creative pressure explained by Itami and Roehl (1987): Organizations tend to privilege the exploitation of the controlled current knowledge, and the exploitation of this very knowledge constitutes at the same time a barrier to innovation. It is necessary, therefore, for public policy to apply "positive" pressure in such a manner as to innovate in a competitive way, that is, create the routines and practices that best ensure the long life of collective innovation capabilities. Supporting

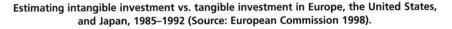

Figure 12.1

Estimating intangible investment vs. tangible investment in Europe, the United States, and Japan, 1985–1992 (Source: European Commission 1998).

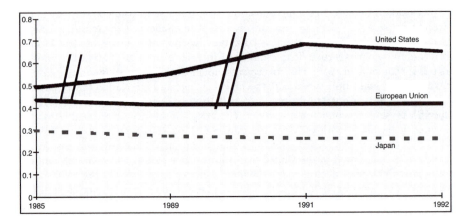

new technology infrastructures and managerial practices represents important aspects to consider.

State of the Art: Europe versus the United States

When comparing European policy with policy in the United States, two interesting points arise: Europe lags behind the United States in terms of investments into IC such as R&D, but Europe seems to be ahead of the United States in embracing the ideas of IC modeling and reporting; in fact, many countries in Europe are developing and experimenting with new approaches and concepts for identifying, managing, and reporting on IC. Here, we discuss these two issues in further detail.

Europe Lags behind in Terms of Investment

In Europe, the debate on the insufficient character of its collective investment in R&D and other intangibles continues. If we look back over the past 15 years, we can observe that this can be observed for most components of IC (specifically for investments into R&D and software). Research conducted on behalf of the European Commission on the impact of the European single market on intangible investments (European Commission 1998[3]) clearly demonstrated that the European Union lagged behind the United States in terms of intangible investment over the period 1985–1992 (see Figures 12.1 and 12.2).

A primary aim of this project was to estimate the level of investment in intangibles by the European Union (12 countries) compared to the United States and Japan. The following investments were considered: R&D, technology payment, software expen-

---

[3] Ahmed Bounfour worked as scientific director for this project.

Figure 12.2

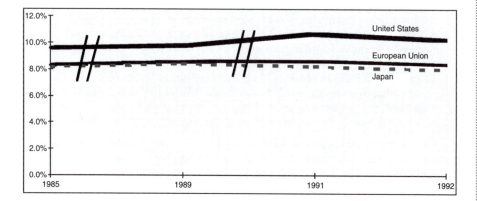

Intangible investment in Europe, United States, and Japan (as pecent of GDP), 1985–1992 (Source: European Commission 1998).

diture, public expenditure on education, and advertising expenditures. From the data available, several important conclusions can be derived:

- In terms of absolute value, the investments in IC increased considerably over the period 1985–1992.
- In terms of relative value (compared to the GDP or gross fixed asset formation), the European Union showed a relatively stable rate of investment over the period as a whole (as a share of the GDP, the ratio was 8.32% in 1992 compared to 8.30% in 1985).
- Compared to the United States and Japan, the European Union is in an intermediate position, below the United States but above Japan.
- In terms of different components of investment, the European Union ratios are below those of the United States and Japan for R&D and software (as share of the GDP) over the considered period.

However, in looking at this data, we must take into account that the R&D market in Europe is still fragmented and a single market has not been achieved completely (at least at the time of this study). The data would also change if we take into account the 10 new member countries that entered the European Union in 2004.

Recent works by the European Working Group on Competitiveness (European Commission 2002) clearly demonstrated the existence of a clear correlation between BERD/GDP (Business Enterprise Research and Development) and annual growth of productivity. This can also be demonstrated by looking at the R&D investments. Over the past decade, the United States invested more in R&D than Europe, and since the mid-1990s the this gap has been growing (Soete 2002). It is interesting that this correlates with the gap in productivity over that period (Meister and Verspagen 2004).

The performance gap between Europe and the United States triggered several policy initiatives taken at the European Union with regards to investments in R&D and other intangibles:

- In January 2000, the European Commission proposed the creation of a European Research Area[4] (also referred to as the *Lisbon agenda*) and subsequently created a set of indicators to benchmark national innovation systems along four perspectives: human resources in RTD (Research and Technology Development), public and private investment in RTD, science and technology productivity, and impact of RTD on competitiveness and employment.
- The Lisbon agenda established a strategic objective for Europe to be the world's most competitive knowledge economy by 2010. To achieve this, a mechanism of coordination, called the "open method of coordination," was put in place among national innovation systems, with the aim of avoiding duplication and increasing convergence and benchlearning ("learning by comparing").
- In 2002, the European Council (Barcelona, March 2002) reconfirmed the objective of all member countries to invest an average of 3% of the GDP in R&D.

Also, in Japan, intangibles are now considered as a driving force for renewing the country's innovation systems. Japan is taking into account various initiatives put in place in Europe and the United States to create an Asian knowledge economy (see, e.g., Masuyama and Vandenbrink 2003).

The United States Lags behind in Terms of Modeling and Reporting Approaches

Indeed, in the field on intangibles' reporting and management, the European Union benefits from a special favorable institutional and experimental context that needs consolidation, better support, and leveraging. This has to be stressed, especially due to the importance of the human capital dimension within the EU socioeconomic context. To a certain extent, intangibles form a European "natural" theme, due to the implicit focus of most of its nations on socioeconomic cohesion. The European "advance" in intangibles modeling and reporting can be illustrated at three levels: definition of taxonomies, experimentation in measurement, and development of microeconomic reporting.

Development of a Taxonomy

The reflection on IC as an autonomous subject started at the beginning of the 1980s, for example, in reports published by the French Commissariat Général au Plan, which led the OECD to publish a first report on the subject in 1987. In the early 1990s, Skandia launched a lexicon and taxonomy of IC (Edvinsson and Malone 1997) Subsequently, the OECD organized and sponsored several workshops and conferences on the topic. There is evidence of a convergence of taxonomies in Europe. As indicated by various reports of European projects on the topic (e.g., Meritum, PRISM), the commonly agreed-on classification of IC is to split it into the following three components: human capital, structural capital, and relational capital.

Prototyping of Measures

Since the mid-1980s, the European national statistical offices in Finland, Sweden, and the Netherlands dedicated a lot of effort to the measurement of IC. INSEE in

---

[4] "Towards a European Research Area," Communication from the Commission to the Council, the European Parliament, the Economic and Social Committee and the Committee of the Regions—COM(2000) 6 (18.01.2000).

France also issued papers on the topic. The statistical agency of Italy is undertaking an exercise designed to quantify the macroeconomic dimension of intangibles. Finally, Eurostat, the statistical office of the European communities, commissioned several studies on the subject. Most of the data available confirm the regular growth of intangible investment within the whole European economy.

Experimentation in Managing and Reporting

Across Europe, several organizations experimented with reporting their IC. The Danish Ministry went further and produced guidelines for both reporting and reading IC statements in 2000. Furthermore, in 2003, the Austrian government passed a law that makes it compulsory for all universities and colleges to publish an annual knowledge capital report, showing knowledge goals, knowledge processes, and knowledge indicators. In addition, the German Ministry of Economy started prototyping such guidelines in 2004.

A Look into the Future

As underlined already, over the past years, several interesting initiatives have been taken at a community level (nations, regions, other nonprofit organizations). Most of these initiatives consisted of analyzing existing data, basically at the input-output level, using existing information. However, we believe that we have to go further, especially by focusing on the organizational and dynamic dimension of socioeconomic performance (e.g., Marr, Schiuma, and Neely 2004). We also have to examine the intellectual capital of cities, regions, and nations as the structural capital to attract and leverage the human capital for the new wealth of nations.

An approach that developed to address this is the intellectual-capital dynamic-value (IC-dVAl®) framework, which helps define metrics from a dynamic perspective (Bounfour 2000, 2003a). This approach has been implemented at both the microeconomic and macroeconomic levels. According to the IC-dVAl® approach, metrics are dynamically defined along four interrelated dimensions of competitiveness:

1. *Resources as inputs.* Resources are inputs to the production process: tangible resources, investment in R&D, acquisition of technology, and the like.
2. *Processes.* Through processes, the deployment of a dynamic strategy founded on intangible factors can be implemented: processes of establishing knowledge networks and competences inside and outside organizations, processes of combining knowledge, just-in-time processes for products and services and the whole of the outputs, processes of motivation and training of personnel, processes for building social capital and trust.
3. *The building of intangible assets (intellectual capital).* These can be built by combining intangible resources. Indeed, combining intangible resources can lead to specific results: collective knowledge, patents, trademarks, reputation, specific routines, and networks of cooperation. For each of these assets, indicators and methods for valuation can be developed.
4. *Outputs.* On this level, the performance of organizations is traditionally measured, through analysis of their products and services' market position. Here, the interest is in indicators: those relating to market share, quality of products and services, establishment of barriers to entry, or establishment of temporary monopolistic positions.

The IC d-VAL® defines and measures IC in terms of relative indexes as well as in monetary terms. The starting point is a clear definition of the main components for the four dimensions: resources, processes, assets, and outputs. Then, a benchmarking process is conducted for these items. Basically we compare the position of a company or a nation to those considered the best performers. The benchmarking exercise leads to calculating ad-hoc performance indexes, as well as a composite index per country, region, or community.

We outline the preliminary results of the application of this framework to Champs-sur-Marne, a small town near Paris[5] (Ibouainene 2001). Champs-sur-Marne is a new city located 25 kilometers east of Paris, with about 25,000 inhabitants. The municipality employs 643 people, of whom 400 are civil servants. The analysis focused mainly on the municipality's five operational departments: Education Department (D1); Children Department (D2); Youth Department (D3); Sports Department (D4); and the Culture Department (D5).

Performance indexes have been calculated by benchmarking these departments' performance with those of similar municipalities (see Table 12.1). In overall terms, the Culture Department (D5) appears to perform best within this municipality, especially with regard to its resources and competences, whereas the Education Department (D1) appears to be in the least favorable position. Departments 2 and 4 appear in an intermediate position. D4 is the best in class for its output, such as for the services supplied the population for sports activities. D2 is number 1 for the processes level, for the way it organizes its activities for young people.

The IC-dVAl® framework has also been used to collect preliminary benchmarking information on the performance of EU innovation systems using the innovation trend chart data as proxy values (Bounfour 2003b). At the macroeconomic level, we can observe that northern European countries are best positioned: Denmark, for the percentage of collaborative innovations among small and medium sized companies (SMEs); the Netherlands, Denmark, and Sweden for the percentage of homes with Internet access; and Finland for information and communication technology (ICT) markets/GDP ratio. The data show that the Nordic countries rank well in Europe (Figure 12.3). This might be related to their good performance at the organizational level but needs further research, particularly to understand how these systems function, what makes them unique, and how path dependent they are.

Any measurement approach has to take these dimensions into account. Indeed, if a naïve perspective were to consider that these countries are the benchmarks for intangibles, the real issue is to document to what extent this might be meaningful for the other EU countries. Could, for instance, a process of "learning by comparing" (bench-learning) be implemented? What capacity do other systems have for absorbing identifiable best-in-class routines, taking into account the difficulties in transferring and comparing practices for managing IC (Marr 2004)?

Conclusion

In this chapter, we demonstrate that IC is a critical resource for cities, regions, and countries in the knowledge economy, which means it should be an important issue for public policy. Several initiatives have been launched in Europe to address this issue, but we feel that there is a need for consolidation of the various approaches and data sets. In a look to the future, we report on some preliminary findings using the

---

[5] Data for this case were collected by Ibouainene in a master's degree project with the aim of implementing the IC-dVAl® approach to a nonprofit organization, the municipality and town hall of Champs-sur-Marne.

Table 12.1

Performance of Five Departments of the City of Marie de Champs (in thousands of euros)

	Partial Indexes of Performance	D1	D2	D3	D4	D5
Macro factors of competitiveness						
Resources and competences	PiR	70	73	56	85	**87**
Processes	PiP	62	**82**	62	70	75
Output	PiO	54	66	70	**71**	69
Overall performance index	OPi	62	73.6	62.6	69	**77**
Macro elements of IC						
Human capital		295	1525	305	1075	1637
Structural capital		124	1052	396	421	1433
Relational capital		Not evaluated	Not evaluated	Not evaluated	Not evaluated	Not evaluated
Total		419	2577	701	1496	**3070**

Note: The assessment of each component of the department's IC has been carried out using a proxy replacement value: the level of expenditures.
Source: Ibouainene (2001).

Figure 12.3

IC performance indexes for European countries (Source: Bounfour 2003b).

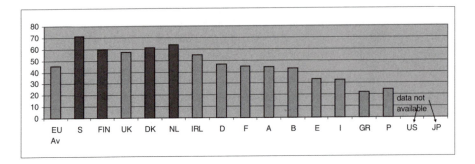

IC-dVAl® approach. However, much of the data used must be estimated. More research and consolidation of data sets would allow us to create more comprehensive databases, which will enable us to conduct further research into the issue of IC and the performance of countries, regions, and cities.

Other approaches have been tested in Israel (Pasher 1998), Norway (Edvinsson and Bounfour 2004), Croatia (Pulic 2003), and Spain (Viedma 2004) and are in progress of addressing the critical dimensions of the new wealth creation of cities, regions, and nations.

Overall, our understanding of the implications of the knowledge economy for public policy is still embryonic. The change in socioeconomic systems all over the world calls for new approaches; it is the role of researchers and policy makers to challenge current models to progress our understanding in this vital field.

References

Abramovitz, M. 1956. "Resource and Output Trends in the United States since 1870." *American Economic Association Papers* 46, no. 2: 5–23.

Amidon, D. 2003. *The Innovation Super Highway.* Boston: Butterworth and Heinemann.

Bontis, N. 2002. *National Intellectual Capital Index: Intellectual Capital Development in the Arab Region.* New York: United Nations.

Bounfour, A. 2000. "Competitiveness and Intangible Resources: Towards a Dynamic View of Corporate Performance." In: *Competitiveness and the Value of Intangibles,* ed. P. Buigues, A. Jacquemin, and J.-F. Marchipont. London: Edward Elgar Publishing Ltd.

———. 2003a. *The Management of Intangibles, the Organisation's Most Valuable Assets.* London and New York: Routledge.

———. 2003b. "The IC-dVAL® Approach." *Journal of Intellectual Capital* 4. no. 3: 396–412.

———. 2003c. "Intangibles and Benchmarking Performance of Innovation Systems in Europe." *The IPTS Report* (May): 32–37.

———, and L. Edvinsson. 2004. *Intellectual Capital for Communities. Nations, Regions, Cities, Districts.* Boston: Butterworth–Heinemann.

Clement, W., G. Hammerer, and K. Schwarz. 1998. *Measuring Intangible Investment, Intangible Investment from an Evolutionary Perspective.* Geneva: OECD.

Club of Rome. 2002. *Statement of the Club of Rome to the World Summit on Sustainable Development.* Rome: Club of Rome.

Danish Agency for Trade and Industry (DATI). 2000. *A Guideline for Intellectual Capital Statements—A Key to Knowledge Management.* Copenhagen: Danish Trade and Industry Development Council.

Dedijer, S. 2002. "Ragusa intelligence and security 1301–1806." *International Journal of Intelligence and Counter Intelligence* 15, no. 1 (Spring).

Dedijer, S. 2003. "Development and Intelligence 2003–2053." Working paper series, 2003/10. Lund, Sweden: Lund Institute of Economic Research, Lund.

Edvinsson, L. 2002. *Corporate Longitude: What you need to know to navigate the knowledge economy.* London: FT Prentice Hall.

Edvinsson, L., and A. Bounfour. 2004. "Assessing National and Regional Value Creation." *Measuring Business Excellence* 8, no. 1: 55–61.

Edvinsson, L., and M. S. Malone. 1997. *Intellectual Capital, Realizing Your Company's True Value by Finding Its Hidden Brainpower.* New York: HarperBusiness.

Edvinsson, L., and C. Stenfelt. 1999. "Intellectual Capital of Nations—for Future Wealth Creation." *Journal of Human Resource Costing and Accounting* 4, no. 1 (Spring).

European Commission. 1998. *Intangible Investments.* The Single Market Review Services, Office for Publications of the European Communities, Kogan Page. Paris: RCS—Research on Competitive Strategies.

——. 2000. *Working Document from the Commission Services, Development of an Open Method of Co-ordination for Benchmarking National Research Policies—Objectives, Methodology and Indicators.* Brussels: European Commission.

——. 2002. "Benchmarking national R&D policies: Strata-Etan Expert Working Group, the Impact of R&D on Competitiveness and Employment (IRCE)." Final report. Brussels: European Commission.

Florida, R., and I. Tinagli. 2004. *Europe in the Creative Class.* London: UK: Demos.

Ibouainene, S. 2001. "Evaluation du capital immatérial d'une organisation non-marchande: La Mairie de Champs-sur-Marne." Master dissertation, University of Marne La Vallee, France.

INSEE. 1995. L'investissement immatériel entre 1970 et 1992, working paper, Paris.

Itami, H., and T. W. Roehl. 1987. *Mobilizing Invisible Assets.* Cambridge, MA: Harvard University Press.

Jensen, R. 1999. *The Dream Society.* New York: McGraw-Hill.

Komninos, N. 2002. *Intelligent cities.* London: Spon Press.

Marr, B. 2004. "Measuring and Benchmarking Intellectual Capital." *Benchmarking—An International Journal.*

Marr, B., G. Schiuma, and A. Neely. 2004. "The Dynamics of Value Creation." *Journal of Intellectual Capital* 5, no. 2: 312–325.

Masuyama S., and D. Vandenbrink, eds. 2003. *Towards a Knowledge-Based Economy, East Asia's Changing industrial Geography.* Tokyo: NRI (Nomura Research Institute), and Singapore: Intsitute of South East Asian Studies.

Meister, C., and B. Verspagen. 2004. *European Productivity Gap: Is R&D the Solution.* MERIT, Infonomics Research Memorandum series, 2004–2005. Meritum Mastricht, Netherlands: MERIT.

Meritum. 2002. *Guidelines for Managing and Reporting on Intangibles (Intellectual Capital Report).* Madrid: Airtel-Vodafone Foundation.

Ministère du Développement Economique et du Plan, Commissariat du Plan. 1995. Call for tenders: L'Entreprise et l'Economie de l'Immatériel, 22 June. Paris.

Nakamura, L. I. 2001. "What is the US Gross Investment in Intangibles? (At Least) One Trillion Dollars a year." Paper given at the Fourth Intangible Conference, New York University, Stern School of Business, May 17–18. *Business Review* (Fourth Quarter): 27–37.

Nelson, R. R., and S. G. Winter. 1982. *An Evolutionary Theory of Economic Change.* Cambridge, MA: Belknap Press and Harvard University Press.

Nonaka, I. 1994. "A Dynamic Theory of Organizational Knowledge Creation." *Organization Science* 5, No. 1 (February).

——, and H. Takeuchi. 1995. *The Knowledge-Creating Company.* Boston Oxford University Press.

OECD. 1992. Technology and the Economy: The Key Relationships. Paris.

O'Mahoney, M., and M. Vecchi. 2000. "Tangible and Intangible Investment and Economic Performance: Evidence from company's Accounts." In: *Competitiveness and the Value of Intangible Assets*, ed. P. Buigues, A. Jaquemin, and J.-F. Machipont, pp. 1999–1223. London: Edward Elgar.

Pasher. E. 1998. *The Intellectual Capital of the State of Israel—The Hidden Values of the Desert.* Herzliyya, Israel: E. Pasher & Associates.

Peneder, M. 2000. "Intangible Assets and the Competitiveness of European Industries." In: *Competitiveness and the Value of Intangible Assets*, ed. P. Buigues, A. Jaquemin, and J.-F. Machipont, pp. 117–153. London: Edward Elgar.

PIMS Associates. 1994. *Building Business for Europe, Evidence from Europe and North America on "Intangible" Factors behind Growth, Competitiveness and Jobs.* London: PIMS Associates.

PRISM. 2003. *Intangibles Report.* Available at www.euintangibles.net.

Pulic. A. 2003. *Efficiency on National and Company Level.* Zagreb: Croatian Chamber of Commerce, available at www.vaic-on.net.

Research on Competitive Strategies (RCS), Ifo Institut, PREST. 2000. *How Esprit Contributed to Building European Industry's Intangible Assets.* Final report, ESPRITCOMP project, 27153, IST Program, Brussels: RCS.

Romer, P. 1991. *Increasing Returns and New Developments in the Theory of Growth.* Barcelona: Spain: Natl Bureall of Economil Res.

Rosembuj, T. 2003. *Intangibles—La fiscalidad del Capital Intelectual.* El Fisco, University of Barcelona, Spain: Publisher.

Soete, L. 2002. "Intangibles: Policy Implications for Europe." In: *The Transparent Enterprise: The Value of Intangibles.* Madrid: Autonomous University of Madrid.

Solow, R. M. 1957. "Technical Progress and Aggregate Production Function." *Review of Economic and Statistics* 39: 312–320.

Suurla, R., M. Markkula, and O. Mustajärvi. 2002. *Developing and Implementing Knowledge Management in the Parliament of Finland.* Helsinki: Parliament of Finland, Committee for the Future. Edita Prima Oy.

Viedma, J. 2004. "CICBS: A Methodology and a Framework for Measuring and Managing Intellectual Capital of Cities, a Practical Application in the City of Mataro." *Knowledge Management Research and Practice* 2, no. 1: 13–13.

A Knowledge-based Perspective on Intellectual Capital

J.-C. Spender
Open University Business School

Bernard Marr
Cranfield School of Management

Introduction

The business world enthusiastically adopted the idea that knowledge has become the most strategic of corporate assets, the principal basis for competitive advantage. This enthusiasm has not, however, been matched by an understanding of how to operationalize knowledge. It seems we argue that knowledge is important largely because it is a different kind of asset. While this is perplexing and suggests that it is important to understand the strategic significance of the different kinds of organizational knowledge, it also raises operational issues for managers.

Attention to the organization's knowledge is not a new phenomenon; organizations have always depended on knowledge. Veblen (1904), in *The Theory of the Business Enterprise*, argues for the importance of the knowledge components of the firm. Bureaucracy is sometimes defined as organization on the basis of knowledge. Likewise, organizations have always relied on innovative ideas and the knowledge of their employees for their competitive advantage. It is often suggested that we live in a new knowledge-intensive period. Although if we look at the history of ideas (e.g., Menand 2001), the nineteenth century seemed as fertile a time for new knowledge and resulting social change as the present. We can also see that the pattern of social change and development of commercial knowledge in Philadelphia at the start of the twentieth century, as a well researched example, was probably as tumultuous as in our own time (Freeman et al. 1992; Spender and Kijne 1996).

But, the manipulation of knowledge and information, the fundamental characteristic of the tertiary sector, is plainly overtaking the manipulation of metal, the essence of the secondary sector, as the source of economic value (Reich 1992). Much of this is evident in the growth of the service sector. An even greater amount seems to be the result of the transformation of all sectors to be more knowledge than capital intensive. This has made today's "business models" quite different from yesterday's, and as a result, today's organizations strive to better understand and manage the relationship between what they know and the value they deliver. The realization that knowledge is an important factor for organizations and critical to their strategic advantage has given organizations new problems; managers want to understand how to manage and measure their knowledge-based assets while, at the same time, increasing pressure is put on managers to measure the benefits and cost effectiveness of their organization's knowledge management initiatives.

In this chapter, we present a knowledge-based perspective on intellectual capital. For this purpose, we first discuss whether knowledge is really more important today. We then outline the discussion about what knowledge is, before we contextualize this in an overview of the evolution of knowledge in business. Next, we discuss the knowledge-based implications for managing and measuring knowledge assets. We conclude with a summary and a look into the future.

Why Is Knowledge So Important Today?

The business environment has changed over the past decades. Whereas booms followed the two World Wars, creating a seller's market in most of the developed countries, global trade gradually changed this toward a buyer's market. Such markets do not absorb all goods produced, they are saturated. Consumers are better informed and more demanding. Differentiation and innovation become critical. This also means that traditional cost-focused management tools do not provide managers adequate information. An understanding of the external competitive forces has to be supplemented by an understanding of the organization's resources and how they can be combined to provide better value.

The general trends include increased globalization. The economic world is "shrinking," and access to tangible resources does not alone provide a sustainable competitive advantage. Traditional assets are increasingly transient. So is technical knowledge. There is improved access to information and knowledge through vastly greater amounts of information technology, most notably the Internet. The increasing collaboration among firms means that firm boundaries are increasingly blurred.

Economists and management scholars have reacted to some of the issues by putting forward new theories of the firm. In 1959, Drucker defined knowledge as an important resource. Machlup was the first modern economist to analyze knowledge and related areas (Machlup 1980). In 1977, Teece reported the results of new research on the transfer of knowledge and its impact on innovation. Following the work of economists like Solow (1957) and Arrow (1962) on "learning curves," there was growing interest in knowledge as a different kind of economic resource. Nonaka and Takeuchi (1995) helped crystallize this with their book about the "knowledge-creating company." Their thesis is that knowledge is the one sure source of lasting competitive advantage. They draw particular attention to the more tacit dimensions of knowledge.

The key theories that contributed to the debate on organizational knowledge include the evolutionary views, the resource-based views, and the knowledge-based views. Managers realize that when formulating a corporate strategy, it is not enough to simply identify the competitive forces, opportunities, and threats of the industry, as suggested by Porter (1980). In addition, managers must identify their organizations' corporate competencies and resources to evaluate their strategic opportunities (Andrews 1971). Different firms develop different distinctive competencies (Selznick 1957), and the question they have to ask themselves is this: Does the organization have the appropriate competence to pursue particular opportunities? Andrews brings the strategic importance of competencies into focus when he states, "opportunism without competence is a path to fairyland" (Andrews 1971). This view of competence-based competition was framed by Penrose (1959) and later enhanced by Wernerfelt (1984), Rumelt (1984), and Barney (1986), who are now generally seen as formulators of the modern resource-based view of the firm (Foss 1997). The resource-based theorists see firms as heterogeneous entities characterized by a unique resource base (Nelson and Winter 1982; Barney 1991). This base increasingly consists of knowledge-based assets (Stewart 1997; Roos et al. 1997; Lev 2001; Sveiby 1997, 2001; Marr and Schiuma 2001). The knowledge of a firm should be the central consideration on which to ground the organization's strategy and the primary basis on which a firm can establish its identity and frame its strategy, as well as one of the primary sources of the firm's profitability (Grant 1991). Therefore, firms need to identify and develop their intellectual resources to establish and maintain a competitive advantage and increase their performance (Petergraf 1993; Prahalad and Hamel 1990; Teece, Pisano, and Shuen 1997). This led to the development of the knowledge-based view of the firm, which considers knowledge the principal source of economic rent (Grant 1991; Spender and Grant 1996 Spender; 1994).

What Is Knowledge?

Knowledge is sometimes treated as an object, which can be collected, stored, and shared within organizations. Another school of thought views knowledge as meaning, which means it cannot be easily transferred unless two parties share some common understanding. Furthermore, scholars often refer to different kinds of knowledge. Here, we briefly outline these different theoretical perspectives.

Knowledge as Object

Most organization theorists and microeconomists treat the firm as a social object to be researched using the methods of positivistic science. Organization theory researchers look "inside" the firm, at the structure and functioning of its constituents. Microeconomists consider the firm's parts as economic assets (constituents of the production function) and focus on the firm's relations to its input and output markets. Both, of course, deal with choice. Microeconomists assume the firm's assets are costly and scarce and are interested in choosing how to allocate them, whether to trade them in the markets or combine them with the production function given. Organization theorists are interested in changing this production function by making choices about the relationships between the organization's parts and resources.

The methodological presupposition for both is that a firm is a member of a class of objects that have common basic properties. From this point of view, firms are not presumed to have fundamentally different properties when they differ in terms of, say, national context, size, age, technology, industry, or product mix. In terms of a theory of the firm, manufacturing firms are like service firms and global firms are like local firms. The research agenda is to reveal the properties and characteristics of this extensive class, thus establishing the theory of the firm.

We can dub this the *objectivist* approach to a theory of the firm. Fitting "knowledge" into this approach has proven difficult, except by treating it, too, as an object, an economic asset with some known structural relationship to the other parts. This leads to a definition of knowledge as "intellectual capital" (IC) and the examination of its management. A firm may have difficulty acquiring and retaining control of its IC or applying it and so generating revenues, which are often referred to as *appropriation issues*. Problems may also occur in trading IC, either across a market or directly with other firms, especially if it has not been legally "fixed" in the form of a patent. Another question is how IC might be acquired under terms that enable the firm to profit from its possession, which is often referred to as *strategic factor market issues*.

In the objectivist tradition, theorists focus on the problems of (a) knowledge's mislocation, being in the wrong place or at the wrong time, and (b) its heterogeneity, especially when it reflects the specialization resulting from the division of labor. Therefore, knowledge assets often need to be communicated, transferred, or re-created at a different location in the firm's heterogeneous "knowledge terrain." This leads to interest in explaining the ease or difficulty of knowledge transfer within the firm. The heterogeneity of the firm's knowledge assets leads to problems of knowledge coordination and integration within the firm. Likewise, the firm seems to be an alternative mechanism for coordinating and integrating knowledge.

The recent interest in knowledge as a factor of production, and the special challenges it presents to management, has provoked new discussion between microeconomists and organization theorists. This is particularly true for economists interested in the circumstances under which firms might be more efficient than markets as factor coordination mechanisms. Thus, one group of economists argues firms exist because they are superior to market mechanisms for coordinating heterogeneous knowledge. Within this framework, both groups of theorists treat knowledge as essentially separable from the people who generate or apply it in the transactions of the market or the firm. For the most part, the focus has been on the theoretical and managerial issues resulting from differences between knowledge and the other factors of production, while keeping the analysis within the familiar framework of managing the latter.

Knowledge as Meaning

Other scholars argue that the objectivist view of knowledge is too narrow and, therefore, the essential managerial and economic issues are missed. The most extreme arguments arise from neo-Wittgensteinian ideas about how knowledge is actually constructed by the knower and is thus inseparable from the knower and her or his processes of knowing. This also relates to Weber's notion of *Verstehen*. Compared with the objectivist view just outlined, this might be dubbed the *interpretivist* view.

Somewhat less extreme would be the suggestion that although knowledge is symbolic in form, such as data or formulae that can be separated from the person writing it down, there are underlying problems about knowing what such symbols actually mean. Therefore, from an interpretivist perspective, the burden of knowledge is more to do with establishing meaning than with the data itself. Wittgenstein argues that it is not possible to write explanations that do not ultimately depend on some sources of meaning lying beyond the reach of such explanation. In the same way, we see communication always requires the receiving person to have some prior knowledge (absorptive capacity) that cannot be made part of the signal sent.

With the notable exception of Edith Penrose (1959) and Veblen before her, microeconomists have not seemed keen to cross the divide between knowledge as object and knowledge as meaning. Indeed, many economists would argue that so long as economics is the study of choice under conditions of scarcity, such a jump is contrary to the axioms of the discipline precisely because meaning cannot be rivalrous, being too flexible, extensible, and impermanent to be made scarce in the same manner as the conventional factors of production.

Organization theorists, on the other hand, have a long history of interest in the problems of meaning, deriving, in particular, from the consequences of the employee's "decision to participate" in the organization. Thus, contemporary organization theory regards employees as role occupants but recognizes they are also individuals with a separate "personal" viewpoint. The decision to participate is the combined adoption of the organization's viewpoint and abandonment of their own. Problems may arise if these views are incompatible.

Meaning versus Objective

Let us summarize the arguments that follow. To investigate knowledge as meaning one must look behind the data and symbols to the processes that determine or shape the meaning attached to them. Knowledge in the objectivist frame is determined by the facts themselves, the naive realist view, or through the processes of science as laid out in the philosophy of science (despite many disputes within the philosophy of science, especially from those post-Kuhnians who see science itself as fundamentally interpretivist). In the objectivist framework, the knower adds nothing to the data, which can therefore be known "objectively" without considering the knowing subject. In contrast, in the interpretivist frame, knowledge is determined by some combination or melding of the phenomena to be known and the knower. Typically, the knower is described in terms of the source of meaning that individuals attach to the phenomena, since such meaning is underdetermined by the phenomenon itself. Some writers speak of the "lenses" through which people view events, data, and other phenomena.

Different Types of Knowledge

The knowledge management field often seems to divide on the question of whether there is more than one kind of knowledge and whether to adopt a one-dimensional or pluralist epistemology. The objectivist position is that there is really only one type, "justified true belief." The rest is ignorance, unjustified or incorrect knowledge, superstition, speculation, conjecture, and the like. Whatever the philosophical, or more correctly, the epistemological problems, they are of little consequence to managers, organization theorists, or economists prepared to take the facts at face value and overlook questions of meaning. For them, there is only one form of knowledge. But, we see that data and meaning can be separated into two distinct kinds of knowledge, one inherent in the phenomena, the other contributed by the knower. This separation has also been explored in terms of the semiotic distinction between a language's sounds or symbols and the ideas to which they refer.

The notion that there might be several types of knowledge is most widely associated with Polanyi's distinction between explicit and tacit forms of knowledge (see, for example, Polanyi 1958, 1966). Despite debate about the precise nature of tacit knowledge and its relationship to explicit knowledge, the distinction is adequate to illustrate the methodological issues of a pluralist epistemology, as opposed to the one-dimensional epistemology of classical theorizing. In the preceding section, the managerial issue is to manage two types of knowledge (data and meaning) and obviously, as a corollary, integrate them and harness the result to the organization's purposes. The same challenge exists if there are separate explicit and tacit types of knowledge.

Some argue Polanyi believed that the differences between explicit and tacit knowledge reflect the dimensions of human knowledge, locating it in a two-dimensional knowledge space. Just as one cannot be without both latitude and longitude if one is on the Earth's surface, so Polanyi argued all human knowledge has both explicit and tacit components. Indeed, one can suggest that the explicit dimension corresponds to the data, communicable through language, while the tacit dimension is the source of its meaning. Others argue that management's task is to make the tacit knowledge explicit and thereby bring it under the organization's control or perhaps, as Nonaka and Takeuchi suggest, structure a controlled interaction between the organization's separate bodies of explicit and tacit knowledge and thereby grow both.

One difference noted between the explicit and tacit types of knowledge has to do with action. Specifically, Polanyi gave us examples of tacit knowledge as the skills necessary for predictable proficient performance. This kind of knowledge is embedded in action. Under most circumstances, an explanation of the performance is not sufficient for someone else to acquire the performance.

There is an interesting puzzle here to do with the world in which action takes place. If the world is well formed, a term of art meaning that it is rationally constructed and bounded, then an explanation may prove adequate. Thus, computer programs, video recorders, and other machines are sold with books of instruction. In principle, nothing can be known about the machine that cannot be reduced to language and so communicated explicitly. Action in such a context may seem simpler than action in the physical world, for that is clearly not well formed, in that it is not wholly comprehended. We are forever open to being surprised by encountering what we do not know. Action in an ill-formed world depends very much on the meaning actors attach to contextual cues. The reason why the explanations of a downhill ski racer are not sufficient to an unskilled skier are that it is not possible to identify all of the processes by which the expert "reads" the hill.

Polanyi's explicit-tacit distinction thus conflates two markedly different ideas. One is that we can know things in ways we cannot express. Tactic knowledge is sometimes defined in terms of its being impossible to communicate. The other idea is that proficient performance may require knowledge that is epistemologically distinct from any knowledge that exists in the realm of thought and symbol, that is, as data or meaning. The relationship between knowledge and action is one of epistemology's oldest puzzles. On the whole, knowledge management researchers have yet to pay adequate attention to the substantial body of work by sociologists and psychologists on the relationship between knowledge and action. Some epistemologists and philosophers have considered this gap; in particular, pragmatists make activity and its consequences the basis for meaning. Managers often adopt pragmatically inclined views of their own knowledge and its relationship to the activities for which they are responsible. So, it is ironic that so much of the work of organization theorists and microeconomists hews to the objectivist approach, thereby separating it from the managers' domain of thought and practice.

How Has Knowledge Evolved in the Business Context?

Next, we present a brief overview of the evolution of the theory of knowledge as a resource for organizations to put the preceding discussion in context. It is less a review of the historic sequence of events and more an outline of the evolution of concepts. Our intention is to highlight the shift of interest from data as an organizational asset toward information and finally knowledge. In our brief discussion, we intend to link the dissimilar concepts to the differences in management concepts and theories of the firm.

Initially, the view of knowledge was as an object or organizational asset, framed by everyday usage and information technology, an implicitly positivistic approach that emphasized the creation of data through measurement and its capture and storage. There was a strong link with information technology as a document and information management system. The data-intensive theory of the firm spun around bureaucratic rationality and a view of the organization as a machine. Data were first generated then stored as input for the production process.

But, as business uncertainty increased, the self-evident nature of data was challenged. A distinction was clarified between data and information—information is more than data. Approaches to the management of knowledge moved away from the data storing toward capturing and mapping information. This more-interpretive approach involved elements of making sense as well as psychological and sociopsychological aspects of information (Weick 1979, 1995).

Davenport and Prusak elaborate this approach with an argument that knowledge is neither data nor information and the difference between them is often a matter of degree (Davenport and Prusak 1998). In their definition, data are described as structured records of transactions, whereas information has the character of a message with a sender and a receiver. Human agency is implied at both ends of the communication. Information must inform; it is data that changes the receiver's perceptions. Knowledge is a "fluid mix of framed experience, values, contextual information, and expert insight that provides a framework for evaluating and incorporating new experiences and information." It originates and is applied in the mind of the knower. In organizations, it often becomes embedded not only in documents or similar inorganic forms and repositories but also in human forms, such as organizational routines, processes, practices, and norms. This is closely aligned with an open systems approach and an organic view of the firm. It supports the evolutionary concepts of the firm, where knowledge is path dependent. Today, this discussion about the nature and creation of knowledge continues on a more epistemological level (e.g., von Krogh, Ichijo, and Nonaka 2000).

Clearly, little attempt has been made to identify the ways the different views of knowledge resources (data, information, knowledge) affect the means we must employ to measure and manage these knowledge resources in our organizations.

What are the Implications for Managing and Measuring?

In this section, we review some of the approaches to measuring and managing knowledge and how they might relate to some of the preceding views on organizational knowledge resources.

Positivistic Views of Organizational Knowledge Assets

The positivistic view of data as a knowledge-based asset allows us to economically value the existing stock of knowledge assets and account for them similarly to financial assets in financial statements. One such approach is *human resource accounting* (HRA), which was introduced several decades ago with the intent of assessing and quantifying the economic value of employees and their knowledge to facilitate better managerial decision making (Sackmann, Flamholz, and Bullen 1989). Bontis et al. (1999) report that none of the HRA experiments has been a long-run success; too many assumptions have to be made, of which some violate common sense.

Another approach is the *Tobin's Q* (Brainard and Tobin 1968; Lerner 1944). It approximates the ratio of the market value of the firm to the replacement cost of its assets. If the latter is lower than the former, the company concerned makes a higher than normal return on its investment. Knowledge-based assets are traditionally associated with high Q values. However, it is difficult if not impossible to find these replacement costs for knowledge-based assets.

Economic value added (EVA), trademarked by Stern Steward and Co., is often suggested as a more comprehensive performance measurement approach, by subtracting operating expenses, taxes, and capital charges from net sales. EVA has been suggested as a substitute measure for the return on organizational intellectual resources by e.g., Marchant and Barsky. To accurately reflect organizational reality, it would be necessary to include up to 164 areas of adjustments, which increases the complexity as well as its vulnerability (Bontis et al. 1999). More important, EVA uses book values of assets as the basis of the calculations. The problem with this approach is that when it comes to knowledge assets, we have no book value, nor do we have accurate surrogates, such as market value or replacement value.

Interpretive View of Organizational Knowledge Assets

The interpretive view of information as a knowledge-based asset allows us to create causal relationships of how information is an input for other higher-level objectives. Knowledge assets are seen as data combined with the meaning that allows organizations to use it as a factor of production.

A tool fitting into this paradigm is the *balanced scorecard* (BSC), with its four measurement perspectives: learning and growth, internal processes, customers, and finances (Kaplan and Norton 1992, 1996). The learning and growth perspective is the natural home for indicators measuring knowledge-based assets, even though Bontis et al. suggest that the meaning of this perspective is not very clear, as it includes information technology and technology as well as human-based assets (Bontis et al. 1999). Especially, the latest publications on the BSC suggest that instead of being just a collection of measures in four perspectives, causal links among the different measures should be established and visualized in so-called strategy maps (Kaplan and Norton 2000, 2003). However, criticism of this approach claims that the assumed relationships in the balanced scorecard are logical rather than causal (Norreklit 2000, 2003).

Other models based on BSC-type approaches, such as the Skandia navigator (Edvinsson and Malone 1997), the intangible asset monitor (Sveiby 1997), and the Ericsson cockpit communicator, fall into this category. However, the argument of simply mapping performance drivers and outcomes seems to be challenged by theories put forward by the resource-based view of the firm (Wernerfelt 1984; Rumelt 1984; Barney 1991). Penrose (1959), for example, argues that resources or assets of firms exist as a bundle; and others (Dierickx and Cool 1989; Lippman and Rumelt 1982) state that these resource bundles affect performance with causal ambiguity and it is difficult to identify how individual resources contribute to success without taking into account the interdependencies with other assets (Alchian and Demsetz 1972).

Organic View of Organizational Knowledge Assets

The organic view of knowledge as a resource views knowledge as a dynamic and tentative combination of data, meaning, and the ability to generate proficient practice. It is a view of knowledge in action that implies embedded skills, organizational routines, and a susceptibility to path dependency. The puzzle, of course, lies in the relationships between these three knowledge types. Nonaka and Takeuchi presume the interchangeability of explicit and tacit knowledge. Roos and Roos (1997) highlight the need for information on the transformations from one intellectual capital category into another, suggesting interdependency of knowledge-based assets. Lev (2001) notes that intangibles, including knowledge, are frequently embedded in physical assets and labor (the tacit knowledge of employees), leading to considerable interaction between tangible and intellectual assets in the creation of value. Spender argues that managers, in pursuit of the organization's rationale and identity, must create contextually contingent syntheses among four basic types of knowledge (Spender 1996a).

If there is more than one type of knowledge, it follows that each type may have to be measured separately. Ways to address this complexity in measurement include *intellectual capital statements*, which provide a narrative approach that tries to capture the interdependencies (Meritum 2002; Mouritsen et al. 2002). The narrative format allows organizations to express the value of their knowledge-based resources and how they interact with other knowledge-based assets to create value. They can then outline their knowledge management initiatives, allowing them to consider a set of measures to track the implementation and evaluate its impact.

Dynamic visualization approaches, such as the *navigator* approach (for example, see Gupta and Roos, 2001, Marr, Grey, and Neely 2003) or the *value creation map* (Marr et al. 2004), extend the cognitive mapping techniques offered by Eden and Spender (1996) and suggest it is possible to map direct as well as indirect dependencies, reflecting the embeddedness and path dependency of knowledge-based assets.

The navigator model is a conceptual map that depicts the presence and importance of tangible and intangible resources and the transformation of these resources in accordance with achieving the organization's strategic intent (Neely et al. 2003). The value creation map follows the same logic but focuses on the knowledge-based assets and the way they interact to directly and indirectly contribute to value creation.

A summary of the different understandings of knowledge together with the associated concepts of management, theories of the firm, and measurement approaches is presented in Table 13.1.

Table 13.1

Views on Knowledge and Associated Measurement Approaches			
Knowledge Management Topic, Context	**Concept of Management**	**Theory of the Firm**	**Measurement Approach**
Data (rules and measurements)	Positivistic (rational decision making)	Machine (bureaucratic rationality)	Economic valuation of IC
Meaning (information)	Interpretive approaches, sense-making, psychological and socio-psychological views	Cognitive lenses, metaphors, expectations	Cause and effect, strategy maps, scorecards
Practice, activity systems, collaboration (proficient practice)	Open systems approaches, organic view	Activity networks, action research, evolutionary concepts, path dependency	Map of dependent and independent relationships, narratives, pattern recognition, complex systems

Conclusion and Look into the Future

The suggestion that there are three rather different types of knowledge assets (positivistic, interpretive, and organic) implies three substantially different approaches to learning and the management of the organization's knowledge processes. Even with some indications of the possible ways of addressing these differences in the previous section, it may be important to get back to the basic philosophical differences between these types of knowledge.

A principal assumption behind the positivist approach is that reality is knowable. Knowledge comprises justified true beliefs about this reality. This relationship between the knower and reality is reflected in the definition of the organization as purposive and goal oriented. The organization's goals are the reality to which it strives. Thus, the positivistic type of knowledge needs to be measured against the organization's goals. These are established prior to the organization's planning and implementation processes, and, in this sense, are independent of them.

The interpretivist approach, in contrast, emerges after the organization and its processes. This type of knowledge is constructed by those observing and experiencing the organization and its processes; it is the result of the managers working to make sense of what they observe. Knowledge is anchored in the mangers themselves and their experience rather than in the organization's prior goals.

It is immediately clear that the knowledge demands of the positivist approach are considerably more severe than those of the interpretive approach. The first emphasizes stability and a notion of change within an established frame of analysis. The second is more flexible. As business uncertainty increases, it is likely that the first eventually will fail, as managers are unable to tease out the complex causal links that give rise to the organization's results. As a result, they will be driven back to trying to make the best sense possible of what is happening, no longer struggling to understand the entire situation.

Simon's notion of "satisficing" embodies this idea (Simon 1957). We see that the interpretive approach assumes that management's knowledge—and, as a result, that of the organization itself—is incomplete. The approach itself is a way of dealing with such incomplete knowledge. Here, the criteria against which one can measure the knowledge is obviously not "the truth," for that is dismissed by assumption as unknowable. Rather the test of the knowledge's quality is an experience-based sense of improvement and understanding: Do we understand the situation better than we did before? The organization's knowledge is tentative, as is the positivist's, but it is not being exposed to falsification. Rather, it is being constructed by analyzing the organization's experiences and applied as the basis for the plan for the next time period. Then, it is measured against the next best alternative, not against a theoretically determined optimum. While the positivistic approach focuses on such an optimal outcome, the interpretive approach suboptimizes.

The organic approach to knowledge takes this separation from the situation of total understanding a step further. To consider an organization "organic" is to endow it with behaviors and characteristics of its own, which are not the immediate result of management's plans. These are readily familiar as the unintended consequences of our plans. The key here is not simply the managers' lack of complete understanding, rather it is their lack of total control over the organization. The criteria against which the mangers' and the organization's knowledge must be measured is not that of total control but of enough control to keep moving toward planned outcomes.

In this chapter, we outline the increasing importance of knowledge-based assets in today's business environment. We offer an integrated set of ways in which knowledge is viewed as an organizational resource: data, information, and proficient practice. These views of organizational knowledge assets are then matched to some existing techniques for measuring knowledge assets in organizations. We believe that the organic view of organizational knowledge most closely reflects the organizational reality today, and we hope to have laid the foundation for further discussion of approaches to measuring knowledge assets embedded in organizational realities. It seems that the time has come to move from the more-simplistic view of data or information assets toward the more-dynamic, path-dependent, and complex role of knowledge in the value creation process of modern businesses.

Acknowledgment

Parts of this chapter are based on an earlier article by the authors (Marr and Spender 2004).

References

Alchian, A. A., and H. Demsetz. 1972. "Production, Information Costs, and Economic Organization." *American Economic Review* 62: 777–795.

Andrews, K. R. 1971. *The Concept of Corporate Strategy*. Homewood, IL: Dow Jones-Irwin.

Arrow, K. 1962. "The Economic Implications of Learning by Doing." *Review of Economic Studies* 29, no. 3: 155–173.

Barney, J. B. 1986. "Strategic Factor Markets: Expectations, Luck and Business Strategy." *Management Science* 32: 231–1241.

———. 1991. "Firm Resources and Sustained Competitive Advantage." *Journal of Management* 17, no. 1: 99–120.

———, and W. G. Ouchi. 1986. *Organizational Economics: Toward a New Paradigm for Understanding and Studying Organizations*. San Francisco: Jossey-Bass.

Bell, D. 1999. *The Coming of Post-Industrial Society: A Venture in Social Forecasting*, special anniversary ed. New York: Basic Books.

Bontis, N., N. C. Dragonetti, K. Jacobsen, and G. Roos. 1999. "The Knowledge Toolbox: A Review of the Tools Available to Measure and Manage Intangible Resources." *European Management Journal* 17, no. 4: 391–402.

Brainard, W., and J. Tobin. 1968. "Pitfalls in Financial Model-Building." *American Economic Review*, 58, no. 2: 99–122.

Brown, M. M., and J. L. Brudney. 2003. "Learning Organizations in the Public Sector?" *Public Administration Review* 63, no. 1: 30–43.

Cabrera, Á., and E. F. Cabrera. 2002. "Knowledge-Sharing Dilemmas." *Organization Studies* 23, no. 5: 687.

Davenport, T. H., and L. Prusak. 1998. *Working Knowledge: How Organizations Manage What They Know*. Boston: Harvard Business School Press.

Dierickx, I., and K. Cool. 1989. "Asset Stock Accumulation and Sustainability of Competitive Advantage." *Management Science* 35, no. 12: 1504–1511.

Drucker, P. F. 1959. "Challenge to Management Science." *Long Range Planning* 5, no. 2: 238–242.

Eden, C., and J. C. Spender, eds. 1996. *Managerial and Organizational Cognition*. London: Sage Publishers.

Edvinsson, L., and M. S. Malone. 1997. *Intellectual Capital: The Proven Way to Establish Your Company's Real Value by Measuring Its Hidden Values*. London: Piatkus.

Foss, N., ed. 1997. *Resources, Firms, and Strategies: A Reader in the Resource-Based Perspective*. Oxford: Oxford University Press.

Freeman, J., et al. 1992. *Who Built America? Working People and the Nation's Economy, Politics, Culture and Society.* New York: Pantheon Books.

Grant, R. M. 1991. "The Resource-Based Theory of Competitive Advantage: Implications for Strategy Formulation." *California Management Review* 33, no. 3: 14–35.

Gupta, O., and G. Roos. 2001. "Mergers and Acquisitions through an Intellectual Capital Perspective." *Journal of Intellectual Capital* 2, no. 3: 297–309.

Kaplan, R. S., and D. P. Norton. 1992. "The Balanced Scorecard—Measures That Drive Performance." *Harvard Business Review* 70, no. 1: 71–79.

———. 1996. *The Balanced Scorecard—Translating Strategy into Action.* Boston: Harvard Business School Press.

———. 2000. "Having Trouble with Your Strategy? Then Map It." *Harvard Business Review* (September–October): 167–176.

———. 2003. *Strategy Maps—Converting Intangible Assets into Tangible Outcomes.* Boston: Harvard Business School Press.

Lerner, A. 1944. *The Economics of Control: Principles of Welfare Economics.* New York: Macmillan.

Lev, B. 2001. *Intangibles: Management, Measurement, and Reporting.* Washington, DC: The Brookings Institution.

Lippman, S. A., and R. P. Rumelt. 1982. "Uncertain Imitability: An Analysis of Interfirm Differences in Efficiency under Competition." *Bell Journal of Economics* 13, no. 2: 418–438.

Machlup, F. 1980. *Knowledge: Its Creation, Distribution, and Economic Significance.* Princeton, NJ: Princeton University Press.

Marr, B., D. Gray, and A. Neely. 2003. "Why Do Firms Measure Their Intellectual Capital." *Journal of Intellectual Capital* 4, no. 4: 441–464.

Marr, B., O. Gupta, S. Pike, and G. Roos. 2003. "Intellectual Capital and Knowledge Management Effectiveness." *Management Decision* 42, no. 8: 771–781.

Marr, B., and G. Schiuma. 2001. "Measuring and Managing Intellectual Capital and Knowledge Assets in New Economy Organisations." In: *Handbook of Performance Measurement,* ed. M. Bourne. London: Gee.

———. 2003. "Business Performance Measurement—Past, Present, and Future." *Management Decision* 41, no. 8: 680–687.

Marr, B., G. Schiuma, and A. Neely. 2004. "The Dynamics of Value Creation: Mapping Your Intellectual Performance Drivers." *Journal of Intellectual Capital* 5, no 2: 312–325.

Marr, B., and J.-C. Spender. 2004. "Measuring Knowledge Assets—Implications of the Knowledge Economy for Performance Measurement." *Measuring Business Excellence* 8, no 1: 18–27.

Menand, L. 2001. *The Metaphysical Club: A Story of Ideas in America.* New York: Farrar, Straus and Giroux.

Meritum. 2002. *Guidelines for Managing and Reporting on Intangibles.* Madrid: Airtel-Vodafone Foundation.

Mouritsen, J., P. N. Bukh, H. T. Larsen, and T. H. Johnson. 2002. "Developing and Managing Knowledge through Intellectual Capital Statements." *Journal of Intellectual Capital* 3, no. 1: 10–29.

Neely, A., B. Marr, G. Roos, S. Pike, and O. Gupta. 2003. "Towards the Third Generation of Performance Measurement." *Controlling* 3–4 (March–April): 61–67.

Nelson, R. R., and S. G. Winter. 1982. *An Evolutionary Theory of Economic Change.* Cambridge, MA: Harvard University Press.

Nonaka, I., and H. Takeuchi. 1995. *The Knowledge-Creating Company: How Japanese Companies Create the Dynamics of Innovation.* New York: Oxford University Press.

Norreklit, H. 2000. "The Balance on the Balanced Scorecard—A Critical Analysis of Some of Its Assumptions." *Management Accounting Research* 11, no 1: 65–88.

———. 2003. "The Balanced Scorecard: What Is the Score? A Rhetorical Analysis of the Balanced Scorecard." *Accounting, Organizations and Society* 28, no. 6: 591–619.

Penrose, E. T. 1959. *The Theory of the Growth of the Firm.* New York: John Wiley.

Petergraf, M. A. 1993. "The Cornerstones of Competitive Advantage: A Resource-Based View." *Strategic Management Journal* 14: 179–188.

Polanyi, M. 1958. *Personal Knowledge: Towards a Post-Critical Philosophy.* Chicago: University of Chicago Press.

———. 1966. *The Tacit Dimension.* Garden City, NY: Doubleday.

Porter, M. E. 1980. *Competitive Strategy.* New York: The Free Press.

Prahalad, C. K., and G. Hamel. 1990. "The Core Competence of the Corporation." *Harvard Business Review* 68, no. 3: 79–91.

Prusak, L. 2001. "Where Did Knowledge Management Come From?" *IBM Systems Journal* 40, no. 4: 1002–1006.

Reich, R. B. 1992. *The Work of Nations: Preparing Ourselves for 21st Century Capitalism.* New York: Vintage Books.

Roos, G., and J. Roos. 1997. "Measuring Your Company's Intellectual Performance." *Long Range Planning* 30, no. 3: 325.

Roos, J., G. Roos, N. C. Dragonetti, and L. Edvinsson. 1997. *Intellectual Capital: Navigating the New Business Landscape.* London: Macmillan.

Rumelt, R. P. 1984. "Towards a Strategic Theory of the Firm." In: *Competitive Strategic Management,* ed. R. B. Lamb. Englewood Cliffs, NJ: Prentice-Hall.

Sackmann, S., E. Flamholz, and M. Bullen. 1989. "Human Resource Accounting: A State of the Art Review." *Journal of Accounting Literature* 8: 23–264.

Selznick, P. 1957. *Leadership in Administration.* New York: Harper and Row.

Simon, H. A. 1957. *The new science of management decision.* New York: Harper.

Solow, R. M. 1957. "Technical Change and the Aggregate Production Function." *Review of Economics and Statistics,* 39: 312–320.

Spender, J.-C. 1994. "Organizational Knowledge, Collective Practice and Penrose Rents." *International Business Review* 3, no. 4: 353–367.

———. 1996a. "Competitive Advantage from Tacit Knowledge? Unpacking the Concept and its Strategic Implications." In: *Organizational Learning and Competitive Advantage,* ed. B. Moingeon and A. Edmondson, pp. 56–73. Thousand Oaks CA: Sage Publications.

———. 1996b. "Villain, Victim or Visionary? F. W. Taylor's Contributions to Organization Theory." In: *Scientific Management: Frederick Winslow Taylor's Gift to the World?* ed. J.-C. Spender and H. Kijne, pp. 1–31. Norwell, MA: Kluwer.

———, and R. M. Grant. 1996. "Knowledge and the Firm: Overview." *Strategic Management Journal* 17: 5–9.

Spender, J. C., and H. Kijne, eds. 1996. *Scientific Management: Frederick Winslow Taylor's Gift to the World?,* Norwell, MA: Kluver.

Stewart, T. A. 1997. *Intellectual Capital: The New Wealth of Organizations.* New York: Doubleday/Currency.

Sveiby, K. E. 1997. "The Intangible Assets Monitor." *Journal of Human Resource Costing & Accounting* 2, no. 1.

———. 2001. "A Knowledge-Based Theory of the Firm to Guide in Strategy Formulation." *Journal of Intellectual Capital* 2, no. 4.

Teece, D. J. 1977. "Technology Transfer by Multinational Firms: The Resource Cost of International Technology Transfer." *Economic Journal* 87: 242–261.

———, G. Pisano, and A. Shuen. 1997. "Dynamic Capabilities and Strategic Management." *Strategic Management Journal* 18, no. 7: 509–533.

Veblen, T. 1965 [1904]. *The Theory of the Business Enterprise.* New York: Augustus M. Kelley.

von Krogh, G., K. Ichijo, and I. Nonaka. 2000. *Enabling Knowledge Creation: How to Unlock the Mystery of Tacit Knowledge and Release the Power of Innovation.* New York: Oxford University Press.

Wernerfelt, B. 1984. "A Resource Based View of the Firm." *Strategic Management Journal* 5, no. 3: 171–180.

Weick, K. E. 1979. *Social Psychology of Organizing,* 2nd ed. Reading, MA: Addison-Wesley.

———. 1995. *Sensemaking in Organizations.* Thousand Oaks, CA: Sage Publications.

An Epistemology Perspective on Intellectual Capital

Göran Roos
Cranfield School of Management

Introduction

This chapter substantiates the claim that the epistemological outlook of people in organizations has a substantial impact on the effectiveness of the firm's value creation and needs to be aligned with both the type of intellectual capital resources that form the basis for the firm's competitive advantage and the type of strategic logics that dominate in the firm.

To do this, we need to first provide three introductions. The first is a brief introduction to the highly complex area of epistemology, where many scholars have been active but complexity still reigns and a full understanding still eludes us. The second is an introduction to the three value creation logics fundamental to understanding different types of firms. The third and final is the introduction to the intellectual capital perspective, which allows for a clear understanding of the types of resources that can form the basis for the firm's competitive advantage.

What Is Epistemology?

The word *epistemology* is derived from the Greek words *episteme* (knowledge) and *logos* (theory). It has been defined as follows: "Epistemology is concerned with understanding the origin, nature and validity of knowledge: it seeks to provide knowledge about knowledge" (von Krogh & Roos 1995). *Epistemology* is further defined by Craib (1992) as "the nature of an explanation: what methodology to use, what logical structure must it have, what proofs are required, or how do we know that our knowledge is knowledge." Therefore, epistemology is concerned with the analysis of what is meant by the term *knowledge* itself. A study of knowledge then runs up against problems of definitions. Wittgenstein pointed out that knowledge is not easily defined in an exact manner (von Krogh & Roos 1995).

Edgar and Sedgwick (1999) set out some questions we can ask about what is meant by the term *knowledge*:

1. What can we be said to know (the limits and scope of knowledge)?
2. What constitutes the reliability of knowledge and what constitutes justification or a warrant for holding a belief and thereby deeming that belief to be "knowledge"?

Plato argued that learning is the process of uncovering what we already know, although at some preconscious level. The empiricists, however, argue that human understanding and hence knowledge is a result of a sense experience alone (Edgar and Sedgwick 1999); that is, what we know is the consequence of our ability to have perceptions of the world via our senses. This is the view taken by philosophers such as Locke, Berkeley, and Hume.

The German philosopher Immanuel Kant argued that there are necessary conditions of knowing that cannot be reduced to mere experience (Edgar and Sedgwick 1999). According to this view, a form of knowledge exists prior to and independent of any empirical knowledge, namely, a priori knowledge.

There is considerable latitude among the human race as to the nature of knowledge, what it means and how it should be managed, if at all. If managers try to impose a model of knowledge and attempt to manage on a basis foreign to the workforce, they will fail. Therefore, to understand people's beliefs and use of knowledge, a grounding in epistemological issues is required.

Organizational Epistemology

Von Krogh and Roos (1995) give meaning to the term *organizational epistemology* as a collection of perspectives, theories, and concepts related to the following sets of issues:

- How and why do individuals within organizations come to know?
- How and why do organizations, as social entities, come to know?
- What counts for knowledge by the individual and the organization?
- What are the impediments to organizational knowledge development?

Von Krogh and Roos claim that organizational epistemology is connected to organizational metaphysics, that is, our understanding of "being" and the "unified whole" as well as our understanding of the basic characteristics of management and organizational studies.

The interrelation of organizational epistemology with the theory of value in organizations is also discussed. This concerns the moral values and principles that constitute how we understand what is good and bad, right and wrong, that is, organizational ethics (von Krogh and Roos 1995). For example, a new organizational epistemology could result in the rethinking of the nature and role of moral concepts and judgments in writing an annual report.

Epistemology in Management

Understanding epistemological assumptions ensures effective knowledge management. The managerial tools and practices employed in a company have to match the specific nature of knowledge (von Krogh and Roos 1996). Von Krogh and Roos set out three distinct epistemologies and state that distinct managerial responsibilities and practices arise from each epistemology (von Krogh, Roos, and Kleine 1998). They argue that the ability to recognize these benefits managers considerably in the following ways:

- Being familiar with different possibilities means having a larger knowledge management repertoire and a better understanding of the limitations of each approach.

Table 14.1

Cognitivist Profile	
Profile Criteria	**Description**
View of one's own organizations	Works like a mainframe computer, information is collected and stored centrally; top management drives processes
Perception of the environment	The environment is pregiven; universal adaptability to the environment is the main task
Notion of knowledge	Knowledge is a fixed and representable entity; knowledge in the form of databases, archives, and manuals can be shared across the organization
Knowledge development	Assimilation and dissemination of incoming information is how the cognitivist develops knowledge
Characteristics of truth	Truth depends on the amount of information.
Adapted from: Von Krogh and Roos 1995.	

- Because knowledge development is contingent (i.e., dependent on the context), researchers as well as managers need to interpret and understand changes in corporate epistemology.
- If we can recognize different epistemologies, we might also be able to choose a distinct mode, depending on the current situation.

Three Epistemologies

The three epistemologies discussed in Varela, Thompson, and Rosch (1991) and von Krogh and Roos (1996) are interpreted by Carter (2002) as follows.

Cognitivist Epistemology

The beginnings of cognitivist epistemology can be traced back to the mid-1950s, when Herbert Simon and others developed a particular way of knowing. Organizations are considered open systems, which develop knowledge by formatting increasingly accurate representations of their predefined worlds (Venzin, von Krogh, and Roos 1998). Data accumulation and dissemination are the major knowledge activities. The cognitivist approach is to equate knowledge with information and data. The truth of knowledge is understood as the degree to which inner representations correspond to the world outside (Venzin et al. 1998). These researchers continue to set out a cognitivist profile, which is shown in Table 14.1. To a cognitivist, the human brain and organization are machines of logic and deduction (von Krogh and Roos 1995).

Connectionist Epistemology

In connectionist epistemology, the process of representing reality is different. This epistemology has many similarities to the cognitivist viewpoint, but there are no universal rules. As rules are team-based, organizations are seen as self-organized networks composed of relationships and driven by communication (Venzin et al. 1998).

Table 14.2

Connectionist Profile	
Profile Criteria	**Description**
View of one's own organization	Individuals are connected mostly through information technology; action is self-organized and steered by local rules that refer to several frames of reference
Perception of the environment	Clusters of the organizational network produce different pictures of the pregiven world
Notion of knowledge	Knowledge resides on the connections of experts and is problem-solution orientated; knowledge depends on the state of the network of interconnected components
Knowledge development	Specific groups develop knowledge relevant to their own environment, as local rules determine how knowledge is accumulated
Characteristics of truth	Experts define what is considered truth in the organization
Adapted from: Von Krogh and Roos 1995.	

Connectionist models are founded on a large number of interacting units that influence one another by sending activation signals down interconnecting pathways. For connectionists, the process of shaping an organization depends not only on the stimuli entering the system but also the system itself. The connectionist profile, as set out by Venzin et al. (1998), is summarized in Table 14.2. Information processing is the basic process of connectionist organizations; the network is key.

Autopoietic Epistemology

The word *autopoietic* derives from the Greek, *auto* (self) and *poiesis* (production). *Autopoiesis*, a term coined by Maturana and Varela (1980), refers to the self-reproduction of living systems. It was redefined by von Krogh and Roos (1995) "as the internal and recursive self-reproduction of the basic elements of a social system to describe their autonomous and self-referential operations."

Autopoietic epistemology provides a fundamentally different understanding of the input coming from outside a system. The input is not information but data. The organization is a system that is simultaneously open (to data) and closed (to information and knowledge). The system is controlled by its rules and organizes itself. Information and knowledge cannot be transmitted easily, since they require internal interpretation within the system according to the individual's rules. Individual knowledge is developed and respected in others. The autopoietic epistemology profile set out by Venzin et al. (1998) is shown in Table 14.3. The cycle of self-production characterizes the theory of autopoiesis (Venzin et al. 1998).

Empirical Findings

Marr, Gupta, Pike, and Roos (2003) gathered a set of data using questionnaires to determine the value beliefs of the various functional groups in companies and their attitudes to knowledge. The questions are repeated, in that respondents are first asked

Table 14.3

	Autopoietic Profile
Profile Criteria	**Description**
View of one's own organization	The company is an autonomous and observing system, built up of individuals, who are considered free agents; management tries to develop opportunities and support organizational members by putting them into action
Perception of the environment	The environment and the organization are coevolving systems
Notion of knowledge	Knowledge is private, respect for different individuals in the organization; knowledge resides in mind, body, and social system
Knowledge development	The process of interpreting incoming data in conversations is the cornerstone; this enables autopoietic systems to make distinctions and create meaning according to observations and previous experiences
Characteristics of truth	Individuals create their own reality; there are many truths within the organization.
Adapted from: Von Krogh and Roos 1995.	

to describe themselves and then how they see the capabilities of their company's knowledge management system.

This methodology has been applied to a number of European companies from various industries. Proceeding in accordance with an agreement for nonspecific attribution, the questionnaire results were coded and analyzed using algorithmic content review to place the respondents' answers on the surface as shown in Figure 14.1.

The survey process was exploratory and therefore not designed to enable statistical treatment of results nor to test or confirm any specific hypothesis. The epistemological results of four firms are shown in the Figures 14.2 and 14.3. In these diagrams, the horizontal-lined areas depict where the responses fell when respondents were considering themselves. The cross-hatched areas depict where the responses fell when respondents were considering their company's knowledge management (KM) system.

These results show the practical importance of epistemology when dealing with knowledge from a managerial perspective. It is obvious, for example, that not taking the epistemological viewpoint into account when designing a knowledge management system is asking for failure.

Value Creation Logics

Here, I provide a short overview of the different value creation logics. The first model is Porter's conventional value chain (1985), in which the output, and the output alone, brings value to the customer (see Figure 14.4). Whatever happens during the process of producing the output is insignificant to the customer who purchases the output. A traditional business, such as a factory, is the typical example of a value chain. The primary resource of the firm cannot be human, as this type of value creation relies on standardized processes and repetition (economies of learning) and mass production (economies of scale). The basis for competitive advantage is more likely to be composed of physical, monetary, organizational, or relational resources.

Figure 14.1

Classes of epistemology.

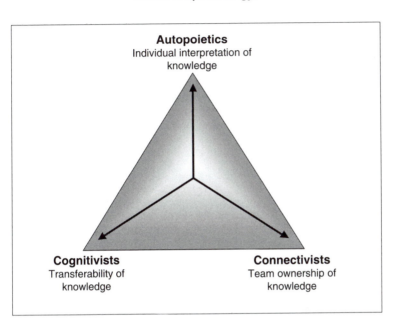

The second value creation logic is the value shop (Figure 14.5), in which the main focus is solving a problem for a client. In contrast to the value chain, the value in a value shop resides not only in the solution itself (the output) but also in the individuals who came up with the solution and the way they reached it. The primary resource and source of competitive advantage is hence most likely to be human but can also be organizational or relational. In any case, the most important resource in a value shop can never be physical or monetary.

The third value creation logic is the value network (Figure 14.6). The basis for value creation in this logic lies in connecting people who wish to be interdependent. Examples of organizations using the value network logic are banks and telecommunications operators. In this logic, the value is created in the actual enabling when connecting customers to each other. The primary resource of a company operating as a value network is therefore most probably its relational or organizational resources. The more subscribers a telecom operator has, the better is the value for the individual subscriber, up until a certain point, where the operator cannot provide its subscribers with satisfactory service. In any case, the primary resource in a value network cannot be monetary, physical, or human.

Empirical Findings

I hold anecdotal evidence for a correlation between the strategic logic of the organization and the epistemological outlook of the organization's senior management. This evidence is based on consulting dialogues with hundreds of senior managers over the last 5 years. The empirical evidence did not allow me to reject my hypothesis

Figure 14.2

Results for service-based Companies (Source: Marr, Gupta, Pike, and Roos 2003).

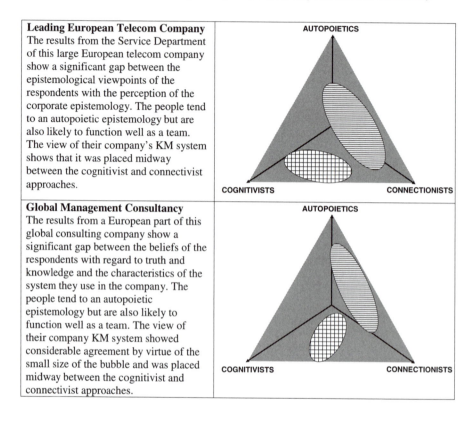

| Leading European Telecom Company
The results from the Service Department of this large European telecom company show a significant gap between the epistemological viewpoints of the respondents with the perception of the corporate epistemology. The people tend to an autopoietic epistemology but are also likely to function well as a team. The view of their company's KM system shows that it was placed midway between the cognitivist and connectivist approaches. | |
| Global Management Consultancy
The results from a European part of this global consulting company show a significant gap between the beliefs of the respondents with regard to truth and knowledge and the characteristics of the system they use in the company. The people tend to an autopoietic epistemology but are also likely to function well as a team. The view of their company KM system showed considerable agreement by virtue of the small size of the bubble and was placed midway between the cognitivist and connectivist approaches. | |

summarized in Figure 14.7. The picture basically states that the higher the alignment is between the pairwise illustrated strategic logics and the epistemological paradigms, the more effective the value creation of the firm.

The Intellectual Capital Perspective of the Firm

The intellectual capital perspective was initially developed as a framework for analyzing the value contribution of intangible assets in an organization. The first major grounding of the work was by Roos and Roos in 1997 and in more theoretical detail by Jay Chatzkel (2002) and Pike, Rylander, and Roos in (2002). This approach developed in parallel with work by Amit and Schoemaker, which shares many features with this view. The intellectual capital approach draws heavily on practical firm experiences (successes and failures).

As with most emerging theories, there are many definitions of *intellectual capital*, but over the last few years, a consensus seems to have formed on dividing a company's resources into three different groups: human resources, comprising the competence (the term is used in a broad sense) of the individual employees; relational resources, which represents all the organization's valuable relationships with

Figure 14.3

Results for production-based companies (Source: Marr, Gupta, Pike, and Roos 2003).

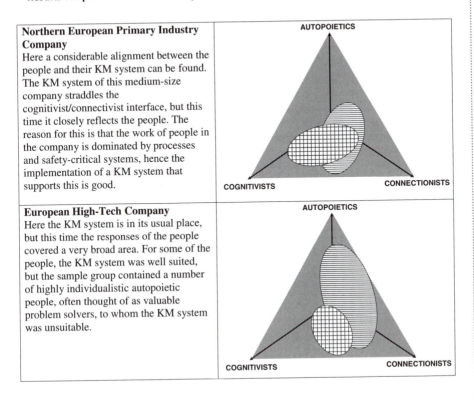

Northern European Primary Industry Company Here a considerable alignment between the people and their KM system can be found. The KM system of this medium-size company straddles the cognitivist/connectivist interface, but this time it closely reflects the people. The reason for this is that the work of people in the company is dominated by processes and safety-critical systems, hence the implementation of a KM system that supports this is good.	AUTOPOIETICS COGNITIVISTS · · · CONNECTIONISTS
European High-Tech Company Here the KM system is in its usual place, but this time the responses of the people covered a very broad area. For some of the people, the KM system was well suited, but the sample group contained a number of highly individualistic autopoietic people, often thought of as valuable problem solvers, to whom the KM system was unsuitable.	AUTOPOIETICS COGNITIVISTS · · · CONNECTIONISTS

customers, suppliers, and other relevant stakeholders; and organizational resources, including processes, systems, structures, documented information, patents, brands, other intellectual property, and other intangibles that are owned by the firm but do not appear on its balance sheet. The resources that actually make up the categories are unique to each organization, as only those resources important for creating value should be included in its distinction tree (Bontis et al. 1999).

The intellectual capital perspective, however, goes beyond the mere presence of a resource; it also considers the organization's ability to transform one resource into another. The presence of resources is not sufficient to create value; for example, there is no correlation between the number of marketing experts in a firm and sales. The importance is in the way resources are deployed, which implies the transformation from one resource into another. Monetary value can be created through selling a process (organizational resources transformed into monetary resources), or new organizational resources can be created through formalizing knowledge into a process (human resources transformed into organizational resources). The impact of these transformations on value creation can be assessed and visualized through the intellectual capital approach with an IC navigator, a model revealing all the value creating resources (tangible and intangible), their transformations, and the relative importance of the resources and transformations for value creation.

Figure 14.4

The value chain (modified after Porter 1985).

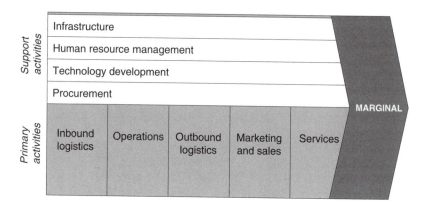

Figure 14.5

The value shop (modified by Roos after Stabell and Fjeldstad 1998).

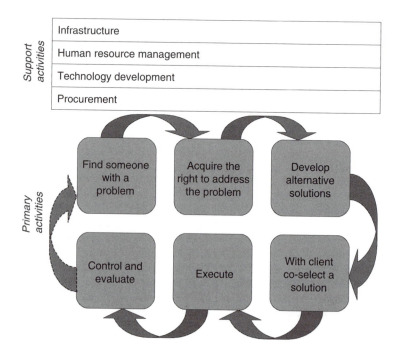

Figure 14.6

The value network (modified by Roos after Stabell and Fjeldstad 1998).

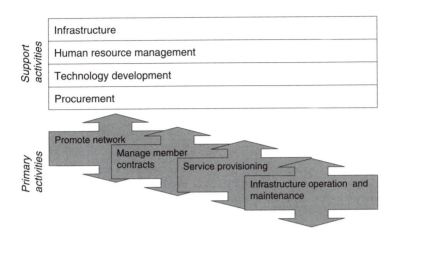

Figure 14.7

Relationship between epistemology and value logic.

Value shop/Autopoietic

Value chain/Cognitivist   Value network/Connectivist

As an example, consider two firms operating in the professional service sector. They may address quite similar markets, but the relative importance of their resources and the way they are deployed may be very different.

Company A might rely heavily on its human and relational resources. This company needs some monetary resources but hardly any physical or organizational resources. The organization is focused around very knowledgeable, competent individuals who use these attributes to form personal relationships with their clients and to deliver value. The firm hires only the best of the best (the people are, after all, its main competitive advantage), it is very flexible, and training takes place through an informal apprenticeship. Growth of this organization may be difficult. It takes place through a kind of replication. This firm probably is a partnership, characterized by internal competition for clients and resources, but restrained by a partnership ethos and an emergent sense of "good manners." The quality of the product or service delivered may vary according to who is doing the job. Marketing and sales are also based on the individuals and often result from their personal prominence and reputation. The organization survives and thrives thanks to low fixed costs and high billing rates and margin. Some of the money earned is used to sustain the relationships with clients and some to maintain and develop the competence of the individual.

Company B operates in the same space, but with a very different value creating mechanism. It places a much larger emphasis on its structural resources and depends less on bright individuals. As this is also a professional service firm, the relationships with customers are obviously still very important. Human resources are relatively less important to value creation here than in the "people-centric" organization. This does not mean that people are not important, but their relative importance is lower. The best people are used to develop processes, which are "activated" by less-skilled employees. This organization is characterized by organizational relationships rather than personal ones. The training and recruitment processes are more formal than in the people-centric organization. Product quality is more standardized, and there is a more system-focused approach. There is more codification and rules, and the company may have higher fixed costs and lower margins than a people-centric one; on the other hand, utilization may be higher. Clearly these two organizations have different assets and philosophies. When presented with strategic alternatives, the relative merits of the different options may be quite different.

Intellectual Capital and Strategic Logics

If we now synthesize the strategic logics perspective with the intellectual capital perspective, we can conclude the type of intellectual capital resources that can form a basis for competitive advantage in each of the strategic logics, as outlined in Figure 14.8, with the value chain, value shop, and value network (from left to right as column headings), and monetary, physical, relational, organizational, and human intellectual capital resources (from top to bottom as row headings).

All the secondary resources might be used as a basis for competitive advantage, but they require higher managerial skill. For example, the orange resources must be on the decreasing marginal part of the network economic behavior to form a basis for competitive advantage in the value chain and on the increasing marginal return part of the network economic behavior in the value shop.

Intellectual Capital and Epistemology

As pointed out already, one strength of the intellectual capital perspective is that it focuses on transformations within and between resource categories. If we now match with these transformations the type of epistemological paradigms held by the individuals involved in executing and managing, we get a clearer picture of how to maximize effectiveness using appropriate epistemological paradigms. The summary is outlined in the Figure 14.9.

Some of these conclusions have been pointed out in earlier articles in implicit or tangential ways (see, e.g., Roos and Roos 1997, p. 419; Sveiby 2001; O'Donnell,

Figure 14.8

Resources and value logics.

	Value Chain	Value Shop	Value Network
Monetary Resources	Primary basis for competitive advantage		
Physical Resources	Primary basis for competitive advantage		
Relational Resources	Secondary basis for competitive advantage	Secondary basis for competitive advantage	Primary basis for competitive advantage
Organizational Resources	Secondary basis for competitive advantage	Secondary basis for competitive advantage	Primary basis for competitive advantage
Human Capital Resources		Primary basis for competitive advantage	

Figure 14.9

Resources and epistemologies.

To: From:	Monetary Resources	Physical Resources	Relational Resources	Organizational Resources	Human Capital Resources
Monetary Resources Physical resources	Cognitivest epistemology		Balanced cognitivist / connectionist epistemology		Balanced cognitivist / autopoietic epistemology
Relational Resources Organizational Resources	Balanced cognitivist / connectionist epistemology		Connectionist epistemology		Balanced connectionist / autopoietic epistemology
Human Capital Resources	Balanced cognitivist / autopoietic epistemology		Balanced connectionist / autopoietic epistemology		Autopoietic epistemology

O'Regan, and Coates 2000; Maula 2000; Jankowicz 2001). But, to my knowledge, this is the first time that it is synthesized in a complete form.

Intellectual Capital, Strategic Logics, and Epistemology

If we now synthesize the table in Figure 14.9 with the managerial epistemological outlook that seems to form a suitable basis for competitive advantage, we get Figure 14.10.

As can be seen from the reasoning in this figure, the understanding of epistemology is crucial in ensuring the effective value creation of the firm through the interaction among its people, its resources, and its strategic logics. A small subset of this issue

Figure 14.10

Intellectual capital, strategic logics, and epistemology.

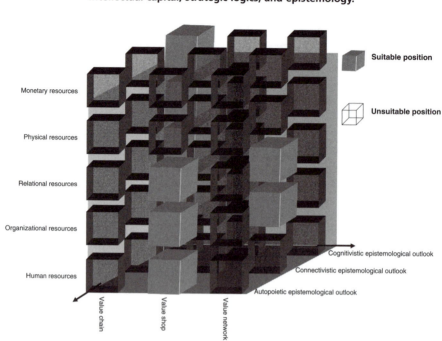

relates to knowledge management. It is highly likely that many failures in knowledge management implementations, for example, are due to differing epistemological worldviews between suppliers and users of knowledge management solutions (for further discussion on the complexities around knowledge management, see, e.g., McAdam and McCreedy 1999; Pike and Roos 2002).

My claim here, "That effectiveness in managing organizations can be substantially improved by aligning the strategic logic of the organization, the intellectual capital resources that form the basis for the organization's competitive advantage, and the epistemological outlook of the people in the organization" cannot be rejected based either on empirical observations or theoretical discussions.

References

Amit, R., and P. J. H. Schoemaker. 1993. "Strategic Assets and Organizational Rents." *Strategic Management Journal* 14: 33–46.

Bainbridge, A., K. Jacobsen, and G. Roos. 2001. "Intellectual Capital Analysis as a Strategic Tool." *Strategy and Leadership Journal* (May).

Bontis, N., N. C. Dragonetti, K. Jacobsen, and G. Roos. 1999. "The Knowledge Toolbox; A Review of the Tools Available to Measure and Manage Intangible Resources." *European Management Journal* (August).

Carter, C. 2002. "Epistemology, Culture and Knowledge Management: Is There a link?" MBA project executed at ICS Ltd., University of Westminster, London.

Chatzkel, J. B. 2002. "Conversation with Göran Roos." *Journal of Intellectual Capital* 3: 2.

Craib, I. 1992. *Modern Social Theory: From Parson to Habermas.* Hemel Hempsted: Harvester-Wheatsheaf.

Edgar, A., and P. Sedgwick, P. 1999. *Cultural Theory: The Key Concepts.* London: Rutledge.

Jankowicz, D. 2001. "Why Does Subjectivity Make Us Nervous? Making the Tacit Explicit." *Journal of Intellectual Capital* 2, no. 1: 61–73.

Marr, B., O. Gupta, S. Pike, and G. Roos. 2003. "Intellectual Capital and Knowledge Management Effectiveness." *Management Decision* 42, no. 8: 771–781.

Maturana, H., and F. Varela. 1980. *Autopoiesis and Cognition: The Realization of the Living.* London: Reidl, D.

Maula, M. 2000. "The Senses and Memory of a Firm—Implications of Autopoiesis Theory for Knowledge Management." *Journal of Knowledge Management* 4, no. 2: 157–161.

McAdam, R., and S. McCreedy. 1999. "A Critical Review of Knowledge Management Models." *The Learning Organization* 6, no. 3: 91–100.

O'Donnell, D., P. O'Regan, and B. Coates. 2000. "Intellectual Capital: A Habermasian Introduction." *Journal of Intellectual Capital* 1 no. 2: 187–200.

Pike, S., and G. Roos. 2002. "Measuring the Impact of Knowledge Management in Companies." Paper presented at the Fifth World Congress on Intellectual Capital, 23rd McMaster Business Conference, January 16–18, Hamilton, Canada.

Pike, S., A. Rylander, and G. Roos. 2002. "Intellectual Capital Management and Disclosure." In: *The Strategic Management of Intellectual Capital and Organizational Knowledge—A Selection of Readings,* ed. N. Bontis and C. Choo. New York: Oxford University Press.

Porter, M. E. 1985. *Competitive Advantage: Creating and Sustaining Superior Performance.* New York: The Free Press.

Roos, G., and L. Fernstrom. 2003. "Differences in Value Creating Logic and Their Managerial Consequences: The Case of Authors, Publishers & Printers." Paper presented at the International Conference, The Future of the Book, Cairns, April.

Roos G., and J. Roos. 1997. "Measuring Your Company's Intellectual Performance." *Long Range Planning* 30, no. 3: 413–426.

Spender, J. C. 1996. "Organisational Knowledge, Learning and Memory: Three Concepts in Search of a Theory." *Journal of Organisational Change Management* 9, no. 1: 63–78.

Stabell, C. B., and Ø. D. Fjeldstad. 1998. "Configuring Value for Competitive Advantage: On Chains, Shops, and Networks." *Strategic Management Journal* 19.

Sveiby, K.-E. 2001. "A Knowledge-Based Theory of the Firm to Guide in Strategy Formulation." *Journal of Intellectual Capital* 2, no. 4: 344–358.

Varela, F. J., E. Thompson, and E. Rosch. 1991. *Embodied Mind: Cognitive Science and Human Experience.* Cambridge, MA: MIT Press.

Venzin, M., G. von Krogh, and J. Roos. 1998. *Future Research into knowledge management.* In: *Knowing in firms, Understanding, Managing and Measuring Knowledge,* ed. G. von Krogh, J. Roos, and D. Kleine. London: Sage.

von Krogh, G., and J. Roos. 1995. *Organisation Epistemology.* London: Macmillan Press.

von Krogh, G., and J. Roos. 1996. "Five Claims of Knowing." *European Management Journal,* no. 14: 423–426.

von Krogh, G., J. Roos, and D. Kleine. 1998. *Knowing in Firms: Understanding, Managing and Measuring Knowledge.* London: Sage Publications.

Part III

Discussion and Final Thoughts

The Evolution and Convergence of Intellectual Capital as a Theme

Bernard Marr
Cranfield School of Management

Introduction

The aim of this final chapter is to synthesize the perspectives outlined in the book and discuss where these different insights lead us. We have seen from the various contributions in this book that the theme of intellectual capital is of significant importance in most disciplines. The chapters summarized how the concept of intellectual capital is addressed in different disciplines and from varying viewpoints. Many of these seem to have evolved with seemingly little awareness or recognition of each other. Only recently have there been interdisciplinary outlets for research on the topic. These publications help facilitate a multidimensional dialogue in this field, but at the same time, they are not necessarily well known across all disciplines. For practicing managers, it is even more difficult to obtain a multidisciplinary overview of the topic, as many publications or conferences are either specialized in certain areas (e.g., accounting or human resources) or treat intellectual capital very superficially. The collection of chapters in this book provides a good starting point for understanding the field as a whole. Here I try to synthesize how the theme of intellectual capital has evolved across different disciplines and perspectives, but first, I will pick up some main issues and suggest possible ways forward.

Evolution of Intellectual Capital as a Theme

When we look at the way the theme of intellectual capital has evolved over time, it is interesting to note that, against many common beliefs, the concept is not a new phenomenon; in fact, the economist Nassau William Senior mentions "intellectual capital" as an important production factor in his book published more than 150 years ago, in 1836. Economists and scholars in the strategy field have long discussed the importance of knowledge-based assets. Table 15.1 outlines a selection of major milestones in the evolution of intellectual capital in management science. It includes a synopsis of the contributions the different authors make, an indication of the main perspective the contribution falls into, and an indication of whether the contribution focuses primarily on the practitioner (P) or academic (A). This is not to deny that publications on the topic have increased exponentially over the past 20 years and made intellectual

Table 15.1

Milestones in the Evolution of Intellectual Capital as a Theme

Work	Argument or Contribution	Perspective	
Senior 1836	Argues that the *intellectual capital* of Great Britain far exceeds all the *material capital*, not only in importance, but in productivity.	Public policy, economics	A
Marshall 1890	Claims that *knowledge* is an important resource and a powerful engine of production.	Economics	A
Veblen 1904	Argues that *knowledge* is the tone-giving force in economic development. Its increase and diffusion contributed to the machine technology and is therefore a determinant of growth in firms.	Economics, general management	A
Drucker 1959	Maintains that the business enterprise of today is an organization of professionals of highly specialized knowledge exercising autonomous, responsible judgment. *Knowledge* is an important resource for organizations, and we need an understanding of the resources available, especially the *human resources: their capabilities* and their limitations.	General management	A
Penrose 1959	In her influential book, she argues that *firms are a collection of resources* bound together by an administrative framework. Resources are split into physical assets and human capital, such as skills and know-how.	Economics	A
Machlup 1962, 1981	Started his economic investigation of innovation and knowledge in 1950, leading to various publications (*The Economic Review of the Patent System*, 1958; *The Production and Distribution of Knowledge in the United States*, 1962) and insights into the economic importance of knowledge. He finished the first 3 volumes of the projected 10-volume series, *Knowledge: Its Creation, Distribution, and Economic Significance*.	Economics	A
Becker 1964	Argues that investment in *human capital*, such as an individual's education and training, is similar to business investments in equipment.	Human resources	A

Work	Argument or Contribution	Perspective	
Accounting Principles Board 1970	The APB published Opinion 17—Intangible Assets, which allowed identifiable intangible assets to be recognized separately, but all costs incurred to develop intangible assets that are not specifically identifiable have to be expensed.	Accounting	P
Itami, 1980 [in Japanese], 1987 [in English]	Asserts that invisible assets, such as information-based assets, which include technology, consumer trust, brand image, corporate culture, and management skills, are the most important resources for organizational long-term success.	General management	A
Teece 1981	Argued that know-how is a resource for firms and plays an important role in the transfer of technology.	Economics, strategy	A
Wernerfelt 1984; Rumelt 1984; Barney 1991	The resource-based view of the firm is framed to challenge the market-based paradigm. Its proponents argue that firms gain a competitive advantage from possessing difficult to replicate resources, which include intangible assets and intellectual capital.	Strategy	A
Flamholtz 1985	Developed the idea of human resource accounting as a way to quantify the effects of human resource strategies and a new way of looking at human resource issues.	Human resources, accounting	P
Romer 1986, 1987, 1992	Developed the new growth theory of the firm, which proves that economic growth is based on knowledge. Knowledge is recognized as a superior part that directs the use of capital, technological development, and quality of labor.	Economics	A
Johnson and Kaplan 1987	Argued that traditional financially focused cost accounting approaches are losing relevance if they continue to ignore other dimensions of organizational performance, such as intangible assets.	Accounting	A
Teece 1987	A book on the competitive challenges of firms. This includes a contribution by Sidney Winter, who argued that knowledge assets and competencies are important strategic assets for firms.	Economics, strategy	A

Table 15.1 *continued*

Milestones in the Evolution of Intellectual Capital as a Theme

Work	Argument or Contribution	Perspective	
Hall 1989, 1992, 1993	In a series of articles, Hall argued that *intellectual assets or intangible assets* are critical value drivers in organizations. Intangible assets drive capability differentials, which in turn drive sustainable competitive advantage, which is why organizations need to bring intangible resources and core competences into their strategic thinking.	Strategy	A
Aaker 1989	Argued that the essence of strategic management should be the development and maintenance of meaningful *assets and skills*, the selection of strategic and competitive arenas to exploit such assets and skills, and the neutralizing of competitors' assets and skills.	General management	A
Prahalad and Hamel 1990	Argued that, in the long run, competitiveness derives from an ability to build the *core competencies* that spawn unanticipated products. The real sources of advantage are to be found in management's ability to consolidate corporatewide technologies and production skills into competencies that empower individual businesses to adapt quickly to changing opportunities.	General management	A
Kaplan and Norton 1992, 1996	The *balanced scorecard* is introduced as a tool to link financial performance with nonfinancial performance dimensions: innovation and learning; internal processes, and customer perspective.	Strategy	P
Kogut and Zander 1992	Argued that firms are a repository of *capabilities*, as determined by the social knowledge embedded in enduring individual relationships structured by organizing principles. Switching to new capabilities is difficult, as neither the knowledge embedded in the current relationships and principles is well understood nor the social fabric required to support the new learning known.	Strategy	A
Hudson 1993	Argued that *intellectual capital* is a personal asset of individuals (a combination of genetic inheritance, education, experience, and attitude about life and business), which every individual has to manage to succeed.	Human resources	P

Work	Argument or Contribution	Perspective	
Grant and Baden-Fuller 1995; Spender and Grant 1996	Building on the ideas of the resource-based view, various authors jointly developed the *knowledge-based view*, arguing that knowledge-based assets are in fact the most critical for gaining a competitive advantage.	Strategy	A
Brooking 1996, 1997	One of the first practitioner publications arguing that firms need to conduct an *IC audit*, to document the intangible assets, their current state, and their value. *Intellectual capital* is defined as market assets, human-centered assets, intellectual property assets, and infrastructure assets.	General management	P
Nonaka and Takeuchi 1995	Building on their work in the early 1990s, they argued that in an economy where the only certainty is uncertainty, the one sure source of lasting competitive advantage is knowledge. However, they argued that often the *tacit and highly subjective knowledge* of employees is the source of real value.	Knowledge management, general management	A
Sveiby 1997	Building on earlier work published in Swedish in the late 1980s ("The New Annual Report" and "The Invisible Balance Sheet"), Sveiby proposes the *intangible assets monitor* as a management control tool with three focal areas: human capital and internally and externally related intangibles.	General management, reporting	P
Edvinsson and Malone 1997; Edvinsson 1997	The Skandia insurance company in Sweden started to use the *Skandia navigator* to report their intellectual capital; similar to the balanced scorecard, it uses different focal areas: financial, customer, human, process, renewal, and development. The first external report appeared in May 1995. Edvinsson (at that time manager of intellectual capital at Skandia) and journalist Malone advocate *intellectual capital reporting* as a new accounting tool to measure the value contained in an organization's structural and human capital.	Reporting	P
Stewart 1997	Building on earlier practitioner publications in *Fortune* magazine (1991, 1994), Stewart argued that *intellectual capital* is the new wealth of organizations.	General management	P

Table 15.1 *continued*

Milestones in the Evolution of Intellectual Capital as a Theme

Work	Argument or Contribution	Perspective	
Roos et al. 1997	The *IC-index* approach is proposed as an attempt to assess intellectual capital strategically. The authors suggest consolidating all individual intellectual capital indicators into a single index to provide a more comprehensive visualization.	Strategy	P
Boisot 1998	Argued that the effective management of knowledge assets is a key requirement for securing competitive advantage. However, the nature of knowledge assets is still poorly understood. Boisot provides a conceptional framework to differentiate knowledge and information assets from physical assets.	Strategy	A
Sullivan 1998, 2000	Provided a set of practical tools and practices to manage intangible assets and intellectual property, such as trade secrets or patents.	Intellectual property, legal	P
Andriessen and Tissen 2000	Introduced the *value explorer* as a practical methodology for managing and valuing intangible assets. Proposed that by answering a set of "new" questions, managers can better understand how to operate in the knowledge economy.	General management	P
Teece 2000	Argued that the essence of the firm in the new economy is its ability to create, transfer, assemble, integrate, protect, and exploit knowledge assets. Introduced and discussed the organization, strategic, and policy dimensions of the management of intellectual capital.	Strategy, public policy	A
Lev 2001	Argued that intangible assets are important nonphysical sources of value (claims to future benefits) generated by innovation (discovery), unique organizational designs, or human resource practices. Intangibles often interact with tangible and financial assets to create corporate value and economic growth.	Economics, accounting	A

Work	Argument or Contribution	Perspective	
SFAS No. 142, "Goodwill and Other Intangible Assets," 2001	Statement of Financial Accounting Standards No. 142 supersedes APB Opinion 17, "Intangible Assets," and requires the discontinuance of the amortization of goodwill and intangible assets with indefinite lives. These assets are subject to an impairment review at least annually.	Accounting	P
Edvinsson 2002; Low and Kalafut 2002	Presented practical thinking and case examples on the importance, development, and management of intellectual capital.	General management	P
Choo and Bontis 2002; Bontis 2002; Hand and Lev 2003	Various edited books attempted to provide wider academic views by publishing selected articles on accounting and the strategic and general management of *intellectual capital*.	Strategy / accounting / general management	A
Chatzkel 2003	A selection of dialogues with leading thinkers and practitioners about the management of *knowledge capital* in firms.	Knowledge management	P
Andriessen 2004	Based on Ph.D. research, the book contains a comprehensive review of tools and approaches to measure and value intellectual capital. It provided a classification of tools to distinguish the many diverse models and puts forward a new approach for valuing intangible assets.	General management	A
Kaplan and Norton 2004	Proposed strategy maps as tools to measure the readiness of intangible assets, which are split into human capital, information capital, and organizational capital.	Strategy	P

capital a much-researched topic; however, as one can see from the table, continuous contributions have been made throughout the past 100 years.

Also interesting to note is that intellectual capital is often referred to as a "practitioner driven concept." It is often argued that the concept of intellectual capital was developed by visionary companies such as Skandia or Dow Chemical, which started to measure and to report their intellectual capital in the 1990s. There was indeed a strong practitioner driven movement in the middle of the 1990s towards tools and approaches for measuring, managing, and reporting intellectual capital. This can be seen in Table 15.1 by the influx of practitioner books starting from 1993. Many of these books proposed classification frameworks of intellectual capital and approaches to measure and manage it. This triggered a seemingly separate intellectual capital movement concerned primarily with practical applications. Most of these approaches were based on the initial experiences of firms and were to a large extent developed in isolation from any academic work done previously.

The first to discuss the topic academically were economists, who highlighted the importance of intellectual capital as a production factor and the different behavior of intellectual capital in comparison to traditional economic assets. A long stream of publications reached its pinnacle in the development of *the new growth theory*, developed by Raul Romer of the University of Stanford, who proved that economic growth is based on knowledge. The theory is in strong opposition to the classical economic theory and based in many respects on the works of the Nobel Prize winner Robert Solow. While the parts of the economic model of Solow are capital, technology, and labor, Romer has added knowledge as another superior part that directs the use of capital, technological development, and quality of labor.

Some of these developments in economics were picked up in the strategic management field. The development of the *resource-based theory* in the 1980s and the *knowledge-based theory* in the 1990s challenged the traditional market-based theories. They argued that a sustainable competitive advantage results from the possession of resources that are inimitable not substitutable, tacit in nature, and synergistic. With this newly developed emphasis on internal resources, special attention was placed on competencies, capabilities, and knowledge-based assets. It is interesting to note that in the strategic management literature, the term *intellectual capital* is rarely used but the same constructs are referred to.

In parallel, there were activities in the field of accounting, with attempts by the major accounting bodies around the world to develop approaches to account for intellectual capital. This was to provide a better picture of firms in which intellectual capital is a major asset but stringent accounting principles prevent recognition of such an asset. This debate has continued since the 1970s, and new guidelines for accounting of intangible assets emerged regularly. Interesting to note is that accountants also rarely refer to intellectual capital, as they seem to prefer the term *intangible assets*. The theme of intangible assets has become a major subject in the accounting field, and conferences and special issues of journals fuel the ongoing debate on the topic.

Accounting takes a statutory inside-out view of the firm to externally disclose performance data in a standardized format driven by accounting rules. However, there is a movement to better *value intellectual capital* from an outside-in perspective. On the one hand, financial analysts, banks, and other investors looked for ways to better understand the potential value of firms; on the other hand, firms wanted to better understand the financial value of their investments in intellectual capital. This need was highlighted with the burst of the dot-com bubble. With the absence of reliable tools to value intellectual capital, speculation led to many firms being overvalued.

However, after the return to reality, many innovative startup firms, even with a sound business case, still find it hard today to secure funding. Approaches discussed in this perspective include EVA™, discounted cash flow, and real options models.

Related to the discussion in accounting and finance has been the work of a group of researchers concerned with the external *reporting* of intellectual capital. Surrendering to the thought that the rigid postulates of accounting do not allow the deserved treatment of intellectual capital, they associated themselves with the more practitioner-orientated management accounting field. The efforts of firms such as Skandia in the 1990s to externally disclose information on their intellectual capital has fueled this debate. This movement resulted in various initiatives in Europe to design guidelines for firms to create intellectual capital reports, most notably, an initiative in Denmark, where many companies experimented with producing and disclosing information on their intellectual capital.

When it comes to *marketing*, it seems that intellectual capital and much of the research just outlined is often ignored. The term *intellectual capital* is rarely used; however, customer relationships and brands are often classified as intellectual capital and definitely represent important intangible assets for firms. One issue in marketing is the drive toward demonstrating the importance of investments into building assets such as brands or relationships with customers. The same issue applies to *human resource management*. However, here, the topic of intellectual capital is addressed but more from a personal perspective: How do we assess the knowledge and capabilities of individuals? It seems that, in both fields, accounting- and finance-driven models hindered development. External valuations of brands or *human resource accounting* were brought into the disciplines from other, maybe more financially and measurement-driven perspectives.

Still another view on intellectual capital that developed in complete isolation is provided by the *legal perspective*. Work in this perspective concerns primarily how to legally protect intellectual capital, such as patents, trademarks, or copyrights, which are generally referred to as intellectual property. With an exception of maybe the pharmaceutical industry, this topic has rarely been discussed outside legal departments. However, many recent publications try to raise awareness among executives about the strategic importance of intellectual property.

Previously, I summarized how intellectual capital as a theme has evolved in different academic disciplines. Many of these disciplines developed the intellectual capital theme in isolation and with little awareness of developments in other fields. The second part of this book includes interdisciplinary views on intellectual capital. These establish starting points for cross-disciplinary knowledge transfer, open new research streams, or provide views that could add insights to new developments.

An interesting development outlined is lifting the level of analysis from an individual or firm level toward an interfirm or even regional or national level of analysis. Closer supply chain integration and more interfirm collaboration mean that intellectual capital issues between firms need to be addressed. On an even higher level is the question of whether we are developing the right intellectual capital in cities, regions, counties, and countries. These are exciting new avenues for future research.

Other interesting insights can be gained from philosophy and epistemology, the oldest disciplines to influence the theme of intellectual capital. Intellectual capital is related to knowledge, and the debate about what knowledge means goes back to Plato (427–347 B.C.), who defined *knowledge* as "justified true belief," which triggered an unremitting epistemological discussion throughout the evolution of philosophy among philosophers including Decartes, Locke, Kant, Hegel, Wittgenstein, and Heidegger, to name just a few. The way we perceive the world and our role in it influences our view of intellectual capital. These insights open up interesting research opportunities and offer new insights into the way intellectual capital is managed, measured, and reported.

Toward Convergence: Some Possible Ways Forward

The multidimensional and diverse nature of thinking on the topic of intellectual capital is appealing; however, as a consequence, there is no cohesive body of literature on intellectual capital. The developments of specialist publications such as the *Journal of Intellectual Capital* (established in 2000) and the *International Journal of Learning and Intellectual Capital* (established in 2004) are attempts to channel diverse thinking into single outlets. However, these journals are still in the process of finding their acknowledged position and have not yet managed to bridge all the disciplinary silos. The diverse nature of thinking on intellectual capital poses many challenges as well as immense opportunities for interdisciplinary and cross-functional learning. Here, I outline some of the major issues to be addressed as well as some possible avenues to take this important field forward.

Terminology and Definitions

The construct of "intellectual capital" has existed in management research for many years. However, different terminology used in different disciplines and different taxonomies of the same constructs cause significant confusion and restrict the potential for generalization and comparison of application and research in this area. To date, there is no commonly agreed-on terminology or definition for the construct "intellectual capital."

Every discipline has different assumptions, and every definition (whether explicit or not) is linked to specific roles of intellectual capital, which in turn are often linked to the disciplinary assumptions. It is important to note that there are no right or wrong definitions of *intellectual capital*; however, what do exist are adequate and inadequate definitions of *intellectual capital*. The least-adequate case occurs when authors fail to define *intellectual capital* at all and leave it to the reader to interpret the construct. This book is meant to highlight the differences in interpretation and therefore the resulting risk of misinterpretation due to a lack of adequate clarification.

It is important that whatever terms we use, such as *intellectual capital, intangible assets,* or *knowledge resources*, we explain what we mean by them. In addition, it would be useful to explain the perspective from which the topic is discussed.

Interdisciplinary Research

The field of intellectual capital seems to offer immense room for knowledge transfer among the individual perspectives and functions outlined in this book. It seems that the theories and insights developed in the economics and strategy perspectives provide a good grounding for other "less-developed" intellectual capital perspectives. Theories such as the new growth theory and the resource-based theory could inform the thinking in disciplines such as marketing, human resources, and accounting.

This book provides a comprehensive overview to the complex and interdisciplinary research and practice on the management, measurement, and reporting of intellectual capital. It is now up to managers and researchers to take the insights from the many perspectives and apply them to further our understanding across disciplines and between academia and practice. I call for more interdisciplinary research projects and more collaboration between academics and managers.

Methodological Implications

It seems that there are different implications for different disciplines and research streams. Next, I outline some implications offering future opportunities.

One opportunity seems to be to empirically test some of the practitioner-driven frameworks. As outlined already, in the middle of the 1990s, many classification and reporting frameworks were developed, sometimes from experience of one or a very small number of firms and other times based only on anecdotal evidence. Many of those frameworks have never been subject to rigorous empirical tests. This offers great opportunities for researchers to test the wider applicability of some of those frameworks.

Another opportunity is to ground some of the practical frameworks in theory. Many theoretical foundations outlined in this book should offer an excellent starting point. Much of the academic work published on intellectual capital is of a theoretical nature and often attempts to build theory. There is immense room for convergence here: The theories developed in academia can be used to ground the practical work; and the practical experience can be used to support or reject theories.

Economics and strategy are the disciplines with the longest track record of research on intellectual capital. However, theory-testing research in these disciplines is traditionally performed using quantitative and large sample methodologies, often using secondary sources of data. It is important that we produce some of those studies; but with the developments of new theories in strategy, for example, these traditional positivistic methods have been questioned. Rouse and Daellenbach (2002; 1999), for instance, argue in their influential (1999) article that research based on the resource-based view must be done not only on organizations but also in organizations, since the research methodologies traditionally used in strategy research do not unambiguously uncover the sources of sustainable advantage. Rouse and Daellenbach continue to argue that uniqueness springing from intangible resources (perhaps, especially forms of knowledge) should form the focus of research. Therefore, generalizable, codifiable knowledge available from secondary sources is probably irrelevant to the core research agenda of the resource-based view (Rouse and Daellenbach 2002).

We need rigorous and theoretically grounded empirical research, provided not only by classic large-sample, cross-sectional research projects, but complemented by rich, longitudinal case studies that allow us to understand the specific context that seems critical for the analysis of intellectual capital. Research methods such as ethnography, participant observation, and other, more-phenomenological approaches might be appropriate.

The Level of Analysis

Most publications on intellectual capital concentrated on the firm level and reported on issues related to the management, measurement, and reporting of intellectual capital. More recently, the level of analysis has been raised. Contributions in this book outline some attempts to address intellectual capital on an interfirm and national or regional level. On the other hand, research on epistemology, for example, is often conducted on a personal level and rarely discussed on an organizational level.

Moving between these different levels of analysis offers exciting new avenues for future research and application. An interesting question that needs further exploration is the applicability of the insights, approaches, and tools developed on a firm level to a regional or national level. On the other side, it would be interesting to apply and test the insights from epistemology and the way we handle and process knowledge on an individual level when looking at higher levels of analysis, such as organizations, cities, regions, and nations.

Theme versus Field

Maybe instead of a field, as often referred to by many practitioners, it might be better to talk about the intellectual capital theme or even a lens that allows us to gain new insights in different disciplines and fields. The challenge here is to learn from each other's insights and develop a greater understanding of intellectual capital without reinventing the wheel. I hope this book provides both managers and academics with a richer insight into the multidimensional nature of intellectual capital as an important construct in today's business context. It is now up to you to take the ideas and insights and utilize them for rigorous research and relevant practical applications.

References

Aaker, D. A. 1989. "Managing Assets and Skills: The Key to a Sustainable Competitive Advantage." *California Management Review* 31, no. 2 (Winter): 91.

Accounting Principles Board (APB). 1970. *APB Opinion 17—Intangible Assets.* New York: American Institute of Certified Public Accountants.

Andriessen, D. 2004. *Making Sense of Intellectual Capital: Designing a Method for the Valuation of Intangibles.* Boston: Butterworth–Heinemann.

Andriessen, D., and R. Tissen. 2000. *Weightless Wealth: Find Your Real Value in a Future of Intangible Assets.* London: FT Prentice Hall.

Barney, J. B. 1991. "Firm Resources and Sustained Competitive Advantage." *Journal of Management* 17, no. 1: 99.

Becker, G. S. 1964. *Human Capital.* New York: Columbia University Press.

Boisot, M. H. 1998. *Knowledge Assets: Securing Competitive Advantage in the Information Economy.* Oxford: Oxford University Press.

Bontis, N., ed. 2002. *World Congress on Intellectual Capital Reading.* Boston: Butterworth–Heinemann.

Brooking, A. 1996. *Intellectual Capital: Core Assets for the Third Millennium Enterprise.* London: Thompson Business Press.

———. 1997. "The Management of Intellectual Capital." *Long Range Planning* 30, no. 3: 364–365.

Chatzkel, J. L. 2003. *Knowledge Capital: How Knowledge-Based Enterprises Really Get Built.* New York: Oxford University Press.

Choo, C. W., and N. Bontis, ed. 2002. *The Strategic Management of Intellectual Capital and Organizational Knowledge.* New York: Oxford University Press.

Drucker, P. F. 1959. "Challenge to Management Science." *Long Range Planning* 5, no. 2: 238–242.

Edvinsson, L. 1997. "Developing Intellectual Capital at Skandia." *Long Range Planning* 30, no. 3: 320–331.

———. 2000. "Some Perspectives on Intangibles and Intellectual Capital 2000." *Journal of Intellectual Capital* 1, no. 1: 12.

———. 2002. *Corporate Longitude: What You Need to Know to Navigate the Knowledge Economy.* London: Bookhouse.

———, and M. S. Malone. 1997. *Intellectual Capital: The Proven Way to Establish Your Company's Real Value by Measuring Its Hidden Values.* London: Piatkus.

Flamholtz, E. 1985. *Human Resource Accounting.* Los Angeles: Jossey-Bass.

Grant, R. M. 1996. "Toward a Knowledge-Based Theory of the Firm." *Strategic Management Journal (1986–1998)* 17 (Winter special issue): 109.
Grant, R. M. 1997. "The Knowledge-Based View of the Firm: Implications for Management Practice." *Long Range Planning* 30, no. 3 (June): 450.
———, and C. Baden-Fuller. 1995. "A Knowledge-Based Theory of Inter-Firm Collaboration." *Academy of Management Journal* (Best Paper Proceedings 1995): 17–21.
Hall, R. 1989. "The Management of Intellectual Assets: A New Corporate Perspective." *Journal of General Management* 15, no. 1: 53.
———. 1992. "The Strategic Analysis of Intangible Resources." *Strategic Management Journal* 13, no. 2 (February): 135.
———. 1993. "A Framework Linking Intangible Resources and Capabilities to Sustainable Competitive Advantage." *Strategic Management Journal* 14, no. 8 (November): 607.
Hand, J., and B. Lev. 2003. *Intangible Assets: Values, Measures, and Risk*. New York: Oxford University Press.
Hudson, W. J. 1993. *Intellectual Capital: How to Build It, Enhance It, Use It*. New York: Wiley.
Itami, H. 1987. *Mobilizing Invisible Assets*. Cambridge, MA: Harvard University Press.
Johnson, T. H., and R. S. Kaplan. 1987. *Relevance Lost: The Rise and the Fall of Management Accounting*. Boston: Harvard Business School Press.
Kaplan, R. S., and D. P. Norton. 1992. "The Balanced Scorecard—Measures That Drive Performance." *Harvard Business Review* 70, no. 1: 71–79.
———. 1996. *The Balanced Scorecard—Translating Strategy into Action*. Boston: Harvard Business School Press.
———. 2004. *Strategy Maps—Converting Intangible Assets into Tangible Outcomes*. Boston: Harvard Business School Press.
Kogut, B., and U. Zander. 1992. "Knowledge of the Firm, Combinative Capabilities, and the Replication of Technology." *Organization Science* 3, no. 3 (August): 383.
Lev, B. 2001. *Intangibles: Management, Measurement, and Reporting*. Washington, DC: The Brookings Institution.
Low, J., and P. Kalafut. 2002. *Invisible Advantage: How Intangibles Are Driving Business Performance*. Cambridge: Perseus.
Machlup, F. 1962. *The Production and Distribution of Knowledge in the United States*. Princeton, NJ: Princeton University Press.
———. 1981. *Knowledge, Its Creation, Distribution, and Economic Significance*. Princeton, NJ: Princeton University Press.
Marshall, A. 1890. *Principles of Economics*. London: Macmillan. Volume I, *Knowledge and Knowledge Production* (1982); Volume II, *The Branches of Learning* (1982); Volume III, *The Economics of Information and Human Capital* (1984, posthumous).
Nonaka, I., and H. Takeuchi. 1995. *The Knowledge-Creating Company: How Japanese Companies Create the Dynamics of Innovation*. Oxford: Oxford University Press.
Penrose, E. T. 1959. *The Theory of the Growth of the Firm*. New York: John Wiley.
Prahalad, C. K., and G. Hamel. 1990. "The Core Competence of the Corporation." *Harvard Business Review* 68, no. 3 (May–June): 79.
Romer, P. 1986. "Increasing Returns and Long-Run Growth." *Journal of Political Economy* 94: 1002–1037.
———. 1987. "Growth Based in Increasing Returns Due to Specialization." *American Economic Review Proceedings* 77: 56–62.
———. 1992. *Increasing Returns and New Developments in the Theory of Growth*, reprint edition. Cambridge, MA: National Bureau of Economic Research.
Roos, J., G. Roos, N. C. Dragonetti, and L. Edvinsson. 1997. *Intellectual Capital: Navigating the New Business Landscape*. London: Macmillan.
Rouse, M. J., and U. S. Daellenbach. 1999. "Rethinking Research Methods for the Resource-Based Perspective: Isolating Sources of Sustainable Competitive Advantage." *Strategic Management Journal* 20, no. 5 (May): 487.

———. 2002. "More Thinking on Research Methods for the Resource-Based Perspective." *Strategic Management Journal* 23, no. 10 (October): 963.

Rumelt, R. P. 1984. "Towards a Strategic Theory of the Firm." In: *Competitive Strategic Management*, ed. R. B. Lamp. Englewood Cliffs, NJ: Prentice-Hall.

Senior, N. W. 1836. *An Outline of the Science of Political Economy.* London: Longman.

SFAF No 142 2001. Goodwill and Intangible Assets, Statemeint of Financial Accounting Standards, Financial Accounting Standards Board.

Spender, J. C., and R. M. Grant. 1996. "Knowledge and the Firm: Overview." *Strategic Management Journal* 17 (Winter): 5–9.

Statement of Financial Accounting Starndards (2001) SFAS No. 142, "Goodwill and Other Intangible Assets". Financial Accounting Standards Bord, Norwalk, CT.

Stewart, T. A. 1991. "Brainpower." *Fortune* (June 3): 44–60.

———. 1994. "Measuring Company IQ." *Fortune* (January): 129.

———. 1997. *Intellectual Capital: The New Wealth of Organizations.* New York: Doubleday/Currency.

Sullivan, P. H. 1998. *Profiting from Intellectual Capital: Extracting Value from Innovation.* New York: Wiley.

———. 2000. *Value-Driven Intellectual Capital: How to Convert Intangible Corporate Assets into Market Value.* New York: Wiley.

Sveiby, K. E. 1997. *The New Organizational Wealth: Managing and Measuring Knowledge-Based Assets.* San Francisco: Barrett-Kohler.

Teece, D. J. 1981. "The Market for 'Know-How' and the Efficient International Transfer of Technology." *Annuals of the American Acadamy of Political and Social Scienc* 458: 81–95.

———, ed. 1987. *The Competitive Challenge: Strategy and Organization for Industrial Innovation and Renewal.* New York: Harper and Row (Ballinger Division).

———. 2000. *Managing Intellectual Capital: Organizational, Strategic, and Policy Dimensions.* Oxford: Oxford University Press.

Veblen, T. 1904. *The Theory of the Business Enterprise.* New York: Augustus M. Kelley.

Wernerfelt, B. 1984. "A Resource-Based View of the Firm." *Strategic Management Journal* 5, no. 2 (April–June): 171.

Index

A

Accounting
cost, 44
creative, 51
gross margins, 21–22
human resource
criticisms of, 99
description of, 98, 189
information, loss of relevance of, 43–44
intangible assets, 42–52, 46–49
metrics for, 20–21
professional organizations for, 43–44
stock market valuations, 21
Accounting Principles Board, 215t
Agglomeration economies, 157
American Institute of Certified Public
Accountants, 43–44
Annual report
information in, 71
intangible assets described in, 69
Applied ideas, 128–129
Appropriability
description of, 17
patents' effect on, 19
regimes, 19
Appropriation, 185
Assets
customer-based, 84
definition of, 113
infrastructure, 59
intangible
accounting for, 42–52, 46–49
annual report provision for, 69
as embedded real options, 66t
balance sheet recognition of, 43, 46
capitalization methods for, 50–51
competitive advantage from, 45
definition of, 30–31
description of, 14–15, 42, 177

future of, 49–52
future profits affected by, 45
human resource as, 32–33, 72, 86
identifiable, 45, 47–48
information about, 49
internally generated, 46–47
investment in, 43
life span of, 47
market value affected by, 45
measurement of, 20
in physical assets, 190
relational resources as, 86–88
reporting of, 49–52
taxation of, 171
valuation of, 148
value captured from, 18
intellectual. *See* Intellectual assets
invisible, 30
knowledge
interpretive view of, 190, 192
organic view of, 190–192
positivistic view of, 189–190, 192
summary of, 192
physical, 57
relational, 84
tangible
definition of, 32
description of, 14–15
replacement value of, 21
Association for Investment Management and
Research, 43–44
Autopoietic epistemology, 199, 200t,
201f

B

Balanced scorecard, 190, 216t
Balance sheets
human capital described in, 97
intangible assets recognized in, 43, 46

Black-Scholes option pricing model
    description of, 62–63
    limitations of, 67
    patent valuation using, 65–66
Book-to-market ratio, 49
Bounded rationality, 8
Brand
    importance of, 89
    measurement of, 90–91
    value and, 89–90
Brand equity, 90
Business knowledge, 118
Business organizations, 3

C
Call options, 62
Capability
    definition of, 30
    dynamic, 30
    information systems, 116–119, 121
Capital
    human
        in balance sheet, 97
        case study examples of, 100–103
        definition of, 96
        description of, 32, 96
        future of, 103
        measurement of, 98–99
        to organizational capital, 116–117, 117f
        in organizations, 97–98
    intellectual. *See* Intellectual capital
    monetary, 32
    organizational
        description of, 22–23, 88
        human capital transformed into,
            116–117, 117f
    physical, 32
Capital markets, 71
Cluster firms
    cognitive dynamics of, 165
    competitive success effects, 156–157
    definition of, 156
    description of, 156
    development of, 157–158
    external network of, 161–162
    features of, 156
    horizontal, 156
    industry, 156
    innovation and, 157
    intellectual capital dimensions of, 158–159
    internal network of, 160–161
    Knoware tree, 158–159
    networking processes of, 161
    regional, 156
    Structural Knoware

    description of, 159
    hardware, 162–163
    netware, 160–162
    software, 163–164
    wetware, 159–160
    summary of, 164–166
    value factors and, 157–158
    vertical, 156
Clustering, 157
Cluster social capital, 164
Codified knowledge, 13, 19, 111, 160
Cognitive maps, 164
Cognitivist epistemology, 198, 201f
Competencies, 119–120
Competition
    competence-based, 184
    knowledge affected by, 14
    option value affected by, 64
    resource-advantage theory applied to,
        85
Competitive advantage, 45, 109, 172, 183
Confidentiality, 128
Connectionist epistemology, 198–199, 199t,
    201f
Context, 115
Contracts, 131–132
Contractual joint ventures, 132
Copyright, 130–131, 138–139
Corporate competencies, 184
Corporate culture, 33–34
Corporate strategy, 28
Cost accounting, 44
Cost capitalization, 50
Creative accounting, 51
Customer-based assets, 84
Customer relationship life-cycle model, 86

D
Data
    cognitivist epistemology view of, 198
    knowledge vs., 189
    positivistic view of, 189
Development costs, 47
Digitization, 116
Discounted cash-flow model, 61–62
Discovery culture, 115
Division of labor, 8
Dynamic capability, 30
Dynamic visualization, 191

E
Earnings information, 44
Earnings management, 50–51
Economic growth, 9–11
Economic value added, 190

Epistemology
  autopoietic, 199, 200t, 201f
  cognitivist, 198, 201f
  connectionist, 198–199, 199t, 201f
  definition of, 196
  empirical findings regarding, 199–200
  intellectual capital and, 206–208
  in management, 197–198
  organizational, 197
  value logic and, 205f
Europe, intellectual capital reporting in, 72–74
European Union, 174–175
Explicit knowledge, 187
Expressive works, 130–131

F
Fair market value, 149
Federal Accounting Standards Board, 149
Financial reporting
  American Institute of Certified Public Accountants concerns, 43–44
  description of, 43
Firm
  intellectual capital perspective of, 202–203, 205–206
  knowledge of, 185
  objectivist approach to, 185
  performance of, legal management effects on, 134–135
  resource-based view of, 215t
Firm clusters
  cognitive dynamics of, 165
  competitive success effects, 156–157
  definition of, 156
  description of, 156
  development of, 157–158
  external network of, 161–162
  features of, 156
  horizontal, 156
  industry, 156
  innovation and, 157
  intellectual capital dimensions of, 158–159
  internal network of, 160–161
  Knoware tree, 158–159
  networking processes of, 161
  regional, 156
  Structural Knoware
    description of, 159
    hardware, 162–163
    netware, 160–162
    software, 163–164
    wetware, 159–160
  summary of, 164–166

  value factors and, 157–158
  vertical, 156
Firm value, 57
Ford Motor Company, 22–23
Four Ps model, 82–83
Functional culture, 115
Functional marketing, 84
Fundamental value, 21

G
General accepted accounting principles, 48, 149
Globalization, 184
Goodwill, 45, 48
Gross margins, 21–22
Growth opportunities, 58

H
Hardware, 162–163
Horizontal clusters of firms, 156
Human capital
  in balance sheet, 97
  case study examples of, 100–103
  definition of, 96
  description of, 32, 96
  future of, 103
  measurement of, 98–99
  organizational capital and, 116–117, 117f
  in organizations, 97–98
Human capital index, 100
Human-centered assets, 59
Human resource(s)
  definition of, 86, 202
  description of, 32–33, 72
  ethical dilemmas, 103
  marketing applications of, 86
  types of, 86
Human resource accounting
  criticisms of, 99
  description of, 98, 189
Human resource costing and accounting, 98–100
Human resource management, 221
Human resource scorecard, 98
Human resources department, 103

I
Imitation, 16–17
Individual learning, 165
Industrial economy
  characteristics of, 42–43
  cost-focused reporting methods in, 42
  knowledge economy vs., 42–43
Industrial property, 138–139
Industry clusters of firms, 156

Industry profitability, 29
Information
  inaccurate, 112
  interpretive view of, 190
  knowledge and, 8, 110–112, 113f
  multiplicative quality of, 114
  poor quality of, 112
  situation of use effects on, 114–115
  time specificity for, 113–114
  valuing of, 113–116
Information and communication
    technologies, 162–163, 170
Information asset management, 109
Information culture, 115
Information resource management, 109
Information systems
  aspects of, 109–110
  as asset, 113
  business knowledge and, 118
  capability, 116–119, 121
  competencies, 119–120
  decision making and, 108, 110
  description of, 107
  functions of, 108
  information technology vs., 108
  as intellectual capital, 107
  management of, 110, 116–117
  strategy development, 120
  summary of, 120–121
  value creation and, 107
  valuing of, 113–116
Information technology
  business value delivered through, 121
  description of, 83
  governance structures, 109
  information systems vs., 108
  platform for, 118
Infrastructure assets, 59
Innovation(s)
  eclectic approaches to study of, 11
  economic growth and, 9–11
  in economic theory, 10–11
  firm clusters and, 157
  historians' comments regarding, 9–11
  intellectual property vs., 18–20
  mapping of, 22
  M-form, 23
  motor assembly line, 22–23
  organizational, 22
  proprietary standards for, 20
  screening criteria for, 142–143
Innovative output, 22
Inquiring culture, 115
Intangible assets
  accounting for, 42–52, 46–49
  annual report provision for, 69

  as embedded real options, 66t
  balance sheet recognition of, 43, 46
  capitalization methods for, 50–51
  competitive advantage from, 45
  definition of, 30–31
  description of, 14–15, 42, 177
  future of, 49–52
  future profits affected by, 45
  human resource as, 32–33, 72, 86
  identifiable, 45, 47–48
  information about, 49
  internally generated, 46–47
  investment in, 43
  life span of, 47
  market value affected by, 45
  measurement of, 20
  in physical assets, 190
  relational resources as, 86–88
  reporting of, 49–52
  taxation of, 171
  valuation of, 148
  value captured from, 18
Intangible assets monitor, 217t
Intangible goods, 125
Intellectual assets
  definition of, 84
  description of, 57–58
  evolution of, 216t
  macroeconomic importance of, 10
  as real options, 65
  valuing of
    description of, 58
    discounted cash-flow model for,
     61–62
    dynamic models, 61–62
    Lev's residual income model for, 60,
     60t
    market-based approach to, 59
    models for, 58
    real options models for, 62–64
    static models for, 58–61
    technology broker model, 58–59
    Tobin's Q model for, 61
    value-based approach to, 59
Intellectual capital
  academic discussions of, 220
  accounting perspective of, 42–52
  analysis levels for, 223–224
  classification of, 96
  as competitive advantage, 172
  definitions of, 31, 45, 125, 137–138, 158,
    202, 222
  description of, 3, 56, 170
  epistemology and, 206–208
  evolution of, 214t–219t, 221–222
  examples of, 36

formal mechanisms for managing,
125–126
history of, 106–107, 214t-219t, 221–222
human capital as, 96–97
identification of, 185
importance of, 38, 56
informal mechanisms for managing,
125–126
information systems as, 107
intellectual property perspective of, 138
interdisciplinary research regarding,
222–223
International Accounting Standard
definition of, 45
investments in, 56
invisibility of, 108
legal instruments for management of
applied ideas, 128–129
contractual joint ventures, 132
contractual relationships for, 131–132
copyright, 130–131, 138
expressive works, 130–131
firm performance affected by, 134–135
formal instruments, 126–131
licenses, 131
passing off, 126–127
patents. *See* Patents
reputation, 126–127
research agreements, 131–132
trade secrets. *See* Trade secrets
uses of, 132–135
management "gathering," 143
marketing and, 91–92, 221
overview of, 74–75
public policy and
description of, 171–173
in Europe, 174–176
models of, 173–174
in United States, 176–180
reporting of
capital market effects, 71
capital reported, 71–72
in Europe, 72–74
future of, 78–79
Maxon Telecom example, 75–78
reasons for, 70–71, 78–79
resource-based view of, 83–84
strategic logics and, 206–207
taxonomies of, 31
terminology associated with, 222
valuation of, 220
value from, 18–20
Intellectual capital audit, 217t
Intellectual-capital dynamic-value framework,
177–178
Intellectual-capital index, 218t

Intellectual capital statements
description of, 74–75, 75f, 191
example of, 76t-77t
future of, 79
purpose of, 78
Intellectual property
assets, 59
background of, 138–139
business value activities, 140–149
competitive assessment, 147–149
defensive activities, 140
definition of, 30–31, 33, 137–138
development of, 138–139
divisions of, 138
example of, 18
future of, 150–151
importance of, 137
innovation vs., 18–20
intellectual capital as viewed by, 138
international agreement on, 139
inventory of, 142
legal activities, 139–140
paradigm of, 138
revenue generated through, 146
screening criteria for, 142–143
strategic value
creation of, 143–145
extraction of, 145–146
types of, 15
valuation of, 147–151
value from, 143
World Intellectual Property Organization,
138–139
Interactive marketing, 83
Internal technology transfer, 23
International Accounting Standards
No. 22, 47
No. 38, 37, 45, 50, 78
*International Journal of Learning and
Intellectual Capital,* 222
Interpretive view, of knowledge assets, 190,
192
Invention
definition of, 128
patented, 129
Invisible assets, 30, 215t

J
Jenkins Report, 70
Joint ventures, 132
Journal of Intellectual Capital, 222

K
Knoware tree, 158–159
Knowledge
appropriability of, 17

Knowledge *(Continued)*
  as assets, 31
  attributes of, 4
  business organization use of, 3
  characteristics of, 112
  codified, 13, 19, 111, 160
  competition effects on, 14
  competitive advantage gained by, 183
  data vs., 189
  definition of, 189, 196–197, 221
  description of, 23–24
  economics of
    concepts involved in, 12–20
    description of, 7–9
  embedding of, 11–12
  evolution of, in business context, 188–189
  explicit, 187
  historical changes in, 184–185
  imitation of, 16–17
  importance of, 183–185
  information and, 8, 110–112, 113f
  interpretivist view of, 186
  as meaning, 186–187
  nature of, 12–16
  negative, 14
  as object, 185–187
  objectivist view of, 186
  observable vs. nonobservable, 13–14
  organizational, 4
  organizational culture effects on, 120
  positive, 14
  present-day views of, 184–185
  process understanding to increase, 16
  replicability of, 16
  scientific, 14
  shared, 33
  situation of use for, 114
  specificity of, 114
  tacit, 13, 19, 160, 187–188
  technological, 4
  transfer of, 13, 16, 112
  types of, 187–188
  value of, 3–4
Knowledge asset map, 159
Knowledge assets
  interpretive view of, 190, 192
  organic view of, 190–192
  positivistic view of, 189–190, 192
  summary of, 192
Knowledge-based theory, 220
Knowledge capital, 106
Knowledge companies, 56
Knowledge economy
  countries with, 170–171
  description of, 42

industrial economy vs., 42–43
Knowledge management
  description of, 111
  information management and, 111–112
Knowledge narrative, 73–74
Knowledge sharing, 111

L
Law of increasing marginal utility, 171
Learning
  description of, 197
  in neoclassical theory, 11
  organizational, 11
Legal instruments, for intellectual capital
    management
  applied ideas, 128–129
  contractual joint ventures, 132
  contractual relationships for, 131–132
  copyright, 130–131, 138
  expressive works, 130–131
  firm performance affected by, 134–135
  formal instruments, 126–131
  licenses, 131
  passing off, 126–127
  patents. *See* Patents
  reputation, 126–127
  research agreements, 131–132
  trade secrets. *See* Trade secrets
  uses of, 132–135
Lev's residual income model, 60, 60t
Licenses, 131
Lisbon agenda, 176

M
Market assets, 59
Market-based approach, to intellectual assets
    valuation, 59
Market-based paradigm, of strategy, 29
Marketing
  description of, 82
  functional, 84
  future of, 91
  human resources applied to, 86
  intellectual capital focus by, 91–92, 221
  interactive, 83
  operational, 84
  origins of, 82–85
  relationship, 86–88
  resource-based view of, 84
  service-centered model of, 91
  of services, 83
  strategic, 84
  task, 84
Marketing mix, 82–83
Market metrics, 20–21

Market relationships, 87
Market value
  description of, 21
  intangible assets' effect on, 45
Marshall, Alfred, 8, 156
Meaning, knowledge as, 186–187
Measurement
  of brand, 90–91
  of human capital, 98–99
  of intangible assets, 20
Mega relationships, 87
Meritum model, 73
M-form, 23
Microeconomists, 185
Mobility barriers, 29
Monetary capital, 32
Monetary value, 203
Monopoly rents, 29
Monte Carlo simulation, 67

N
Nano relationships, 87
Narratives, 103
National Cooperative Research Act of 1984,
  6
Navigator model, 191
Negative knowledge, 14
Net present value, 22, 148–149
Netware, 160–162

O
Object, knowledge as, 185–187
Operand resources, 91
Operant resources, 91
Operational marketing, 84
Option premium, 62
Option pricing models
  Black-Scholes
    description of, 62–63
    limitations of, 67
    patent valuation using, 65–66
  description of, 62
Organic view, of knowledge assets, 190–192
Organization(s)
  human capital in, 97–98
  information cultures in, 115
Organizational assets
  classification of, 31–32
  taxonomy of, 31–32
Organizational capital
  description of, 22–23, 88
  human capital transformed into, 116–117,
    117f
Organizational culture, 120
Organizational epistemology, 197

Organizational innovation, 22
Organizational key resources, 37
Organizational knowledge, 4
Organizational learning, 11
Organizational resources, 33, 88–91, 203
Organizational routines, 163–164
Outcomes, 115

P
Passing off, 126–127
Patents
  Black-Scholes option pricing model for
    valuation of, 65–66
  description of, 15, 19
  disadvantages of, 133
  issuance count for, 22
  legal protection of, 128, 133
  questions regarding, 134
  term of protection for, 128
  trade secrets vs., 128–129
  violation of, 129
Performance drivers, 33
Performance indexes, 178
Physical assets, 57, 190
Physical capital, 32
Portfolio administration, 139–140
Positive knowledge, 14
Positivistic view, of knowledge assets,
  189–190, 192
PRISM model, 72–73
Process technology, 13
Process understanding, 16
Property rights
  description of, 15
  imitation affected by, 17
Proprietary standards, 20
Public goods, 14
Public policy
  description of, 171–173
  in Europe, 174–176
  models of, 173–174
  in United States, 176–180
Put options, 62

R
Real options
  description of, 63–64
  intangible assets as, 66t
  intellectual assets as, 65
Real options models, for intellectual asset
    valuation
  description of, 62–64
  limitations of, 66–67
Regional clusters of firms, 156
Relational assets, 84

Relational learning, 165
Relational resources, 32, 202–203
Relationship economies, 86
Relationship marketing, 86–88
Relationship value, 88
Replicability of knowledge, 16
Reporting, of intellectual capital
 capital market effects, 71
 capital reported, 71–72
 description of, 221
 in Europe, 72–74
 future of, 78–79
 Maxon Telecom example, 75–78
 reasons for, 70–71, 78–79
Reputation protection, 126–127
Research agreements, 131–132
Research and development
 activities associated with, 5
 Black-Scholes option pricing model for
  valuation of, 65–66
 growth opportunities and, 58
 history of, 5–6
 modern changes in, 6
 organizing of, 6
 outsourcing of, 6
 purpose of, 5
 by universities, 6
Resource(s)
 architecture of, 35–36
 definition of, 30, 85
 dynamic view of, 91
 examples of, 30
 human
  definition of, 86, 202
  description of, 32–33, 72
  ethical dilemmas, 103
  marketing applications of, 86
  types of, 86
 interdependence of, 35f
 operand, 91
 operant, 91
 organizational, 33, 37, 88–91, 203
 relational, 32, 86–88, 202–203
 value of, 34
Resource-advantage theory, 85
Resource-based paradigm, of strategy, 29–30, 34
Resource-based theory, 220
Resource stock map, 36, 37f-38f
Return on relationships, 88
Reverse engineering, 13–14

S
Scalability, 16
Scarcity rents, 30

Scientific knowledge, 14
Services, 83
Shared knowledge, 33
Sharing culture, 115
Simulation models, 67
Smith, Adam, 7–8
Sociocultural values, 164
Solow model, 9–10
Spillovers, 11
Spin-off, 146
Standards, 20
Startups, 7
Statement of Financial Accounting Standards
 description of, 43
 No. 2, 47
 No. 141, 48
 No. 142, 219t
Stock market valuations, 21
Strategic assets, 30
Strategic factor market issues, 185
Strategic logics, 206–207
Strategic marketing, 84
Strategic value creation
 description of, 30
 drivers of, 106
 dynamic nature of, 33–35, 36–37
 identifying of, 35–37
 information systems and, 107
 mapping of, 35–37
 principles of, 84
 through intellectual property, 143–145
Strategy
 corporate, 28
 definition of, 28
 description of, 223
 development of, 29–30
 information systems, 120
 market-based paradigm of, 29
 resource-based paradigm of, 29–30
Strategy maps, 33, 34f
Structural Knoware
 description of, 159
 hardware, 162–163
 netware, 160–162
 software, 163–164
 wetware, 159–160
Structured records of transactions, 110
Success maps, 33
Supply management, 36
Sustainable competitive advantage, 30, 109

T
Tacit knowledge, 13, 19, 160, 187–188
Tangible assets
 definition of, 32

description of, 14–15
replacement value of, 21
Tangible goods, 125
Task marketing, 84
Technological innovation
   eclectic approaches to study of, 11
   economic growth and, 9–11
   in economic theory, 10–11
   historians' comments regarding, 9–11
   paradigmatic nature of, 14
Technological knowledge
   description of, 4
   positive externalities of, 10
Technological paradigm, 14
Technology broker model, 58–59
Technology development, 11
Technology transfer, 23
Territory infrastructure, 162–163
30R approach, 87
Tobin's Q
   description of, 21, 49, 189
   intellectual asset valuation using,
      61
Trademarks, 126–127
Trade secrets
   description of, 15
   patents vs., 128–129
   protection of, 19, 128
   violation of, 129
Transformation, 115
Transport infrastructure, 162

U
Universities, 6

V
Valuation
   fair market value, 149
   of information, 113–116
   of intangible assets, 148
   of intellectual assets
      description of, 58
      discounted cash-flow model for, 61–62
      dynamic models, 61–62

Lev's residual income model for, 60, 60t
   market-based approach to, 59
   models for, 58
   real options models for, 62–64
   static models for, 58–61
   technology broker model, 58–59
   Tobin's Q model for, 61
   value-based approach to, 59
   of intellectual capital, 220
   of intellectual property, 147–151
Value
   brands and, 89–90
   to buyer, 150
   from intellectual capital, 18–20
   from intellectual property, 143
   to owner, 150
Value-based approach, to intellectual assets
   valuation, 59
Value chain, 200, 204f
Value creation
   description of, 30
   drivers of, 106
   dynamic nature of, 33–35, 36–37
   identifying of, 35–37
   information systems and, 107
   logics, 200–202
   mapping of, 35–37
   principles of, 84
Value creation map, 191
Value drivers
   description of, 36, 49
   intangible assets as, 49–51
Value network, 201, 205f
Value shop, 201, 204f
Value streams, 148
Venture capital, 7
Vertical clusters of firms, 156
Vertical integration, 36

W
Wetware, 159–160
Work ethics, 164
World Intellectual Property Organization,
   138–139